THE
DURHAM
REPORT

**Report on Matters Related to
Intelligence Activities and Investigations
Arising Out of the 2016 Presidential
Campaigns**

United States Department of Justice

Office of Special Counsel
John H. Durham

Department of Justice, 2CON
145 N Street, NE
Washington, D.C. 20002

May 12, 2023

TO: ATTORNEY GENERAL MERRICK B. GARLAND

FROM: JOHN H. DURHAM
             SPECIAL COUNSEL

SUBJECT: REPORT ON MATTERS RELATED TO INTELLIGENCE ACTIVITIES AND INVESTIGATIONS ARISING OUT OF THE 2016 PRESIDENTIAL CAMPAIGNS

The attached report is submitted to the Attorney General pursuant to 28 C.F.R. § 600.8(c), which states that, "[a]t the conclusion of the Special Counsel's work, he . . . shall provide the Attorney General a confidential report explaining the prosecution or declination decisions reached by the Special Counsel." In addition to the confidential report required by section 600.8(c), the Attorney General has directed that the Special Counsel, "to the maximum extent possible and consistent with the law and the policies and practices of the Department of Justice, shall submit to the Attorney General a final report . . . in a form that will permit public dissemination."[1] This two-part report (Unclassified Report and Classified Appendix) is presented in fulfillment of these requirements and sets forth our principal findings and recommendations concerning the matters that were the subject of our review. The principal report is confidential, but contains no classified information based on thorough, coordinated reviews of the information contained therein by the appropriate authorities within the Federal Bureau of Investigation, the Central Intelligence Agency, and the National Security Agency. The Classified Appendix likewise has been coordinated with those same agencies for classification purposes.

We note that the Classified Appendix contains some information that is derived from Foreign Intelligence Surveillance Act ("FISA") authorities. Accordingly, to the extent the Department determines that it is appropriate to share information contained in the Classified Appendix with congressional or other government entities outside of the Department, steps will need to be taken in accordance with that Act and any relevant Orders that have been issued by the Foreign Intelligence Surveillance Court.

---

[1] Office of the Att'y Gen., Order No. 4878-2020, Appointment of Special Counsel to Investigate Matters Related to Intelligence Activities and Investigations Arising Out of the 2016 Presidential Campaigns ¶ (f) (Oct. 19, 2020).

Finally, we want to thank you and your Office for permitting our inquiry to proceed independently and without interference as you assured the members of the Senate Judiciary Committee would be the case during your confirmation hearings to become Attorney General of the United States.

Report on Matters Related to Intelligence Activities and Investigations Arising Out of the 2016 Presidential Campaigns

Special Counsel John H. Durham

Submitted Pursuant to 28 C.F.R. § 600.8(c)

Washington, D.C.

May 12, 2023

TABLE OF CONTENTS

INTRODUCTION

This report is submitted to the Attorney General pursuant to 28 C.F.R. § 600.8(c), which states that, "[a]t the conclusion of the Special Counsel's work, he . . . shall provide the Attorney General a confidential report explaining the prosecution or declination decisions reached by the Special Counsel." In addition to the confidential report required by section 600.8(c), the Attorney General has directed that the Special Counsel, "to the maximum extent possible and consistent with the law and the policies and practices of the Department of Justice, shall submit to the Attorney General a final report, and such interim reports as he deems appropriate, in a form that will permit public dissemination."[1] This report is in fulfillment of these requirements and sets forth our principal findings and recommendations concerning the matters that were the subject of our review. Section I briefly describes the scope of our investigation, and Section II is an Executive Summary of this report. Section III describes the laws and Department and Federal Bureau of Investigation ("FBI") policies that applied to, or were addressed in, our investigation. Section IV summarizes the facts and evidence that we found and describes our prosecution and declination decisions. In Section V, we provide some observations on issues pertinent to our areas of inquiry.

I. THE SPECIAL COUNSEL'S INVESTIGATION

In March 2019, Special Counsel Robert S. Mueller, III concluded his investigation into the Russian government's efforts to interfere in the 2016 presidential election, "including any links or coordination between the Russian government and individuals associated with the Trump Campaign." That investigation "did not establish that members of the Trump Campaign conspired or coordinated with the Russian government in its election interference activities."[2] Following Special Counsel Mueller's report, on May 13, 2019, Attorney General Barr "directed United States Attorney John Durham to conduct a preliminary review into certain matters related to the 2016 presidential election campaigns," and that review "subsequently developed into a criminal investigation."[3] On February 6, 2020, the Attorney General appointed Mr. Durham "as Special Attorney to the Attorney General pursuant to 28 U.S.C. § 515."[4] On October 19, 2020, the Attorney General determined that, "in light of the extraordinary circumstances relating to these matters, the public interest warrants Mr. Durham continuing this investigation pursuant to the powers and independence afforded by the Special Counsel regulations." Relying on "the authority vested" in the Attorney General, "including 28 U.S.C. §§ 509, 510, and 515," the

---

[1] Office of the Att'y Gen., Order No. 4878-2020, Appointment of Special Counsel to Investigate Matters Related to Intelligence Activities and Investigations Arising Out of the 2016 Presidential Campaigns ¶ (f) (Oct. 19, 2020) (hereinafter "Appointment Order").

[2] 1 Robert Mueller, *Report on the Investigation into Russian Interference in the 2016 Presidential Election* 1-2 (2019) (hereinafter "*Mueller Report*"); *see also id.* at 173.

[3] *Appointment Order* (introduction). When Mr. Durham was asked to lead the review, he was serving as the United States Attorney for the District of Connecticut. Before May 2019, Mr. Durham had been asked by Attorneys General of both major political parties, namely Janet Reno, Judge Michael Mukasey, Eric Holder, and Senator Jeff Sessions, to conduct other sensitive investigations for the Department.

[4] Letter from the Attorney General to United States Attorney John Durham (Feb. 6, 2020).

Attorney General ordered the appointment of the Special Counsel "in order to discharge the [Attorney General's] responsibility to provide supervision and management of the Department of Justice, and to ensure a full and thorough investigation of these matters."[5] The Order stated:

> The Special Counsel is authorized to investigate whether any federal official, employee, or any other person or entity violated the law in connection with the intelligence, counter-intelligence, or law-enforcement activities directed at the 2016 presidential campaigns, individuals associated with those campaigns, and individuals associated with the administration of President Donald J. Trump, including but not limited to Crossfire Hurricane and the investigation of Special Counsel Robert S. Mueller, III.[6]

"If the Special Counsel believes it is necessary and appropriate," the Order further provided, "the Special Counsel is authorized to prosecute federal crimes arising from his investigation of these matters." The Order also provided that "28 C.F.R. §§ 600.4 to 600.10 are applicable to the Special Counsel."[7]

---

[5] *Appointment Order* (introduction).

[6] *Appointment Order* ¶ (b).

[7] *Id.* ¶¶ (c)-(d). We have not interpreted the Order as directing us to investigate the Department's handling of matters associated with the investigation of former Secretary of State Hillary Clinton's use of a private email server. For a review of those matters, *see* Office of the Inspector General, U.S. Department of Justice, *A Review of Various Actions by the Federal Bureau of Investigation and Department of Justice in Advance of the 2016 Election* (June 2018). We also have not interpreted the Order as directing us to consider the handling of the investigation into President Trump opened by the FBI on May 16, 2017. *See* FBI EC from Counterintelligence, *Re: [Redacted] Foreign Agents Registration Act – Russia; Sensitive Investigative Matter* (May 16, 2017). (The following day, the Deputy Attorney General appointed Special Counsel Mueller "to investigate Russian interference with the 2016 presidential election and related matters." *See* 1 *Mueller Report* at 11-12 (describing the authorities given to Special Counsel Mueller). Finally, we have not interpreted the Order as directing us to consider matters addressed by the former United States Attorney for the District of Utah or by the former United States Attorney for the Eastern District of Missouri, other than those relating to Crossfire Hurricane or the FISA applications targeting Carter Page. For accounts of these matters in the news media, *see* Thomas Burr & Pamela Manson, *U.S. Attorney for Utah Is Investigating GOP-Raised Concerns About the FBI Surveilling Trump Aide and About Clinton's Uranium Ties*, Salt Lake Tribune (Mar. 29, 2018), https://www.sltrib.com/news/2018/03/29/us-attorney-for-utah-huber-probing-gop-raised-concerns-about-the-fbi-surveilling-trump-aide-ignoring-clinton-uranium-ties/; Charlie Savage et al., *Barr Installs Outside Prosecutor to Review Case Against Michael Flynn, Ex-Trump Adviser*, N.Y. Times (Feb. 14, 2020), https://www.nytimes.com/2020/02/14/us/politics/michael-flynn-prosecutors-barr.html.

On December 21, 2020, the Attorney General delegated certain authority to use classified information to the Special Counsel.[8]

After the inauguration of President Biden, Attorney General Garland met with the Office of Special Counsel ("OSC" or "the Office"). The Office very much appreciates the support, consistent with his testimony during his confirmation hearings, that the Attorney General has provided to our efforts and the Department's willingness to allow us to operate independently.

The Special Counsel structured the investigation in view of his power and authority "to exercise all investigative and prosecutorial functions of any United States Attorney."[9] Like a U.S. Attorney's Office, the Special Counsel's Office considered in the course of its investigation a range of classified and unclassified information available to the FBI and other government agencies. A substantial amount of information and evidence was immediately available to the Office at the inception of the investigation as a result of numerous congressional investigations[10] and Special Counsel Mueller's investigation. The examinations by the Office of the Inspector General ("OIG") of the Crossfire Hurricane investigation, the Foreign Intelligence Surveillance Act ("FISA") applications targeting Carter Page, and other matters provided additional evidence and information,[11] as did an internal report prepared by the FBI's Inspection Division.[12] The Office reviewed the intelligence, counterintelligence, and law-enforcement activities directed at the 2016 Trump campaign and individuals associated either with the campaign or with the Trump administration in its early stages. The Office structured its work around evidence for possible use in prosecutions of federal crimes (assuming that one or more crimes were identified that warranted prosecution). The Office exercised its judgment regarding what to investigate but

---

[8] Office of the Att'y Gen., Order No. 4942-2020, *Delegation to John Durham, Special Counsel, Authority to Use Classified Information* (Dec. 21, 2020). The Special Counsel has not used this authority.

[9] 28 C.F.R. § 600.6.

[10] *See, e.g.*, Senate Select Committee on Intelligence, S. Rep. No. 116-290, 116th Cong., 2d Sess. (2020) (hereinafter "*SSCI Russia Report*").

[11] *See* OIG, U.S. Department of Justice, *Review of Four FISA Applications and Other Aspects of the FBI's Crossfire Hurricane Investigation* at xiii-xiv, 414 (Dec. 8, 2019) (redacted version) (hereinafter "*OIG Review*" or "*Redacted OIG Review*"), https://www.justice.gov/storage/120919-examination.pdf; OIG, U.S. Department of Justice, *Management Advisory Memorandum for the Director of the Federal Bureau of Investigation Regarding the Execution of Woods Procedures for Applications Filed with the Foreign Intelligence Surveillance Court Relating to U.S. Persons* (Mar. 30, 2020) (hereinafter "*OIG Management Advisory Memorandum*"); OIG, U.S. Department of Justice, *Audit of the Federal Bureau of Investigation's Execution of Its Woods Procedures for Applications Filed with the Foreign Intelligence Surveillance Court Relating to U.S. Persons* (Sept. 2021) (hereinafter "*Audit of 29 Applications*").

[12] FBI Inspection Division, Internal Affairs Section, *Closing Electronic Communication for Case ID # [redacted]* (Nov. 15, 2021) (hereinafter "*Inspection Division Report*" or "*FBI Inspection Division Report*").

did not investigate every public report of an alleged violation of law in connection with the intelligence and law enforcement activities directed at the 2016 presidential campaigns.

In addition to the Special Counsel, the Office has been staffed by experienced FBI and Internal Revenue Service Criminal Investigation Division Agents; Department attorneys and prosecutors; support personnel; and contractor employees.

The Office's investigation was broad and extensive. It included investigative work both domestically and overseas. It entailed obtaining large document productions from businesses, firms, government agencies, universities, political campaigns, internet service providers, telephone companies, and individuals. The Office interviewed hundreds of individuals, many on multiple occasions. The Office conducted the majority of interviews in classified settings; for some interviewees and their counsel security clearances needed to be obtained. The Office conducted interviews in person and via video link, with the vast majority of the latter occurring after the COVID-19 pandemic-related closures began in March 2020. Although a substantial majority of individuals voluntarily cooperated with the Office, some only provided information under a subpoena or grant of immunity. Some individuals who, in our view, had important and relevant information about the topics under investigation refused to be interviewed or otherwise cooperate with the Office. As of April 2023, with two trials completed, the Office has conducted more than 480 interviews; obtained and reviewed more than one million documents consisting of more than six million pages; served more than 190 subpoenas under the auspices of grand juries; executed seven search warrants; obtained five orders for communications records under 18 U.S.C. § 2703(d); and made one request to a foreign government under a Mutual Legal Assistance Treaty.

The Office would like to express its appreciation to, among others, the FBI's Office of General Counsel ("OGC")[13] and Inspection Division; the Litigation Technology Support Services Unit in the National Security Division ("NSD"); the eDiscovery Team in the Office of the Chief Information Officer of the Justice Management Division ("JMD"); and JMD's Service Delivery Staff. The NSD and JMD entities created and maintained the databases and technology infrastructure needed to organize and review the large amount of data we obtained. The Office would also like to express its appreciation to the Department's Office of Privacy and Civil Liberties for its guidance on appropriate information to include in a public report.

---

[13] The FBI's OGC produced more than 6,580,000 pages of documentation in response to our multiple requests. We note that it did so at the same time it was coping with the personnel shortages brought about by the COVID-19 crisis, working to comply with various production demands from congressional committees, and addressing requests from other government entities. Moreover, FBI leadership made it clear to its personnel that they were to cooperate fully with our inquiry, which, in all but a few instances involving some personnel in the Counterintelligence Division, proved to be the case. In those few instances in which individuals refused to cooperate, FBI leadership intervened to urge those individuals to agree to be interviewed. Similarly, both the Central Intelligence Agency ("CIA") and the National Security Agency ("NSA") made their employees available for interview, including former CIA Director John Brennan and former NSA Director Mike Rogers, who voluntarily made themselves available for interviews.

The Office has concluded its investigation into whether "any federal official, employee, or any other person or entity violated the law in connection with the intelligence, counter-intelligence, or law-enforcement activities directed at the 2016 presidential campaigns, individuals associated with those campaigns, and individuals associated with the administration of President Donald J. Trump."

This report is a summary. It contains, in the Office's judgment, that information necessary to account for the Special Counsel's prosecution and declination decisions and describe the investigation's main factual results. It then sets forth some additional observations.

The Office made its criminal charging decisions based solely on the facts and evidence developed in the investigation and without fear of, or favor to, any person. What is stated below in the *Mueller Report* is equally true for our investigation:

> This report describes actions and events that the Special Counsel's Office found to be supported by the evidence collected in our investigation. In some instances, the report points out the absence of evidence or conflicts in the evidence about a particular fact or event. In other instances, when substantial, credible evidence enabled the Office to reach a conclusion with confidence, the report states that the investigation established that certain actions or events occurred. A statement that the investigation did not establish particular facts does not mean there was no evidence of those facts.[14]

Conducting this investigation required us to consider U.S. criminal laws, the Constitutional protections our system provides to individuals, and the high burden placed on the government to prove every element of a crime "beyond a reasonable doubt." Moreover, the law does not always make a person's bad judgment, even horribly bad judgment, standing alone, a crime. Nor does the law criminalize all unseemly or unethical conduct that political campaigns might undertake for tactical advantage, absent a violation of a particular federal criminal statute. Finally, in almost all cases, the government is required to prove a person's actual criminal intent – not mere negligence or recklessness – before that person's fellow citizens can lawfully find him or her guilty of a crime. The Office's adherence to these principles explains, in numerous instances, why conduct deserving of censure or disciplinary action did not lead the Office to seek criminal charges.

There are also reasons why, in examining politically-charged and high-profile issues such as these, the Office must exercise – and has exercised – special care. First, juries can bring strongly held views to the courtroom in criminal trials involving political subject matters, and those views can, in turn, affect the likelihood of obtaining a conviction, separate and apart from the strength of the actual evidence and despite a court's best efforts to empanel a fair and impartial jury. Second, even when prosecutors believe that they can obtain a conviction, there are some instances in which it may not be advisable to expend government time and resources on a criminal prosecution, particularly where it would create the appearance – even if unfounded – that the government is seeking to criminalize the behavior of political opponents or punish the activities of a specific political party or campaign. At the same time, prosecutors should not shy

---

[14] 1 *Mueller Report* at 2.

away from pursuing justifiable cases solely due to the popularity of the defendant or the controversial nature of the government's case.

The *Principles of Federal Prosecution* provide the following pertinent guidance on this point, which informed the Special Counsel's charging and declination decisions:

> Where the law and the facts create a sound, prosecutable case, the likelihood of an acquittal due to unpopularity of some aspect of the prosecution or because of the overwhelming popularity of the defendant or his/her cause is not a factor prohibiting prosecution. For example, in a civil rights case or a case involving an extremely popular political figure, it might be clear that the evidence of guilt— viewed objectively by an unbiased factfinder—would be sufficient to obtain and sustain a conviction, yet the prosecutor might reasonably doubt, based on the circumstances, that the jury would convict. In such a case, despite his/her negative assessment of the likelihood of a guilty verdict (based on factors extraneous to an objective view of the law and the facts), the prosecutor may properly conclude that it is necessary and appropriate to commence or recommend prosecution and allow the criminal process to operate in accordance with the principles set forth here.[15]

The decision of whether to bring criminal charges in any given matter thus is a complicated one that is neither entirely subjective nor mechanistic. If this report and the outcome of the Special Counsel's investigation leave some with the impression that injustices or misconduct have gone unaddressed, it is not because the Office concluded that no such injustices or misconduct occurred. It is, rather, because not every injustice or transgression amounts to a criminal offense, and criminal prosecutors are tasked exclusively with investigating and prosecuting violations of U.S. criminal laws. And even where prosecutors believe a crime occurred based on all of the facts and information they have gathered, it is their duty only to bring criminal charges when the evidence that the government reasonably believes is *admissible in court* proves the offense beyond a reasonable doubt.

Both Attorneys General Barr and Garland have stated that one of their most important priorities is to ensure the proper functioning and administration of federal law by government agencies. Indeed, the first goal of the Department's current *Strategic Plan* is to uphold the rule of law:

> We will continue our work to ensure that the public views the Department as objective, impartial, and insulated from political influence. . . .

> The Justice Department['s] . . . foundational norms . . . include the principled exercise of discretion; independence from improper influence; treating like cases alike; and an unwavering commitment to following the facts and the law. Reaffirming and, where necessary, strengthening the Justice Department policies

---

[15] *Principles of Federal Prosecution*, Section 9-27.220.

that are foundational to the rule of law – many of which were initially adopted in the aftermath of Watergate – is essential to this effort.[16]

In the aftermath of Crossfire Hurricane and the FISA surveillances of Page, the Department has adopted other important policies. We discuss them, and possible additional changes, in portions of the report that follow.

II.   EXECUTIVE SUMMARY

The public record contains a substantial body of information relating to former President Trump's and the Trump Organization's relationships with Russian businesses, Russian business people, and Russian officials, as well as separate evidence of Russia's attempts to interfere in the 2016 presidential election. These and related subjects are well-documented in the careful examinations undertaken by (i) the Department's Office of the Inspector General of issues related to the FBI's Crossfire Hurricane investigation and its use of Foreign Intelligence Surveillance Act ("FISA") authorities,[17] (ii) former FBI Director Robert Mueller as detailed in his report entitled "*Report on the Investigation into Russian Interference in the 2016 Presidential Election,*" issued in March 2019,[18] and (iii) the *Senate Select Committee on Intelligence entitled, "Russian Active Measures Campaigns and Interference in the 2016 U.S. Election.*"[19] The scope of these earlier inquiries, the amount of important information gathered, and the contributions they have made to our understanding of Russian election interference efforts are a tribute to the diligent work and dedication of those charged with the responsibility of conducting them. Our review and investigation, in turn has focused on separate but related questions, including the following:

- Was there adequate predication for the FBI to open the Crossfire Hurricane investigation from its inception on July 31, 2016 as a full counterintelligence and Foreign Agents

---

[16] U.S. Department of Justice, *FYs 2022 – 2026 Strategic Plan* at 15. *See* Attorney General Message – DOJ Strategic Plan (July 1, 2022), https://www.justice.gov/opa/pr/attorney-general-merrick-b-garland-announces-department-justice-2022-26-strategic-plan. *See also* U.S. Department of Justice, OIG, *Department of Justice Top Management and Performance Challenges 2021* ("One important strategy that can build public trust in the Department is to ensure adherence to policies and procedures designed to protect DOJ from accusations of political influence or partial application of the law"), https://oig.justice.gov/reports/top-management-and-performance-challenges-facing-department-justice-2021; Attorney General Memorandum, *Additional Requirements for the Opening of Certain Sensitive Investigations* at 1 (Feb. 5, 2020) ("While the Department must respond swiftly and decisively when faced with credible threats to our democratic processes, we also must be sensitive to safeguarding the Department's reputation for fairness, neutrality, and nonpartisanship") (hereinafter "*Sensitive Investigations Memorandum*").

[17] *See supra* footnote 11.

[18] *See supra* footnote 2.

[19] *See supra* footnote 10; *see also* Intelligence Community Assessment, *Assessing Russian Activities and Intentions in Recent U.S. Elections* (Jan. 6, 2017).

Registration Act ("FARA") investigation given the requirements of *The Attorney General's Guidelines for FBI Domestic Operations* and FBI policies relating to the use of the least intrusive investigative tools necessary?[20]

- Was the opening of Crossfire Hurricane as a full investigation on July 31, 2016 consistent with how the FBI handled other intelligence it had received *prior to* July 31, 2016 concerning attempts by foreign interests to influence the Clinton and other campaigns?

- Similarly, did the FBI properly consider other highly significant intelligence it received at virtually the same time as that used to predicate Crossfire Hurricane, but which related not to the Trump campaign, but rather to a purported Clinton campaign plan "to vilify Donald Trump by stirring up a scandal claiming interference by Russian security services," which might have shed light on some of the Russia information the FBI was receiving from third parties, including the Steele Dossier, the Alfa Bank allegations and confidential human source ("CHS") reporting? If not, were any provable federal crimes committed in failing to do so?

- Was there evidence that the actions of any FBI personnel or third parties relating to the Crossfire Hurricane investigation violated any federal criminal statutes, including the prohibition against making false statements to federal officials? If so, was that evidence sufficient to prove guilt beyond a reasonable doubt?

- Was there evidence that the actions of the FBI or Department personnel in providing false or incomplete information to the Foreign Intelligence Surveillance Court ("FISC") violated any federal criminal statutes? If so, was there evidence sufficient to prove guilt beyond a reasonable doubt?

Our findings and conclusions regarding these and related questions are sobering.

State of Intelligence Community Information Regarding Trump and Russia Prior to the Opening of Crossfire Hurricane

As set forth in greater detail in Section IV.A.3.b, before the initial receipt by FBI Headquarters of information from Australia on July 28, 2016 concerning comments reportedly made in a tavern on May 6, 2016 by George Papadopoulos, an unpaid foreign policy advisor to the Trump campaign, the government possessed no verified intelligence reflecting that Trump or the Trump campaign was involved in a conspiracy or collaborative relationship with officials of the Russian government.[21] Indeed, based on the evidence gathered in the multiple exhaustive and costly federal investigations of these matters, including the instant investigation, neither U.S. law enforcement nor the Intelligence Community appears to have possessed any actual evidence of collusion in their holdings at the commencement of the Crossfire Hurricane investigation.

---

[20] *See The Attorney General's Guidelines for FBI Domestic Operations* § I.C.2 (Sept. 29, 2008) (hereinafter "*AGG-Dom*"); FBI, *Domestic Investigations and Operations Guide* § 4.4 (Mar. 3, 2016) (hereinafter "*DIOG*").

[21] *See infra* § IV.A.3.b.

<u>The Opening of Crossfire Hurricane</u>

As set forth in greater detail in Section IV, the record in this matter reflects that upon receipt of unevaluated intelligence information from Australia, the FBI swiftly opened the Crossfire Hurricane investigation. In particular, at the direction of Deputy Director Andrew McCabe, Deputy Assistant Director for Counterintelligence Peter Strzok opened Crossfire Hurricane immediately.[22] Strzok, at a minimum, had pronounced hostile feelings toward Trump.[23] The matter was opened as a full investigation without ever having spoken to the persons who provided the information. Further, the FBI did so without (i) any significant review of its own intelligence databases, (ii) collection and examination of any relevant intelligence from other U.S. intelligence entities, (iii) interviews of witnesses essential to understand the raw information it had received or (iv) using any of the standard analytical tools typically employed by the FBI in evaluating raw intelligence. Had it done so, again as set out in Sections IV.A.3.b and c, the FBI would have learned that their own experienced Russia analysts had no information about Trump being involved with Russian leadership officials, nor were others in sensitive positions at the CIA, the NSA, and the Department of State aware of such evidence concerning the subject. In addition, FBI records prepared by Strzok in February and March 2017 show that at the time of the opening of Crossfire Hurricane, the FBI had no information in its holdings indicating that at any time during the campaign anyone in the Trump campaign had been in contact with any Russian intelligence officials.[24]

The speed and manner in which the FBI opened and investigated Crossfire Hurricane during the presidential election season based on raw, unanalyzed, and uncorroborated intelligence also reflected a noticeable departure from how it approached prior matters involving possible attempted foreign election interference plans aimed at the Clinton campaign. As described in Section IV.B, in the eighteen months leading up to the 2016 election, the FBI was required to deal with a number of proposed investigations that had the potential of affecting the election. In each of those instances, the FBI moved with considerable caution. In one such matter discussed in Section IV.B.1, FBI Headquarters and Department officials required defensive briefings to be provided to Clinton and other officials or candidates who appeared to be the targets of foreign interference. In another, the FBI elected to end an investigation after one of its longtime and valuable CHSs went beyond what was authorized and made an improper

---

[22] Peter Strzok, *Compromised: Counterintelligence and the Threat of Donald J. Trump* at 115 (Houghton Mifflin Harcourt 2020) (hereinafter "Strzok, *Compromised*").

[23] Strzok and Deputy Director McCabe's Special Assistant had pronounced hostile feelings toward Trump. As explained later in this report, in text messages before and after the opening of Crossfire Hurricane, the two had referred to him as "loathsome," "an idiot," someone who should lose to Clinton "100,000,000 – 0," and a person who Strzok wrote "[w]e'll stop" from becoming President. Indeed, the day before the Australian information was received at FBI Headquarters, Page sent a text message to Strzok stating, "Have we opened on him yet? [angry-faced emoji]" and referenced an article titled *Trump & Putin. Yes, It's Really a Thing*.

[24] *See* SENATE-FISA2020-001163 (Annotated version of article titled *Trump Campaign Aides Had Repeated Contacts With Russian Intelligence*, N.Y. Times (February 14, 2017); FBI-EMAIL-428172 (Annotated version of article titled *Obama Administration Rushed to Preserve Intelligence of Russian Election Hacking*, N.Y. Times (Mar. 1, 2017).

and possibly illegal financial contribution to the Clinton campaign on behalf of a foreign entity as a precursor to a much larger donation being contemplated. And in a third, the Clinton Foundation matter, both senior FBI and Department officials placed restrictions on how those matters were to be handled such that essentially no investigative activities occurred for months leading up to the election. These examples are also markedly different from the FBI's actions with respect to other highly significant intelligence it received from a trusted foreign source pointing to a Clinton campaign plan to vilify Trump by tying him to Vladimir Putin so as to divert attention from her own concerns relating to her use of a private email server. Unlike the FBI's opening of a full investigation of unknown members of the Trump campaign based on raw, uncorroborated information, in this separate matter involving a purported Clinton campaign plan, the FBI never opened any type of inquiry, issued any taskings, employed any analytical personnel, or produced any analytical products in connection with the information. This lack of action was despite the fact that the significance of the Clinton plan intelligence was such as to have prompted the Director of the CIA to brief the President, Vice President, Attorney General, Director of the FBI, and other senior government officials about its content within days of its receipt. It was also of enough importance for the CIA to send a formal written referral memorandum to Director Comey and the Deputy Assistant Director of the FBI's Counterintelligence Division, Peter Strzok, for their consideration and action.[25] The investigative referral provided examples of information the Crossfire Hurricane fusion cell had "gleaned to date."[26]

The Crossfire Hurricane Investigation

Within days after opening Crossfire Hurricane, the FBI opened full investigations on four members of the Trump campaign team: George Papadopoulos, Carter Page, Paul Manafort, and Michael Flynn.[27] No defensive briefing was provided to Trump or anyone in the campaign concerning the information received from Australia that suggested there might be some type of collusion between the Trump campaign and the Russians, either prior to or after these investigations were opened. Instead, the FBI began working on requests for the use of FISA authorities against Page and Papadopoulos. The effort as related to Papadopoulos proved

---

[25] Memorandum from the CIA to the Director of the Federal Bureau of Investigation, *Re: [Redacted] CROSSFIRE HURRICANE [redacted]* (Sept. 7, 2016) (sent to the Director of the FBI and to the attention of Peter Strzok, Deputy Assistant Director for Operations Branch I, Counterintelligence Division)) (redacted version) (hereinafter "*Referral Memo*").

[26] The *Referral Memo* states that the FBI made a verbal request for examples of relevant information the fusion cell had obtained. *Id.* at 2. In his July 26, 2021 interview with the Office, Supervisory Analyst Brian Auten advised that on the Friday before Labor Day, which was September 2, 2016, CIA personnel briefed Auten and Intelligence Section Chief Moffa (and possibly FBI OGC Unit Chief-1) at FBI Headquarters on the Clinton intelligence plan. Auten advised that at the time he wanted to see an actual investigative referral memo on the information. OSC Report of Interview of Brian Auten dated July 26, 2021 at 7.

Separately, we note that the masked identities used in this report do not necessarily correspond to those used in any other document such as the *OIG Review*.

[27] *See infra* §§ IV.A.3 and 4.

unsuccessful.[28] Similarly, the initial effort directed at Page was unsuccessful until the Crossfire Hurricane investigators first obtained what were designated as "Company Intelligence Reports" generated by Christopher Steele. As set forth in Sections IV.D.1.b.ii and iii and in brief below, the Steele Reports were first provided to the FBI in early July 2016 but, for unexplained reasons, only made their way to the Crossfire Hurricane investigators in mid-September. The reports were ostensibly assembled based on information provided to Steele and his company by a "primary sub source," who the FBI eventually determined in December 2016 was Igor Danchenko.

Our investigation determined that the Crossfire Hurricane investigators did not and could not corroborate any of the substantive allegations contained in the Steele reporting. Nor was Steele able to produce corroboration for any of the reported allegations, even after being offered $1 million or more by the FBI for such corroboration.[29] Further, when interviewed by the FBI in January 2017, Danchenko also was unable to corroborate any of the substantive allegations in the Reports. Rather, Danchenko characterized the information he provided to Steele as "rumor and speculation"[30] and the product of casual conversation.[31]

Section IV.D.1.h describes other efforts undertaken by the Crossfire Hurricane investigators working on the Page FISA application. Those efforts included having CHSs record conversations with Page, Papadopoulos and a senior Trump foreign policy advisor. The FBI's own records and the recordings establish that Page made multiple exculpatory statements to the individual identified as CHS-1, but the Crossfire Hurricane investigators failed to make that information known to the Department attorneys or to the FISC. Page also made explicit statements refuting allegations contained in the Steele reporting about his lack of any relationship with Paul Manafort, but the FBI failed to follow logical investigative leads related to those statements and to report to Department lawyers what they found. Similarly, multiple recordings of Papadopoulos were made by CHS-1 and a second CHS, in which Papadopoulos also made multiple exculpatory statements that were not brought to the attention of the Department lawyers or the FISC.

Furthermore, our investigation resulted in the prosecution and conviction of an FBI OGC attorney for intentionally falsifying a document that was material to the FISC's consideration of one of the Page FISA applications.[32]

The Steele Dossier

In the spring of 2016, Perkins Coie, a U.S.-based international law firm, acting as counsel to the Clinton campaign, retained Fusion GPS, a U.S.-based investigative firm, to conduct

---

[28] OSC Report of Interview of Chicago Agent-1 on Aug. 7, 2019 at 4.

[29] SCO-101648 (Email from Special Agent-2 to Supervisory Special Agent-1, Strzok, Auten, Case Agent-1, Acting Section Chief-1 & Handling Agent-1 dated Oct. 4, 2016); *United States v. Igor Danchenko*, 21-CR-245 (E.D. Va.) Trial Transcript 10/11/2022 PM at 81:7-20 (hereinafter "*Danchenko* Tr.").

[30] SCO_005801 (Interview of Igor Danchenko Electronic Communication dated 02/09/17) at 39.

[31] SCO_105282 (CHS Reporting Document dated 06/01/2017) at 1.

[32] *See infra* § IV.D.2.a.

opposition research on Trump and his associates. In mid-May 2016, Glenn Simpson of Fusion GPS met with Steele in the United Kingdom and subsequently retained Steele and his firm, Orbis Business Intelligence ("Orbis"), to investigate Trump's ties to Russia.[33] Steele described himself as a former intelligence official for the British government,[34] and was also at the time an FBI CHS. Beginning in July 2016 and continuing through December 2016, the FBI received a series of reports from Steele and Orbis that contained derogatory information about Trump concerning Trump's purported ties to Russia. As discussed in Section IV.D.1.b.ii, Steele provided the first of his reports to his FBI handler on July 5th. These reports were colloquially referred to as the "Steele Dossier" or "Steele Reports."

As noted, it was not until mid-September that the Crossfire Hurricane investigators received several of the Steele Reports.[35] Within days of their receipt, the unvetted and unverified Steele Reports were used to support probable cause in the FBI's FISA applications targeting Page, a U.S. citizen who, for a period of time, had been an advisor to Trump. As discussed later in the report, this was done at a time when the FBI knew that the same information Steele had provided to the FBI had also been fed to the media and others in Washington, D.C.[36]

In particular, one allegation contained in an undated Steele Report, identified as 2016/095, described a "well-developed conspiracy of co-operation" between Trump, his campaign, and senior Russian officials. This allegation would ultimately underpin the four FISA applications targeting Page. Specifically, the allegation stated:

> Speaking in confidence to a compatriot *in late July 2016, Source E, an ethnic Russian close associate of Republican US presidential candidate Donald TRUMP,* admitted that there was a well-developed conspiracy of co-operation between them and the Russian leadership. This was managed on the TRUMP side by the Republican candidate's campaign manager, Paul MANAFORT, who was using foreign policy advisor, Carter PAGE, and others as intermediaries. The two sides had a mutual interest in defeating Democratic presidential candidate Hillary CLINTON, whom President PUTIN apparently both hated and feared.[37]

---

[33] Glenn Simpson & Peter Fritsch, *Crime in Progress: Inside the Steele Dossier and the Fusion GPS Investigation of Donald Trump* at 69-70 (2019) (hereinafter "*Crime in Progress*").

[34] Steele has testified in prior legal proceedings that between 1987 and 2009 that he was an intelligence professional working for the British government. Trial Testimony of Christopher Steele, *Peter Aven, et al. v. Orbis Bus. Intel. Ltd.*, Claim No. HQ18M01646 (hereinafter "*Steele Transcript*") (Mar. 17, 2020) at 147-48.

[35] While Steele first provided several of his Reports to his FBI handler in July 2016, the transmittal of these Reports to FBI Headquarters and the Crossfire Hurricane team met an inexplicable delay. This delay is discussed in Section IV.D.1.b.iii.

[36] *See infra* § IV.D.1.

[37] SCO-105084 (Documents Known to the FBI Comprising the "Steele Dossier") at 9 ("Company Intelligence Report 2016/095") (Emphasis added, capitalization in original).

Igor Danchenko – Steele's Primary Sub-Source

As noted, the FBI attempted, over time, to investigate and analyze the Steele Reports but ultimately was not able to confirm or corroborate any of the substantive allegations contained in those reports. In the context of these efforts, and as discussed in Sections IV.D.1.b.ix and x, the FBI learned that Steele relied primarily on a U.S.-based Russian national, Igor Danchenko, to collect information that ultimately formed the core allegations found in the reports. Specifically, our investigation discovered that Danchenko himself had told another person that he (Danchenko) was responsible for 80% of the "intel" and 50% of the analysis contained in the Steele Dossier.[38][39]

In December 2016, the FBI identified Danchenko as Steele's primary sub-source. Danchenko agreed to meet with the FBI and, under the protection of an immunity letter, he and his attorney met with the Crossfire Hurricane investigators on January 24, 25, and 26, 2017. Thereafter, from January 2017 through October 2020, and as part of its efforts to determine the truth or falsity of specific information in the Steele Reports, the FBI conducted multiple interviews of Danchenko regarding, among other things, the information he provided to Steele. As discussed in Section IV.D.1.b.ix, during these interviews, Danchenko was unable to provide any corroborating evidence to support the Steele allegations, and further, described his interactions with his sub-sources as "rumor and speculation" and conversations of a casual nature.[40] Significant parts of what Danchenko told the FBI were inconsistent with what Steele told the FBI during his prior interviews in October 2016 and September 2017. At no time, however, was the FISC informed of these inconsistencies. Moreover, notwithstanding the repeated assertions in the Page FISA applications that Steele's primary sub-source was based in Russia, Danchenko for many years had lived in the Washington, D.C. area. After learning that Danchenko continued to live in the Washington area and had not left except for domestic and foreign travel, the FBI never corrected this assertion in the three subsequent Page FISA renewal applications. Rather, beginning in March 2017, the FBI engaged Danchenko as a CHS and began making regular financial payments to him for information – none of which corroborated Steele's reporting.

---

[38] *Danchenko* Government Exhibit 1502 (LinkedIn message from Danchenko dated Oct. 11, 2020).

[39] Our investigators uncovered little evidence suggesting that, prior to the submission of the first Page FISA application, the FBI had made any serious attempts to identify Steele's primary sub-source other than asking Steele to disclose the identities of his sources, which he refused to do. The reliability of Steele's reporting depended heavily on the reliability of his primary sub-source because, as represented to the FISC, Steele's source reporting was principally derived from the primary sub-source, who purportedly was running a "network of sub-sources." *In re Carter W. Page*, Docket No. 16-1182, at 16 n.8 (FISC Oct. 21, 2016). The failure to identify the primary sub-source early in the investigation's pursuit of FISA authority prevented the FBI from properly examining the possibility that some or much of the non-open source information contained in Steele's reporting was Russian disinformation (that wittingly or unwittingly was passed along to Steele), or that the reporting was otherwise not credible.

[40] *See supra* footnotes 30 and 31.

The Unresolved Prior FBI Counterintelligence Investigation of Danchenko

Importantly, and as discussed in Section IV.D.1.c, the FBI knew in January 2017 that Danchenko had been the subject of an FBI counterintelligence investigation from 2009 to 2011. In late 2008, while Danchenko was employed by the Brookings Institution, he engaged two fellow employees about whether one of the employees might be willing or able in the future to provide classified information in exchange for money. According to one employee, Danchenko believed that he (the employee) might be following a mentor into the incoming Obama administration and have access to classified information. During this exchange, Danchenko informed the employee that he had access to people who were willing to pay for classified information. The concerned employee passed this information to a U.S. government contact, and the information was subsequently passed to the FBI. Based on this information, in 2009 the FBI opened a preliminary investigation into Danchenko. The FBI converted its investigation into a full investigation after learning that Danchenko (i) had been identified as an associate of two FBI counterintelligence subjects and (ii) had previous contact with the Russian Embassy and known Russian intelligence officers. Also, as discussed in Section IV.D.1.c, at that earlier time, Agents had interviewed several former colleagues of Danchenko who raised concerns about Danchenko's potential involvement with Russian intelligence. For example, one such colleague, who had interned at a U.S. intelligence agency, informed the Office that Danchenko frequently inquired about that person's knowledge of a specific Russian military matter.

Meanwhile in July 2010, the FBI initiated a request to use FISA authorities against Danchenko, which was subsequently routed to Department attorneys in August 2010. However, the investigation into Danchenko was closed in March 2011 after the FBI incorrectly concluded that Danchenko had left the country and returned to Russia.

Our review found no indication that the Crossfire Hurricane investigators ever attempted to resolve the prior Danchenko espionage matter before opening him as a paid CHS. Moreover, our investigation found no indication that the Crossfire Hurricane investigators disclosed the existence of Danchenko's unresolved counterintelligence investigation to the Department attorneys who were responsible for drafting the FISA renewal applications targeting Carter Page. As a result, the FISC was never advised of information that very well may have affected the FISC's view of Steele's primary sub-source's (and Steele's) reliability and trustworthiness. Equally important is the fact that in not resolving Danchenko's status vis-à-vis the Russian intelligence services, it appears the FBI never gave appropriate consideration to the possibility that the intelligence Danchenko was providing to Steele – which, again, according to Danchenko himself, made up a significant majority of the information in the Steele Dossier reports – was, in whole or in part, Russian disinformation.

Danchenko's Relationship with Charles Dolan

During the relevant time period, Danchenko maintained a relationship with Charles Dolan, a Virginia-based public relations professional who had previously held multiple positions and roles in the Democratic National Committee ("DNC") and the Democratic Party. In his role as a public relations professional, Dolan focused much of his career interacting with Eurasian clients, with a particular focus on Russia. As described in Section IV.D.1.d.ii, Dolan previously conducted business with the Russian Federation and maintained relationships with several key Russian government officials, including Dimitry Peskov, the powerful Press Secretary of the Russian Presidential Administration. A number of these Russian government officials with whom Dolan maintained a relationship – and was in contact with at the time Danchenko was collecting information for Steele – would later appear in the Dossier.

In the summer and fall of 2016, at the time Danchenko was collecting information for Steele, Dolan traveled to Moscow, as did Danchenko, in connection with a business conference. As discussed in Section IV.D.1.d.iii, the business conference was held at the Ritz Carlton Moscow, which, according to the Steele Reports, was allegedly the site of salacious sexual conduct on the part of Trump. Danchenko would later inform the FBI that he learned of these allegations through Ritz Carlton staff members. Our investigation, however, revealed that it was Dolan, not Danchenko, who actually interacted with the hotel staff identified in the Steele Reports, so between the two, Dolan appears the more likely source of the allegations.

As discussed in Section IV.D.1.d.vi, our investigation also uncovered that Dolan was the definitive source for at least one allegation in the Steele Reports. This allegation, contained in Steele Report 2016/105, concerned the circumstances surrounding the resignation of Paul Manafort from the Trump campaign. When interviewed by the Office, Dolan admitted that he fabricated the allegation about Manafort that appeared in the Steele Report. Our investigation also revealed that, in some instances, Dolan independently received other information strikingly similar to allegations that would later appear in the Steele Reports. Nevertheless, when interviewed by the FBI, Danchenko denied that Dolan was a source for any information in the Steele Reports.

Furthermore, as discussed in Section IV.D.1.d.iii, during the relevant time period, Dolan maintained a business relationship with Olga Galkina, a childhood friend of Danchenko, who, according to Danchenko, was a key source for many of the allegations contained in the Steele Reports. In fact, when Galkina was interviewed by the FBI in August 2017, she admitted to providing Dolan with information that would later appear in the Steele Reports.

The FBI's Failure to Interview Charles Dolan

Our investigation revealed that the Crossfire Hurricane investigators were aware of Dolan and his connections to Danchenko and the Steele Reports. In fact, as discussed in Section IV.D.1.b.v, in early October 2016, Steele informed the FBI that Dolan was a person who might have relevant information about Trump. The FBI interviewed hundreds of individuals through the course of the Crossfire Hurricane and later investigations, and yet it did not interview Dolan as a possible source of information about Trump. Our investigators interviewed Dolan on several occasions, as well as the two other persons mentioned by Steele. Dolan initially denied being a source of information for the Steele Reports. When, however, he was shown a particular Steele Report relating to Paul Manafort and his resignation as Trump's campaign manager, along with related emails between himself and Danchenko in August 2016, he acknowledged that the reporting mirrored the information he had provided to Danchenko. Dolan acknowledged to the Office that he fabricated this information. Although both Steele and Olga Galkina suggested to the FBI that Dolan may have had information related to the Steele Reports, our investigation was not able to definitively show that Dolan was the actual source – whether wittingly or unwittingly – for any additional allegations set forth in the Steele Reports. Regardless, in light of the foregoing, there does not appear to have been an objectively sound reason for the FBI's failure to interview Dolan.

15

Danchenko's Claims Regarding Sergei Millian

Perhaps the most damning allegation in the Steele Dossier reports was Company Report 2016/95, which Steele attributed to "Source E," one of Danchenko's supposed sub-sources. This report, portions of which were included in each of the four Page FISA applications, contributed to the public narrative of Trump's conspiring and colluding with Russian officials. As discussed in Section IV.D.1.f, Danchenko's alleged source for the information (Source E) was an individual by the name of Sergei Millian who was the president of the Russian-American Chamber of Commerce in New York City and a public Trump supporter. The evidence uncovered by the Office showed that Danchenko never spoke with Sergei Millian and simply fabricated the allegations that he attributed to Millian.

When interviewed by Crossfire Hurricane investigators in late January 2017, Danchenko said that Source E in Report 2016/95 sounded as though it was Sergei Millian. As discussed in Section IV.D.1.f.i, Danchenko stated that he never actually met Millian. Instead, he said that in late-July 2016 he received an anonymous call from a person who did not identify himself, but who spoke with a Russian accent. Danchenko further explained that he thought it might have been Millian – someone Danchenko previously had emailed twice and received no response – after watching a *YouTube* video of Millian speaking. Thus, as detailed in Section IV.D.1.f.i, the total support for the Source E information contained in Steele Report 2016/95 is a purported anonymous call from someone Danchenko had never met or spoken to but who he believed might be Sergei Millian – a Trump supporter – based on his listening to a *YouTube* video of Millian. Unfortunately, the investigation revealed that, instead of taking even basic steps, such as securing telephone call records for either Danchenko or Millian to investigate Danchenko's hard-to-believe story about Millian, the Crossfire Hurricane investigators appear to have chosen to ignore this and other red flags concerning Danchenko's credibility, as well as Steele's.[41]

The Alfa Bank Allegations

The Office also investigated the actions of Perkins Coie attorney Michael Sussmann and others in connection with Sussmann's provision of data and "white papers" to FBI General Counsel James Baker purporting to show that there existed a covert communications channel between the Trump Organization and a Russia-based bank called Alfa Bank. As set forth in Section IV.E.1.c.iii, in doing so he represented to Baker by text message and in person that he was acting on his own and was not representing any client or company in providing the information to the FBI. Our investigation showed that, in point of fact, these representations to Baker were false in that Sussmann was representing the Clinton campaign (as evidenced by, among other things, his law firm's billing records and internal communications).[42] In addition, Sussmann was representing a second client, a technology executive named Rodney Joffe (as evidenced by various written communications, Sussmann's subsequent congressional testimony, and other records).

---

[41] As noted in Section IV.D.2.f, a federal grand jury in the Eastern District of Virginia returned a five-count indictment against Danchenko charging him with making false statements. A trial jury, however, found that the evidence was not sufficient to prove his guilt beyond a reasonable doubt. *See United States v. Igor Danchenko*, 21-CR-245 (E.D. Va.).

[42] *Sussmann* Government Exhibit 553 (Perkins Coie billing records for HFA).

Cyber experts from the FBI examined the materials given to Baker and concluded that they did not establish what Sussmann claimed they showed. At a later time, Sussmann made a separate presentation regarding the Alfa Bank allegations to another U.S. government agency and it too concluded that the materials did not show what Sussmann claimed. In connection with that second presentation, Sussmann made a similar false statement to that agency, claiming that he was not providing the information on behalf of any client.

With respect to the Alfa Bank materials, our investigation established that Joffe had tasked a number of computer technology researchers who worked for companies he was affiliated with, and who had access to certain internet records, to mine the internet data to establish "an inference" and "narrative" tying then-candidate Trump to Russia. In directing these researchers to exploit their access in this manner, Joffe indicated that he was seeking to please certain "VIPs," in context referring to individuals at Perkins Coie who were involved in campaign matters and the Clinton campaign. During its investigation, the Office also learned that, after the 2016 presidential election, Joffe emailed an individual and told that person that "[he - Joffe] was tentatively offered the top [cybersecurity] job by the Democrats when it looked like they'd win."

As explained in Section IV.E.1.c.i, the evidence collected by the Office also demonstrated that, prior to providing the unfounded Alfa bank claims to the FBI, Sussmann and Fusion GPS (the Clinton campaign's opposition research firm) had provided the same information to various news organizations and were pressing reporters to write articles about the alleged secret communications channel. Moreover, during his September 2016 meeting at the FBI, Sussmann told Baker that an unnamed news outlet was in possession of the information and would soon publish a story about it. The disclosure of the media's involvement caused the FBI to contact the news outlet whose name was eventually provided by Sussmann in the hope of delaying any public reporting on the subject. In doing so it confirmed for the *New York Times* that the FBI was looking into the matter. On October 31, 2016, less than two weeks before the election, the *New York Times* and others published articles on the Alfa Bank matter and the Clinton campaign issued tweets and public statements on the allegations of a secret channel of communications being used by the Trump Organization and a Russian bank - allegations that had been provided to the media and the FBI by Fusion GPS and Sussmann, both of whom were working for the Clinton campaign.

Conclusion

Based on the review of Crossfire Hurricane and related intelligence activities, we conclude that the Department and the FBI failed to uphold their important mission of strict fidelity to the law in connection with certain events and activities described in this report. As noted, former FBI attorney Kevin Clinesmith committed a criminal offense by fabricating language in an email that was material to the FBI obtaining a FISA surveillance order. In other instances, FBI personnel working on that same FISA application displayed, at best, a cavalier attitude towards accuracy and completeness. FBI personnel also repeatedly disregarded important requirements when they continued to seek renewals of that FISA surveillance while acknowledging – both then and in hindsight – that they did not genuinely believe there was probable cause to believe that the target was knowingly engaged in clandestine intelligence

17

activities on behalf of a foreign power, or knowingly helping another person in such activities.[43] And certain personnel disregarded significant exculpatory information that should have prompted investigative restraint and re-examination.[44]

Our investigation also revealed that senior FBI personnel displayed a serious lack of analytical rigor towards the information that they received, especially information received from politically affiliated persons and entities. This information in part triggered and sustained Crossfire Hurricane and contributed to the subsequent need for Special Counsel Mueller's investigation. In particular, there was significant reliance on investigative leads provided or funded (directly or indirectly) by Trump's political opponents. The Department did not adequately examine or question these materials and the motivations of those providing them, even when at about the same time the Director of the FBI and others learned of significant and potentially contrary intelligence.[45]

In light of the foregoing, there is a continuing need for the FBI and the Department to recognize that lack of analytical rigor, apparent confirmation bias, and an over-willingness to rely on information from individuals connected to political opponents caused investigators to fail to adequately consider alternative hypotheses and to act without appropriate objectivity or restraint in pursuing allegations of collusion or conspiracy between a U.S. political campaign and a foreign power. Although recognizing that in hindsight much is clearer, much of this also seems to have been clear at the time. We therefore believe it is important to examine past conduct to identify shortcomings and improve how the government carries out its most sensitive functions. Section V discusses some of these issues more fully.

This report does not recommend any wholesale changes in the guidelines and policies that the Department and the FBI now have in place to ensure proper conduct and accountability in how counterintelligence activities are carried out. Rather, it is intended to accurately describe the matters that fell under our review and to assist the Attorney General in determining how the Department and the FBI can do a better, more credible job in fulfilling its responsibilities, and in analyzing and responding to politically charged allegations in the future. Ultimately, of course, meeting those responsibilities comes down to the integrity of the people who take an oath to follow the guidelines and policies currently in place, guidelines that date from the time of Attorney General Levi and that are designed to ensure the rule of law is upheld. As such, the answer is not the creation of new rules but a renewed fidelity to the old. The promulgation of additional rules and regulations to be learned in yet more training sessions would likely prove to be a fruitless exercise if the FBI's guiding principles of "Fidelity, Bravery and Integrity" are not

---

[43] *See, e.g.,* OSC Report of Interview of Supervisory Special Agent-2 on May 5, 2021 at 1-2; OSC Report of Interview of Supervisory Special Agent-3 on Mar. 18, 2021 at 2-3.

[44] *See, e.g.,* FBI-EC-00008439 (Lync message exchange between Case Agent-1 and Support Operations Specialist-1 dated 09/27/2016); E2018002-A-002016 (Handwritten notes of FBI OGC Unit Chief-1 dated 10/12/2016); FBI-LP-00000111 (Handwritten notes of Lisa Page dated 10/12/2016); OSC Report of Interview of OI Attorney-1 on July 1, 2020 at 2-7.

[45] *See infra* § IV.B.1.

engrained in the hearts and minds of those sworn to meet the FBI's mission of "Protect[ing] the American People and Uphold[ing] the Constitution of the United States."[46]

III. APPLICABLE LAWS AND DEPARTMENT AND FBI POLICIES

This section begins by summarizing some of the *Principles of Federal Prosecution*, which govern all federal prosecutions. Next, this section describes the laws and policies that we considered in the course of our investigation. These include the requirements that apply to the FBI's assessments and investigations of counterintelligence matters, most of which are found in guidelines promulgated by the Attorney General and FBI policies, and the legal standards for conducting electronic surveillance under FISA. This section concludes by describing the principal statutes that we used to evaluate possible criminal conduct for prosecution: 18 U.S.C. § 1001(a)(2) (false statements); 18 U.S.C. § 1621(2) (perjury); 18 U.S.C. § 1519 (falsification of records); 18 U.S.C. § 242 (violation of civil rights); 18 U.S.C. §§ 241, 371 (conspiracy); 18 U.S.C. § 1031(a) (fraud against the United States); 52 U.S.C. §§ 30116, 30121(a) (campaign contributions); 18 U.S.C. §§ 1956-57 (money-laundering); and 18 U.S.C. § 793(d) (transmission of classified information).

A. Principles of Federal Prosecution

In deciding whether to exercise prosecutorial authority with respect to the statutes discussed below, the Office has been guided by the *Principles of Federal Prosecution* set forth in the *Justice Manual*.[47] Those principles include:

1. Determination to prosecute

A determination to prosecute represents a policy judgment that the fundamental interests of society require the application of federal criminal law to a particular set of circumstances. The attorney for the government should commence or recommend federal prosecution if he/she believes that the person's conduct constitutes a federal offense, and that the admissible evidence will probably be sufficient to obtain and sustain a conviction, unless (i) the prosecution would serve no substantial federal interest; (ii) the person is subject to effective prosecution in another jurisdiction; or (iii) there exists an adequate non-criminal alternative to prosecution.[48]

2. Substantial federal interest

In determining whether a prosecution would serve a substantial federal interest, the attorney for the government should weigh all relevant considerations, including:

> Federal law enforcement priorities, including any federal law enforcement
> initiatives or operations aimed at accomplishing those priorities;
> The nature and seriousness of the offense;
> The deterrent effect of prosecution;

---

[46] *See* Mission Statement of the Federal Bureau of Investigation, https://www.fbi.gov/about/mission.

[47] U.S. Department of Justice, *Justice Manual* § 9-27.000 (Feb. 2018), https://www.justice.gov/jm/jm-9-27000-principles-federal-prosecution#9-27.001.

[48] *Justice Manual* §§ 9-27.001; 9-27.220.

The person's culpability in connection with the offense;
The person's history with respect to criminal activity;
The person's willingness to cooperate in the investigation or prosecution of others;
The person's personal circumstances;
The interests of any victims; and
The probable sentence or other consequences if the person is convicted.[49]

3. *Most serious, readily provable offense*

During our investigation, the *Justice Manual* provided that once the decision to prosecute has been made, the attorney for the government should charge and pursue the most serious, readily provable offenses. By definition, the most serious offenses are those that carry the most substantial guidelines sentence, including mandatory minimum sentences.[50]

4. *Unpopularity*

Where the law and the facts create a sound, prosecutable case, the likelihood of an acquittal due to unpopularity of some aspect of the prosecution or because of the overwhelming popularity of the defendant or his/her cause is not a factor prohibiting prosecution.[51] This provision from the *Justice Manual* is quoted more fully in section I.

5. *Interests of uncharged parties*

In all public filings and proceedings, federal prosecutors should remain sensitive to the privacy and reputation interests of uncharged third parties. In the context of public plea and sentencing proceedings, this means that, in the absence of some significant justification, it is not appropriate to identify (either by name or unnecessarily specific description), or cause a defendant to identify, a third-party wrongdoer unless that party has been officially charged with the misconduct at issue.[52]

As a series of cases makes clear, there is ordinarily "no legitimate governmental interest served" by the government's public allegation of wrongdoing by an uncharged party, and this is true "[r]egardless of what criminal charges may . . . b[e] contemplated by the Assistant United States Attorney against the [third-party] for the future."[53] Courts have applied this reasoning to preclude the public identification of unindicted third-party wrongdoers in plea hearings, sentencing memoranda, and other government pleadings.[54]

---

[49] *Id.* § 9-27.230.

[50] *Id.* § 9-27.300. This charging policy has since been revised. *See* Att'y Gen., General Department Policies Regarding Charging, Pleas, and Sentencing Memorandum (Dec. 16, 2022).

[51] *Justice Manual* § 9-27.220.

[52] *Id.* § 9-27.760.

[53] *In re Smith*, 656 F.2d 1101, 1106-07 (5th Cir. 1981).

[54] *Justice Manual* § 9-27.760. *See Finn v. Schiller*, 72 F.3d 1182, 1189 (4th Cir. 1996) ("Overzealous prosecutors must not be allowed to file sweeping statements of fact alleging violations of various laws by unindicted individuals. A primary purpose of Rule 6 is to protect

In a similar vein, Deputy Attorney General Rosenstein stated that "we do not hold press conferences to release derogatory information about the subject of a declined criminal investigation." He went on to say that "[d]erogatory information sometimes is disclosed in the course of criminal investigations and prosecutions, but we never release it gratuitously."[55]

B. **The FBI's Assessment and Investigation of Counterintelligence Matters**

This subsection describes the requirements that apply to the FBI's assessments and investigations of counterintelligence matters. The *AGG-Dom* gives the FBI a broad mandate to "detect, obtain information about, and prevent and protect against federal crimes and threats to the national security."[56] These crimes and threats include espionage and other intelligence activities and foreign computer intrusions.[57] The *AGG-Dom* provides that "[t]hese Guidelines do not authorize investigating or collecting or maintaining information on United States persons solely for the purpose of monitoring activities protected by the First Amendment or the lawful exercise of other rights secured by the Constitution or laws of the United States."[58]

The requirements of the *AGG-Dom* are implemented and expanded upon in FBI policy.[59] In its investigative activities, the FBI is to use less intrusive investigative techniques where feasible, and investigative activity is broken down into various levels. There are also requirements in separate guidelines approved by the Attorney General governing the FBI's use of confidential human sources ("CHSs").[60] In 2020, the Department imposed additional requirements for politically sensitive assessments and investigations and for applications under FISA.

---

the unindicted . . . ."); *United States v. Anderson*, 55 F. Supp. 2d 1163 (D. Kan 1999); *United States v. Smith*, 992 F. Supp. 743 (D.N.J. 1998). The Fifth Circuit has stated:

> Nine of the ten persons named in the indictment were active in the Vietnam Veterans Against the War, an anti-war group. The naming of appellants as unindicted conspirators was not an isolated occurrence in time or context. . . . There is at least a strong suspicion that the stigmatization of appellants was part of an overall governmental tactic directed against disfavored persons and groups. Visiting opprobrium on persons by officially charging them with crimes while denying them a forum to vindicate their names, undertaken as extra-judicial punishment or to chill their expressions and associations, is not a governmental interest that we can accept or consider.

United States v. Briggs, 514 F.2d 794, 805-06 (5th Cir. 1975) (footnote omitted).

[55] Memorandum for the Attorney General from Rod J. Rosenstein, Deputy Attorney General, *Restoring Public Confidence in the FBI* at 1 (May 9, 2017).

[56] *AGG-Dom* § II.

[57] *Id.* § VII.S.

[58] *Id.* § I.C.3.

[59] *See* FBI, *Domestic Investigations and Operations Guide* (Mar. 3, 2016) (hereinafter "*DIOG*").

[60] These are discussed in Subsection 3 below.

1. Use of least intrusive means

The President has directed that the Intelligence Community "shall use the least intrusive collection techniques feasible within the United States or directed against United States persons abroad."[61] The Intelligence Community includes the intelligence elements of the FBI. The *AGG-Dom* implements this provision and observes that:

> The conduct of investigations and other activities . . . may present choices between the use of different investigative methods that are each operationally sound and effective, but that are more or less intrusive, considering such factors as the effect on the privacy and civil liberties of individuals and potential damage to reputation.[62]

There is additional discussion of requirements for a "sensitive investigative matter" or "SIM," principally in the *DIOG*. One category of SIM is a matter involving a political candidate or a "domestic political organization or individual prominent in such an organization."[63] The definition of a SIM also includes "any other matter which, in the judgment of the official authorizing an investigation, should be brought to the attention of FBI Headquarters and other Department of Justice officials."[64] It goes on to explain:

- In a SIM, "particular care should be taken when considering whether the planned course of action is the least intrusive method if reasonable based on the circumstances of the investigation."[65]

---

[61] Executive Order 12333 § 2.4 (Dec. 4, 1981).

[62] *AGG-Dom* § I.C.2.a.

[63] *DIOG* § 10.1.2.1; *see also AGG-Dom* § VII.N.

[64] *AGG-Dom* § VII.N. The *DIOG* says that, "[a]s a matter of FBI policy, 'judgment' means that the decision of the authorizing official is discretionary." *DIOG* § 10.1.2.1. For preliminary or full investigations involving SIMs, there are notice requirements:

> An FBI field office shall notify FBI Headquarters and the United States Attorney or other appropriate Department of Justice official of the initiation by the field office of a predicated investigation involving a sensitive investigative matter. If the investigation is initiated by FBI Headquarters, FBI Headquarters shall notify the United States Attorney or other appropriate Department of Justice official of the initiation of such an investigation. If the investigation concerns a threat to the national security, an official of the National Security Division must be notified. The notice shall identify all sensitive investigative matters involved in the investigation.

AGG-Dom § II.B.5.

[65] *DIOG* § 10.1.3.

- More generally, "when First Amendment rights are at stake, the choice and use of investigative methods should be focused in a manner that minimizes potential infringement of those rights."[66]

- "If . . . the threat is remote, the individual's involvement is speculative, and the probability of obtaining probative information is low, intrusive methods may not be justified, and, in fact, they may do more harm than good."[67]

The *DIOG* says that the FBI will "[a]pply best judgment to the circumstances at hand to select the most appropriate investigative means to achieve the investigative goal."[68] At the same time, it "shall not hesitate to use any lawful method . . . even if intrusive, where the degree of intrusiveness is warranted in light of the seriousness of a criminal or national security threat."[69] The factors that may support the use of more intrusive collection techniques include operational security.[70]

2. *Levels of investigation*

One significant way that the *AGG-Dom* and the *DIOG* implement the least intrusive means requirement is by describing four different levels of activity. The first is activity that the FBI may conduct without any formal opening or authorization process and is referred to as "activities authorized prior to opening an assessment."[71] The other, more formalized levels of activity are assessment, preliminary investigation, and full investigation. As the level increases, the FBI may use a broader range of techniques:

a. Activity authorized before opening an assessment

The *DIOG* states that "[w]hen initially processing a complaint, observation, or information," an FBI employee may take limited steps to evaluate the information. These include looking at government records and at commercially and publicly available information. The employee may also "[c]onduct a voluntary clarifying interview of the complainant or the person who initially furnished the information . . . for the sole purpose of eliminating confusion in the original allegation or information provided." The *DIOG* explains that "[t]hese activities may allow the FBI employee to resolve a matter without the need to conduct new investigative activity."[72] New investigative activity requires the opening of an assessment or predicated investigation.[73]

---

[66] *Id.* § 4.4.4.

[67] *Id.*

[68] *Id.* § 4.1.1(F) (bolding omitted).

[69] *AGG-Dom* § I.C.2.a.

[70] *DIOG* § 4.4.4.

[71] *See id.* § 5.1.

[72] *DIOG* § 5.1.1.

[73] *Id.*

b. Assessment

The FBI may open an assessment if it has an authorized purpose and a clearly defined objective. No particular factual predication is required, but the basis for opening an assessment "cannot be arbitrary or groundless speculation." In addition to the techniques that are authorized without opening an assessment, in an assessment the FBI may recruit and use CHSs, conduct physical surveillance in 72-hour increments, and obtain some grand jury subpoenas. An FBI employee should be able to explain the reason for the use of particular investigative methods.[74]

c. Preliminary investigation

The factual predicate required to open a preliminary investigation is "information or an allegation" that a federal crime or threat to the national security "may be" occurring. Authorized investigative methods include undercover operations, trash covers, consensual monitoring, pen registers, national security letters, and polygraphs. The FBI may also conduct physical searches and use monitoring devices that do not require judicial authorization. A preliminary investigation is to last a relatively short time and lead either to closure or a full investigation.[75]

d. Full investigation

The standard for opening a full investigation is "an articulable factual basis for the investigation that reasonably indicates that . . . [a]n activity constituting a federal crime or a threat to the national security . . . is or may be occurring . . . and the investigation may obtain information relating to the activity."[76] The *DIOG* gives as examples of sufficient predication to open a full investigation:

- "[C]orroborated information from an intelligence agency" stating "that an individual is a member of a terrorist group."

- "[A]n analyst discovers on a blog a threat to a specific home builder and additional information connecting the blogger to a known terrorist group."[77]

The FBI may use "all lawful methods" in a full investigation, including court-authorized electronic surveillance and physical searches.[78]

3. *The Confidential Human Source Guidelines*

In addition to the *AGG-Dom*, the Attorney General has approved separate guidelines governing the FBI's use of human sources. The guidelines in place at the time of Crossfire

---

[74] *Id.* §§ 5.1; 18.5; 18.5.8.3.2.

[75] *See id.* § 6.7.2 ("Extensions of preliminary investigations beyond one year are discouraged and may only be approved . . . for 'good cause'"); *see also id.* § 6.7.2.1 (describing "good cause" and focusing on need to move to a full investigation or to closure); *AGG-Dom* § II.B.4.a.ii (requiring approval to extend a preliminary investigation beyond six months).

[76] *Id.* §§ II.B.3.a; II.B.4.b.i.

[77] *DIOG* § 7.5.

[78] *AGG-Dom* § II.B.4.b.ii; *see also id.* § V.A.11-13.

Hurricane required the validation of a CHS when the person was opened as a source.[79] Validation included documenting the person's criminal record and motivation for providing information."[80] Because a source's reliability can change, the guidelines directed the FBI to review each CHS's file "at least annually" and "ensure that all available information that might materially alter a prior validation assessment . . . is promptly reported" to a supervisor and documented.[81]

The guidelines also required that an FBI agent instruct the CHS.[82] Because the instructions are important, another agent or official was to be present as a witness.[83] The agent was to direct the CHS to provide truthful information and to "abide by the instructions of the FBI."[84] If the FBI compensated the CHS, the CHS was "liable for any taxes that may be owed."[85] The guidelines explained that "[t]he content and meaning of each of the . . . instructions must be clearly conveyed" to the CHS.[86] Immediately afterward, the agent "shall require" the CHS "to acknowledge his or her receipt and understanding of the instructions."[87]

---

[79] *The Attorney General's Guidelines Regarding the Use of FBI Confidential Human Sources* § II.A (Dec. 13, 2006), *as amended by* Attorney General Orders 3019-2008 (Nov. 26, 2008) and 3596-2015 (Nov. 18, 2015) (hereinafter "*2006 CHS Guidelines*"). In 2020, the Attorney General approved new CHS guidelines. *The Attorney General's Guidelines Regarding the Use of FBI Confidential Human Sources* (Dec. 23, 2020) (hereinafter "*2020 CHS Guidelines*"). The *2020 Guidelines* are discussed below in Section III.B.5.b.

[80] The guidelines required the following information as part of the initial validation:

> whether the person has a criminal history, is reasonably believed to be the subject or target of a pending criminal investigation, is under arrest, or has been charged in a pending prosecution;

> the person's motivation for providing information or assistance, including any consideration sought from the government for this assistance; [and]

> . . . .

> any other information that is required to be documented . . . pursuant to . . . FBI policies.

2006 CHS Guidelines § II.A.3.c; A.3.d; A.3.f.

[81] *Id.* § II.C. The FBI was to establish procedures to ensure the prompt reporting of information that might alter a prior assessment. *See id.* § II.C.2.

[82] *Id.* § II.B.1.

[83] *Id.*

[84] *Id.* § II.B.1.a; B.1.d.

[85] *Id.* § II.B.2.f.

[86] *Id.* § II.B.3.

[87] *Id.*

The guidelines did not include an explicit requirement to document whether the person had previously been a source of an intelligence or law enforcement agency.[88] Moreover, the FBI was not required to seek or obtain the approval of the Department before using sources to record conversations and obtain information not only from targets of its investigations in Crossfire Hurricane (such as Page and Papadopoulos) but also from a senior campaign official to whom its sources had access.[89]

4. Analytic integrity

The FBI's Counterintelligence Division is an operational component, whereas a separate Directorate of Intelligence provides analytic support.[90] The Counterintelligence Division's policy guidance says that "*[e]ffective* . . . operations are based on integration" of personnel from the two entities who work "toward common goals." Division personnel "must cultivate and develop relationships" with Directorate of Intelligence elements "in order to maximize operational performance." Case agents "should rely on" the Directorate of Intelligence "for strategic and tactical guidance on targeting priorities, *the generation of source debriefing packages, the evaluation of source reporting*, preparation of various raw intelligence dissemination products, and the identification of intelligence gaps."[91]

For the Intelligence Community as a whole, Congress has directed the Director of National Intelligence ("DNI") to assign a person or entity "to be responsible for ensuring that finished intelligence products . . . are timely, objective, independent of political considerations, based upon all sources of available intelligence, and employ the standards of proper analytic tradecraft."[92] The Intelligence Community's Analytic Standards say that analysts "must perform their functions with objectivity and with awareness of their own assumptions and reasoning."[93] They are to "employ reasoning techniques and practical mechanisms that reveal and mitigate bias."[94] Moreover, "[a]ll IC analytic products" should be "[i]ndependent of political consideration" and "not be distorted by . . . advocacy of a particular . . . agenda . . . or policy viewpoint."[95]

Responding to a congressional inquiry, the Intelligence Community's Analytic Ombudsman documented "a few incidents" from 2020 "where individuals, or groups of

---

[88] *See id.* § II.A.3.

[89] *See AGG-Dom* §§ V.A.4; VII.O (authorizing consensual monitoring as a technique and requiring Department approval in a "sensitive monitoring circumstance," but not including the monitoring of campaign officials as such a circumstance); *see also Redacted OIG Review* at 30.

[90] The Directorate of Intelligence is part of the FBI's Intelligence Branch. *See FBI Leadership & Structure – Intelligence Branch*, https://www.fbi.gov/about/leadership-and-structure.

[91] FBI Counterintelligence Division, *Counterintelligence Division Policy Directive and Policy Guide* § 5.1 (Nov. 1, 2018) (emphases added).

[92] 50 U.S.C. § 3364(a).

[93] Intelligence Community Directive 203, *Analytic Standards* at 2 (Jan. 2, 2015).

[94] *Id.*

[95] *Id.*

individuals, [took] willful actions that . . . had the effect of politicizing intelligence, hindering objective analysis, or injecting bias into the intelligence process." The Ombudsman's assessment mentioned the reluctance of China analysts "to have their analysis brought forward because they tended to disagree with the Administration's policies." On the other hand, Russia analysts were frustrated because management was "slowing down or not wanting to take their analysis to customers, claiming that it was not well received."[96] The assessment also has a section entitled "historical context." It discusses the politicization of intelligence about Iraq in 2003, but it does not mention Crossfire Hurricane or the Carter Page FISA.[97] The assessment paraphrases former intelligence official Neil Wiley:

> [I]ntelligence is the only great function of state that does not come to top decision makers with an agenda . . . . The purpose of intelligence is to provide objective, unbiased, and policy-neutral assessments. We are, perhaps, most important to decision makers when we bring to them the bad news . . . . This . . . sometimes demands moral courage to carry out. Other institutions are inherently political and are much less likely to bring bad news. If we lose that objectivity, or even are perceived to have lost it, we have endangered the entire reason for us to exist.[98]

5. *Recently upgraded protections*

a. Investigative activities

The *Sensitive Investigations Memorandum*, promulgated by the Attorney General in 2020, imposes additional approval requirements for politically sensitive activities. If the FBI takes "exploratory investigative steps relating to" a presidential candidate, a senior staff member, or an advisor, it must give prompt written notice to the appropriate Assistant Attorney General and U.S. Attorney. The Attorney General explained that "this includes any person who has been publicly announced by a campaign as a staffer or member of an official campaign advisory committee or group." The same notice requirement applies if the FBI opens an assessment of such a person. If the FBI opens either a preliminary or full investigation of such a person, then

---

[96] Barry Zulauf, *Independent IC Analytic Ombudsman's [sic] on Politicization of Intelligence* at 3 (Jan. 6, 2021) (attached to letter from Zulauf to Senators Rubio and Warner (Jan. 6, 2021).

[97] *See id.* at 8.

[98] *Id.* at 9 (italics omitted).

notice to the Department is not enough; the Attorney General must approve the opening of the investigation.[99]

The memorandum also directs:

- Department components to "review their existing policies governing notification, consultation, and/or approval of politically sensitive investigations," provide a summary of those policies, and recommend "any necessary changes or updates."[100]

- The Department to study, after the 2020 elections, "its experiences and consider whether changes" to the requirements in the memorandum are necessary.[101]

The Attorney General recently reaffirmed the need to adhere to the requirements of the *Sensitive Investigations Memorandum* that govern "the opening of criminal and counter-intelligence investigations by the Department . . . related to politically sensitive individuals and entities."[102]

b. CHS guidelines and policy

In 2020, following various OIG reviews, the FBI undertook a "comprehensive review" of the *2006 CHS Guidelines* "to ensure that the FBI's source validation process was wholly refocused, revised, and improved across the FBI."[103] The *2020 CHS Guidelines* thus provide additional direction to the FBI in the handling of human sources. They require information about whether the CHS "is reasonably believed to be a current or former subject or target of an FBI investigation."[104] There is also a new requirement for information about a source's reporting relationship with other government agencies.[105] At the time when the Attorney General approved the *Guidelines*, he also directed that "pending further guidance" he or the Deputy Attorney General must approve "any use" of a CHS "to target a federal elected official or political campaign . . . for the purposes of investigating political or campaign activities."[106]

---

[99] *Sensitive Investigations Memorandum* at 2 & n.3.

[100] *Id.* at 3.

[101] *Id.*

[102] Attorney General Memorandum, *Election Year Sensitivities* (May 25, 2022).

[103] Stephen C. Laycock, Memorandum to the Attorney General, *Re: Proposed Revisions to the Attorney General Guidelines Regarding the Use of FBI's Confidential Human Sources* (Dec. 23, 2020).

[104] *2020 CHS Guidelines* § II.A.3.c.

[105] *Id.* § II.A.3.d.

[106] Letter from Attorney General William Barr to FBI Director Christopher Wray (Dec. 23, 2020).

The FBI's *Confidential Human Source Policy Guide*[107] also includes new or strengthened requirements and implements portions of the *Sensitive Investigations Memorandum*. Its requirements include:

- Identifying the specific source-related activities in which FBI intelligence analysts and other non-agent personnel may engage.[108] For example, an intelligence analyst may only contact a CHS or a potential CHS in the presence of a case agent, and an analyst may only accompany an agent to a debriefing of a CHS with supervisory approval.[109]

- Requiring information about "[a]ll likely motivations the CHS could have for providing information."[110]

- Enhancing the requirements for source validation reviews.

- Requiring detailed information and additional approvals in a request to reopen a CHS who was previously closed for cause, either by the FBI or another agency.[111]

Finally, the *CHS Policy Guide* requires a CHS to be treated as "sensitive" and thus subject to more controls based on *either* the position the source holds or the position held by someone the source is reporting on.[112] So, for example, even though a CHS may not hold a position in a campaign, if the source is reporting on such a person he/she would still be treated as sensitive. Post-Crossfire Hurricane, the *Guide* now provides this example:

> A CHS with indirect access to a U.S. Presidential campaign is tasked to report on campaign activities involving possible cooperation with foreign entities to influence the outcome of a U.S. Presidential election. The CHS had only indirect access, but his or her affiliation nevertheless enabled the CHS to be tasked to collect information on the campaign.[113]

 c. Defensive briefings

The OIG's review of Crossfire Hurricane discusses defensive briefings for those who may be targets of nefarious activities by foreign powers and, specifically at the time of the

---

[107] FBI, *Confidential Human Source Policy Guide* (Dec. 15, 2021) (hereinafter "*CHS Policy Guide*").

[108] *Id.* §§ 2.2.3; 2.2.3.1.

[109] *Id.* § 2.2.3.1.

[110] *Id.*

[111] *Id.* §§ 4.3; 4.5.1; *see also* § 4.5.2 (when a closed CHS from one field office is opened in another, the new office "must promptly be provided with any information that reflects negatively upon the reliability of the CHS").

[112] *See id.* § 7.19; *see also* § 6.1 (explaining § 7.19). There is also now a requirement for approval by the Assistant Director of Intelligence. *See* § 7.19.2.1 (requiring an electronic communication to the Assistant Director of the Directorate of Intelligence before the approval request goes to the Director and the Department).

[113] *Id.* § 7.19.1.3.

investigation, the possibility of conducting a defensive briefing for the Trump campaign on Russian activities. The *Review* says that:

> We did not identify any Department or FBI policy that applied to this decision and therefore determined that the decision whether to conduct defensive briefings in lieu of opening an investigation, or at any time during an investigation, was a judgment call that is left to the discretion of FBI officials.

It went on to suggest that it would be desirable to give "senior Department leadership the opportunity . . . to consult with the FBI about whether to conduct a defensive briefing in a circumstance such as this one."[114]

The Department and the FBI have taken steps to address this issue. First, the Attorney General has instructed the FBI Director to promulgate procedures concerning defensive briefings. The purpose of this requirement is "[t]o address concerns" that U.S. persons "may become unwitting participants in an effort by a foreign power to influence an election or the policy or conduct" of the government.[115] Second, the FBI has established a Foreign Influence Defensive Briefing Board ("FIDBB"). The FBI is

> continuing [its] newly implemented review process for malign foreign influence defensive briefings, and in particular briefings to Legislative and Executive Branch officials. This will encompass actions taken after receipt of specific threat information that identifies malign foreign influence operations – that is, foreign operations that are subversive, undeclared, coercive, or criminal – including convening the [FIDBB] to evaluate whether and how to provide defensive briefings to affected parties. *To determine whether notification is warranted and appropriate in each case, the FIDBB uses consistent, standardized criteria* guided by principles that include, for example, the protection of sources and methods and the integrity and independence of ongoing criminal investigations and prosecutions.[116]

C. The Foreign Intelligence Surveillance Act ("FISA")

FISA permits the government to seek authority from the FISC to use a range of investigative techniques.[117] For the installation and use of pen register and trap and trace devices, which are relatively unintrusive, FISA requires that the information likely to be obtained

---

[114] *See Redacted OIG Review* at 348 & n.482.

[115] Attorney General Memorandum, *Supplemental Reforms to Enhance Compliance, Oversight, and Accountability with Respect to Certain Foreign Intelligence Activities of the Federal Bureau of Investigation* at 3 (Aug. 31, 2020) (hereinafter "*Supplemental Reforms Memorandum*").

[116] *See Redacted OIG Review*, Appendix 2, The FBI's Response to the Report, at 433 (Dec. 6, 2019) (emphasis added).

[117] FISA contains provisions related to numerous intelligence collection activities. The principal provisions of the statute are codified at 50 U.S.C. §§ 1801-1812; 1821-1829; 1841-1846; 1861-1864; 1871-1874; 1881-1881g; 1885-1885c.

is relevant to an FBI investigation.[118] For electronic surveillance, which is among the most intrusive techniques available to the FBI, the requirements are more extensive. We describe below some of the findings required by the statute, FISA's First Amendment proviso, and the certification by a high-ranking Executive Branch official.[119] This subsection concludes by summarizing some of the Executive Branch's requirements for FISA applications, many of which have been added in recent years.

1. *Required findings*

FISA requires the government submit an application to the FISC describing the target of the surveillance, the techniques that will be used, and other matters.[120] An FBI agent or other federal official swears to the truth of the facts in the application.[121]

The FISC may authorize electronic surveillance if there is probable cause to believe that the target of the surveillance is an agent of a foreign power.[122] For a U.S. person, there are at least two additional related requirements. First, as the House Intelligence Committee's 1978 report on FISA explains, "[a]s a matter of principle . . . no United States citizen . . . should be targeted for electronic surveillance . . . absent some showing that he at least may violate the laws of our society."[123] Second, the person must be knowingly engaged in the specified conduct. Thus, a U.S. person may be an agent of a foreign power if the person is knowingly engaged in clandestine intelligence gathering activities on behalf of a foreign power, or knowingly helping another person in such activities, provided that the activities involve or may involve a violation of U.S. criminal law.[124]

The *House Report* goes on to explain how foreign powers may engage both in intelligence gathering and other nefarious intelligence activities:

---

[118] *See* 50 U.S.C. §1842(c) (requiring that the applicant certify that "the information likely to be obtained . . . is relevant to an ongoing investigation to protect against international terrorism or clandestine intelligence activities, provided that such investigation of a United States person is not conducted solely upon the basis of activities protected by the [F]irst [A]mendment").

[119] This subsection focuses on those provisions of FISA and related procedures most relevant to the Crossfire Hurricane investigation and to the observations in section V. It discusses FISA's requirements for electronic surveillance. FISA contains comparable provisions governing physical searches conducted for foreign intelligence purposes. *See* 50 U.S.C. §§ 1821-25. As pertinent to this report, Carter Page was a target of both electronic surveillance and physical search.

[120] *See* 50 U.S.C. § 1804(a).

[121] *See id.* ("Each application for an order approving electronic surveillance . . . shall be made by a Federal officer in writing upon oath or affirmation to a judge").

[122] *Id.* § 1805(a)(2)(A).

[123] H.R. Rep. No. 95-1283, 95th Cong., 2d Sess., Pt. 1, at 36 (1978) (hereinafter "*House Report*"). The *Report* also says that a citizen "should be able to know that his government cannot invade his privacy with the most intrusive techniques if he conducts himself lawfully."

[124] *See* 50 U.S.C. §§ 1801(b)(2)(A) and (E).

Not only do foreign powers engage in spying in the United States to obtain information, they also engage in activities which are intended to harm the Nation's security by affecting the course of our Government, the course of public opinion, or the activities of individuals. Such activities may include political action (recruiting, bribery or influencing of public officials to act in favor of the foreign power), disguised propaganda (including the planting of false or misleading articles or stories), and harassment, intimidation, or even assassination of individuals who oppose the foreign power. Such activity can undermine our democratic institutions as well as directly threaten the peace and safety of our citizens.[125]

Consistent with this discussion, a U.S. person engaged in political action or other non-intelligence gathering activity also may fall within the definition of an agent of a foreign power. This is the case if the person knowingly aids or abets, or conspires with:

> any person who . . . pursuant to the direction of an intelligence service or network of a foreign power, knowingly engages in *other clandestine intelligence activities* for or on behalf of such foreign power, which activities *involve or are about to involve* a violation of the criminal statutes of the United States.[126]

Because these other activities may come closer to activity protected by the First Amendment, the required level of criminal involvement is higher in this definition. The *House Report* explains that:

> [T]he activities engaged in must presently involve or be about to involve a violation of Federal criminal law. Again, this is a higher standard than is found in the other definitions, where the activities "may" involve a violation of law. In this area where there is close [sic] line between protected First Amendment activity and the activity giving rise to surveillance, it is most important that where surveillance does occur the activity be such that it involves or is about to involve a violation of a Federal criminal statute.[127]

The *House Report* also discusses the "aiding or abetting" provision at length and says that FISA:

> allows surveillance of any person, including a U.S. person, who knowingly aids or abets any person in the conduct of activities described . . . . The knowledge requirement is applicable to both the status of the person being aided by the proposed subject of the surveillance *and the nature of the activity being promoted.* This standard requires the Government to establish probable cause that the prospective target knows both that the person with whom he is conspiring or whom he is aiding or abetting is engaged in the described activities as an agent of

---

[125] *House Report* at 41.

[126] 50 U.S.C. § 1801(b)(2)(B) (emphases added).

[127] *House Report* at 42.

a foreign power and that his own conduct is assisting or furthering such activities.[128]

The Report goes on to explain how the earlier surveillance of Martin Luther King, which was justified based on his association with members of the Communist Party, would not meet this standard:

> An illustration of the "knowing" requirement is provided by the case of Dr. Martin Luther King. Dr. King was subjected to electronic surveillance on "national security grounds" when he continued to associate with two advisers whom the Government had apprised him were suspected of being American Communist Party members and by implication, agents of a foreign power. Dr. King's mere continued association and consultation with those advisers, despite the Government's warnings, would clearly not have been a sufficient basis under this bill to target Dr. King as the subject of electronic surveillance.

> Indeed, even if there had been probable cause to believe that the advisers alleged to be Communists were engaged in criminal clandestine intelligence activity for a foreign power within the meaning of this section, and even if there were probable cause to believe Dr. King was aware they were acting for a foreign power, *it would also have been necessary under this bill to establish probable cause that Dr. King was knowingly engaged in furthering his advisers' criminal clandestine intelligence activities.* Absent one or more of these required showings, Dr. King could not have been found to be one who knowingly aids or abets a foreign agent.

> As noted above, however, the "knowing" requirement can be satisfied by circumstantial evidence, and there is no requirement for the Government to disprove lack of knowledge where the circumstances were such that a reasonable man would know what he was doing.[129]

The King excerpt underscores the need for the target to be knowingly furthering the criminal clandestine intelligence activities of those whom he is aiding, but it also explains that such knowledge may be inferred.

2. Protection of First Amendment activities

In enacting FISA, Congress recognized that "there may often be a narrow line between covert action and lawful activities undertaken by Americans in the exercise of their [F]irst [A]mendment rights."[130] FISA thus includes a provision similar to the one found in the *AGG-Dom* and prohibits any U.S. person from being "considered . . . an agent of a foreign power solely upon the basis of activities protected by the [F]irst [A]mendment."[131] The *House Report* explains that "[t]his provision is intended to reinforce the intent of the committee that lawful

---

[128] *Id.* at 44 (emphasis added).

[129] *Id.* at 44-45 (emphases added).

[130] *House Report* at 41.

[131] 50 U.S.C. § 1805(a)(2)(A); *cf. AGG-Dom* § I.C.3.

political activities should never be the sole basis for a finding of probable cause to believe that a U.S. person is . . . an agent of a foreign power."[132]

3. *Certification by Executive Branch official*

An application for electronic surveillance under FISA requires a certification by the Director of the FBI or a similar official. The official must certify that a significant purpose of the electronic surveillance is to obtain foreign intelligence information.[133] One definition of foreign intelligence found in the statute is "information with respect to a foreign power or foreign territory that . . . is necessary to . . . the national defense or security of the United States . . . or the conduct of the foreign affairs of the United States."[134] The *House Report* says that this category includes information necessary to national defense or security and the conduct of foreign affairs.[135] It does "not include information solely about the views . . . or activities of . . . private citizens concerning the foreign affairs or national defense of the United States."[136] Another definition of foreign intelligence is information "necessary . . . to protect against . . . clandestine intelligence activities by an intelligence service or network of a foreign power or by an agent of a foreign power."[137] The certifying official must designate the type or types of foreign intelligence information sought, and include an explanation of the basis for that certification.[138]

The official must also certify that the foreign intelligence sought cannot be obtained by normal investigative techniques, and the official must explain the basis for that certification.[139] In other words, the official must explain why the government cannot obtain the information sought through other, less intrusive techniques, such as checking government records and publicly available information, interviewing the target of the surveillance, or using informants. "This requirement," the *House Report* says, "is particularly important in those cases when U.S. citizens or resident aliens are the target of the surveillance."[140]

The certification requirement thus applies to the purpose of the surveillance and to the use of electronic surveillance as an investigative technique. By its terms, it does not apply to the accuracy of the factual information in the application. That is addressed by the sworn statement of an FBI agent or other federal official,[141] and by the Executive Branch requirements described below.

---

[132] *House Report* at 80.

[133] 50 U.S.C. § 1804(a)(6)(B).

[134] *Id.* § 1801(e)(2).

[135] *House Report* at 49.

[136] *Id.*

[137] 50 U.S.C. § 1801(e)(1)(C).

[138] *Id.* §§ 1804(a)(6)(D) and (a)(6) (E)(i).

[139] *Id.* §§ 1804(a)(6)(C) and (a)(6)(E)(ii).

[140] *House Report* at 76.

[141] *See supra* § III.C.1.

4. *Executive Branch requirements*

Over 20 years ago, the FBI adopted procedures designed to ensure the accuracy of the information contained in FISA applications. These are often referred to as the "Woods Procedures," after their principal author.[142] The recent OIG reviews of the Page and other FISA applications raised concerns about compliance with the Woods Procedures and the accuracy and completeness of the information in FISA applications.[143] As a result, the Department has made numerous filings with the FISC, and the FISC has also directed that changes be made:[144]

- For all applications, the FBI now requires that both an agent and a supervisor must affirm that the Office of Intelligence ("OI") of NSD, which represents the Government before the FISC, "has been apprised of all information that might reasonably call into question the accuracy of the information in the application or otherwise raise doubts about the requested probable cause findings or the theory of the case."[145]

- Before the government files an application for electronic surveillance of a federal elected official, a candidate for federal office, or a staffer of such a person, the Attorney General has directed that an FBI field office not involved in the investigation must "review[] the case file and evaluate[] the proposed filing for accuracy and completeness."[146]

The Attorney General also has imposed other limitations on applications for electronic surveillance in politically sensitive matters:

- <u>Defensive briefings</u>. Before the government files an application with the FISC, the FBI Director must consider "conducting a defensive briefing of the target." Then, either the FBI must conduct a briefing or, "if the Director determines that such a briefing is not appropriate," the Director must document that determination in writing.[147] This is in addition to the general requirement described above for the FBI to establish procedures for defensive briefings.

- <u>Duration of surveillance</u>. The maximum duration the government may seek from the FISC for a surveillance is 60 days. This is shorter than the statutorily permitted 90-day maximum for surveillance of a U.S. person. In addition, every 30 days, the government

---

[142] For a description of the Woods Procedures and a discussion of accuracy issues and the FISC, *see* 1 David Kris & Douglas Wilson, *National Security Investigations & Prosecutions* § 6.3 (2019).

[143] *E.g., Redacted OIG Review* at viii-x; *Audit of 29 Applications* at i.

[144] *See, e.g., In re Accuracy Concerns Regarding FBI Matters Submitted to the FISC*, Corrected Op. and Order at 4, Misc. No. 19-02 (FISC Mar. 5, 2020); *In re Carter W. Page,* Order Regarding Handling and Disposition of Information at 1, Nos. 16-1182, 17-52, 17-375, and 17-679 (FISC Jan. 7, 2020).

[145] Declaration of Christopher W. Wray, *In Re Accuracy Concerns*, Docket No. Misc. 19-02, at 3 (Jan. 10, 2020) (hereinafter "*Wray Declaration*").

[146] *Supplemental Reforms Memorandum* at 2.

[147] *Id.*

must report to the FISC "on the results of the approved surveillance and the continued need for such authority."[148]

D. Statutes Used to Evaluate Possible Criminal Conduct

This section begins with a brief description of the burden of proof that the government faces in every criminal case. It then describes the principal statutes that we considered to evaluate possible criminal conduct and exactly what must be proven beyond a reasonable doubt in order for a jury to convict.

1. Standard of proof beyond a reasonable doubt

The government has the burden of proving that a defendant committed any criminal offense beyond a reasonable doubt. A standard jury instruction on reasonable doubt is:

> The government has the burden of proving [name of defendant] guilty beyond a reasonable doubt. In civil cases, it is only necessary to prove that a fact is more likely true than not, or, in some cases, that its truth is highly probable. In criminal cases such as this one, the government's proof must be more powerful than that. It must be beyond a reasonable doubt. Reasonable doubt, as the name implies, is a doubt based on reason—a doubt for which you have a reason based upon the evidence or lack of evidence in the case. If, after careful, honest, and impartial consideration of all the evidence, you cannot say that you are firmly convinced of the defendant's guilt, then you have a reasonable doubt.

> Reasonable doubt is the kind of doubt that would cause a reasonable person, after careful and thoughtful reflection, to hesitate to act in the graver or more important matters in life. However, it is not an imaginary doubt, nor a doubt based on speculation or guesswork; it is a doubt based on reason. The government is not required to prove guilt beyond all doubt, or to a mathematical or scientific certainty. Its burden is to prove guilt beyond a reasonable doubt.[149]

2. False statements

The principal federal statute criminalizing false statements to government investigators is 18 U.S.C. § 1001. As relevant here, subsection 1001(a)(2) makes it a crime "in any matter within the jurisdiction of the executive . . . branch of the Government" knowingly and willfully to "make [] any materially false, fictitious, or fraudulent statement or representation." The government must prove five elements beyond a reasonable doubt to obtain a conviction under this provision: .

> *First*, the defendant made a statement or representation;

> *Second*, the statement or representation was false, fictitious or fraudulent;

> *Third*, this statement or representation was material;

---

[148] *Id.* at 3.

[149] *Criminal Jury Instructions for the District of Columbia* 2.108 (5th ed. 2014).

Fourth, the false, fictitious or fraudulent statement was made knowingly and willfully; and

Fifth, the statement or representation was made in a matter within the jurisdiction of the executive branch of the government.[150]

The *Mueller Report* contains additional discussion of these requirements:

> An FBI investigation is a matter within the Executive Branch's jurisdiction. *United States v. Rodgers*, 466 U.S. 475, 479 (1984). The statute also applies to a subset of legislative branch actions—*viz.*, administrative matters and "investigation[s] or review[s]" conducted by a congressional committee or subcommittee. 18 U.S.C. § 1001(c)(1) and (2); *see United States v. Pickett*, 353 F.3d 62, 66 (D.C. Cir. 2004).
>
> Whether the statement was made to law enforcement or congressional investigators, the government must prove beyond a reasonable doubt the same basic non-jurisdictional elements: the statement was false, fictitious, or fraudulent; the defendant knew both that it was false and that it was unlawful to make a false statement; and the false statement was material. *See, e.g., United States v. Smith*, 831 F.3d 1207, 1222 n.2[7] (9th Cir. 2017) (listing elements); *see also* Ninth Circuit Pattern Instruction 8.73 & cmt. (explaining that the section 1001 jury instruction was modified in light of the Department of Justice's position that the phrase "knowingly and willfully" in the statute requires the defendant's knowledge that his or her conduct was unlawful). In the D.C. Circuit, the government must prove that the statement was actually false; a statement that is misleading but "literally true" does not satisfy section 1001(a)(2). *See United States v. Milton*, 8 F.3d 39, 45 (D.C. Cir. 1993); *United States v. Dale*, 991 F.2d 819, 832-33 & n.22 (D.C. Cir. 1993). For that false statement to qualify as "material," it must have a natural tendency to influence, or be capable of influencing, a discrete decision or any other function of the agency to which it is addressed. *See United States v. Gaudin*, 515 U.S. 506, 509 (1995); *United States v. Moore*, 612 F.3d 698, 701 (D.C. Cir. 2010).[151]

3. *Perjury*

18 U.S.C. § 1621 provides that:

Whoever--

(1) having taken an oath before a competent tribunal, officer, or person, in any case in which a law of the United States authorizes an oath to be administered, that he will testify, declare, depose, or certify truly, or that any written testimony, declaration, deposition, or certificate by him subscribed, is true, willfully and

---

[150] *See generally* 2 *Modern Federal Jury Instructions* ¶ 36.01, Instruction 36-9: "Elements of the Offense."

[151] 1 *Mueller Report* at 191-92.

contrary to such oath states or subscribes any material matter which he does not believe to be true; or

(2) in any declaration, certificate, verification, or statement under penalty of perjury as permitted under section 1746 of title 28, United States Code, willfully subscribes as true any material matter which he does not believe to be true;

is guilty of perjury . . . .

18 U.S.C. § 1623(a) provides that:

Whoever under oath (or in any declaration, certificate, verification, or statement under penalty of perjury as permitted under section 1746 of title 28, United States Code) in any proceeding before or ancillary to any court or grand jury of the United States knowingly makes any false material declaration or makes or uses any other information, including any book, paper, document, record, recording, or other material, knowing the same to contain any false material declaration, shall be fined under this title or imprisoned not more than five years, or both.

The Department's *Criminal Resources Manual* states that sections 1621 and 1623 share four common elements. The government must prove each element beyond a reasonable doubt. The Manual summarizes these elements as follows:

The first element of a perjury offense is that the defendant must be under oath during his testimony, declaration or certification, unless the perjurious statement is an unsworn declaration permitted by 28 U.S.C. § 1746.

The second essential element . . . is that the defendant must have made a false statement.

The third element . . . is proof of specific intent, that is, that the defendant made the false statement with knowledge of its falsity, rather than as a result of confusion, mistake or faulty memory.

The false statement must be material to the proceedings.[152]

In addition to the text quoted above, the Manual explains each of the requirements in more detail as well as the differences among the statutory provisions.

4. Falsification of records

18 U.S.C. § 1519 imposes criminal liability on any person who:

knowingly . . . falsifies [] or makes a false entry in any record, document, or tangible object with the intent to impede, obstruct, or influence the investigation or proper administration of any matter within the jurisdiction of any department or

---

[152] U.S. Department of Justice, *Criminal Resources Manual* §§ 1744-48, Elements of Perjury (Dec. 7, 2018) (archived content), https://www.justice.gov/archives/usam/criminal-resource-manual-1744-elements-perjury.

agency of the United States . . . or in relation to or contemplation of any such matter.

The government must prove three elements beyond a reasonable doubt to obtain a conviction under section 1519:

First, the defendant knowingly falsified a document;

Second, the defendant did so with the intent to impede, obstruct, or influence an investigation [or] the proper administration of a matter; and

Third, the investigation or matter was within the jurisdiction of the Department, the FBI, or another federal department or agency.[153]

5. *Obstruction of justice*

There are several statutes that cover conduct intended to obstruct or impede government investigations.[154] 18 U.S.C. § 1512(c)(2) is an omnibus obstruction-of-justice provision that covers a range of obstructive acts directed at pending or contemplated official proceedings. 18 U.S.C. §§ 1503 and 1505 also offer broad protection against obstructive acts directed at pending grand jury, judicial, administrative, and congressional proceedings, and they are supplemented by a provision in section 1512(b) aimed specifically at conduct intended to prevent or hinder the communication to law enforcement of information related to a federal crime. The *Mueller Report* describes these requirements and noted that "[t]hree basic elements are common to the obstruction statutes pertinent to the Office's charging decisions: an obstructive act; some form of nexus between the obstructive act and an official proceeding; and criminal (*i.e.*, corrupt) intent."[155]

6. *Violation of civil rights*

18 U.S.C. § 242 makes it a crime for anyone, acting under color of law, willfully to deprive any person of a right secured by the Constitution or laws of the United States. The government must prove three elements beyond a reasonable doubt to obtain a conviction under section 242:

First, the defendant deprived the person of an identified right, such as the right to due process of law, secured by the Constitution or laws of the United States.

Second, the defendant acted willfully, that is, the defendant committed such act or acts with a bad purpose to disobey or disregard the law, specifically intending to deprive the person of that right. To find that the defendant was acting willfully, it is not necessary for the government to prove that the defendant knew the specific constitutional provision or federal law that his or her conduct violated. But the defendant must have a specific intent to deprive the person of a right protected by the Constitution or federal law.

---

[153] *See generally Model Crim. Jury Instr.* 8th Cir. 6.18.1519 (2020).

[154] *See* 18 U.S.C. §§ 1503, 1505, 1512(b)(3), 1512(c)(2).

[155] 1 *Mueller Report* at 192.

Third, the defendant acted under color of law. Acting "under color of law" means acts done under any state law, county or city ordinance, or other governmental regulation, and acts done according to a custom of some governmental agency. It means that the defendant acted in his or her official capacity or else claimed to do so, but abused or misused his or her power by going beyond the bounds of lawful authority.[156]

7. *Conspiracy to violate civil rights*

18 U.S.C. § 241 makes it a crime to conspire to deprive a person of his or her civil rights. The government must prove three elements beyond a reasonable doubt to obtain a conviction under section 241:

First, the defendant entered into a conspiracy to injure, oppress, threaten, or intimidate a named victim;

Second, the defendant intended to interfere with the named victim's exercise or enjoyment of a right that is secured (or protected) by the Constitution (or laws) of the United States; and

Third, the named victim was present in any state, district, or territory of the United States.[157]

8. *General conspiracy statute*

A conspiracy under 18 U.S.C. § 371 requires the government to prove four elements beyond a reasonable doubt:

First, two or more persons in some way agreed to try to accomplish a shared and unlawful plan;

Second, the defendant knew the unlawful purpose of the plan and willfully joined in it;

Third, during the conspiracy, one of the conspirators knowingly engaged in at least one overt act as described in the indictment; and

Fourth, the overt act was committed at or about the time alleged and with the purpose of carrying out or accomplishing some object of the conspiracy.[158]

In addition to criminalizing an agreement whose object is to violate a federal criminal law, section 371 also criminalizes a conspiracy "to defraud the United States, or any agency thereof for any manner or for any purpose." This may also include interfering with the performance of official duties by government officials.[159]

---

[156] *See, e.g., Pattern Crim. Jury Instr.* 5th Cir. 2.12 (2019).

[157] *See Modern Federal Jury Instructions-Criminal*, LexisNexis Form 485-17-33 (Elements of the Offense).

[158] *See, e.g., Pattern Crim. Jury Instr.* 11th Cir. OI O13.1 (WL 2020).

[159] *See United States v. Klein*, 247 F.2d 908, 916 (2d Cir. 1957); Practical Law Securities & White Collar Crime, *Conspiracy Charges: Overview*, w-009-8988 (WL 2022).

9. *Campaign contributions*

52 U.S.C. § 30116(a)(1)(A) provides that "no person shall make contributions to any candidate and his authorized political committees with respect to any election for Federal office which, in the aggregate, exceed $2,000." The term "person" includes "an individual, partnership, committee, association, corporation, labor organization, or any other organization or group of persons."[160] "Contributions" are defined as, "any gift . . . or deposit of . . . anything of value made by any person for the purpose of influencing any election for Federal office."[161] Contributions do not include, "the value of services provided without compensation by any individual who volunteers on behalf of a candidate or political committee."[162] Section 30116(c) provides for adjustments for inflation, stating that limitations for contributions by persons to federal candidates are adjusted every two years.[163] The limitation for an individual donor to a candidate committee for the 2015-2016 election cycle was $2,700.[164]

Violations of section 30116 by a person qualify as a crime if, (1) the violation involved at least the amount specified in a calendar year, and (2) the violation was committed knowingly and willfully.[165]

10. *Campaign contributions by foreign nationals*

52 U.S.C. § 30121(a)(1)(A) makes it a crime for "a foreign national, directly or indirectly . . . to make a contribution or donation of money or other thing of value, or to make an express or implied promise to make a contribution or donation, in connection with a Federal . . . election." Subsection (a)(2) makes it a crime for any person to solicit, accept, or receive such a contribution or donation.

11. *Fraud against the United States*

18 U.S.C. § 1031(a) imposes criminal liability on:

Whoever knowingly executes, or attempts to execute, any scheme or artifice with the intent—

> (1) to defraud the United States; or
>
> (2) to obtain money or property by means of false or fraudulent pretenses, representations, or promises,

---

[160] 52 U.S.C. § 30101(11).

[161] *Id.* § 30101(8)(A)(i).

[162] *Id.* § 30101(8)(B)(i).

[163] *Id.* § 30116(c).

[164] Federal Election Commission, *Archive of Contribution Limits*, https:www.fec.gov/help-candidates-and-committees/candidate-taking-receipts/archived-contribution-limits/.

[165] 52 U.S.C. § 30109(d)(1)(A).

in any grant, contract . . . or other form of Federal assistance . . . if the value of such grant, contract . . . or other form of Federal assistance . . . is $1,000,000 or more . . . .

The government must prove three elements beyond a reasonable doubt to obtain a conviction under section 1031(a):

First, the defendant knowingly used or tried to use a scheme with the intent to defraud the United States or to get money or property by using materially false or fraudulent pretenses, representations, or promises;

Second, the scheme took place as a part of acquiring property, services, or money as a contractor with the United States or as a subcontractor or a supplier on a contract with the United States; and

Third, the value of the contract or subcontract was $1,000,000 or more.[166]

12. *Money-laundering*

18 U.S.C. § 1956(a)(1)(A) imposes criminal liability on:

Whoever, knowing that the property involved in a financial transaction represents the proceeds of some form of unlawful activity, conducts or attempts to conduct such a financial transaction which in fact involves the proceeds of specified unlawful activity--

(i) with the intent to promote the carrying on of specified unlawful activity; or

(ii) with intent to engage in conduct constituting a violation of section 7201 or 7206 of the Internal Revenue Code of 1986.

To obtain a conviction under section 1956(a)(1)(A), the government must prove the following three elements beyond a reasonable doubt:

First, the defendant conducted (or attempted to conduct) a financial transaction involving property constituting the proceeds of specified unlawful activity;

Second, the defendant knew that the property involved in the financial transaction was the proceeds of some form of unlawful activity; and

Third, the defendant acted either with the intent to promote the carrying on of specified unlawful activity or with the intent to engage in conduct violating certain provisions of the Internal Revenue Code.[167]

18 U.S.C. § 1957 imposes criminal liability on:

Whoever . . . knowingly engages or attempts to engage in a monetary transaction in criminally derived property of a value greater than $10,000 and is derived from

---

[166] *See Pattern Crim. Jury Instr.* 11th Cir. OI O43 (WL 2020).

[167] *See 3 Modern Federal Jury Instructions-Criminal* P 50A.01 (Lexis).

specified unlawful activity [and does so either] in the United States or in the special maritime and territorial jurisdiction of the United States [or] outside the United States and such special jurisdiction, but the defendant is a United States person.

To obtain a conviction under section 1957, the government must prove the following five elements beyond a reasonable doubt:

First, the defendant engaged (or attempted to engage) in a monetary transaction in or affecting interstate commerce;

Second, the monetary transaction involved criminally derived property of a value greater than $10,000;

Third, the property was derived from specified unlawful activity;

Fourth, the defendant acted knowingly, that is, with knowledge that the transaction involved proceeds of a criminal offense; and

Fifth, the transaction took place in the United States, or the defendant is a U.S. person. [168]

Finally, 18 U.S.C. § 1956(h) imposes criminal liability on any person who conspires to commit any offense defined in section 1956 or 1957. To obtain a conviction under section 1956(h), the government must prove the following three elements beyond a reasonable doubt:

First, two or more persons reached an agreement to commit one of the specified offenses;

Second, the defendant voluntarily and intentionally joined in the agreement or understanding, either at the time it was first reached or at some later time while it was still in effect; and

Third, at the time the defendant joined in the agreement or understanding, he/she knew the purpose of the agreement or understanding. [169]

13. *Disclosure of national defense information*

18 U.S.C. § 793(d) imposes criminal liability on:

Whoever, lawfully having possession of, access to, control over, or being entrusted with any document, writing, code book, signal book, sketch, photograph, photographic negative, blueprint, plan, map, model, instrument, appliance, or note relating to the national defense, or information relating to the national defense which information the possessor has reason to believe could be used to the injury of the United States or to the advantage of any foreign nation, willfully communicates, delivers, transmits or causes to be communicated, delivered, or transmitted or attempts to communicate, deliver, transmit or cause to be communicated, delivered or transmitted the same to any person not entitled to

---

[168] *See* 3 *Modern Federal Jury Instructions-Criminal* P 50A.06 (Lexis).

[169] *See Modern Federal Jury Instructions-Criminal* 6.18.1956K (8th Cir.) (Lexis 2022).

receive it, or willfully retains the same and fails to deliver it on demand to the officer or employee of the United States entitled to receive it.

Modern Federal Jury Instructions summarizes the elements that the government must prove beyond a reasonable doubt to obtain a conviction under section 793(d):

First, that the defendant had lawful . . . possession of (or access to or control over) [describe document].

Second, that the [document] was related to the national defense.

Third, that the defendant had reason to believe that the document could be used to the injury of the United States or to the advantage of [name of foreign country].

Fourth, that on [insert date], the defendant willfully communicated (or delivered or transmitted or caused to be communicated, delivered, or transmitted or attempted to communicate, deliver or transmit) the document to [name of person], who was not entitled to receive it.[170]

IV.   BACKGROUND FACTS AND PROSECUTION DECISIONS

This section begins by providing factual information about the FBI's New York Field Office ("NYFO") investigation of Carter Page in the spring of 2016 (Subsection A.1); the text messages between certain FBI officials that on their face show a predisposition to investigate Trump (Subsection A.2); and the predication, opening, and conduct of the Crossfire Hurricane investigation (Subsections A.3 through A.5). This part concludes with a comparison of some of the FBI's investigative decisions related to Clinton with some of those related to Trump (Subsection A.6). The remaining parts of this section each include a factual background and then describe the prosecutive decisions the Office made. The first addresses an investigative referral of a possible Clinton "campaign plan" (Subsection B). The next is an extensive discussion of the FISA applications targeting Page (Subsection C). The last part of this section covers conduct by private-sector actors in connection with Crossfire Hurricane and related subjects (Subsection D). In describing these matters, this section does not endeavor to repeat or restate all the information that the Office and others[171] have covered and made public. Instead, it aims to add to that body of information, include additional relevant facts, and explain the prosecutive decisions we made.

The *Appointment Order* authorized the Special Counsel "to prosecute federal crimes arising from his investigation" of the matters assigned to him.[172] What is stated in the *Mueller Report* is equally true for our investigation:

In deciding whether to exercise this prosecutorial authority, the Office has been guided by the Principles of Federal Prosecution set forth in the Justice . . . Manual. In particular, the Office has evaluated whether the conduct of the

---

[170] 1 *Modern Federal Jury Instructions-Criminal* § 29.04 (2022).

[171] These include most notably the OIG in its comprehensive reports, the *Mueller Report*, the *SSCI Russia Report*, and the *FBI Inspection Division Report*.

[172] *Appointment Order* ¶ (b).

individuals considered for prosecution constituted a federal offense and whether admissible evidence would probably be sufficient to obtain and sustain a conviction for such an offense. Where the answer to those questions was yes, the Office further considered whether the prosecution would serve a substantial federal interest, the individuals were subject to effective prosecution in another jurisdiction, and there existed an adequate non-criminal alternative to prosecution.[173]

These considerations, as explained below, led the Office to charge three individuals with making false statements. The Office considered whether other individuals, including individuals in the government, made false statements to the FBI, the OIG, or congressional committees or whether, during the course of the Office's investigation, other individuals interviewed either omitted material information or provided false information. Again, what is stated in the *Mueller Report* is also true for our investigation:

> Applying the Principles of Federal Prosecution, the Office did not seek criminal charges against any individuals other than those listed above. In some instances, that decision was due to evidentiary hurdles to proving falsity. In others, the Office determined that the witness ultimately provided truthful information and that considerations of culpability, deterrence, and resource preservation weighed against prosecution.[174]

The Office determined that other matters it investigated either did not involve the commission of a federal crime or that our evidence was not sufficient to obtain and sustain a criminal conviction.

In addition to its prosecution and declination decisions, the Office made the following referrals to other entities:

- A referral on June 30, 2020 to the FBI's Washington Field Office ("WFO") regarding a matter related to an existing counterintelligence investigation.

- A referral in December 2020 to OI of information relevant to the accuracy of information contained in four non-Page FISA applications.

- Referrals of two matters on December 14, 2022 to the Inspector General of the Department of Defense with a copy to the General Counsel of the Defense Intelligence Agency. One matter involved the execution of a contract between DARPA and the Georgia Institute of Technology; and a separate matter involved the irregular conduct in 2016 of two former employees of the Department of Defense.

- A referral to the FBI's OGC and Inspection Division of an FBI agent for failing to document properly the known history of Igor Danchenko upon his opening as an FBI CHS.

---

[173] 1 *Mueller Report* at 174 (citations omitted). For a discussion of the *Principles of Federal Prosecution, see supra* § III.A; *Justice Manual* § 9-27.220 (2018).

[174] 1 *Mueller Report* at 198-99.

- A referral to the FBI's OGC and Inspection Division of the same FBI agent for questionable instructions given to Danchenko regarding the taxability of cash payments made to him by the FBI.

In addition to the referrals described above, the Office also provided information to the FBI's Inspection Division regarding certain activities by current and former FBI employees.

A. The Crossfire Hurricane Investigation

1. New York Field Office investigation of Page

In late March 2016, Carter Page, an American energy consultant, was named a foreign policy advisor to the Donald Trump 2016 presidential campaign. Page's prior business experience was largely focused on Russian and Eurasian energy issues, and as such, he frequently interacted with various Russian nationals. Based on his previous Russian contacts, Page was known to the FBI and had been interviewed on three occasions between 2009 and 2013 by the NYFO. In 2015, Page was again interviewed by the FBI in connection with the indictment of three Russian intelligence officers in the Southern District of New York. According to the criminal complaint and subsequently returned indictment in that case, Page had been approached by the intelligence officers in an apparent failed recruitment effort.[175] In the criminal complaint, one intelligence officer referred to Page, anonymized as "Male-1," as an "idiot," and Page does not seem to have been receptive to the recruitment efforts.[176] Page was interviewed by prosecutors as a possible government witness in that case.[177] One defendant, Evgeny Buryakov, pleaded guilty before trial and was sentenced to 30 months of imprisonment.[178] The two other defendants in the case were protected by diplomatic immunity and are no longer in the United States.[179]

In April 2016, shortly after Page was named as an advisor to the Trump campaign, the NYFO opened a counterintelligence investigation of him. According to the case agent in the matter ("NYFO Case Agent-1"), in opening the investigation, the FBI was not so

---

[175] *See* Sealed Complaint, *United States v. Evgeny Buryakov, "a/k/a Zhenya," et al.* (S.D.N.Y.) ¶¶ 1-4 (Jan. 3, 2015) (hereinafter "*Buryakov Complaint*") (the *Buryakov Complaint* has been unsealed.); *see* U.S. Department of Justice, Office of Public Affairs, *Attorney General Holder Announces Charges Against Russian Spy Ring in New York City* (Jan. 26, 2015); *see generally Redacted OIG Review* at 61-62 (describing Russian activities in New York and the FBI's interviews of Page).

[176] *See Buryakov Complaint* at 12-13, ¶¶ 32-34; *see also* Ellen Nakashima, Devlin Barrett & Adam Entous, *FBI Obtained FISA Warrant to Monitor Former Trump Advisor Carter Page*, Wash. Post (Apr. 11, 2017) (quoting one of the "Russian spy suspects" as saying that Page was an "idiot").

[177] OSC Report of Interview of NYFO Case Agent-1 on Sept. 5, 2019 at 2.

[178] U.S. Department of Justice, U.S. Attorney's Office Southern District of New York, Russian Banker Sentenced in Manhattan Federal Court to 30 Months in Prison for Conspiring to Work for Russian Intelligence (May 25, 2016).

[179] *Id.* at 4; Nate Raymond, *Russian banker accused by U.S. of spy role gets two-and-a-half years prison*, Reuters (May 25, 2016).

concerned about Page, but rather it was concerned about the Russians reaching out to Page.[180] Moreover, NYFO Case Agent-1 told the Office that there were no plans to seek FISA coverage on Page.[181] NYFO Case Agent-1 and her FBI supervisor informed the OIG that Page's role as a foreign policy advisor "did not influence their decision to open a case on Page."[182] It may, however, have affected the timing of the case opening and increased interest in him. Indeed, Director Comey had earlier in April "requested relevant information pertaining to any Presidential candidate."[183] In line with that directive, Comey was briefed on the Page investigation, which a week later was described as a "top priority" for the Director.[184] At that time, FBI personnel in Washington prepared a counterintelligence report on Page for the Director.[185] In July, the same personnel described the Page case, "and ones like it" as, "a top priority for Director Comey."[186] In any event, despite Page's role as a publicly named foreign policy advisor, the FBI did not open the investigation as a "Sensitive Investigative Matter" or SIM.[187]

A few months later, shortly after the FBI opened the Crossfire Hurricane investigation at FBI Headquarters and the four sub-files, including on Page, the NYFO's investigation of Page was transferred to the Crossfire Hurricane investigation at FBI Headquarters.[188]

2. *Evidence of predisposition to investigate Trump*

The record reviewed by the Office demonstrated a rather clear predisposition on the part of at least certain FBI personnel at the center of Crossfire Hurricane to open an

---

[180] OSC Report of Interview of NYFO Case Agent-1 on Sept. 5, 2019 at 2.

[181] *Id.*

[182] *Redacted OIG Review* at 63; *see also id.* at 62 (noting supervisor's view that investigation should have been opened earlier).

[183] FBI-AAA-21-0000829 (Email from Headquarters Supervisory Special Agent-1 to Auten & others dated 04/01/2016). Comey declined through counsel to be interviewed by the Office. Counsel indicated his client had previously testified in various Congressional hearings and been interviewed by various government entities on all matters relating to Crossfire Hurricane.

[184] *Id.*; FBI-AAA-21-0000798 (Email to Headquarters Supervisory Special Agent-1, Auten & others dated 04/07/2016); FBI-AAA-21-0000828 (Email from Headquarters Supervisory Special Agent-1 to Auten & others dated 07/01/2016).

[185] FBI-AAA-21-0000798 (Email to Headquarters Supervisory Special Agent-1, Auten & others dated 04/07/2016).

[186] FBI-AAA-21-0000828 (Email from Headquarters Supervisory Special Agent-1 to Auten & others dated 07/01/2016).

[187] *See* OSC Report of Interview of NYFO Case Agent-1 on Sept. 5, 2019 at 3; *Redacted OIG Review* at 62-63.

[188] *Redacted OIG Review* at 63.

investigation of Trump. For example, Peter Strzok [189] and Lisa Page[190] were directly involved in matters relating to the opening of Crossfire Hurricane. Strzok was the Agent who both wrote and approved the electronic communication opening the matter from the very start as a full investigation rather than an assessment or preliminary investigation. At the time, Page was serving as Deputy Director Andrew McCabe's Special Assistant, and, according to Strzok, it was McCabe who directed that the Crossfire Hurricane investigation be "opened immediately" after information described more fully below was received from Australian authorities in late July 2016.[191] Over a period of months prior to the opening of Crossfire Hurricane, Strzok and Page had exchanged numerous messages, which are already in the public domain and express a very clear prejudice against Trump. For example:

August 16, 2015:

Strzok: [Bernie Sanders is] an idiot like Trump.[192]

December 20, 2015 (After exchanging an article about Trump):

Page: What an utter idiot.
Strzok: No doubt.[193]

March 3, 2016:

Page: God [T]rump is a loathsome human.
Strzok: Yet he may win [the Republican nomination]. Good for Hillary.
Page: It is.
Strzok: Would he be a worse president than [C]ruz?
Page: Trump? Yes, I think so.
Strzok: I'm not sure. Omg [Trump's] an idiot.
Page: He's awful.
Strzok: America will get what the voting public deserves.
Page: That's what I'm afraid of.

---

[189] Strzok was a Section Chief and later the Deputy Assistant Director in the FBI's Counterintelligence Division. (For the positions held by those involved in the Crossfire Hurricane investigation, see the chart in the *Redacted OIG Review* at 81-82.) Strzok agreed to provide information to the Office concerning matters related to the FBI's Alfa Bank investigation, but otherwise declined to be interviewed by the Office on matters related to his role in the Crossfire Hurricane investigation.

[190] Page was an attorney in FBI's OGC who was detailed as a Special Assistant to Deputy Director McCabe's Office.

[191] Strzok, *Compromised* at 115.

[192] FBI-0008217 (Office of Professional Responsibility [OPR] letter to Strzok dated 08/08/2016) at 4.

[193] *Id.*

Strzok: God, Hillary should win 100,000,000 – 0.[194]

May 3, 2016:

Page: And holy [expletive] Cruz just dropped out of the race. It's going to be a Clinton Trump race. Unbelievable.

Strzok: What?!?!??

Page: You heard that right my friend.

Strzok: I saw [T]rump won, figured it would be a bit. Now the pressure really starts to finish [the Clinton email investigation] . . .

Page: It sure does.[195]

July 18, 2016 (During the Republican National Convention):

Strzok: Oooh, TURN IT ON, TURN IT ON!!! THE DOUCHE BAGS ARE ABOUT TO COME OUT. You can tell by the excitable clapping.

Page: And wow, Donald Trump is an enormous d*uche.

July 19, 2016:

Strzok: Hi. How was Trump, other than a douche?

Page: Trump barely spoke, but the first thing out of his mouth was "we're going to win soooo big." The whole thing is like living in a bad dream.[196]

July 21, 2016:

Strzok: Trump is a disaster. I have no idea how destabilizing his Presidency would be.[197]

July 27, 2016:

Page: Have we opened on him yet? Trump & Putin. Yes, It's Really a Thing http://talkingpointsmemo.com/edblog/trumpputin-yes-it-s-really-a-thing

Strzok: Opened on Trump? If Hillary did, you know 5 field offices would . . .[198]

---

[194] *Id.* at 5.

[195] *Id.*

[196] *Id.* at 6.

[197] *Id.*

[198] *Id.* at 7 (ellipses in original); *see also* Letter from Jill C. Tyson, Office of Congressional Affairs, FBI, to Senator Ron Johnson, Chairman of the Committee on Homeland Security and Governmental Affairs (Oct. 23, 2020) (attachment), https://www.grassley.senate.gov/imo/media/doc/lync_text_messages_of_peter_strzok_from_2-13-16_to_12-6-17.pdf.

(As discussed more fully below, the next day, July 28, 2016, FBI Headquarters received the Australian information that formed the basis for the opening of Crossfire Hurricane. On Sunday, July 31, 2016, Strzok, as he has written he was directed to do by McCabe, immediately opened Crossfire Hurricane. He both drafted and approved (with the authorization of Assistant Director Priestap) the Crossfire Hurricane opening communication.)[199]

August 8, 2016:

Page:	[Trump's] not going to become president, right? Right?!
Strzok:	No. No, he's not. We'll stop it.[200]

Similarly, and as discussed in more detail below, FBI OGC attorney Kevin Clinesmith made troubling statements demonstrating a blatant political bias against Trump. Clinesmith, who played a central role in the Page FISA process, on the day after Trump's election as President, stated to fellow FBI personnel, among other things, "viva le resistance,"[201] an obvious reference to those individuals opposed to Trump.

Although those involved in opening the Crossfire Hurricane investigation denied that bias against Trump was a factor in opening the investigation,[202] the communications quoted

---

[199] *Redacted OIG Review* at 53, 58. Regarding Strzok's having direct access to McCabe, when asked if he was aware of people going around him to the 7th Floor, (meaning jumping the chain of command and going to the FBI Executive Offices on the 7th floor), Priestap replied, "oh, yeah." While Priestap stated he could not remember the specifics, Lisa Page was a concern, without question, in this respect. In addition, there were multiple times when Strzok mentioned something to Priestap and shared it with Page who, in turn, shared the information with Deputy Director McCabe. There were also instances when Strzok shared information directly with McCabe before Priestap could provide the information to McCabe himself. Priestap said these actions drove him "insane." He also told the Office that Strzok was the worst offender in this regard and that these events occurred mostly when he (Priestap) wanted to go in one direction and they (Page and Strzok) disagreed and thus went around him. *See* OSC Report of Interview of E.W. Priestap on June 2, 2021 at 3.

Priestap agreed to provide information to the Office concerning matters related to the FBI's Alfa Bank investigation, but otherwise declined to be interviewed by the Office on matters related to his role in the Crossfire Hurricane investigation.

[200] FBI-0008217 (Office of Professional Responsibility Letter to Strzok dated 08/08/2016 at 7); *see also* Letter from Jill C. Tyson, Office of Congressional Affairs, FBI, to Senator Ron Johnson, Chairman of the Committee on Homeland Security and Governmental Affairs (Oct. 23, 2020) (attachment).

[201] FBI-AAA-EC-00006440 (Lync message exchange between Clinesmith and FBI OGC Unit Chief-1 dated 11/22/2016).

[202] *See, e.g.,* Strzok, *Compromised* at 345-46; OSC Report of Interview of Supervisory Special Agent-1 on June 17, 2019 at 5; OSC Report of Interview of FBI OGC Unit Chief-1 on Aug. 29, 2019 at 10; OSC Report of Interview of Supervisory Special Agent-2 on May 5, 2021 at 8; OSC Report of Interview of Brian Auten on July 26, 2021 at 16.

above quite clearly show, at least on the part of certain personnel intimately involved in the matter, a predisposition to open an investigation into Trump.

3. *The opening of Crossfire Hurricane*

The FBI opened Crossfire Hurricane as a full counterintelligence investigation "to determine whether individual(s) associated with the Trump campaign [were] witting of and/or coordinating activities with the Government of Russia."[203] The starting point for the Office's inquiry was to examine what information was known or available to the FBI about any such ties as of July 31, 2016, prior to opening Crossfire Hurricane. That question then divided itself into two related questions: (i) what was the information that predicated the opening of the investigation and (ii) did that information support such an investigation being opened not as an "assessment" or "preliminary" investigation, but from the start as a "full" investigation. In exploring these questions, we determined the following:

a. The information used to predicate Crossfire Hurricane

In March 2016, the Trump campaign identified George Papadopoulos as a foreign policy advisor.[204] Papadopoulos had previously worked as an energy consultant, with a particular focus on projects in the Eastern Mediterranean.[205] At the time of his appointment, Papadopoulos was employed in the United Kingdom at the London Center of International Law Practice.[206] Among Papadopoulos's acquaintances in London was a diplomat from another country ("Foreign Government-1 Diplomat-1"). Foreign Government-1 Diplomat-1 was familiar with an Australian diplomat ("Australian Diplomat-1").[207] On May 6, 2016, by prearrangement, Foreign Government-1 Diplomat-1 introduced Papadopoulos to Australian Diplomat-1.[208] On May 10, 2016, Papadopoulos and Australian Diplomat-1 met again, and this time they were joined by

---

[203] FBI-0002784 (FBI EC from Counterintelligence, *Re: Crossfire Hurricane* dated July 31, 2016 at 3-4) (hereinafter "*Crossfire Hurricane Opening EC*" or "*Opening EC*").

[204] Missy Ryan & Steven Mufson, *One of Trump's Foreign Policy Advisers Is a 2009 College Grad Who Lists Model UN As a Credential*, Wash. Post (Mar. 22, 2016).

[205] FBI-AAA-02-0019485 (Crossfire Hurricane Papadopoulos Profile dated 08/05/2016); *See also SSCI Russia Report*, pt. 5, at 471.

[206] FBI-AAA-02-0019485 (Crossfire Hurricane Papadopoulos Profile dated 08/05/2016); *SSCI Russia Report*, pt. 5, at 470.

[207] OSC Report of Interview of Australian Diplomat-1 on Oct. 09, 2019 at 1-2; *SSCI Russia Report*, pt. 5, at 487.

[208] OSC Report of Interview of Australian Diplomat-1 on Oct. 09, 2019 at 2; FBI-0002775 (FBI interview of Australian diplomats dated Aug. 11, 2016 at 1-2) (hereinafter "*Australia 302*").

Australian High Commissioner Alexander Downer.[209] Both meetings were over drinks in public settings.[210]

The Australian diplomats were interested in meeting with Papadopoulos because of his role in the Trump campaign, and much of the conversation centered on the upcoming U.S. election.[211] Over two months later, on July 26, 2016, Australia provided the U.S. Embassy in London certain information its diplomats had memorialized at or around the time of the meetings with Papadopoulos. The next day, the State Department passed this information on to the FBI's Legal Attaché assigned to the Embassy in London ("UK Legat-1").[212]

"Paragraph Five" was the name given to the raw information provided by the Australian government and included in a May 16, 2016 cable that documented the diplomats' encounters with Papadopoulos.[213] Paragraph Five is an abstract from the cable and was quoted verbatim in the *Crossfire Hurricane Opening EC*, stating in its entirety that:

> Mr[.] Papadopoulos was, unsurprisingly, confident that Mr[.] Trump could win the election. He commented that the Clintons had "a lot of baggage" and suggested the Trump team had plenty of material to use in its campaign. He also suggested the Trump team had received some kind of suggestion from Russia that it could assist this process with the anonymous release of information during the campaign that would be damaging to Mrs[.] Clinton (and President Obama). It was unclear whether he or the Russians were referring to material acquired publicly of [sic] through other means. It was also unclear how Mr[.] Trump's team reacted to the offer. We note the Trump

---

[209] *Australia 302* at 2-3. Australia has released a redacted version of a cable describing the meeting with Papadopoulos. Cable from London (Alexander Downer) to Canberra, *Re: UK: US: Donald Trump – Views from Trump's Adviser* (May 11, 2016), https://www.dfat.gov.au/sites/default/files/dfat-foi-1801-f1852.pdf. Sky News has also interviewed Downer about the meeting. Jack Crowe, *Ex-Australian Diplomat Explains Why He Turned Papadapoulos [sic] Info over to FBI*, Yahoo! News (May 10, 2019), https://www.yahoo.com/video/ex-australian-diplomat-explains-why-164317262.html. In its report, the SSCI includes a detailed description of the meetings between Papadopoulos and the Australian diplomats. *See SSCI Russia Report*, pt. 5, at 487-89.

The information that the Australian diplomats provided to the U.S. Embassy and the FBI is described in SCO-010930 (FBI EC from London, *Re: Legat London information from U.S. Embassy London Deputy Chief of Mission* dated July 28, 2016) (hereinafter "*London EC*").

[210] *Australia 302* at 1-2.

[211] *See London EC at 2; Australia 302* at 1; OSC Report of Interview of Alexander Downer on Oct. 09, 2019 at 1; OSC Report of Interview of Australian Diplomat-1 on Oct. 09, 2019 at 1.

[212] OSC Report of Interview of UK Legat-1 on May 28, 2019 at 1-2; *London EC* at 2; *see also Redacted OIG Review* at 50-52.

[213] OSC Report of Interview of FBI OGC Unit Chief-1 on Aug. 29, 2019 at 3.

team's reaction could, in the end, have little bearing of [sic] what Russia decides to do, with or without Mr[.] Trump's cooperation.[214]

The Australian account reflects that two meetings of a casual nature took place with Papadopoulos.[215] These meetings were documented by Downer on May 11, 2016 and by Australian Diplomat-1 later in the month.[216] Both diplomats advised that prior to the Spring of 2016, Papadopoulos was unknown to them.[217] Notably, the information in Paragraph Five does not include any mention of the hacking of the DNC, the Russians being in possession of emails, or the public release of any emails. In addition, when interviewed by the Office, Downer stated that he would have characterized the statements made by Papadopoulos differently than Australian Diplomat-1 did in Paragraph 5. According to Downer, Papadopoulos made no mention of Clinton emails, dirt or any specific approach by the Russian government to the Trump campaign team with an offer or suggestion of providing assistance. Rather, Downer's recollection was that Papadopoulos simply stated "the Russians have information" and that was all.[218]

As recounted to the FBI on August 2, 2016, by Australian Diplomat-1, the substance of Paragraph Five was written in a "purposely vague" way.[219] This was done because Papadopoulos left a number of things unexplained and "did not say he had direct contact

_____

[214] *London EC*, at 2-3; *see also Crossfire Hurricane Opening EC* at 3 (also quoting the Paragraph Five information); *Redacted OIG Review* at 52, 55.

[215] We note there is an inconsistency in the statements given by Australian Diplomat-1 and former-High Commissioner Downer to the Crossfire Hurricane interviewers in August 2016 and what they told the Office when interviewed in October 2019. Australian Diplomat-1 and Downer were interviewed together in August 2016, and, according to the FD-302 prepared afterward by Supervisory Special Agent-1, Papadopoulos made the statements about the Russians during the May 6, 2016 introductory meeting when he met only with Australian Diplomat-1. When the two diplomats were interviewed separately by the Office in October 2019, investigators were advised that Papadopoulos made the statements in front of both Australian Diplomat-1 and Downer during the second meeting on May 10, 2016.

[216] The meetings with Papadopoulos took place on May 6 and 10, 2016. *Australia 302* at 1-2. The Australian diplomats documented the meetings in two cables dated May 11 and May 16, 2016; OSC Report of Interview of Alexander Downer on Oct. 9, 2019 at 2; OSC Report of Interview of Australian Diplomat-1 on Oct. 9, 2019 at 3.

[217] OSC Report of Interview of Alexander Downer on Oct. 09, 2019 at 1; OSC Report of Interview of Australian Diplomat-1 on Oct. 09, 2019 at 1-2.

[218] OSC Report of Interview of Alexander Downer on Oct. 09, 2019 at 2 (and related field notes); Downer also is reported to have stated in an interview that in talking with Papadopoulos there was "no suggestion that there was collusion between Donald Trump or Donald Trump's campaign and the Russians." Brooke Singman, *Diplomat Who Helped Launch Russia Probe Speaks Out, Defends Role*, Fox News (May 10, 2019), https://www.foxnews.com/politics/former-ausralian-diplomat-alexander-downer-defends-work-pushes-back-on-claim-he-tried-to-trap-papadopoulos.

[219] *Australia 302* at 2.

with the Russians."[220] The impression Papadopoulos made on the Australian diplomats was wide ranging. On the one hand, he "had an inflated sense of self," was "insecure," and was "trying to impress."[221] On the other hand, he was "a nice guy," was "not negative," and "did not name drop."[222] Downer noted that he

> was impressed Papadopoulos acknowledged his lack of expertise and felt the response was uncommon for someone of Papadopoulos' age, political experience and for someone thrust into the spotlight overnight. Many people in a similar position would represent themselves differently and [Downer] would have sniffed them out. If [Downer] believed Papadopoulos was a fraud [he] would not have recorded and reported on the meeting [he] had with Papadopoulos.[223]

Downer also said that he "did not get the sense Papadopoulos was the middle-man to coordinate with the Russians."[224]

The Australian diplomats would later inform the FBI, and subsequently the Office, that the impetus for passing the Paragraph Five information in late-July was the public release by WikiLeaks (on July 22, 2016) of email communications that had been hacked from the DNC servers.[225] As far as the Office's investigation was able to determine, Papadopoulos's comments did not undergo any additional analysis or scrutiny by Australian intelligence officials.

b. The lack of intelligence information supporting the premise of Crossfire Hurricane

As an initial matter, there is no question that the FBI had an affirmative obligation to closely examine the Paragraph Five information. The Paragraph Five information, however, was the sole basis cited by the FBI for opening a full investigation into individuals associated with the ongoing Trump campaign.[226] Significantly, the FBI opened a full investigation before any preliminary discussions or interviews were undertaken with either the Australian diplomats or Papadopoulos. Further, the *Opening EC* does not describe any collaboration or joint assessments of the information with either friendly foreign intelligence services or other U.S. intelligence agencies. In effect, within three days of its receipt of the Paragraph Five reporting, the FBI determined,[227] without further analysis, that the

---

[220] *Id.*

[221] *Id.* at 2-3.

[222] *Id.*

[223] *Id.*

[224] *Id.* at 3.

[225] *See Australia 302* at 4; OSC Report of Interview of Alexander Downer on Oct. 09, 2019 at 2-3.

[226] *See supra* §§ III.B.1 – 3.

[227] Regarding who on the 7th floor was involved in the decision making, McCabe informed the OIG that Director Comey "was engaging on a very regular basis" with the team after the

Australian information was an adequate basis for the opening of a full investigation into whether individuals associated with an ongoing presidential campaign were "witting of and/or coordinating activities with the Government of Russia."[228]

In his interview with the Office, Executive Assistant Director for National Security Michael Steinbach commented on the sufficiency of the information in the *Opening EC*, stating that it was "poorly written."[229] Steinbach added that the EC should not be read to suggest that the FBI was investigating the Trump campaign, but only those potential subjects within the campaign whose activities justified inquiry.[230] Steinbach was also questioned separately by the OIG on the amount of information that should normally be included in an EC opening a counterintelligence case. He stated that it should be a logical summary sufficient to justify the opening. Steinbach told the OIG, by way of an example, "It's, hey look, I have Mike Steinbach on this date met with a Russian who we know is associated with this intelligence organization. And, lay that out, and open a PI (preliminary investigation)."[231]

Although not referenced in the *Opening EC*, FBI officials have later pointed to the importance of the Australian information when viewed in conjunction with Russia's likely connections to the WikiLeaks disclosures and its efforts to interfere with the 2016 U.S. elections.[232] In addition, Trump had also stated in a recently televised campaign speech, "Russia, if you're listening, I hope you're able to find the 30,000 emails that are missing,"[233]

Paragraph Five information had been received. OIG Interview of Andrew McCabe dated Aug. 15, 2019 at 16.

[228] *Crossfire Hurricane Opening EC* at 3-4.

[229] OSC Report of Interview of Michael Steinbach on Aug. 12, 2019 at 2.

[230] *Id.* at 3.

[231] OIG Interview of Michael Steinbach on June 20, 2019 at 22-28.

[232] *See, e.g.*, OSC Report of Interview of FBI OGC Unit Chief-1 on August 29, 2019 at 4; OSC Report of Interview of Supervisory Special Agent-1 on June 17, 2019 at 2; *see generally Redacted OIG Review* at 351-52. There were also at least some activities involving the Trump campaign and Russians that did not become public, and were not known to the FBI, until much later. For example, on June 9, 2016, senior representatives of the campaign met briefly with a private Russian lawyer, Natalia Veselnitskaya, and others at the Trump Tower. 1 *Mueller Report* at 110, 117. Veselnitskaya "had previously worked for the Russian government and maintained a relationship with that government throughout this period of time." *Id.* at 110. The initial email to Donald Trump Jr. proposing the meeting said that the Crown prosecutor of Russia was offering to provide the campaign with documents and information that would incriminate Clinton. *Id.* The meeting at the Trump Tower only became public over a year later. *Id.* at 121.

[233] *Donald Trump on Russian & Missing Hillary Clinton Emails*, YouTube Channel C-SPAN, posted 7/27/16, *available at* https://www.youtube.com/watch?v=3kxG8uJUsWU (starting at 0:41). The *Mueller Report* states that this statement was "apparently a reference" to emails stored on a personal server that Clinton used while she was Secretary of State. 1 *Mueller Report* at 49. Strzok stated in his book *Compromised: Counterintelligence and the Threat of Donald J.*

a widely reported statement that appears to have referred to emails stored on the personal server that Clinton used while Secretary of State.[234]

The evidence the Office reviewed shows that there were internal discussions with FBI Headquarters executives, including the Deputy Director, about the decision to open Crossfire Hurricane. The executives were unanimous in supporting the opening of the investigation and there is no indication that these discussions contemplated anything short of an immediate full investigation, such as an assessment or preliminary investigation, into the meaning, credibility, and underpinnings of the statements attributed to Papadopoulos.[235] The personnel involved in the decision to open a full investigation have stated that they acted within the FBI's governing principles as set forth in the *AGG-Dom* and *DIOG* that required an authorized purpose and an "articulable factual basis for the investigation that reasonably indicates" that an activity constituting a federal crime or a national security threat "may be" occurring. But notably the *DIOG* also explicitly cautions FBI employees to avoid reputational risk to those being investigated by, among other things, specifying different standards for opening an assessment, a preliminary investigation, and a full investigation, with a corresponding continuum of permissible investigative activities. That measured approach does not appear to have been followed with respect to Crossfire Hurricane. Instead, as described above, on a Sunday and just three days after receiving the unanalyzed information from Australia, Strzok authored and approved the Crossfire Hurricane opening EC.[236] Thus, a full counterintelligence investigation into a SIM[237] was triggered, at the height of a political campaign, before any dialogue with Australia or the Intelligence Community, and prior to any critical analysis of the information itself or the potential for the risk

---

Trump at 109, as well as to the OIG that Australian High Commissioner Downer was prompted to turn over the Paragraph Five information upon seeing Trump's televised news conference during which Trump made his "Russia, if you're listening" comment. Strzok, *Compromised* at 109; OIG Interview of Peter Strzok on May 8, 2018 at 15. Strzok's version of this is factually inaccurate and contrary to the FBI's report of the August 2, 2016 interview of Downer and Australian Diplomat-1, an interview that Strzok himself conducted. The report of interview does not refer to Trump's news conference or the missing Clinton emails. *See Australian 302.* Moreover, Downer and Australian officials came to the U.S. Embassy with the Paragraph Five information on July 26th - one day *before* Trump's televised news conference. As referenced above in footnote 189, Strzok declined to be interviewed by the Office on this and other subjects.

[234] *See* 1 *Mueller Report* at 49.

[235] *Redacted OIG Review* at 53-54.

[236] *Crossfire Hurricane Opening EC* at 1. The speed of this action sharply contrasts with Strzok's decision-making in the referral in September 2016 of a matter involving former Congressman Anthony Weiner's laptop computer. In that instance, according to the OIG, the FBI and Strzok did not act for over a month to pursue legal process to review thousands of missing Clinton emails found on Weiner's laptop. The OIG sharply criticized the FBI, and particularly Strzok, for this delay. As discussed more fully below, the immediate opening of Crossfire Hurricane as a full investigation contrasts with the care taken in connection with the investigation of the Clinton Foundation and other matters.

[237] *See supra* § III.B.1 for a discussion of the requirements for sensitive investigative matters.

of error or disinformation, issues that appropriately are addressed during assessments or preliminary investigations.

The information from Papadopoulos was, in the words of one FBI executive, "a tipping point."[238] When interviewed by the OIG, FBI Deputy General Counsel Trisha Anderson stated that it would have been a dereliction of duty had the FBI not opened Crossfire Hurricane.[239] For his part, FBI General Counsel James Baker told the OIG that "[t]he opening of an investigation . . . [a]nd doing it quickly is a good thing for oversight because it forces the institution of the FBI and eventually the Department of Justice . . . to have appropriate management controls over what's going on."[240] In this regard, the *OIG Review* found that in early August 2016, after the opening of Crossfire Hurricane, NSD officials "were briefed on at least two occasions" about the investigation.[241]

FBI officials have acknowledged that they were aware that the information concerning Papadopoulos did not come from Australia's intelligence services, but rather from Australian diplomats who were previously unknown to the FBI personnel handling the Paragraph Five information.[242] In various interviews, several FBI officials have opined that the FBI was justified in opening Crossfire Hurricane as a full investigation because, in part, the information was given to the FBI from a trusted partner and therefore was deemed reliable.[243] Although this sentiment is understandable, the FBI's well-placed trust in a foreign partner should not equate to confidence in the shared information itself. Australia could not and did not make any representation about the credibility of the information. Although the Counterintelligence Division did eventually seek information about Papadopoulos,[244] the Office found no indications from witness testimony, electronic communications, emails, calendar entries, or other documentation that, at the time, the FBI gave any consideration to the actual trustworthiness of the information the diplomats

---

[238] *Redacted OIG Review* at 53.

[239] *Id.* at 54.

[240] *See* OIG Interview of James Baker on May 17, 2019 at 44; OSC Report of Interview of James Baker on Feb. 7, 2020 at 6. Baker's point is a reasonable one regarding the oversight value of opening an investigation, but we note that it would and should apply equally to the opening of a preliminary investigation or an assessment.

[241] *Redacted OIG Review* at 58 n.176 ("Notes and testimony reflect that in early August, NSD officials were briefed on at least two occasions" about the investigation).

[242] *See, e.g.*, OSC Report of Interview of Supervisory Special Agent-1 on July 22, 2020 at 1.

[243] U.S. Senate Judiciary Cmte. Staff Interview of Jonathan Moffa on September 9, 2020 at 65-66, 71-72.

[244] *See, e.g.*, FBI-AAA-02-0019550 (Email from Special Agent-2 to Supervisory Special Agent-1, Case Agent-1 & Laycock dated 08/05/2016); FBI-AAA-02-0019485 (Crossfire Hurricane Papadopoulos Profile dated 08/05/2016).

received from Papadopoulos - an individual whom they described as, among other things, "insecure" and "trying to impress" them.[245]

The information from Papadopoulos was clearly raw and unevaluated. It was not the product of normal Intelligence Community collection and analysis, and it lacked the standard caveats accompanying uncorroborated information from an individual whose information was being seen for the first time. The information – involving an ongoing presidential campaign – was precisely the kind of unevaluated information that required rigorous analysis in order to assess its relevance and value.[246] Nevertheless, the FBI predicated Crossfire Hurricane and its subsequent investigative activities, including the use of CHSs, undercover operations and FISA coverage, on the statements attributed to Papadopoulos.

Thus, at the time of opening Crossfire Hurricane, the FBI had (i) publicly available information concerning Papadopoulos's role in the campaign as a volunteer foreign policy adviser, (ii) information obtained from Papadopoulos by the Australian diplomats, (iii) information about Russia's likely election interference activities, (iv) Trump's public statements about Russia, and (v) unvetted media reporting on possible ties between Trump and Russian businessmen.[247] Significantly, beyond this, the FBI's Counterintelligence Division and its Crossfire Hurricane investigators did not possess any intelligence or other vetted, corroborated information regarding Trump or his campaign staff colluding with the Russian government.[248] The FBI OGC Unit Chief who advised on many Crossfire Hurricane matters and approved the case being opened as a SIM, ("FBI OGC Unit Chief-1") noted that she lacked "knowledge of alleged . . . ties between the Trump campaign and Russia prior to the

---

[245] *See supra* § IV.A.3.a (discussing the views of Papadopoulos held by the Australian diplomats and noting his strengths and weaknesses). Understandably, as noted below, when Crossfire Hurricane was opened, serious efforts were made to keep the investigation quiet so as not to interfere with the upcoming election. Ultimately, however, the Mueller investigation reported that:

> When interviewed, Papadopoulos and the Campaign officials who interacted with him told the [Mueller] Office that they could not recall Papadopoulos' sharing the information that Russia had obtained "dirt" on candidate Clinton in the form of emails or that Russia could assist the Campaign through the anonymous release of information about Clinton. . . . No documentary evidence, and nothing in the email accounts or other communications facilities reviewed by the [Mueller] Office, shows that Papadopoulos shared this information with the Campaign.

1 *Mueller Report* at 93-94.

[246] *See* discussion of analytic requirements *supra* § III.B.3.

[247] *See Redacted OIG Review* at 351-52.

[248] In early July 2016, the NYFO received some of the reports that later came to be known as the "Steele dossier." The Office found no evidence, however, suggesting that Strzok, who wrote and approved the *Crossfire Hurricane Opening EC*, was aware of those reports when he opened the investigation, and the Crossfire Hurricane investigators did not receive the reports until mid-September. *See Redacted OIG Review* at v.

[Crossfire Hurricane] investigation being formally opened."[249] The *FBI Inspection Division Report* describes similar statements by others. As noted in that FBI internal review, "[t]his total lack of intelligence did not appear to have been considered significant [ ]"[250] when opening a full investigation on persons associated with an active presidential campaign.

As the record now reflects, at the time of the opening of Crossfire Hurricane, the FBI did not possess any intelligence showing that anyone associated with the Trump campaign was in contact with Russian intelligence officers at any point during the campaign.[251] Moreover, the now more complete record of facts relevant to the opening of Crossfire Hurricane is illuminating. Indeed, at the time Crossfire Hurricane was opened, the FBI (albeit not the Crossfire Hurricane investigators) was in possession of some of the Steele Reports. However, even if the Crossfire Hurricane investigators were in possession of the Steele Reports earlier, they would not have been aware of the fact that the Russians were cognizant of Steele's election-related reporting. The *SSCI Russia Report* notes that "[s]ensitive reporting from June 2017 indicated that a [person affiliated] to Russian Oligarch 1 was [possibly aware] of Steele's election investigation as of early July 2016."[252] Indeed, "an early June 2017 USIC report indicated that two persons affiliated with [Russian Intelligence Services] *were aware of* Steele's election investigation in early July 2016."[253] Put more pointedly, Russian intelligence knew of Steele's election investigation for the Clinton campaign by no later than early July 2016. Thus, as discussed in Section IV.D.1.a.3, Steele's sources may have been compromised by the Russians at a time prior to the creation of the Steele Reports and throughout the FBI's Crossfire Hurricane investigation.

c. Interview of the Australian diplomats

On August 2, 2016, two days after opening Crossfire Hurricane, Strzok and Supervisory Special Agent-1 met in London with the Australian diplomats to assess and clarify exactly what had been said by Papadopoulos in May and provided to the U.S. government in July.

In preparation for their interview, Strzok and Supervisory Special Agent-1 sought the assistance of the FBI's Assistant Legal Attaché in London ("UK ALAT-1"). UK ALAT-1's primary FBI responsibilities in London included, among other things, collaboration and information-sharing with British Intelligence Service-1. In UK ALAT-1's interview with the Office, he pointed out the inherent importance of sharing information with the British intelligence service that related to potential Russian intelligence activity in the United Kingdom.[254] Thus, UK ALAT-1 briefed the British intelligence service about

---

[249] U.S. House of Representatives Cmte. on the Judiciary Interview of FBI OGC Unit Chief-1 on Oct. 23, 2018 at 145.

[250] *FBI Inspection Division Report* at 125.

[251] This is shown by an analysis in early 2017 of what the FBI knew about articles published in the *New York Times*. It is described later in this report in connection with other matters from that time period. *See infra* § IV.D.1.a.iii.

[252] *SSCI Russia Report* at 885 (emphasis added).

[253] *Id.*

[254] OSC Report of Interview of UK ALAT-1 on June 4, 2019 at 1.

Papadopoulos's allegations involving possible Russian influence in the Trump campaign. Given the nature of the allegations and the speed with which Strzok and Supervisory Special Agent-1 needed his assistance, UK ALAT-1 assumed that the FBI's interview of the Australian diplomats was exceptionally critical.[255] UK ALAT-1 also believed that the Crossfire Hurricane investigators likely were in possession of compelling facts beyond what UK ALAT-1 understood from the substance of Papadopoulos's claims in Paragraph Five.[256] Nevertheless, UK ALAT-1's independent impression of the predication for the investigation was echoed by Supervisory Special Agent-1 in a Lync exchange with UK ALAT-1 during which the predication was referred to as "thin."[257] UK ALAT-1 also recalled Strzok making a comment in the taxi on their way to the Australian High Commission to the effect that "there's nothing to this, but we have to run it to ground."[258] These exchanges with Supervisory Special Agent-1 and Strzok resonated with UK ALAT-1 because, in sharing the Papadopoulos information with his British Intelligence Service-1 counterparts at the time, they expressed real skepticism about the motivations and reliability of Papadopoulos.[259] UK ALAT-1 told the Office that British Intelligence Service-1 did not assess the information about the Russians and Trump, attributed to Papadopoulos, to be particularly valuable intelligence.[260] Indeed, he told the FBI's Inspection Division investigators that "the British could not believe the Papadopoulos bar conversation was all there was,"[261] and they were convinced the FBI must have had more information that it was holding back.[262]

As it relates to predication for opening Crossfire Hurricane as a full investigation, after Strzok and Supervisory Special Agent-1 had traveled to London and interviewed the Australian diplomats on August 2, 2016, the following Lync exchange between UK ALAT-1 and Supervisory Special Agent-1 on August 11, 2016 is instructive:

UK ALAT-1:   Dude, are we telling them [British Intelligence Service-1] everything we know, or is there more to this?

Supervisory Special Agent-1: that's all we have

Supervisory Special Agent-1: not holding anything back

UK ALAT-1:   Damn that's thin

Supervisory Special Agent-1: I know

---

[255] *Id.* at 1-2.

[256] *Id.*

[257] FBI-AAA-EC-00000365 (Lync exchange between Supervisory Special Agent-1 and UK ALAT-1 dated 08/11/2016).

[258] OSC Report of Interview of UK ALAT-1 on June 4, 2019 at 2.

[259] *Id.* at 3.

[260] *Id.*

[261] *FBI Inspection Division Report* at 224 (quoting UK ALAT-1).

[262] *Id.* at 225.

Supervisory Special Agent-1: it sucks[263]

UK ALAT-1 went on to tell the Inspection Division that in discussing the matter with a senior British Intelligence Service-1 official, the official was openly skeptical, said the FBI's plan for an operation made no sense, and asked UK ALAT-1 why the FBI did not just go to Papadopoulos and ask him what they wanted to know,[264] a sentiment UK ALAT-1 told investigators that he shared.[265]

Later in the Fall of 2016, UK ALAT-1 was at FBI Headquarters with some of his British Intelligence Service-1 counterparts. While there, members of the Crossfire Hurricane team played the audio/visual recordings of CHS-1's August 20, 2016 meeting with Carter Page. UK ALAT-1 said the effect on the British Intelligence Service-1 personnel was not positive because of the lack of any evidence coming out of the conversation.[266] UK ALAT-1 told the OIG that after watching the video one of his British colleagues said, "For [expletive] sake, man. You went through a lot of trouble to get him to say nothing." At a later point in time, after the Mueller Special Counsel team was in place, UK ALAT-1 said that "the Brits finally had enough," and in response to a request for some assistance "[a British Intelligence Service-1 person] basically said there was no [expletive] way in hell they were going to do it."[267]

From his vantage point, UK ALAT-1 saw that FBI executive management was pushing the matter so hard that "there was no stopping the train," and he told the OIG that," I mean it was, this thing was coming. So my job was to grease the skids for it, and that's what I did."[268]

Had the Crossfire Hurricane investigators attempted to critically assess the information from Papadopoulos through FBI holdings and standard requests to other government agencies for information about Trump and Russian intelligence activities involving Trump, they would have learned:

- Jonathan Moffa served as the Chief of the FBI's Counterintelligence Analysis Section throughout 2016. Moffa was a career FBI Intelligence Analyst who began working as a full-time FBI counterespionage analyst in 2004,[269] and, prior to being selected for the Section Chief position in January 2016, had been Chief of the Russian Analysis Unit for approximately four years. Moffa advised investigators that he had heard nothing about Trump and Russia until events began to be reported in July 2016.[270]

---

[263] FBI-AAA-EC-00007239 (Aug. 11, 2016 at 14:40:27)

[264] *FBI Inspection Division Report* at 224 (quoting UK ALAT-1).

[265] *Id.* at 227.

[266] *Id.* at 208.

[267] *Id.* at 233.

[268] *Id.* at 225.

[269] The Counterintelligence Analysis Section that Moffa headed throughout 2016 had responsibility for covering Russia intelligence matters, among those of other countries.

[270] *See* Section IV.A.1 regarding pre-July 2016 efforts.

- The FBI Intelligence Analyst who had perhaps the most in-depth knowledge of particularly sensitive Russian intelligence information in FBI holdings during the relevant time period disclosed that she never saw anything regarding any Trump election campaign conspiracy with the Russians, nor did she see anything in FBI holdings regarding Carter Page, Michael Flynn, George Papadopoulos, or Paul Manafort[271] engaging in any type of conspiracy with the Russians regarding the election.[272]

- Similarly, DNI James Clapper testified before Congress on the subject of Trump and Russia and he answered "no" when asked if he was aware of any such evidence.[273] The former DNI reconfirmed this fact when he was interviewed by the Office and advised that he knew of no direct evidence that would meet the legal standard of conspiracy or collusion on Trump's part.

- Admiral Mike Rogers served as the Director of NSA during the relevant time period. When asked about any awareness he had of any evidence of collusion as asserted in the Steele Reports, he stated that he did not recall any intelligence that supported the collusion assertions in that reporting, nor did he have any discussions during the Summer of 2016 with his counterparts in the intelligence community about collusion between the Russians and any Republicans.[274]

- Victoria Nuland served as Undersecretary for Political Affairs at the Department of State during the relevant time frame. A career employee of the Department of State and one of its most experienced Russian observers, she told our investigators that she never saw any U.S. government proof of the allegations contained in the Steele reporting regarding Trump and Russian officials,[275] and further stated that to her recollection no information regarding a well-coordinated conspiracy between Trump and the Russians had ever come across her desk,[276] with one exception. Nuland advised that she had received a two-page

---

[271] The Intelligence Analyst did, however, find some information related to Manafort that was not connected to the election or the presidential campaign. OSC Interview Report of Headquarters Analyst-3 on Aug. 14, 2019 at 4.

[272] OSC Reports of Interview of Headquarters Analyst-3 on Aug. 14, 2019 at 4; Dec. 10, 2019 at 4; and Feb. 19, 2020 at 7.

[273] U.S. House of Representatives Executive Session, Permanent Select Committee on Intelligence Interview of James Clapper on July 17, 2017 at 26, 87-89; OSC Report of Interview of James Clapper on December 13, 2021 at 5.

[274] OSC Report of Interview of Mike Rogers on Aug. 1, 2019 at 2, 5.

[275] OSC Report of Interview of Victoria Nuland on Nov. 30, 2021 at 5-6.

[276] Nuland also pointed out, however, that, if reporting is about a U.S. person, "it is heavily redacted and compartmented before it would come to her attention" and that it was possible that "she would not have seen all the information." She said that "[t]he masking rules are followed when it comes to providing intelligence reporting" and that she "would have had no national security reason to see reporting on the sex-related allegations concerning an American businessman." In her view, for the State Department, "it was not intelligence" if it pertained to U.S. persons. *Id.* at 6, 8.

summary of the Steele allegations from Jonathan Winer, who in 2016 was serving as Secretary of State Kerry's Special Envoy to Libya.[277] Winer told Nuland that Winer had prepared the summary from his review of the Steele reporting while he was at Steele's country house in the United Kingdom. Nuland thought Winer had passed the summary to her sometime in July 2016.[278]

- CIA Director John Brennan and Deputy Director David Cohen were interviewed by the Office and were asked about their knowledge of any actual evidence of members of the Trump campaign conspiring or colluding with Russian officials. When Brennan was provided with an overview of the origins of the Attorney General's Review after Special Counsel Mueller finding a lack of evidence of collusion between the Trump campaign and Russian authorities, Brennan offered that "they found no conspiracy."[279] [280] (In fact, Special Counsel Mueller's report explicitly states that "[u]ltimately, [his] investigation did not establish that the [Trump] Campaign coordinated or conspired with the Russian government in its election-interference activities."[281]) Relatedly, however, shortly after Special Counsel Mueller delivered his report to the Attorney General and the Attorney General had issued a short summary of the Report's findings, Brennan appeared on MSNBC's *Morning Joe* program, where he stated that "[he] suspected there was more than there actually was" with regard to collusion between the Trump campaign and Russia in the 2016 election, thus suggesting that he had no actual knowledge of such information.[282] Moreover, Deputy Director Cohen advised that he had no recollection of knowing anything Trump was doing with Putin, as opposed to what Putin and the Russians were doing to interfere in the election. Cohen stated that if there were such

---

[277] Nuland thought the summary was more on the order of four pages, but others believed it was two pages. *Id.* at 4.

[278] *Id.*

[279] OSC Report of Interview of John Brennan on Aug. 21, 2020 at 1.

[280] Prior to the release of the *Mueller Report*, and specifically in an August 16, 2018 opinion piece, the former Director had characterized the claims of then-President Trump that there was no collusion with Russia as, "in a word, hogwash." https://www.nytimes.com/2018/08/16/opinion/john-brennan-trump-russia-collusion-security-clearance.html.

[281] 1 *Mueller Report* at 173; *see also* 1 *Mueller Report* at 1-2 ("Although the investigation established that the Russian government perceived it would benefit from a Trump presidency and worked to secure that outcome, and that the Campaign expected it would benefit electorally from information stolen and released through Russian efforts, the investigation did not establish that members of the Trump Campaign conspired or coordinated with the Russian government in its election interference activities."); 1 *Mueller Report* at 9 ("Further, the evidence was not sufficient to charge that any member of the Trump Campaign conspired with representatives of the Russian government to interfere in the 2016 election.")

[282] MSNBC, "Morning Joe," March 25, 2019 at 8:24 a.m. ET; *see also* RealClear Politics, *Brennan: 'Relieved' There Was Not a Criminal Conspiracy with Russia, 'Good News for the Country,'* March 25, 2019.

knowledge, it would have been included in a formal referral to the FBI. In addition, if the CIA had become aware of any U.S. person being involved in a criminal conspiracy, it would have sent the information to the FBI in a formal referral. He advised that he was not aware of any such referrals in this matter.[283]

In any event, within days after opening Crossfire Hurricane, the FBI learned from interviewing the Australian diplomats that there were reasons to be unsure about what to make of the information from Papadopoulos. Not only had Supervisory Special Agent-1 and Strzok told UK ALAT-1 that what they had was "thin," but one of the Australian diplomats had told Strzok and Supervisory Special Agent-1 in their interview that the Paragraph Five information was written in an intentionally vague way because of what Papadopoulos did and did not say. Nonetheless, shortly thereafter, the FBI opened full investigations of Papadopoulos, Carter Page, General Michael Flynn, and Paul Manafort.[284] All four were U.S. persons associated with the Trump campaign and all of them (other than Papadopoulos) had "either ties to Russia or a history of travel to Russia."[285]

In July 2016, in addition to receiving the first several Steele reports, the FBI received a separate stream of information regarding Trump from a former FBI CHS. Specifically, an FBI supervisor from a New England field office ("New England Supervisory Special Agent-1") was contacted unexpectedly by the former CHS with whom the supervisor had worked many years earlier when assigned to a different field office on matters related to Russian organized crime. New England Supervisory Special Agent-1 agreed to meet his former CHS on July 21, 2016. At that meeting, the CHS told New England Supervisory Special Agent-1 that he/she had been contacted by a colleague who owns an investigative firm and who was looking into Trump's various business contacts and ventures in Russia.[286] The former CHS did not identify the investigative firm that day, except to say that the firm had been hired by the DNC and another unnamed individual.[287] The former CHS then provided New England Supervisory Special Agent-1 with a list of approximately 45 individuals and entities who reportedly had surfaced in the firm's investigation of Trump's ties to Russia.[288]

---

[283] OSC Report of Interview of David Cohen on Feb. 2, 2022 at 7-8.

[284] FBI-0002788 (Crossfire D. Opening Electronic Communication dated 08/10/2016); FBI-0007869 (Crossfire F. Opening Electronic Communication dated 08/10/2016); FBI-0007875 (Crossfire T. Opening Electronic Communication dated 08/10/2016); FBI-0007873 (Crossfire R. Opening Electronic Communication dated 08/16/2016). As noted above, the NYFO had already opened an investigation of Page. In addition, in January 2016, the FBI's Criminal Investigation Division had opened an investigation into allegations of money laundering and tax evasion by Manafort. *Redacted OIG Review* at 291.

[285] *Redacted OIG Review* at 59-60; *see also* U.S. Senate Judiciary Cmte. Staff Interview of Jonathan Moffa on September 9, 2020 at 77-80.

[286] FBI-EMAIL-197479 (Email from New England Supervisory Special Agent-1 to New England Supervisory Special Agent-2 dated 07/29/2016).

[287] *Id.*

[288] *Id.*

The list was comprised mostly of Russian individuals and entities and immediately raised "red flags" for New England Supervisory Special Agent-1, who believed it was necessary to get the information into the right hands as soon as possible.[289] Following the July 21, 2016 meeting, New England Supervisory Special Agent-1 emailed a counterintelligence colleague about the meeting and forwarded the list of names he had received. Within a few days, New England Supervisory Special Agent-1's email and the investigative firm's list of names made its way to FBI Headquarters and to the Crossfire Hurricane investigators.[290]

The former CHS reached out to New England Supervisory Special Agent-1 again on August 23, 2016, telling him that he/she had reviewed a large volume of material that the investigative firm had compiled and the former CHS passed on more information from that effort.[291] New England Supervisory Special Agent-1 in turn passed the information directly to an Agent on the Crossfire Hurricane team ("Special Agent-2").[292] Then, one month later, on September 23, 2016,[293] the former CHS reached out yet again, prompting New England Supervisory Special Agent-1 to email the Crossfire Hurricane investigators again, to report that the CHS has more information on Trump's reported ties to Russia.[294]

Months later, on January 11, 2017, after the Steele Dossier had been made public, New England Supervisory Special Agent-1 asked Supervisory Special Agent-1 if anything was "to be gleaned from" the information he provided in July.[295] It was at that time that Supervisory Special Agent-1 let New England Supervisory Special Agent-1 know that his team had received the same information through a separate reporting stream from a different source, in context being Steele.[296] Supervisory Special Agent-1 further advised that the second source was working with the same investigative firm that had given the information to the former CHS. Sometime later, New England Supervisory Special Agent-1 had learned that his former CHS had developed the information related to Trump while working with Glenn Simpson and Fusion GPS. Thus, it appears that in July 2016 the FBI had not yet determined that the dual reporting it was receiving actually was coming from the same source – that is, Simpson and Fusion GPS.

---

[289] OSC Report of Interview of New England Supervisory Special Agent-1 on Sept. 1, 2020 at 2-3.

[290] FBI-AAA-02-0018017 (Email from Moffa to Auten, Strzok & Supervisory Special Agent-1 dated 08/02/2016).

[291] FBI-EMAIL-262171 (Email from New England Supervisory Special Agent-1 to Special Agent-2 dated 08/23/2016).

[292] *Id.*

[293] Interestingly, September 23, 2016 was the same day that Michael Isikoff's *Yahoo! News* article was published.

[294] FBI-EMAIL-242390 (Email from New England Supervisory Special Agent-1 to Supervisory Special Agent-1 dated 09/23/2016).

[295] FBI-EMAIL-038612 (Email from New England Supervisory Special Agent-1 to Supervisory Special Agent-1 dated 01/11/2017).

[296] FBI-EMAIL-028908 (Email from Supervisory Special Agent-1 to New England Supervisory Special Agent-1, Supervisory Special Agent-3, Auten, Case Agent-1 & others dated 01/11/2017).

Further, it does not appear that the FBI was aware of the fact that essentially the same information the former CHS was providing to New England Supervisory Special Agent-1 was being provided to the media by Simpson and Fusion GPS. This was a pattern similar to that later employed in the Alfa Bank matter when the Alfa Bank allegations were provided to members of the media by Fusion GPS and then to the FBI through Michael Sussmann.[297]

4. *Other investigative activity prior to the receipt of the Steele Reports*

Between the time the FBI opened the Crossfire Hurricane investigation and when Crossfire Hurricane investigators first received the Steele Reports in mid-September 2016,[298] the FBI took the following investigative steps:

- As discussed above, Strzok and Supervisory Special Agent-1 met with Australian officials to verify the information provided by Papadopoulos.

- Records and open source data were checked on the four Crossfire Hurricane subjects.

- Travel of the subjects was monitored.

- Some records were obtained from other federal agencies and a foreign government.

- FBI CHSs and UCEs were used to engage with some of the subjects.[299]

The *OIG Review* provides the following succinct summary of the FBI's investigative activity prior to the receipt of the Steele Reports:

> [B]y the date the Crossfire Hurricane team received the six Steele reports on September 19, the investigation had been underway for approximately 6 weeks and the team had opened investigations on four individuals: Carter Page, George Papadopoulos, Paul Manafort, and Michael Flynn. In addition, during the prior 6 weeks, the team had used CHSs to conduct operations against Page, Papadopoulos, and a high-level Trump campaign official, although those operations *had not resulted in the collection of any inculpatory information.*[300]

FBI personnel told the OIG that "[t]he FBI did not use national security letters or compulsory process prior to obtaining the first FISA orders."[301] FBI Deputy General Counsel Anderson said that "early on . . . FBI managers . . . 'took off the table any idea of legal process' . . . because the FBI was 'trying to move very quietly.'"[302] Similarly,

---

[297] *See infra* § IV.E.1.c.

[298] The Steele Dossier is described in detail in Section IV.D.1.b.

[299] *See Redacted OIG Review* at 78-80; 355-56.

[300] *Id.* at 101 (emphasis added).

[301] *Id.* at 78.

[302] *Id.* (quoting FBI Deputy General Counsel Trisha Anderson); *see also id.* at 69 (describing statements by Comey and Deputy Director McCabe on the importance of keeping the investigation covert).

"[m]embers of the Crossfire Hurricane team told [the OIG] that they avoided the use of compulsory legal process to obtain information at this time in order to prevent any public disclosure of the investigation's existence and to avoid any potential impact on the election."[303] Notably absent from the list of investigative steps taken were the following non-public, non-compulsory options:

- Interviewing Page, particularly once the FBI's interest in him was publicly disclosed by the media.[304] In fact, two days after this disclosure, Page wrote to Director Comey offering to be interviewed, but the FBI elected not to do so.[305]

- Asking Page, who volunteered to be interviewed and had spoken with the FBI when asked to do so on prior occasions, if he would consent to a polygraph exam or provide access to relevant electronic records.

- Using other standard investigative techniques not requiring a court order.

- Interviewing Papadopoulos, the actual source of the Paragraph Five information.[306] [307]

Another step that the Crossfire Hurricane investigators could have taken, but chose not to take, was the use of pen registers and trap and trace devices. Although FISA authorizes the government to obtain a pen register when "the information likely to be obtained . . . is relevant to an ongoing investigation to protect against . . . clandestine intelligence activities,[308] Case Agent-1 told the OIG that he saw pen registers as a "criminal authority."[309] FBI OGC Unit Chief-1 could not understand why investigators working on

---

[303] *Id.* at 78, 355; *see also* OIG Interview of Case Agent-1 on Aug. 28, 2018 at 69 (expressing concern about the risk of disclosure of subpoenas).

[304] *See* Michael Isikoff, *U.S. Intel Officials Probe Ties Between Trump Adviser and Kremlin, Yahoo! News* (Sept. 23, 2016) (hereinafter "Isikoff, *Officials Probe Ties*").

[305] Letter from Carter Page to FBI Director Comey (Sept. 25, 2016). As discussed below, the FBI did not interview Page until Comey approved the interview in March 2017. *See infra* § IV.D.1.h.ii.

[306] As noted below, when Crossfire Hurricane was opened, an important goal was to keep the investigation secret. By September 23, 2016, however, the investigation was made public via Isikoff's article attributing the information to a "senior U.S. law enforcement official." *See infra* § IV.D.1.h.ii.

[307] As noted, Australian High Commissioner Downer told Strzok and Supervisory Special Agent-1 that he did not get the sense that Papadopoulos was the middle man coordinating with the Russians. *See supra* footnote 224.

[308] *See supra* § III.C.

[309] OIG Interview of Case Agent-1 on Aug. 28, 2018 at 69.

Crossfire Hurricane were not seeking authority to use pen registers and trap and trace devices.[310]

In terms of the analytical capabilities that were applied to Crossfire Hurricane, Lisa Page testified that the FBI used "line level analysts who [were] super experts on Russia."[311] The FBI's *Inspection Division Report* found, however, that the intelligence analysts "selected for Crossfire Hurricane were uniformly inexperienced" and that "[n]one of them were subject matter expert analysts."[312] Aside from Auten, the most experienced analyst had less than nine months of experience working in that capacity, two had less than four months experience, and two came straight from analyst training.[313]

The analysis done in Crossfire Hurricane was also limited by the Counterintelligence Division's failure to integrate the Directorate of Intelligence into the investigation as required by policy.[314] Rather, in at least one instance, Assistant Director of the Counterintelligence Division Bill Priestap appears to have deliberately shut down the involvement of the Directorate of Intelligence in an enhanced validation review of Christopher Steele, a key source.[315]

B. The FBI's and the Department's Disparate Treatment of Candidates Clinton and Trump

In the course of the Office's investigation, we learned of allegations involving possible attempted foreign election influence activities associated with entities related to Clinton, in addition to the allegations related to Trump. The Office sought to determine, to the extent possible, if the actions taken by the FBI (and in certain instances, the Department) to address the allegations were consistent with those taken by the FBI relating to the allegations of Russian foreign election influence attached to the Trump campaign in July 2016. Comparing the respective investigative activity was significant to the investigation since it could support or undercut allegations of institutional bias against either candidate. As an initial matter, given the

---

[310] FBI-AAA-EC-00006440 (Lync message exchange between Clinesmith and FBI OGC Unit Chief-1 dated 10/03/2016). In referring to Crossfire Hurricane investigators, FBI OGC Unit Chief-1 inquired of Clinesmith "[W]hy aren't they getting PR/TTs [pen registers/trap and trace devices]? UGH!"

[311] U.S. House of Representatives Cmte. on the Judiciary Interview of Lisa Page on July 16, 2018 at 157.

[312] *FBI Inspection Division Report* at 17.

[313] *Id.*

[314] *See supra* § IV.A.3.b.

[315] U.S. Senate Cmte. on the Judiciary Interview of Supervisory Special Agent-1 on Aug. 27, 2020 at 91-105 (agent left the Crossfire Hurricane investigation because he "had a professional disagreement with stopping the enhanced validation review"); *see also* OSC Report of Interview of Supervisory Special Agent-1 on July 22, 2020 at 2-3; OSC Report of Interview of Jonathan Moffa on Oct. 28, 2020 at 15; OSC Report of Interview of Supervisory Special Agent-3 on Mar. 18, 2021 at 2; OSC Report of Interview of Headquarters Analyst-1 on Dec. 16, 2020 at 2. As described above, *see supra* § III.B.3, the *CHS Policy Guide* appears to give the Assistant Director for Intelligence an approval role for a source like Steele.

68

particular nature of the allegations related to each campaign, attempting to view the FBI's investigative activity in an "apples to apples" approach is undoubtedly an imperfect method to analyze whether the FBI engaged in disparate treatment of the campaigns. Nevertheless, the comparisons are instructive, and below we discuss our observations regarding the investigative approach to allegations of foreign election influence against each campaign.

1. *The threat of foreign election influence by Foreign Government-2*

Beginning in late 2014, before Clinton formally declared her presidential candidacy, the FBI learned from a well-placed CHS ("CHS-A") that a foreign government ("Foreign Government-2") was planning to send an individual ("Non-U.S. Person-1") to contribute to Clinton's anticipated presidential campaign, as a way to gain influence with Clinton should she win the presidency.[316] The FBI's independent corroboration of this information is discussed in the Classified Appendix.

Upon receipt of this information and the predication it provided, Field Office-1 sought to have one of two other better-positioned and higher-resourced field offices open a counterintelligence or public corruption investigation into these allegations, but Counterintelligence Division Executive Management directed Field Office-1 to open a full counterintelligence investigation into the matter.[317]

Field Office-1 sought FISA coverage of Non-U.S. Person-1, almost immediately, in order to obtain access to his/her email accounts and to conduct a search of him/her as soon as he/she arrived in the United States.[318] Although Field Office-1 attempted to obtain expedited approval for the FISA authorization,[319] the certified copy of the application was sent by OI to the FBI Headquarters for final approval where it remained, according to Field Office-1 SAC-1, "in limbo" for approximately four months.[320] According to another agent, the application lingered because "everyone was 'super more careful'" and "scared with the big name [Clinton]" involved.[321] "[T]hey were pretty 'tippy-toeing' around HRC because there was a chance she would be the next President." [322] Similarly, Field Office-1 SAC-1 told investigators that, when

---

[316] *See* FBI-AAA-12-0023529 (Classified Codeword-1 Investigation Chronology); *see also*, FBI-AAA-03-0000482 (Email from Comey to Field Office-1 SAC-1 & others dated 04/14/2015); OSC Report of Interview of Headquarters Supervisory Special Agent-4 on May 28, 2020 at 5.

[317] *Id.*; OSC Report of Interview of Field Office-1 Handling Agent-1 on April 23, 2020 at 1; OSC Report of Interview of Headquarters Supervisory Special Agent-4 on May 28, 2020 at 5.

[318] FBI-AAA-03-0000482 at 0000483, Email from Field Office-1 SAC-1 to FBI Director James Comey, April 14, 2015.

[319] FBI-AAA-12-0023529 (Codename-1 Investigation Chronology).

[320] FBI-AAA-03-0000482 at 0000483, Email from Field Office-1 SAC-1 to FBI Director James Comey, April 14, 2015.

[321] OSC Report of Interview of Headquarters Supervisory Special Agent-4 dated May 28, 2020 at 8.

[322] OSC Report of Interview of Headquarters Supervisory Special Agent-4 dated May 28, 2020 at 9.

she spoke with the Counterintelligence Division Assistant Director and Deputy Assistant Director, they alluded to the fact that they did not want a presidential candidate on tape, even though Field Office-1 SAC-1 believed that was a very remote possibility.[323] According to the records the Office reviewed, it appears that the delay also may have been partially attributable to a decision to await the confirmation of the incoming Attorney General.[324] The FISA was ultimately conditioned on the requirement that the FBI give defensive briefings to the various public officials and candidates of both political parties, including Clinton, targeted by Foreign Government-2.[325]

On December 16, 2014, FBI OGC Section Chief Rick McNally summarized his conversation with Stuart Evans, the Deputy Assistant Attorney General responsible for OI, about the proposed activities:

> I spoke to Stu Evans, he suggested that we can go back to him rather than calling the AAG. BUT, the question was not about PC (no legal issue)[[326]] it was about what was the FBI's thinking about this case, specifically whether or not we think that the politician's staff and the politician are complicit with the target, meaning that the pol and staff know that the target is working for a foreign government and has some bad intent, or alternatively, do we think that the pol and staff are unwitting, and if they are unwitting, are we considering some sort of defensive brief to the politician or staff to mitigate risk. . . .[327]

Certain critical activity in the investigation was delayed for months due to, among other things, concerns that "a politician [Clinton] [was] involved," and that the investigation might interfere with a presumed future presidential campaign. In line with the directive, the FBI ultimately provided defensive briefings to the officials or their representatives, though it took

---

[323] OSC Report of Interview of Field Office-1 SAC dated Sept. 10, 2020 at 1.

[324] *Id.* at 3.

[325] FBI-AAA-12-0023531 (Classified Codeword-1 Investigation Chronology). The need for a defensive briefing had been discussed by the Department and the FBI even before the announcement of Clinton's candidacy in April 2015. Ultimately, one was provided to her representatives in October 2015. *Id.* at 0023531-32.

[326] *See also* OSC Report of Interview of OI Attorney-2 on August 12, 2021 at 1 (probable cause was "solid" with "plenty of corroborative evidence") and ("it was normal to 'pause' FISAs when they involved politicians because those types of investigations are sensitive"); *see also* OSC Report of Interview of Stuart Evans on June 17, 2020, at 5.

[327] Email from Richard McNally to Kevin Clinesmith, Headquarters Supervisory Special Agent-4 & others dated 12/16/2014.

approximately 11 months from the receipt of the original allegations.[328] Clinton elected to receive the defensive briefing through her personal attorneys.[329]

The use of defensive briefings in 2015 contrasts with the FBI's failure to provide a defensive briefing to the Trump campaign approximately one year later when Australia shared the information from Papadopoulos. Significant to the question of whether a defensive briefing was appropriate here - as it was determined to be just months earlier when a defensive briefing was given to Clinton via her lawyers - is the fact that Australia had specifically noted, "[i]t was unclear whether [Papadopoulos] or the Russians were referring to material acquired publicly of [sic] through other means."[330] Further, the Office's investigation revealed that the FBI engaged in what were likely very limited discussions as to whether any such briefing was appropriate. Deputy Director McCabe informed the OIG that he did not remember participating in *any* discussions about providing a defensive briefing as an alternative to opening the full counterintelligence investigation.[331] McCabe noted that, at the time Crossfire Hurricane was opened, the FBI had "[t]o do some work to have a better understanding of what [it had] before tak[ing] a step as overt as providing a defensive briefing because the . . . briefing could . . . eliminate . . . or reduce your ability to get to the bottom of the threat."[332] On the other hand, Assistant Director for Counterintelligence Priestap said that he discussed the issue of defensive briefings with others.[333] He explained that the FBI provides

---

[328] OSC Report(s) of Interview(s) of Field Office-1 Handling Agent-1 on April 23, 2020 and May 5, 2020; OSC Report of Interview of Headquarters Supervisory Special Agent-4 on May 28, 2020 at 5 – 7; OSC Report of Interview of David Archey on June 21, 2021 at 1 – 3 (discussing the rationale for the debriefings regarding the threat from Foreign Government-2 and ECs documenting the September 1, 2015 briefing to a designated staffer on behalf of an elected official within the Republican party, and the October 15, 2015 defensive briefing Archey provided to Clinton's personal attorneys).

[329] *See* SENATE-FISA2020-001321 (Declassified defensive brief EC dated 10/22/2015).

[330] *London EC* at 2-3.

[331] OIG Interview of Andrew McCabe on Aug. 15, 2019 at 118; *see also* OSC Report of Interview of Special Agent-2 on June 25, 2020 at 2 (Special Agent-2 did not recall any internal FBI discussions suggesting a defensive briefing to the Trump campaign); OSC Report of Interview of Brian Auten on July 26, 2021 at 12 (Auten did not recall conversations about a defensive briefing regarding the information from Australia); OSC Report of Interview of Supervisory Special Agent-1 on July 22, 2020 at 5-6 (Supervisory Special Agent-1 did not recall any consideration being given to conducting straightforward defensive briefings to candidate Trump or members of his team regarding this information); OIG Interview of James Comey on Feb. 28, 2019 at 102-108 (Comey stated that he had no memory of any discussion of a defensive briefing to the Trump campaign).

[332] OIG Interview of Andrew McCabe on Aug. 15, 2019 at 118-119.

[333] OIG Interview of E.W. "Bill" Priestap on Aug. 22, 2018 at 4; *see also Redacted OIG Review* at 55.

defensive briefings when we obtain information indicating a foreign adversary is trying or will try to influence a specific U.S. person and when there is no indication that that specific U.S. person could be working with the adversary.

. . . [W]e had no indication as to which person in the Trump campaign allegedly received the offer from the Russians. . . .

. . . . Because the possibility existed that someone on the Trump campaign could have taken the Russians up on their offer, I thought it was wise to open an investigation to look into the situation.[334]

How these observations can be reconciled with the defensive briefings previously provided to Clinton and others is unclear. The FBI's decision to conduct defensive briefings in the investigation of Foreign Government-2's foreign influence efforts is curious given that defensive briefings could reduce the likelihood of success of any investigation into the foreign influence allegations [335] and that candidates and public officials might then be less likely to interact with representatives of Foreign Government-2. The decision to provide defensive briefings to Clinton and others seems to conflict directly with McCabe's notion that providing "a defensive briefing [to the Trump campaign] . . . could . . . eliminate . . . or reduce your ability to get to the bottom of the threat."

Similarly, with respect to the Trump campaign, Priestap's twofold concern that (i) the FBI was unaware of which member of the Trump campaign allegedly received the

---

[334] OIG Interview of E.W. "Bill" Priestap on Aug. 22, 2018 at 4-5; *see also* OIG Interview of E.W. "Bill" Priestap on Aug. 13, 2018 at 45-48; *Redacted OIG Review* at 55. Similarly, General Counsel Baker advised that there was some limited discussion about providing a defensive briefing to the Trump campaign regarding the Papadopoulos information; however, in his words, there was also the thought that "why hasn't anyone from the Trump campaign reported this information to the FBI?" Baker advised the FBI felt it did not know to whom in the Trump campaign it could provide a defensive briefing as there was uncertainty about who could be trusted with the information. Additionally, there was some concern about tipping off the Russians if they became aware the FBI had learned of its scheme through a briefing provided to the Trump campaign. Baker advised the FBI did not wish to "mess up" the political process by going overt with its investigation. He also advised that the FBI needed to do more work, figure things out and come up with a strategic plan before deciding how to proceed. He said part of that plan may have included providing a defensive briefing to the campaign. OSC Interview Report of James Baker on Feb. 7, 2020 at 8-9; *see also* OSC Interview Report of Case Agent-1 on June 19, 2019 at 3 (Case Agent-1 recalled a "notional idea of going directly to the Trump campaign leadership with a briefing about the intelligence threats").

[335] *See* OSC Report of Interview of Headquarters Supervisory Special Agent-4 on May 28, 2020 at 6-7 ("it was important to know if the [Clinton] people being targeted for foreign influence knew of the targeting. Headquarters Supervisory Special Agent-4 did not think they had any information one way or the other on that issue."); *see also* OSC Report of Interview of Field Office-1 Handling Agent-1 on April 23, 2020 at 3 (Field Office-1 Handling Agent-1 "was ok with the defensive briefings because he felt the common goal was to neutralize [Foreign Government-2's] intent to interfere with the election.")

offer from the Russian government and (ii) the possibility existed that the campaign had ultimately taken Russia up on the purported offer is also unpersuasive when viewed in light of the planned activity of Foreign Government-2 given the unknowns that existed in that investigation. Nevertheless, the FBI went forward with defensive briefings in that investigation – an investigation predicated on the receipt of corroborated information – but failed to conduct defensive briefings to the Trump campaign, an investigation predicated on less certain information.[336]

The FBI's and the Department's measured approach to these foreign influence allegations involving Clinton also stands in stark contrast to the speed with which the FBI undertook to include the Steele Report allegations in the FISA request it submitted to OI targeting Page. Indeed, as discussed below in Section IV.D.1.b.iii, the Crossfire Hurricane investigators received the initial Steele Reports on September 19, 2016 and within two days had included portions of those allegations in the draft Page FISA submission. As noted below, approximately one month later, on October 21, 2016, the FISC signed the initial authorization.

During the period between the drafting of the initial FISA request and the approval of the application by the Deputy Attorney General, Evans (who was previously consulted regarding the allegation of Foreign Government–2's foreign influence effort directed at Clinton and others) raised concerns in a call with FBI Special Assistant Lisa Page about (among other things) Steele's personal bias, unknown sourcing, and that the use of FISA authorities was bad from a policy perspective, to which Page's notes appear to indicate in response:

> We accept info from biased people all the time.
> Would look terrible if we pull our punch due to policy/political concern.
> We believe the info & sourcing is good.
> As leaks continue to trickle, is one of the only opportunities to see reflections.[337]

Despite the concerns raised by Evans, the FBI and the Department proceeded to obtain authority from the FISC to conduct surveillance of Page slightly more than one month after the Crossfire Hurricane investigators first received the Steele Reports. The speed with which surveillance of a U.S. person associated with Trump's campaign was authorized – in the face of the unverified Steele Reports and in the absence of a defensive briefing being provided to then-candidate Trump – are difficult to explain compared to the FBI's and Department's actions nearly two years earlier when confronted with

---

[336] *See* OSC Report of Interview of Field Office-1 Handling Agent-1 on May 5, 2020 ("[P]olitics was a concern" because approval for a certain activity was "inexplicably stalled" and "[CD AD] Coleman's call to [Field Office-1 SAC-1] about the case where he said he didn't want to drag the Bureau into a firestorm."); *see also* OSC Report of Interview of [Field Office-1 SAC-1] on September 10, 2020 at 1 - 2 (although the SAC "was never told why HQ would not support the [sensitive investigative technique]A" and "Coleman and [CD Deputy Assistant Director Robert] Jones alluded to the fact they didn't want a presidential candidate on tape," the SAC attributed the delay not to the candidate involved, but alternatively, to the identity of Foreign Government-2, the turnover in management at FBI Headquarters, or a bias against Field Office-1).

[337] FBI-LP-00000111-112.

corroborated allegations of attempted foreign influence involving Clinton, who at the time was still an undeclared candidate for the presidency.

2. *The threat of foreign election influence by Foreign Government-3*

In addition to advising the FBI of foreign influence efforts by Foreign Government-2, CHS-A also provided information to the FBI about reported foreign election influence efforts targeting the Clinton campaign in November 2015 (and possibly the Trump campaign in March 2016) by a different foreign country ("Foreign Government-3").[338] A Foreign Government-3 insider ("Insider-1"), who was known to the FBI to have foreign intelligence and criminal connections, had solicited CHS-A to set up a meeting with candidate Clinton because Insider-1 wanted to propose "something" that CHS-A understood to be campaign contributions on behalf of Foreign Government-3 in exchange for the protection of Foreign Government-3's interests should Clinton become President.[339]

Although this information pertained to a foreign influence threat from a different country, the handling agent for CHS-A continued to work this threat under the existing counterintelligence case for the threat CHS-A reported regarding Foreign Government-2. The handling Agent consulted with FBI OGC and the Counterintelligence Division at Headquarters to seek to renew the Otherwise Illegal Activity ("OIA") authority the CHS had to make introductions at a prior fundraising event scheduled for December 2014 that involved a representative of Foreign Government-2.[340]

According to CHS-A, Insider-1, on behalf of Foreign Government-3, sought access through CHS-A, to a Clinton campaign fundraising event in the Fall of 2015.[341] Although CHS-A was initially advised by an individual associated with the fundraising efforts that Insider-1 could attend, that individual consulted with the campaign and disinvited Insider-1 to the event because of the perceived negative attention a foreign national might attract.[342] According to CHS-A, the fundraising contact suggested CHS-A schedule a separate meeting for Insider-1.[343] Field Office-1 renewed the OIA from late 2014 for the CHS to attend the late November 2015

---

[338] CHS-A Source File, Sub R – Serial 206, OIA Serial 4 (approved 11/19/2015); Sub V Serial 400.

[339] CHS-A Source File, Sub R – Serial 206, OIA Serial 4 (approved 11/19/2015).

[340] FBI-AAA-03-0000514 et seq.; *see also* OSC Report of Interview of Field Office-1 Handling Agent-3 on April 14, 2020 at 3.

[341] CHS-A Source file, Sub R- Serial 207.

[342] CHS-A Source file, Sub R- Serial 207; *see also* FBI-AAA-03-0001188 (Email from Headquarters Supervisory Special Agent-4 to Field Office-1 Handling Agent-3 & others dated 01/15/2016).

[343] FBI-AAA-03-0001188 (Email from Headquarters Supervisory Special Agent-4 to Field Office-1 Handling Agent-3 & others dated 01/15/2016); CHS-A Source file, Sub R Serial 207. The Office found no evidence that candidate-Clinton ever met with Insider-1.

event and make introductions on behalf of Insider-1, but ultimately CHS-A did not attend the event.[344]

CHS-A, however, did attend a fundraiser in January 2016, after providing same-day notice and receiving the approval of his FBI handling agent.[345] CHS-A reported in an email that Insider-1 "got cold feet" and was not going to attend, but the source file report indicates Insider-1 was told by a representative of Clinton not to attend.[346] When Insider-1 decided not to attend, he/she asked CHS-A to deliver a message of support. CHS-A provided the draft message to the handling agent, who received same-day approval from FBI OGC for the CHS to deliver the message at the event scheduled for later that day.[347]

However, without the knowledge or prior approval of the handling agent, CHS-A had made a $2700 campaign contribution (the maximum amount at the time for an individual contribution) prior to the event, which CHS-A indicated he/she "made on [his/her] [credit] card" on behalf of Insider-1.[348] If true, the campaign contribution on behalf of a foreign national would violate Title 52 USC Section 30121 ("Contributions and donations by foreign nationals"). However, despite CHS-A's claim that the contribution was made in his/her personal name, the Federal Election Commission records reviewed did not reveal any contribution in CHS-A's name. Rather, Commission records corroborate a contribution paid by a credit card in the name of a close associate (who was a U.S. person) of CHS-A. CHS-A also told the handling agent that "[t]hey [the campaign] were okay with it. [...] yes they were fully aware from the start" of the contribution being made on behalf of a foreign interest and CHS-A offered to provide a copy of the credit card charges.[349] Despite this offer by CHS-A to provide a copy of the credit card charges, we did not find any indication that the handling agent asked for or otherwise secured a copy.

---

[344] *See* FBI-AAA-03-0000514 (Email from Clinesmith to Field Office-1 Handling Agent-3, Headquarters Supervisory Special Agent-4 & others dated 11/19/2015); *see also* OIA Serial 4 dated 11/19/2015; *see also* FBI-AAA-EC-00000983 (Lync exchange between Headquarters Supervisory Special Agent-4 & Field Office-1 Handling Agent-3 dated 01/19/2016) (CHS did not attend the 11/30/2015 event).

[345] FBI_DOJ_2019_CFH_005507 at 1-3, 6 (CHS informed handling agent on 1/13/2016: "I just got to DC, will be meeting Hillary today. [Insider-1] was suppose[d] to join me but [Insider-1] got cold feet [...]. [Insider-1] asked me to relay a message and setup a meeting. That should be okay right?" Agent replied on 1/13/2016 that it was fine to deliver that message.)

[346] CHS-A Source File Sub R Serial 208.

[347] FBI_DOJ_2019_CFH_005507 at 3 ("The message is [head] [of Foreign Government-3] fully supports you and wants closer cooperation once you are president. He has always believed you would be the perfect candidate and has been following your campaigning closely. [Foreign Government-3] and US have a [ ] and is the only standing fort against [third country]. [Insider-1] would like to sit with you and or your staff to discuss regional affairs. If it's possible for me to get a contact or arrange a meeting. Would that be okay?"); *see* CHS-A Source File Sub-V Serial 384, and Sub R Serial 208.

[348] FBI_DOJ_2019_CFH_005507 at 7.

[349] *Id.* at 6-7.

When interviewed by the Office about this contribution, one of CHS-A's FBI handlers could not explain why this apparent illegal contribution was not documented in FBI records.[350] Although the handling agent at the time asked CHS-A about the payment,[351] there is no indication that the agent documented the contribution in the CHS's source file.[352] Moreover, despite the CHS telling the handling agent that the CHS was going to Insider-1's house "after the event to update [him/her]," [353] there was no follow up by the handling agent to document that in the source file.[354] In fact, the handling agent subsequently told the CHS to stay away from all events relating to Clinton's campaign.[355]

The Counterintelligence Division Unit Chief ("Headquarters Unit Chief-2") also did not recall the campaign contribution, despite being shown an FBINET Lync chat dated at the time of the events between himself and Headquarters Supervisory Special Agent-4, in which Headquarters Unit Chief-2 wrote "just spoke with the [Field Office-1] ASAC" and asked Headquarters Supervisory Special Agent-4, "do we know who made the $2700 donation, CHS, CHS's boss, or CHS on behalf of [Insider-1]? We'll have to have an answer for that by the morning."[356] In 2021, at the time of the Office's interview of Headquarters Unit Chief-2, his SAC was the former ASAC of Field Office-1 with whom the Lync indicated Headquarters Unit Chief-2 had spoken about this matter at the time of the events in January 2016. Field Office-1 Supervisory Special Agent-1, who oversaw the investigation, also had no recollection about why this contribution was not documented in CHS-A's source file, nor considered as reportable unauthorized illegal activity by CHS-A.[357] Also, Field Office-1 ASAC-1 had no recollection of the payment by CHS-A, and did not know why it was not documented in the source file.[358]

Although Field Office-1 had documented reporting from CHS-A regarding the threat to the Clinton campaign, and subsequently to the Trump campaign, of Foreign Government-3's

---

[350] OSC Report of Interview of Field Office-1 Handling Agent-2 on May 5, 2021 at 3.

[351] FBI_DOJ_2019_CFH_005507 at 6 ("I also need to know how the money ($2700) was donated on behalf of [Insider-1]. Did it come out of your pocket? How was it paid? Was there any mention of the donation being on behalf of [Insider-1] BEFORE the contribution was made? Was the money returned?").

[352] OSC Report of Interview of Field Office-1 Handling Agent-3 on September 22, 2020 at 3 ("[Field Office-1 Handling Agent-3] could not recall if he documented the $2700 payment in [the Source File] or not. He did not make a conscious decision to not document the payment.").

[353] FBI_DOJ_2019_CFH_005507 at 2.

[354] OSC Report of Interview of Field Office-1 ASAC-1 on July 7, 2021 at 5 (the handling Agent's ASAC did not know why CHS-A's purported visit to Insider-1 after the January 13, 2016 fundraising event was not documented in an FBI record).

[355] FBI_DOJ_2019_CFH_005507 at 6; see also Source file Sub xxx Serial 384.

[356] OSC Report of Interview of Headquarters Unit Chief-2 on April 22, 2021 at 4; FBI-AAA-EC-00000983 (Lync exchange between Headquarters Supervisory Special Agent-4 & Headquarters Unit Chief-2 dated 01/19/2016).

[357] OSC Report of Interview of Field Office-1 Supervisory Special Agent-1 on April 8, 2021 at 5.

[358] OSC Report of Interview of Field Office-1 ASAC-1 on July 7, 2021 at 4 - 5.

foreign election influence efforts, Field Office-1 did not open a separate investigation into this threat.[359] Nor did Field Office-1 "consider this information as to whether it would be a good idea to let [Insider-1] get close to HRC in an operation or that [Insider-1] might be a foreign influence threat to the presidential candidates worthy of continued scrutiny."[360] Field Office-1 also did not document the unauthorized illegal activity by CHS-A in connection with making a campaign contribution purportedly on behalf of Insider-1.[361] Instead, the FBI effectively removed their sole source of insight into this threat when the handling agent, responding to direction, admonished CHS-A:

> do NOT attend any more campaign events, set up meetings, or anything else relating to [Clinton's] campaign. We need to keep you completely away from that situation. I don't know all the details, but it's for your own protection."[362]

Moreover, despite removing their source of insight into this threat, and DAD Archey's belief that "the FBI protects the candidates by doing defensive briefings,"[363] the FBI did not provide the Clinton campaign or the Trump campaign a defensive briefing regarding Foreign Government-3's foreign election influence efforts.[364]

Contrasted with the FBI's rapid opening of Crossfire Hurricane, the FBI appears to have made no effort to investigate the possible illegal campaign contribution (which allegedly was a precursor to the contribution of a significant sum of money by Insider-1 on behalf of Foreign Government-3) or the Clinton campaign's purported acceptance of a campaign contribution that was made by the FBI's own long-term CHS on behalf of Insider-1 and, ultimately, Foreign Government-3.

---

[359] OSC Report of Interview of Field Office-1 Supervisory Special Agent-1 on April 8, 2021 at 4 (The Field Office never opened a counterintelligence case on [Insider-1] because [Insider-1] lived in areas outside Field Office-1's area of responsibility).

[360] OSC Report of Interview of Field Office-1 Supervisory Special Agent-1 on April 8, 2021 at 4.

[361] OSC Report of Interview of Field Office-1 Supervisory Special Agent-1 on April 8, 2021 at 5, (Headquarters Supervisory Analyst-1 "did not know why this action was not documented in a FD-1023 and stated that it should have been because it was Unauthorized Illegal Activity (UIA) and not within the scope of what [CHS-A] was allowed to do in the OIA.")

[362] FBI_DOJ_2019_CFH 005512; see also OSC Report of Interview of Field Office-1 Supervisory Special Agent-1 on April 8, 2021 at 5 ("Their plan, however, was to move [CHS-A] away from the political matters so they could fully utilize [CHS-A] in overseas national security matters.").

[363] OSC Report of Interview of David Archey on June 21, 2021 at 4.

[364] This conclusion by the Office is based on the Office's review of available documentation in the source file, Sentinel, and electronic communications of FBI personnel. Neither Archey nor Field Office-1 ASAC-1 recalled this threat reporting nor offered an explanation as to the absence of defensive briefings. See OSC Report of Interview of David Archey on June 21, 2021 at 5; see also OSC Report of Interview of Field Office-1 ASAC-1 on July 7, 2021 at 5.

3. *Allegations involving the Clinton Foundation*

Beginning in January 2016, three different FBI field offices, the New York Field Office ("NYFO"), the Washington Field Office ("WFO"), and the Little Rock Field Office ("LRFO"), opened investigations into possible criminal activity involving the Clinton Foundation.[365] The LRFO case opening communication referred to an intelligence product and corroborating financial reporting that a particular commercial "industry likely engaged a federal public official in a flow of benefits scheme, namely, large monetary contributions were made to a non-profit, under both direct and indirect control of the federal public official, in exchange for favorable government action and/or influence."[366] The WFO investigation was opened as a preliminary investigation, because the Case Agent wanted to determine if he could develop additional information to corroborate the allegations in a recently-published book, *Clinton Cash* by Peter Schweizer, before seeking to convert the matter to a full investigation.[367] Additionally, the LRFO and NYFO investigations included predication based on source reporting that identified foreign governments that had made, or offered to make, contributions to the Foundation in exchange for favorable or preferential treatment from Clinton.[368]

With three different FBI field offices having opened investigations related to the Clinton Foundation, there was a perceived need to conduct coordination meetings between the field offices, FBI Headquarters, and appropriate United States Attorney's offices and components from the Department. These meetings likely were deemed especially important given that the investigations were occurring in an election year in which Clinton was a declared candidate for President. Several of those meetings are described in more detail below.

On February 1, 2016, a meeting was held to discuss the Foundation investigations. Present for the meeting from the FBI were, among others, Executive Assistant Director Randy Coleman, Criminal Investigative Division Assistant Director Joe Campbell and Acting OGC Section Chief-1. Those present from the Department included Criminal Division Assistant Attorney General Leslie Caldwell and Public Integrity Section Chief Ray Hulser.[369] When

---

[365] OSC Report of Interview of Ray Hulser on July 8, 2020 at 1; OSC Report of Interview of Headquarters Unit Chief-3 on January 28, 2020 at 1; *see also*, 58A-WF-6930742 Serial 1 (opened 1/29/2016); FBI_DOJ_2019_CFH_002365 (58A-LR-6912913 Serial 1 opened 01-27-2016) (opening EC is almost identical to opening EC for 58A-LR-2187489, opened July 2017 and containing no reference to 58A-LR-6912913); 58A-NY-6888608 Serial 1 (opened 1/22/2016).

[366] FBI_DOJ_2019_CFH_002365 at 2.

[367] *See* Email from WFO Clinton Foundation Case Agent-1 to WFO ASAC-1 dated 09/01/2017; *see generally*, OSC Report of Interview of WFO Clinton Foundation Case Agent-1 on August 20, 2020.

[368] *See* FBI_DOJ_2019_CFH_002365 at 2 (referring without specific CHS references to an intelligence product from January 2016), and 58A-NY-6888608 Serial 1 at 4. WFO's Opening EC (58A-WF-6930742 Serial 1) mentions leveraging CHSs from a different pending investigation but does not incorporate by reference any CHS reporting.

[369] OSC Report of Interview of Acting OGC Section Chief-1 on Sept. 9, 2020 at 2; OSC Report of Interview of Randall Coleman on August 12, 2019 at 1.

interviewed by the Office, Hulser noted, in sum, that the FBI briefing was poorly presented and that there was insufficient predication for at least one of the investigations due to its reliance on allegations contained in a book. Hulser also downplayed the information provided by the NYFO CHS and recalled that the amount involved in the financial reporting was "de minimis."[370]

Although Hulser declined prosecution on behalf of the Public Integrity Section, he told the Office he "made it clear, however, that his decision was not binding on the various U.S. Attorneys' Offices or FBI field divisions."[371] Acting OGC Section Chief-1 recalled that the Department's reaction to the Clinton Foundation briefing was "hostile."[372]

Three weeks later, on February 22, 2016, another meeting was convened at FBI Headquarters to discuss the Foundation investigations.[373] The meeting was chaired by McCabe.[374] Present for the meeting from the FBI were, among others, Coleman, Campbell, and representatives from the affected field offices, including then-WFO Assistant Director-in-Charge ("ADIC") Paul Abbate.[375] Representatives from the Department and the affected U.S. Attorney's offices were also present.[376] At the meeting, McCabe initially directed the field offices to close their cases, but following objections, agreed to reconsider the final disposition of the cases.[377] In his interview with the Office, Abbate described McCabe as "negative," "annoyed," and "angry."[378] According to Abbate, McCabe stated "they [the Department] say there's nothing here" and "why are we even doing this?"[379] At the close of the meeting, Campbell directed that for any overt investigative steps to be taken, the Deputy Director's approval would be required.[380] This restriction on overt investigative activity essentially

---

[370] OSC Report of Interview of Ray Hulser on July 8, 2020 at 1-2. We note that the financial reporting concerning the Clinton Foundation was not available to show Hulser at the time of his interview to help refresh any recollections he might have. The Office, however, separately reviewed the material to understand the allegations that caused the reporting to be made in the summer of 2015. The reporting, which in itself is not proof of wrongdoing, was a narrative describing multiple funds transfers, some of which involved international bank accounts that were suspected of possibly facilitating bribery or gratuity violations. The transactions involved occurred between 2012 and 2014, and totaled hundreds of thousands of dollars.

[371] Id. at 1.

[372] OSC Report of Interview of Acting OGC Section Chief-1 on Sept. 9, 2020 at 2.

[373] Id.

[374] Id.

[375] Id.; OSC Report of Interview of Paul Abbate on March 18, 2020 at 2.

[376] OSC Report of Interview of Acting OGC Section Chief-1 on Sept. 9, 2020 at 2.

[377] Id.; OSC Report of Interview of Paul Abbate on March 18, 2020 at 2.

[378] OSC Report of Interview of Paul Abbate on March 18, 2020 at 2.

[379] Id.

[380] Id.

remained in place until August 2016. Abbate recalled that FBI personnel from the field offices left the meeting frustrated with the limitations placed on them by the Deputy Director.[381]

According to NYFO Assistant Director in Charge Diego Rodriguez, Coleman called him on behalf of Director Comey around May and directed the NYFO to "cease and desist" from the Foundation investigation due to some undisclosed counterintelligence concern.[382] Coleman informed Rodriguez that Comey wanted to consult with Associate Deputy Attorney General David Margolis regarding the referenced counterintelligence matter.[383] The Office was not able to determine what the counterintelligence issue raised by Comey was.[384]

On August 1, 2016, a video teleconference meeting ("VTC") was held wherein the WFO and LRFO cases were directed to be closed and consolidated into the NYFO investigation.[385] During this VTC, the NYFO was given authorization to seek subpoenas from the U.S. Attorneys' offices in the Southern and Eastern Districts of New York ("SDNY" and "EDNY").[386] However, both SDNY and EDNY declined to issue subpoenas to the NYFO, despite previously expressing support for the investigation.[387]

Once again, the investigative actions taken by FBI Headquarters in the Foundation matters contrast with those taken in Crossfire Hurricane. As an initial matter, the NYFO and WFO investigations appear to have been opened as preliminary investigations due to the political sensitivity and their reliance on unvetted hearsay information (the *Clinton Cash* book) and CHS reporting.[388] By contrast, the Crossfire Hurricane investigation was *immediately* opened as a full investigation despite the fact that it was similarly predicated on unvetted hearsay information. Furthermore, while the Department appears to have had legitimate concerns about the Foundation investigation occurring so close to a presidential election, it does not appear that similar concerns were expressed by the Department or FBI regarding the Crossfire Hurricane investigation. Indeed, in short order after opening the Crossfire Hurricane file and its four sub-files, the FBI was having one of its long-time CHSs meet not with just one Trump campaign

---

[381] *Id.*

[382] OSC Report of Interview of Diego Rodriguez on August 12, 2019 at 2; *see also* OSC Report of Interview of Diego Rodriguez on January 16, 2020 at 1-2.

[383] *Id.* at 2.

[384] Mr. Margolis unfortunately passed away in July 2016. Comey declined to be interviewed by the Office.

[385] 58A-NY-6888608 Serial 6; OSC Report of Interview of Headquarters Unit Chief-3 on January 28, 2020 at 3.

[386] 58A-NY-6888608 Serial 6.

[387] OSC Report of Interview of Acting OGC Section Chief-1 on Sept. 9, 2020 at 3; OSC Report of Interview of Diego Rodriguez on January 16, 2020 at 1; *see also* OSC Report of Interview of NYFO Clinton Foundation Case Agent-1 on January 15, 2020 at 1–2; OSC Report of Interview of Patrick Fallon on September 29, 2020 at 2.

[388] *See* Email from WFO Clinton Foundation Case Agent-1 to WFO ASAC-1 dated 09/01/2017; *see generally* OSC Report of Interview of WFO Clinton Foundation Case Agent-1 on August 20, 2020.

associate, but meet and record conversations with three such insiders. And a little more than a month after opening the Crossfire Hurricane file on Page, a "senior U.S. law enforcement official" was publicly reported as confirming for Michael Isikoff and *Yahoo! News* that the FBI had Page on its radar screen.[389]

In the end, the perceived difference between the approaches taken and mindsets of FBI personnel central to both the Clinton and Trump matters is well-captured in a February 24, 2016 email between McCabe's Special Assistant Lisa Page and Strzok. Prior to the FBI's interview of Clinton in the investigation of her use of a private email server while she was serving as Secretary of State, the following exchange took place:

Page: One more thing: [Clinton] may be our next president. The last thing you need [is] going in there loaded for bear. You think she's going to remember or care that it was more doj than fbi?

Strzok: Agreed . . . .[390]

C. **Investigative Referral of Possible Clinton Campaign Plan**

1. *Factual background*

The Office also considered as part of its investigation the government's handling of certain intelligence that it received during the summer of 2016. That intelligence concerned the purported "approval by Hillary Clinton on July 26, 2016 of a proposal from one of her foreign policy advisors to vilify Donald Trump by stirring up a scandal claiming interference by the Russian security services."[391] We refer to that intelligence hereafter as the "Clinton Plan intelligence." DNI John Ratcliffe declassified the following information about the Clinton Plan intelligence in September 2020 and conveyed it to the Senate Judiciary Committee:

- In late July 2016, U.S. intelligence agencies obtained insight into Russian intelligence analysis alleging that U.S Presidential candidate Hillary Clinton had approved a campaign plan to stir up a scandal against U.S. Presidential candidate Donald Trump by tying him to Putin and the Russians' hacking of the Democratic National Committee. The IC does not know the accuracy of this allegation or the extent to which the Russian intelligence analysis may reflect exaggeration or fabrication.

- According to his handwritten notes, CIA Director Brennan subsequently briefed President Obama and other senior national security officials on the intelligence, including the "alleged approval by Hillary Clinton on July 26, 2016 of a proposal from one of her foreign policy advisors to vilify Donald Trump by stirring up a scandal claiming interference by Russian security services."

---

[389] *See* Isikoff, *Officials Probe Ties*.

[390] FBI-0008217 (Office of Professional Responsibility (OPR) letter to Strzok dated Feb. 24, 2016 at 4) FBI-0008217-240 at 0008220.

[391] Letter from John Ratcliffe, DNI, to Sen. Lindsay Graham (Sept. 29, 2020) (hereinafter *"Ratcliffe Letter"*); Notes of John O. Brennan, declassified by DNI Ratcliffe on October 6, 2020 (hereinafter *"Brennan Notes"*).

- On 07 September 2016, U.S. intelligence officials forwarded an investigative referral to FBI Director James Comey and Deputy Assistant Director of Counterintelligence Peter Strzok regarding "U.S. Presidential candidate Hillary Clinton's approval of a plan concerning U.S. Presidential candidate Donald Trump and Russian hackers hampering U.S. elections as a means of distracting the public from her use of a private mail server."[392]

The Clinton Plan intelligence was relevant to the Office's investigation for two reasons.

First, the Clinton Plan intelligence itself and on its face arguably suggested that private actors affiliated with the Clinton campaign were seeking in 2016 to promote a false or exaggerated narrative to the public and to U.S. government agencies about Trump's possible ties to Russia. Given the significant quantity of materials the FBI and other government agencies did in fact receive during the 2016 presidential election season and afterwards that originated with and/or were funded by the Clinton campaign or affiliated persons (*i.e.*, the Steele Dossier reports, the Alfa Bank allegations, and the Yotaphone allegations), the Clinton Plan intelligence prompted the Office to consider (i) whether there was in fact a plan by the Clinton campaign to tie Trump to Russia in order to "stir[] up a scandal" in advance of the 2016 presidential election, and (ii) if such a plan existed, whether an aspect or component of that plan was to intentionally provide knowingly false and/or misleading information to the FBI or other agencies in furtherance of such a plan.[393]

Second, the Clinton Plan intelligence was also highly relevant to the Office's review and investigation because it was part of the mosaic of information that became known to certain U.S. officials at or before the time they made critical decisions in the Crossfire Hurricane case and in related law enforcement and intelligence efforts. Because these officials relied, at least in part, on materials provided or funded by the Clinton campaign and/or the DNC when seeking FISA warrants against a U.S. citizen (*i.e.*, the Steele Dossier reports) and taking other investigative steps, the Clinton Plan intelligence had potential bearing on the reliability and credibility of those materials. Put another way, this intelligence—taken at face value—was arguably highly relevant and exculpatory because it could be read in fuller context, and in combination with other facts, to suggest that materials such as the Steele Dossier reports and the Alfa Bank allegations (discussed below and in greater detail in Section IV.E.1) were part of a political effort to smear a political opponent and to use the resources of the federal government's law enforcement and intelligence agencies in support of a political objective. The Office therefore examined whether, and precisely when, U.S. law enforcement and intelligence officials became aware of the Clinton Plan intelligence; whether they vetted and analyzed the intelligence to understand its potential

---

[392] *Referral Memo.*

[393] To be clear, the Office did not and does not view the potential existence of a political plan by one campaign to spread negative claims about its opponent as illegal or criminal in any respect. As prosecutors and the Court reminded the jury in the *Sussmann* trial, opposition research is commonplace in Washington, D.C. and elsewhere, is conducted by actors of all political parties, and is not a basis in and of itself for criminal liability. Rather, only if the evidence supported the latter of the two conditions described above—*i.e.*, if there was an intent by the Clinton campaign or its personnel to knowingly provide false information to the government—would such conduct potentially support criminal charges.

significance; and whether those officials, in turn, incorporated the intelligence into their decision-making regarding the investigation of individuals who were part of the Trump campaign and had possible ties to Russian election interference efforts.

As was declassified and made public previously, the purported Clinton Plan intelligence was derived from insight that "U.S. intelligence agencies obtained into Russian intelligence analysis."[394] Given the origins of the Clinton Plan intelligence as the product of a foreign adversary, the Office was cognizant of the statement that DNI Ratcliffe made to Senate Judiciary Chairman Lindsey Graham in a September 29, 2020 letter: "The [intelligence community] *does not know the accuracy of this allegation* or the extent to which the Russian intelligence analysis may reflect exaggeration or fabrication."[395]

Recognizing this uncertainty, the Office nevertheless endeavored to investigate the bases for, and credibility of, this intelligence in order to assess its accuracy and its potential implications for the broader matters within our purview.

Given the significance of the Clinton Plan intelligence, and the need to protect sources and methods of the Intelligence Community, we report the results of our investigation in bifurcated fashion. More specifically:

(1) This section describes in unclassified form the circumstances in which U.S. officials received and acted on (or failed to act upon) the Clinton Plan intelligence, as well as the nature and significance of their reactions to it;

(2) The Classified Appendix to this report provides further information about (i) the details of the Clinton Plan intelligence; (ii) facts that heightened the potential relevance of this intelligence to the Office's inquiry; and (iii) the Office's efforts to verify or refute the key claims found in this intelligence.

a. Relevant facts

Before addressing the U.S. government's receipt and handling of the Clinton Plan intelligence, we reiterate below the description of that intelligence as declassified by the DNI in his September 29, 2020 letter to Chairman Graham. Ratcliffe's letter stated, in part, as follows:

> In late July 2016, U.S. intelligence agencies obtained insight into Russian intelligence analysis alleging that U.S Presidential candidate Hillary Clinton had approved a campaign plan to stir up a scandal against U.S. Presidential candidate Donald Trump by tying him to Putin and the Russians' hacking of the Democratic National Committee.[396]

As described herein and in the Classified Appendix, U.S. officials described the Clinton Plan intelligence in various other ways in their official notes and documents. As described more fully in the Classified Appendix, there were specific indications and additional facts that heightened the potential relevance of this intelligence to the Office's inquiry.

---

[394] *Ratcliffe Letter.*

[395] *Id.* (emphasis added).

[396] *Id.*

i. *Receipt of the Clinton Plan intelligence*

The Intelligence Community received the Clinton Plan intelligence in late July 2016.[397] The official who initially received the information immediately recognized its importance— including its relevance to the U.S. presidential election— and acted quickly to make CIA leadership aware of it.[398] Materials obtained from former Director Brennan's office holdings reflect that he personally received a copy of the intelligence.[399] When interviewed, Brennan generally recalled reviewing the materials but stated he did not recall focusing specifically on its assertions regarding the Clinton campaign's purported plan.[400] Brennan recalled instead focusing on Russia's role in hacking the DNC.[401]

On July 28, 2016, Director Brennan met with President Obama and other White House personnel, during which Brennan and the President discussed intelligence relevant to the 2016 presidential election as well as the potential creation of an inter-agency Fusion Cell to synthesize and analyze intelligence about Russian malign influence on the 2016 presidential election.[402] Brennan's recollection was that he spoke with Director Comey on the morning of July 29, 2016, to brief him on his July 28th meeting with the President.[403] Brennan could not recall when he actually saw the Clinton Plan intelligence, but he did not think he had the information when he spoke to Comey on that morning.

Immediately after communicating with the President, Comey, and DNI Clapper to discuss relevant intelligence, Director Brennan and other agency officials took steps to ensure that dissemination of intelligence related to Russia's election interference efforts, including the Clinton Plan intelligence, would be limited to protect sensitive information and prevent leaks.[404] Brennan stated that the inter-agency Fusion Cell, a team to synthesize and analyze pertinent intelligence on Russian malign influence activities related to the presidential election, was put in motion after his meeting with President Obama on July 28th. Email traffic and witness interviews conducted by the Office reflect that at least some CIA personnel believed that the Clinton Plan intelligence led to the decision being made to set up the Fusion Cell.[405]

---

[397] *Id.*; *see also* OSC Report of Interview of IC Officer #6 on Aug. 19, 2020 at 11.

[398] OSC Report of Interview of IC Officer #6 on Aug. 19, 2020 at 4.

[399] OSC Report of Interview of John Brennan on Aug. 21, 2020 at 7-8; 16-17.

[400] *Id.* at 8-9.

[401] *Id.*

[402] OSC Report of Interview of John Brennan on Aug. 21, 2020 at 8; Email from OGA Liaison-1 to OGA employees dated 08/02/2016; Notes of Retired CIA Employee-2 dated 07/28/2016.

[403] OSC Report of Interview of John Brennan on Aug. 21, 2020 at 8.

[404] *Id.*

[405] OSC Report of Interview of I.C. Officer #6 on Aug. 19, 2020 at 4; OSC Report of Interview of I.C. Officer #12 on Dec. 23, 2020 at 3.

On August 3, 2016, within days of receiving the Clinton Plan intelligence, Director Brennan met with the President, Vice President and other senior Administration officials, including but not limited to the Attorney General (who participated remotely) and the FBI Director, in the White House Situation Room to discuss Russian election interference efforts.[406] According to Brennan's handwritten notes and his recollections from the meeting, he briefed on relevant intelligence known to date on Russian election interference, including the Clinton Plan intelligence.[407] Specifically, Director Brennan's declassified handwritten notes reflect that he briefed the meeting's participants regarding the "alleged approval by Hillary Clinton on 26 July of a proposal from one of her [campaign] advisors to vilify Donald Trump by stirring up a scandal claiming interference by the Russian security services."[408]

iii.   FBI awareness

The Office was unable to determine precisely when the FBI first obtained any of the details of the Clinton Plan intelligence (other than Director Comey, who attended the August 3, 2016 briefing). It appears, however, that this occurred no later than August 22, 2016. On that date, an FBI cyber analyst ("Headquarters Analyst-2") emailed a number of FBI employees, including Supervisory Intelligence Analyst Brian Auten and Section Chief Moffa, the most senior intelligence analysts on the Crossfire Hurricane team, to provide an update on Russian intelligence materials.[409] The email included a summary of the contents of the Clinton Plan intelligence.[410] The Office did not identify any replies or follow-up actions taken by FBI personnel as a result of this email.

When interviewed by the Office, Auten recalled that on September 2, 2016 – approximately ten days after Headquarters Analyst-2's email – the official responsible for overseeing the Fusion Cell briefed Auten, Moffa, and other FBI personnel at FBI Headquarters regarding the Clinton Plan intelligence.[411] Auten did not recall any FBI "operational" personnel (*i.e.*, Crossfire Hurricane Agents) being present at the meeting.[412] The official verbally briefed the individuals regarding information that the CIA planned to send to the FBI in a written investigative referral, including the Clinton Plan intelligence information.[413] Auten recalled thinking at the meeting that he wanted to see the formal *Referral Memo* containing the Clinton

---

[406] OSC Report of Interview of John Brennan on Aug. 21, 2020 at 7; *Brennan Notes*; Notes of Retired CIA Employee-2 dated August 3, 2016 (brief-back notes of Brennan post-White House meeting).

[407] *Brennan Notes.*

[408] *Id.*

[409] FBI-JCM-0004364 (Email from Headquarters Analyst-2 to Brian Auten, Jonathan Moffa & others dated 08/22/2016.).

[410] *Id.*

[411] OSC Report of Interview of Brian Auten on July 26, 2021 at 7, 13.

[412] *Id.* at 7.

[413] *Id.*

Plan intelligence.[414] Separate and apart from this meeting, FBI records reflect that by no later than that same date (September 2, 2016), then-FBI Assistant Director for Counterintelligence Bill Priestap was also aware of the specifics of the Clinton Plan intelligence as evidenced by his hand-written notes from an early morning meeting with Moffa, DAD Dina Corsi and Acting AD for Cyber Eric Sporre.[415] The Office was unable to determine the exact contours of Priestap's knowledge, however, in part, because he declined to be interviewed by the Office on this subject.[416]

iv.   CIA referral and dissemination

Five days later, on September 7, 2016, the CIA completed its *Referral Memo* in response to an FBI request for relevant information reviewed by the Fusion Cell.[417] The CIA addressed the *Referral Memo* to the FBI Director and to the attention of Deputy Assistant Director Peter Strzok. The *Referral Memo*, which mentioned the Clinton Plan intelligence, stated, in part:

> Per FBI verbal request, CIA provides the below examples of information the CROSSFIRE HURRICANE fusion cell has gleaned to date [Source revealing information redacted]:
>
> [] An exchange . . . discussing US presidential candidate Hillary Clinton's approval of a plan concerning US presidential candidate Donald Trump and Russian hackers hampering US elections as a means of distracting the public from her use of a private email server. According to open sources, Guccifer 2.0 is an individual or group of hackers whom US officials believe is tied to Russian intelligence services. Also, per open sources, Guccifer 2.0 claimed credit for hacking the Democratic National Committee (DNC) this year.[418]

None of the FBI personnel who agreed to be interviewed could specifically recall receiving this *Referral Memo*, nor did anyone recall the FBI doing anything in response to the *Referral Memo*. Auten stated that it was possible he hand-delivered this *Referral Memo* to the FBI, as he had done with numerous other referral memos,[419] and noted that he typically shared referral memos with the rest of the Crossfire Hurricane investigative team, although he did not recall if he did so in this instance.[420]

In late September 2016, high-ranking U.S. national security officials, including Comey and Clapper, received an intelligence product on Russian interference in the 2016 presidential election that included the Clinton Plan intelligence.[421] The Office did not identify any further

---

[414] *Id.*

[415] Handwritten notes of E.W. Priestap dated 09/02/2016.

[416] *Id.*

[417] *Referral Memo.*

[418] *Id.*

[419] OSC Report of Interview of Brian Auten on July 26, 2021 at 13.

[420] *Id.*

[421] Intelligence Community Document-1.

actions that the CIA or FBI took in response to this intelligence product as it related to the Clinton Plan intelligence.

> v. *Awareness by the Crossfire Hurricane investigators*

The Office located no evidence that in conducting the Crossfire Hurricane investigation the FBI considered whether and how the Clinton Plan intelligence might impact the investigation. No FBI personnel who were interviewed by the Office recalled Crossfire Hurricane personnel taking any action to vet the Clinton Plan intelligence.[422] For example, Brian Auten stated that he could not recall anything that the FBI did to analyze, or otherwise consider the Clinton Plan intelligence, stating that it was "just one data point."[423]

This stands in sharp contrast to its substantial reliance on the uncorroborated Steele Reports, which at least some FBI personnel appeared to know was likely being funded or promoted by the Clinton campaign. For example:

- During a meeting in London on July 5, 2016, Steele provided his first Report to Handling Agent-1. Handling Agent-1's notes from the meeting reflect that "HC" was aware of his (Steele's) "Brit firm seeking info."[424] While Handling Agent-1 did not have an independent recollection of Steele explicitly stating that "HC" referred to Hillary Clinton, he could think of no other individual – in that context – to whom "HC" could possibly refer.[425]

- On September 23, 2016, Strzok sent a Lync message to Brian Auten regarding the Michael Isikoff article that stated, "Looking at the Yahoo article. I can definitely say at a minimum [Steele's] reports should be viewed as intended to influence as well as to inform."[426]

- On October 11, 2016, Strzok sent a Lync message to OGC attorney Kevin Clinesmith noting that Steele's "unnamed client" was "presumed to be connected to the [Clinton] campaign in some way[.]"[427]

Nor did the Office identify any evidence that the FBI disclosed the contents of the Clinton Plan intelligence to the OI attorneys working on FISA matters related to Crossfire Hurricane. Similarly, the FBI did not disclose any of the Clinton Plan intelligence materials to the FISC (despite relying on the uncorroborated Steele reporting in its FISA applications

---

[422] *See, e.g.*, OSC Report of Interview of Headquarters Analyst-2 on Feb. 25, 2020 at 11; OSC Report of Interview of Jonathan Moffa on Feb. 28, 2020 at 2-4.

[423] OSC Report of Interview of Brian Auten on July 26, 2021 at 13.

[424] Handwritten notes of Handling Agent-1 at 4.

[425] OSC Report of Interview of Handling Agent-1 on Mar. 1, 2022 at 2.

[426] FBI-AAA-EC-00006182 (Lync Message Exchange between Strzok and Auten dated 09/23/16).

[427] FBI-AAA-EC-00006440 (Lync Message Exchange between Strzok and Clinesmith on 10/11/16).

concerning Carter Page), and we uncovered no evidence that anyone at the FBI considered doing so.

The Office showed portions of the Clinton Plan intelligence to a number of individuals who were actively involved in the Crossfire Hurricane investigation. Most advised they had never seen the intelligence before, and some expressed surprise and dismay upon learning of it. For example, the original Supervisory Special Agent on the Crossfire Hurricane investigation, Supervisory Special Agent-1, reviewed the intelligence during one of his interviews with the Office.[428] After reading it, Supervisory Special Agent-1 became visibly upset and emotional, left the interview room with his counsel, and subsequently returned to state emphatically that he had never been apprised of the Clinton Plan intelligence and had never seen the aforementioned *Referral Memo*.[429] Supervisory Special Agent-1 expressed a sense of betrayal that no one had informed him of the intelligence. When the Office cautioned Supervisory Special Agent-1 that we had not verified or corroborated the accuracy of the intelligence and its assertions regarding the Clinton campaign, Supervisory Special Agent-1 responded firmly that regardless of whether its contents were true, he should have been informed of it.[430]

Former FBI General Counsel Baker also reviewed the Clinton Plan intelligence during one of his interviews with the Office.[431] Baker stated that he had neither seen nor heard of the Clinton Plan intelligence or the resulting *Referral Memo* prior to his interview with the Office. He acknowledged the significance of the reporting and explained that had he known of it during the Crossfire Hurricane investigation, he would have viewed in a different and much more skeptical light (i) information the FBI received from Steele concerning Trump's purported ties to Russia and (ii) information received from attorney Michael Sussmann that purported to show a secret communications channel between the Trump Organization and Alfa Bank.[432]

> vi.   *Other evidence obtained by the Office that appears to be relevant to an analysis of the Clinton Plan intelligence*

As discussed above, according to the declassified Clinton Plan intelligence, on July 26, 2016, Clinton allegedly approved a proposal from one of her foreign policy advisors to tie Trump to Russia as a means of distracting the public from her use of a private email server. The Office interviewed a number of individuals connected with the campaign as part of its investigation into the Clinton Plan intelligence. One foreign policy advisor ("Foreign Policy Advisor-1") stated that she did not specifically remember proposing a "plan" to Clinton or other campaign leadership to "stir up a scandal" by tying Trump to Putin or Russia.[433] Foreign Policy Advisor-1 stated, however, that it was possible that she had proposed ideas on these topics to the campaign's leadership, who may have approved those ideas.[434] Foreign Policy Advisor-1

---

[428] OSC Report of Interview of Supervisory Special Agent-1 on July 22, 2020 at 7.

[429] *Id.*

[430] *Id.*

[431] OSC Report of Interview of James Baker on June 18, 2020 at 4.

[432] *Id.*

[433] OSC Report of Interview of Foreign Policy Advisor-1 on July 21, 2021 at 7.

[434] *Id.*

recalled conversations with others in the campaign expressing their genuine concerns that the DNC hack was a threat to the electoral system, and that Trump and his advisors appeared to have troubling ties to Russia.[435] Foreign Policy Advisor-1 said it was also possible someone proposed an idea of seeking to distract attention from the investigation into Clinton's use of a private email server, but she did not specifically remember any such idea.[436] Foreign Policy Advisor-1 advised that she did not recall the FBI coming up in any campaign conversations she had.[437]

Records obtained from Foreign Policy Advisor-1 reflect that on July 27, 2016 – the day following candidate Clinton's purported authorization of the plan – Foreign Policy Advisor-1 circulated a draft public statement to certain of her colleagues. In the email circulating the draft statement, Foreign Policy Advisor-1 urged her colleagues to sign the draft statement, which criticized Trump for his comments about the NATO alliance and asserted that Trump's public statements concerning NATO were too friendly towards Russia. In her cover email, Foreign Policy Advisor-1 wrote, in part:

> We are writing to enlist your support for the attached public statement. Both of us are Hillary Clinton supporters and advisors but hope that this statement could be signed by a bipartisan group[.] Donald Trump's repeated denigration of the NATO Alliance, his refusal to support our Article 5 obligations to our European allies and his kid glove treatment of Russia and Vladimir Putin are among the most reckless statements made by a Presidential candidate in memory.[438]

During the same week, Clinton's campaign manager, Robby Mook, stated in media interviews that the campaign believed that the Russian government had carried out the DNC hack to assist Trump's electoral chances, and that Trump had made troubling statements concerning Russia.[439]

During an interview of former Secretary Clinton, the Office asked if she had reviewed the information declassified by DNI Ratcliffe regarding her alleged plan to stir up a scandal between Trump and the Russians.[440] Clinton stated it was "really sad," but "I get it, you have to go down every rabbit hole." She said that it "looked like Russian disinformation to me; they're very good at it, you know." Clinton advised that she had a lot of plans to win the campaign, and anything that came into the public domain was available to her.

In addition, the Office interviewed several other former members of the Clinton campaign using declassified materials[441] regarding the purported "plan" approved by Clinton.

---

[435] *Id.*

[436] *Id.*

[437] *Id.*

[438] XXXX-0014561 (Email from Foreign Policy Advisor-1 dated July 27, 2016).

[439] Jeremy Herb, *Mook Suggests Russians Leaked DNC Emails to Help Trump*, Politico (July 24, 2016); Jessie Hellmann, *Clinton Campaign Manager Questions Russian Involvement in Email Leak*, The Hill (July 24, 2016).

[440] OSC Report of Interview of Hillary Clinton on May 11, 2022 at 6.

[441] *See Ratcliffe Letter.*

The campaign Chairperson, John Podesta, stated that he had not seen the declassified material before, characterized the information as "ridiculous," and denied that the campaign was involved in any such "plan."[442] Jake Sullivan, the campaign Senior Policy Advisor, stated that he had not seen the intelligence reporting before and had no reaction to it other than to say, "that's ridiculous."[443] Although the campaign was broadly focused on Trump and Russia, Sullivan could not recall anyone articulating a strategy or "plan" to distract negative attention away from Clinton by tying Trump to Russia, but could not conclusively rule out the possibility.[444] The campaign Communications Director, Jennifer Palmieri, who was shown the *Referral Memo*,[445] stated that she had never seen the memorandum before, found its contents to be "ridiculous," and could not recall anything "like this" related to the campaign.[446] She stated that Podesta, Mook, Sullivan and herself were aware of a project involving ties between Trump and Russia being conducted by Perkins Coie, the campaign law firm, but she did not think Clinton was aware of it, nor did she receive any direction or instruction from Clinton about the project.[447]

Another foreign policy advisor ("Foreign Policy Advisor-2") confirmed that the campaign was focused on Trump and Russia, but that focus was due to national security concerns and not designed to distract the public from Clinton's server issue.[448] Foreign Policy Advisor-2 stated that she did not have a conversation with Clinton about a plan involving Trump and Russia during the Democratic convention, that she did not remember Clinton approving anything concrete, but that she would not necessarily have been involved in such strategy conversations.[449]

The Office's review of certain communications involving Foreign Policy Advisor-1 and Foreign Policy Advisor-2, however, arguably provide some support for the notion that the Clinton campaign was engaged in an effort or plan in late July 2016 to encourage scrutiny of Trump's potential ties to Russia, and that the campaign might have wanted or expected law enforcement or other agencies to aid that effort, in part, by concluding that the Russians were responsible for the hack.

For example, on July 5, 2016, Foreign Policy Advisor-2 sent an email to three other campaign advisors ("Individual-1," "Individual-2," and "Individual-3") in which she wrote:

> We're looking for ways to build on Franklin Foer's great (and scary) piece on Trump and Russia.[450] One thing I've heard from a few folks is that the Russia

---

[442] OSC Report of Interview of John Podesta on Jan. 19, 2022 at 5.

[443] OSC Report of Interview of Jake Sullivan on Nov. 12, 2021 at 3-4.

[444] *Id.*

[445] *Referral Memo.*

[446] OSC Report of Interview of Jennifer Palmieri on Nov. 10, 2021 at 4.

[447] *Id.* at 1-2

[448] OSC Report of Interview of Foreign Policy Advisor-2 on Mar. 28, 2022 at 4.

[449] *Id.*

[450] In its June 2020 issue, the *Atlantic* had published an article by Franklin Foer titled "*Putin is Well on His Way to Stealing the Next Election: RIP Democracy.*"

desk at State has been tracking (and sounding an internal alarm) about parallels between rhetoric/words/methods that Trump uses and Putin-supported European right-wing candidates. I'm told it goes beyond just populist stuff. I'd love to get my hands on details of what they are seeing - can one of you help run this down? I imagine INR or IC [Intelligence Community] types might also have some insight - obviously need to be a bit careful here but eager to get specifics or details.[451]

Foreign Policy Advisor-2 stated that she did not speak with anyone at the State Department about this issue.[452] The information she mentioned in this email regarding the State Department's Russia desk came from an outside advisor who formerly worked at the State Department ("Outside Advisor-1").[453]

In addition, on July 25, 2016, Foreign Policy Advisor-1 had the following text message exchange with Foreign Policy Advisor-2:

[Foreign Policy Advisor-2]:	Can you see if [Special Assistant to the President and National Security Council member] will tell you if there is a formal fbi or other investigation into the hack?
[Foreign Policy Advisor-1]:	[She] won't say anything more to me. Sorry. Told me [she] went as far as [she] could.
[Foreign Policy Advisor-2]:	Ok. Do you have others who might?
[Foreign Policy Advisor-1]:	Has [Individual-2] tried [her]? Curious if [she] would react differently to [Individual-2]? I can also try OVP [Office of the Vice President]. They might say more.
[Foreign Policy Advisor-2]:	I don't know if he has but can ask. Would also be good to try ovp, and anyone in IC [intelligence community]
[Foreign Policy Advisor-1]:	Left messages for OVP but politico just sent me a push notification stating that they are indeed investigating.
[Foreign Policy Advisor-2]:	Fbi just put our [sic] statement. Thx[454]

In sum, Foreign Policy Advisor-1's July 27, 2016 email to her colleagues regarding Trump, Russia and NATO – the day after Clinton purportedly approved a plan to tie Trump to Russia – is consistent with the substance of the purported plan. In addition, Foreign Policy

---

[451] XX_DOJ_000003 (Email from Foreign Policy Advisor-2 dated July 5, 2016).

[452] *Id.*

[453] *Id.*

[454] XX_DOJ_000022-23 (Text message exchange between Foreign Policy Advisor-1 and Foreign Policy Advisor-2 dated 07/25/2016).

Advisor-1's text message exchange with Foreign Policy Advisor-2 supports the notion that at least some officials within the campaign were seeking information about the FBI's response to the DNC hack, which would be consistent with, and a means of furthering, the purported plan. Moreover, the campaign's funding of the Steele Reports and Alfa Bank allegations as described in greater detail in Sections IV.D.1.b.ii and IV.E.1.b provide some additional support for the credibility to the information set forth in the Clinton Plan intelligence.

      vii.   *Other events occurring at the time of the purported approval of the Clinton Plan intelligence*

As set forth in Section IV.D.1.h.i, some of the significant Steele Dossier reporting related to Carter Page and his alleged role as a conduit for passing Russian information between Paul Manafort and the Trump campaign. This uncorroborated allegation is significantly undercut by the evidence examined by the Office and that, at the time, was in the possession of the Crossfire Hurricane investigators. As discussed below, this evidence was never presented to OI or the FISC at *any time* during the pendency of the Page FISA surveillance.

Furthermore, the evidence gathered by the Office revealed a concerted effort on the part of Fusion GPS in late July 2016 – *i.e.*, the same timeframe the Clinton Plan intelligence was purportedly approved – to communicate with the press regarding the Page allegations in the Steele reporting. For example:

- On July 19, 2016, Peter Fritsch of Fusion GPS emailed Steve LeVine, identified in his signature block as a Washington correspondent for *Quartz*, and asked of LeVine "have you ever come across this cat carter page? He strikes me as a fraud . . . ."[455] Mr. LeVine responded that he knew Page, he (LeVine) was on vacation, but would reach out when he returned.[456]

- On July 22, 2016, Fritsch emailed Franklin Foer of *Slate* stating "now we need to do the next level, which is in the works." Foer responded, "Good deal – what's the next level? And is it a sex scandal?" Fritsch replied, "it's who carter page met with in early july and what they talked about."[457]

- On July 25, 2016, Mark Hosenball of *Reuters* sent Glenn Simpson at Fusion GPS an email stating "if you have stuff on the Carter Page guy, including his most recent Russian excursion, pls. send. Doing two Russian hacking stories today and might be able to do another as early as tomorrow."[458]

---

[455] SCID_00034478.

[456] *Id.*

[457] SCID_00034501. Notably, in an uncorroborated Steele Report dated just three days earlier, in what Steele designated as "Company Intelligence Report 2016/94," dated July 19, 2016, it was alleged that Page had met secretly with "SECHIN and senior Kremlin Internal Affairs official, DIVYEKIN."

[458] SC-00082677.

- On July 26, 2016, Fritsch emailed Jay Solomon of the *Wall Street Journal* and wrote:

  > "OTR the easy scoop waiting for confirmation: that dude carter page met with igor sechin when he went to moscow earlier this month. sechin discussed energy deals and possible lifting of sanctions on himself et al. he also met with a senior kremlin official called divyekin who told page they have good kompromat on hillary and offered to help. he also warned page they have good kompromat on the donald. i know of one person who is chasing this and has asked kremlin re these meets. the response: there was no meeting between sechin and page "at the kremlin." uh, well, ok . . . maybe somewhere else? no comment. needless to say, a senior trump advisor meeting with a former kgb official close to putin, who is on the treasury sanctions list, days before the republican convention and a big russian-backed wikileak would be huge news."[459]

  > That same day, Solomon responded, "Page is neither confirming nor denying." Fritsch replied "call adam schiff or difi [in context, Sen. Diane Feinstein] for that matter. i bet they are concerned about what page was doing other than giving a speech over 3 days in moscow."[460]

  > Fritsch later emailed Solomon that "its kind of hard to believe that the wsj is ignoring the russia stuff. literally everyone is chasing this [expletive] now."[461]

- Also, on July 26, 2016 – the date of the purported approval of the Clinton Plan intelligence – Fritsch reached back out to Steve LeVine of *Quartz*, and wrote *"[S]o carter page is of some urgency now. Can you talk?"*[462] LeVine replied that he could and asked if Fritsch wanted to talk by phone.[463]

- On that same date, July 26, 2016, Glenn Simpson emailed Jane Mayer of *New Yorker* magazine with the subject line "Carter Page." Simpson wrote, "Jane – I understand that you are interested in him."[464] Two days later, Mayer responded to Simpson advising him that her editor, among others, was "interested in setting up an off the record meeting to discuss stories, and learn more about your research."[465]

---

[459] SCID_00034363.

[460] *Id.*

[461] *Id.* (emphasis added).

[462] SCID_00034478 (emphasis added).

[463] *Id.*

[464] SC-00082579.

[465] *Id.*

- On July 28, 2016, Simpson sent Jake Berkowitz, an employee at Fusion GPS, an email with the subject line "carter page TLO/ clear."[466] Simpson asked Berkowitz to send "the carter page TLO/clear" to Tom Hamburger "asap" at the *Washington Post*.[467] Later that same day, Berkowitz sent Hamburger a copy of the "carter page clear" information.[468]

- Importantly, on the very next day, July 29, 2016, Hamburger emailed Simpson with subject line "Re: fyi, we are getting kick back to the idea," and wrote *"That Page met with Sechin and Ivanov, 'It's [expletive]. Impossible,' said one of our Moscow sources."*[469] Simpson responded to Hamburger's email and stated "ok."[470] Hamburger then emailed Simpson "FYI, passed on by another reporter who likely doesn't like this story. Just letting you know. . . ."[471]

Thus, in one day – and months before the Crossfire Hurricane investigators used the alleged Page meetings in its initial and subsequent renewal FISA applications – a Moscow-based U.S. media source for the *Washington Post* appears to have been able to debunk to its satisfaction the Page meetings.

Several weeks later, on September 16, 2016, Fritsch emailed Michael Isikoff of *Yahoo! News*. As discussed below, on September 23, 2016, Isikoff was the first journalist to publish an article about the alleged meetings between Page and Sechin. Fritsch wrote, "Glenn [Simpson] says you may soon break the carter page story? I ask cuz if so I'm gonna stiff-arm someone else chasing…"[472] Isikoff replied, "got it, am going to talk to glenn [Simpson] on [sic] a bit."[473] Thereafter, on September 20, 2016, Simpson sent Isikoff a Word document identified as a transcript of Page's July 7, 2016 speech in Moscow.[474]

The above-quoted emails from Fusion GPS to members of the media are a sampling of the correspondence regarding Carter Page that the Clinton/DNC-funded Fusion GPS sent to various members of the media from late July 2016 (the purported date the Clinton Plan intelligence was approved) through the fall of 2016.

In addition, as relates to the Clinton Plan intelligence and as discussed in detail in Section IV.E.1.c.iii below, on September 19, 2016, Michael Sussmann, a lawyer at Perkins Coie, the firm that was then serving as counsel to the Clinton campaign, met with James Baker, the FBI

---

[466] SC-00082631. Simpson's reference to "TLO/clear" appears to refer to two commercially available databases that provide information on, among other things, individuals, businesses and assets.

[467] *Id.*

[468] *Id.*

[469] SC-00082576 (emphasis added).

[470] *Id.*

[471] *Id.*

[472] SCID_00034257.

[473] *Id.*

[474] SCID_00024621.

General Counsel, at FBI Headquarters in Washington, D.C. Sussmann provided Baker with purported data and "white papers" that allegedly demonstrated a covert communications channel between the Trump Organization and a Russia-based bank, Alfa Bank.[475] Sussmann's billing records reflect that he was regularly billing the Clinton campaign for his work on the Alfa Bank allegations.[476] Importantly, on July 29, 2016 – three days after the purported approval of the Clinton Plan intelligence – Michael Sussmann and Marc Elias, the General Counsel to the Clinton campaign, met with Fusion GPS personnel in Elias's office at Perkins Coie. Sussmann billed his time in this meeting to the Clinton campaign under the category "General Political Advice."[477] Thereafter, on July 31, 2016, Sussmann billed the Clinton campaign for twenty-four minutes with the billing description, "communications with Marc Elias regarding server issue." In compiling and disseminating the Alfa bank allegations, Sussmann consistently met and communicated with Elias.[478]

On October 31, 2016 – a little over one week before the election – multiple media outlets reported that the FBI had received and was investigating allegations concerning a purported secret channel between the Trump Organization and Alfa Bank.[479] On that day, the *New York Times* published an article titled *Investigating Donald Trump, F.B.I. Sees No Clear Link to Russia*.[480] The article stated that the FBI possessed information concerning "what cyber experts said appeared to be a mysterious back channel between the Trump Organization and Alfa Bank."[481] The article further reported that the FBI "had spent weeks examining computer data showing an odd stream of activity to a Trump Organization server," and that the *New York Times* had been provided computer logs that evidenced this activity.[482] The article also noted that the FBI had not found "any conclusive or direct link" between Trump and the Russian government and that "Hillary Clinton's supporters . . . pushed for these investigations."[483] On the same date, *Slate* published an article titled *Was a Trump Server Communicating with Russia?* that likewise discussed at length the allegations that Sussmann provided to the FBI.[484]

Notably, also on that day, *Mother Jones* published David Corn's article titled *A Veteran Spy Has Given the FBI Information Alleging a Russian Operation to Cultivate Donald Trump: Has the Bureau Investigated this Material?"* The *Mother Jones* piece referenced the Foer *Slate*

---

[475] Indictment, *United States v. Sussmann*, No. 1:21-cr-00582-CRC (D.D.C. September 16, 2021) (hereinafter "*Sussmann Indictment*" or "*Indictment*") at ¶¶ 3, 27.

[476] *Id.* at ¶¶ 4, 20, 24, 25, 26, 29, 37.

[477] *Id.* at ¶ 20.

[478] *Id.* at ¶¶ 19, 20, 21, 24, 25, 26, 33.

[479] *Id.* at ¶ 1.

[480] Eric Lichtblau & Steven Lee Myers, *Investigating Donald Trump, F.B.I. Sees No Clear Link to Russia*, N.Y. Times (Oct. 31, 2016).

[481] *Id.*

[482] *Id.*

[483] *Id.*

[484] Franklin Foer, *Was a Trump Server Communicating with Russia?*, Slate (Oct. 31, 2016).

article on Alfa Bank and also disclosed that it had reviewed memos prepared by the "former western intelligence official." Corn included information in his October 31, 2016 article that referenced the Isikoff's earlier *Yahoo! News* piece on Carter Page and the Russians. In addition, the Corn article contained allegations that were consistent with those contained in some of the Steele Dossier reports that eventually were published in January 2017 by *BuzzFeed*.[485]

In the months before the publication of these articles, Sussmann had communicated with the media and provided them with the Alfa Bank data and allegations.[486] Sussmann also kept Marc Elias apprised of his efforts, and Elias, in turn, communicated with the Clinton campaign's leadership about potential media coverage of these issues.[487]

On September 1, 2016, Sussmann met with the *New York Times* reporter who published the aforementioned article and billed his time to the Clinton campaign.[488] On September 15, 2016, Elias provided an update to the Clinton campaign regarding the Alfa Bank allegations and the not-yet-published *New York Times* article, sending an email to senior members of the Clinton campaign, which he billed to the campaign as "re: Alfa Article."[489]

On the same day that these articles were published, the Clinton campaign posted a tweet through Clinton's Twitter account that stated: "Computer scientists have apparently uncovered a covert server linking the Trump Organization to a Russian-based Bank."[490] The tweet included a statement from Clinton campaign advisor Jake Sullivan that made reference to the media coverage of the article and stated, in relevant part, that the allegations in the articles "could be the most direct link yet between Donald Trump and Moscow[,] that "[t]his secret hotline may be the key to unlocking the mystery of Trump's ties to Russia[,]" and that "[w]e can only assume that federal authorities will now explore this direct connection between Trump and Russia as part of their existing probe into Russia's meddling in our elections." The fact that the Clinton campaign immediately issued a tweet concerning the articles – after funding the Alfa Bank allegations and receiving foreknowledge of the articles from Sussmann and Elias – tends to

---

[485] According to Glenn Simpson and Peter Fritsch, on September 21, 2016, Steele flew to Washington, D.C. at the urging of Fusion GPS to meet with reporters. *Crime in Progress* at 109. The following day, Simpson and Steele, who was only speaking "on background" with the background information being attributed to a "former, senior western intelligence official," met with reporters in staggered intervals at the Tabard Inn. *Id.* at 109-110. Among the reporters who attended the Tabard presentations were Eric Lichtblau from the *New York Times* and Michael Isikoff of *Yahoo! News*. *Id.* at 110. The next day, September 23, 2016, Isikoff's *Yahoo! News* article focusing on Carter Page and the Russians was published. *Id.* at 111. The article reported that Senate minority leader Harry Reid had written to Director Comey about the need for the FBI to investigate Page and "'significant and disturbing ties' between the Trump campaign and the Kremlin." The article also reported that a "senior U.S. law enforcement official" confirmed that Page was on the radar screen and being looked at. *See* Isikoff, *Officials Probe Ties*.

[486] *Sussmann Indictment* at ¶¶ 24, 25, 26, 27, 33-38.

[487] *Id.* at ¶ 25.

[488] *Id.*

[489] *Id.*

[490] Twitter, @HillaryClinton 10/31/2016 8:36 p.m. Tweet.

96

support the notion that the Alfa Bank allegations were part of a Clinton campaign plan to tie Trump to Russia.

2. *Prosecution decisions*

The aforementioned facts reflect a rather startling and inexplicable failure to adequately consider and incorporate the Clinton Plan intelligence into the FBI's investigative decision-making in the Crossfire Hurricane investigation. Indeed, had the FBI opened the Crossfire Hurricane investigation as an assessment and, in turn, gathered and analyzed data in concert with the information from the Clinton Plan intelligence, it is likely that the information received would have been examined, at a minimum, with a more critical eye. A more deliberative examination would have increased the likelihood of alternative analytical hypotheses and reduced the risk of reputational damage both to the targets of the investigation as well as, ultimately, to the FBI.

The FBI thus failed to act on what should have been – when combined with other, incontrovertible facts – a clear warning sign that the FBI might then be the target of an effort to manipulate or influence the law enforcement process for political purposes during the 2016 presidential election. Indeed, CIA Director Brennan and other intelligence officials recognized the significance of the intelligence by expeditiously briefing it to the President, Vice President, the Director of National Intelligence, the Attorney General, the Director of the FBI, and other senior administration officials.[491] Whether or not the Clinton Plan intelligence was based on reliable or unreliable information, or was ultimately true or false, it should have prompted FBI personnel to immediately undertake an analysis of the information and to act with far greater care and caution when receiving, analyzing, and relying upon materials of partisan origins, such as the Steele Reports and the Alfa Bank allegations. The FBI also should have disseminated the Clinton Plan intelligence more widely among those responsible for the Crossfire Hurricane investigation so that they could effectively incorporate it into their analysis and decision-making, and their representations to the OI attorneys and, ultimately, the FISC.[492]

Whether these failures by U.S. officials amounted to criminal acts, however, is a different question. In order for the above-described facts to give rise to criminal liability under federal civil rights statutes, the Office would need to, for example, identify one or more persons who (i) *knew* the Clinton campaign intended to falsely accuse its opponent with specific information or allegations, (ii) intentionally disregarded a particular civil right of a particular person (such as the right to be free of unreasonable searches or seizures), and (iii) then intentionally aided that effort by taking investigative steps based on those allegations while knowing that they were false.

In order to prove a criminal violation of the false statements and/or obstruction statutes by a government official, the Office would need to prove that the official willfully and intentionally failed to inform the FISC or caused another to fail to inform the FISC of the Clinton Plan intelligence in order to conceal that information from the Court. Similarly, to prove a

---

[491] *See Ratcliffe Letter*; *Brennan Notes*.

[492] *See* OSC Report of Interview of James Baker on June 11, 2020 at 2 (stating that he would have remembered if he had seen the Clinton Plan intelligence reporting and would have considered it significant); OSC Report of Interview of Supervisory Special Agent-1 on July 22, 2022 at 7.

criminal violation of the perjury statutes, the Office would need to prove, among other things, that the official made a false statement to the Court "with knowledge of its falsity, rather than as a result of confusion, mistake, or faulty memory."[493]

Although the evidence we collected revealed a troubling disregard for the Clinton Plan intelligence and potential confirmation bias in favor of continued investigative scrutiny of Trump and his associates, it did not yield evidence sufficient to prove beyond a reasonable doubt that any FBI or CIA officials[494] intentionally furthered a Clinton campaign plan to frame or falsely accuse Trump of improper ties to Russia. Nor did it reveal sufficient evidence to prove that the omission of the Clinton Plan intelligence from applications to the FISC was a conscious or intentional decision, much less one intended to influence the Court's view of the facts supporting probable cause.

Moreover, any attempted prosecution premised on the Clinton Plan intelligence would face what in all likelihood would be insurmountable classification issues given the highly sensitive nature of the information itself.

In sum, the government's handling of the Clinton Plan intelligence may have amounted to a significant intelligence failure and a troubling instance in which confirmation bias and a tunnel-vision pursuit of investigative ends may have caused government personnel to fail to appreciate the extent to which uncorroborated reporting funded by an opposing political campaign was intended to influence rather than inform the FBI. It did not, all things considered, however, amount to a provable criminal offense.

D. The Carter Page FISA Applications

On April 1, 2016, Perkins Coie, a law firm acting as counsel to the Clinton campaign, "Hillary for America," retained Fusion GPS, a Washington, D.C.-based investigative firm, to conduct opposition research on Trump and his associates.[495] Shortly thereafter, Fusion GPS hired Christopher Steele and his U.K.-based firm, Orbis Business Intelligence, to investigate Trump's ties to Russia. At the time, Steele, who again has stated that he was formerly an intelligence professional for the British government,[496] was an FBI CHS. Beginning in July 2016 and continuing through December 2016, Steele and Fusion GPS prepared a series of reports containing derogatory information about purported ties between Trump and Russia. According to the reports, important connections between Trump and Russia ran through campaign manager Paul Manafort and foreign policy advisory Carter Page.

Steele provided the reports to the Department, the FBI, the State Department, members of Congress, and multiple media outlets. Steele styled the reports "Company Intelligence Reports," and each report contained an identifying number (*e.g.*, Company Intelligence Report 2016/095). Collectively, these reports came to be known colloquially as the "Steele Dossier," and we refer to them in this report as the "Steele Dossier" or the "Steele Reports." The reports played an

---

[493] *See supra* § III.D.3 (quoting the Department's *Criminal Resources Manual*).

[494] Indeed, as noted above, the CIA acted with dispatch to bring the information to the attention of the highest levels of the U.S. government.

[495] SC-00004920 (Consulting Agreement dated Apr. 1, 2016).

[496] *See supra* at footnote 34.

98

important role in applications submitted to the FISC targeting Page, a U.S. person. The FBI relied substantially on the reports to assert probable cause that Page was knowingly engaged in clandestine intelligence activities on behalf of Russia, or knowingly helping another person in such activities. As discussed in more detail below, the FBI was not able to corroborate a single substantive allegation contained in the Steele Reports, despite protracted efforts to do so. The Steele Reports themselves, however, were not the only issue that we considered in connection with the Page FISA applications.

This section begins by discussing probable cause and the Page FISA applications. It then focuses on the Steele Reports and the subsources that Steele allegedly used:

- The FBI's relationship with Steele and its handling of the Steele Reports (Subsection V.D.1.b).
- The prior counterespionage investigation of Igor Danchenko, Steele's primary subsource for his reporting (Subsection V.D.1.c).
- Danchenko's relationship with Charles Dolan, one of Danchenko's subsources (Subsection V.D.1.d).
- The FBI's failure to investigate Dolan's possible role as a subsource for Danchenko (Subsection V.D.1.e).
- Danchenko's purported contact with Sergei Millian, another subsource that Danchenko claimed to have received information from (Subsection V.D.1.f).

This section then turns to other aspects of the Page FISA applications:

- Information about Page's role as a source of another U.S. government agency (Subsection V.D.1.g).
- Meetings between FBI CHSs and Papadopoulos, Page, and a senior Trump campaign official (Subsection V.D.1.h).
- Other shortcomings in the Page FISA applications (Subsection V.D.1.i).

This section concludes with a discussion of the factors that the Office considered in its prosecution and declination decisions related to the Page FISA applications.

A few additional aspects of the FISA applications are discussed in the Classified Appendix.

1. Factual background

a. "Probable Cause" and the Page FISA applications

"Omissions of material fact," the FISC has stated, "were the most prevalent and among the most serious problems with the Page applications."[497] The OIG, for its part, found in its review of the applications targeting Page "at least 17 significant errors or omissions" and "so many basic and fundamental errors."[498] These were "made by three separate, hand-picked teams on one of the most sensitive FBI investigations that was briefed to the highest levels within the

---

[497] *In re Accuracy Concerns Regarding FBI Matters Submitted to the FISC*, Corrected Op. and Order at 4, Misc. No. 19-02 (FISC Mar. 5, 2020).

[498] *Redacted OIG Review* at xiii-xiv; *see also id.* at 413.

FBI."[499] The *OIG Review* also found that FBI personnel "did not give appropriate attention to facts that cut against probable cause."[500]

Also of concern, and the focus of this section, is that several Crossfire Hurricane investigators were skeptical of the information used in the Page FISA applications and, particularly as time went on, believed that Page *was not* acting as an agent of Russia and *was not* a threat to national security. Nevertheless, despite the surveillance's lack of productivity, FBI management directed the Crossfire Hurricane investigators to renew the Page surveillance three times.

i.   The lead up to the initial Page FISA application

As has been noted by several individuals, including Deputy Director McCabe, the FISA on Page would not have been authorized without the Steele reporting.[501] Indeed, prior to receipt of the Steele Reports, the FBI had drafted a FISA application on Page that FBI OGC determined lacked sufficient probable cause.[502] Within two days of their eventual receipt by Crossfire Hurricane investigators, however, information from four of the Steele Reports was being used to buttress the probable cause in the initial draft FISA application targeting Page.[503] [504] Yet even prior to the initial application, the Page case agent, Case Agent-1, recognized that the FBI's reliance on the uncorroborated and unvetted Steele Reports could be problematic.

Indeed, on September 27, 2016, Case Agent-1 exchanged the following FBI Lync messages with another employee assisting with Crossfire Hurricane ("Support Operations Specialist-1"):

> Support Operations Specialist-1:   Hopefully [Steele] can get more detailed info though

---

[499] *Id.* at xiv.

[500] *Redacted OIG Review* at 413; *see also id.* at xiii.

[501] When asked during his HPSCI testimony whether the initial Page FISA had sufficient probable cause without the Steele Report information, McCabe stated, "Let me be clear. I don't want to rely on implication. My position is that anything less than the package that went to the FISA court would not have been enough. We put in that information that we thought was necessary." U.S. House of Representatives Permanent Select Cmte. On Intelligence Interview of Andrew McCabe on Dec. 19, 2017 at 109.

[502] In her interview with the Office, FBI OGC Unit Chief-1 described the probable cause without the Steele reporting as a "close call." OSC Report of Interview of FBI OGC Unit Chief-1 on August 29, 2019 at 6-7. FBI OGC Unit Chief-1 informed the OIG that the Steele reporting "pushed it over." OIG Interview of FBI OGC Unit Chief-1 on June 1, 2018 at 83.

[503] FBI-EMAIL-385532 (Email from Case Agent-1 to FBI OGC Unit Chief-1 & Clinesmith dated 9/21/16) (stating that Case Agent-1 had "repackaged the information from the Rome Source [Steele] and put it in the application.")

[504] David Laufman, the then-Chief of the Department's Counterespionage and Export Control Section, referred to the FISA targeting Page as "predicated on [the] [Steele] reporting." DOJ-NSD-00060564 (Notes of David Laufman dated 3/27/2017).

Case Agent-1:	Yeah, exactly. Dates, times, etc, would be key
Support Operations Specialist-1:	Yeah – it just goes down to how confident we are in that reporting
Support Operations Specialist-1:	There aren't a WHOLE lot of details in it
Case Agent-1:	haha, true.
Support Operations Specialist-1:	Which is just what worries me a bit
Support Operations Specialist-1:	Hopefully the sources sub-sources are legit
Support Operations Specialist-1:	They seem legit based on past reporting
Case Agent-1:	Yeah, no kidding. What was strange was that [British Intelligence Services] don't seem to want to deal with the guy.
Support Operations Specialist-1:	But there aren't many specifics in this reporting that couldn't be expanded on from open source
Case Agent-1:	Not sure why.
Support Operations Specialist-1:	Yeah that's weird too
Support Operations Specialist-1:	If he has the sub-source network that he claims to have (and the reporting suggests), you would think they'd be interested in him.
Support Operations Specialist-1:	Though, maybe these are newly developed since he went to [British Intelligence Services]?
Case Agent-1:	Yeah that's the weird thing. [Handling Agent-1] said it was the OC angle and that they're not too interested, but that still seems odd
Case Agent-1:	*Who knows. We may have to take a calculated risk with the reporting, if we're pressed for time.*[505]

This exchange between Case Agent-1 and Support Operations Specialist-1 underscores the fact that Case Agent-1, the principal contributor of the factual information contained in the

---

[505] FBI-AAA-EC-00008439 (Lync message exchange between Case Agent-1 and Support Operations Specialist-1 dated 09-27-2016) (capitalization in original; emphasis added).

request for the initial Page FISA application, had clearly recognized issues with using the Steele Report information due to the uncorroborated nature of the allegations and the lack of insight into the reliability of Steele's sub-sources. Indeed, an experienced counterintelligence agent like Case Agent-1 was no doubt aware of the need to evaluate the credibility and reliability of human source information.

The OI attorney who was responsible for preparing the initial FISA application ("OI Attorney-1"), recalled being constantly pressured to advance the FISA and FBI executive management being invoked as the reason for the pressure.[506] OI Attorney-1 advised the Office that FBI OGC attorney Kevin Clinesmith informed him that Director Comey "wants to know what's going on," and that Deputy Director McCabe asked who the FBI needed to speak with at DOJ "to get this going."[507] McCabe confirmed this basic push by the FBI and Comey when he was interviewed by the OIG investigators. McCabe told the interviewers that there was a lot of back-and-forth between the Crossfire Hurricane investigators and OI regarding "[w]hen are we going to get it? When are we going to get it?" and that Comey repeatedly asked him "where is the FISA, where is the FISA? What's the status with the, with the Page FISA?" McCabe noted that the FISA was something McCabe definitely knew Comey wanted.[508]

This recollection also is consistent with email traffic and other FBI records in which the inclination on the part of Department personnel to move cautiously and FBI executives to move quickly are made clear. For example, on October 12, 2016, a meeting took place involving AD Priestap, DAD Strzok, FBI OGC Unit Chief-1 and the Deputy Director's Special Assistant Lisa Page. Page's notes from the meeting reflect that Deputy Assistant Attorney General Evans had spoken with Strzok the night before and raised concerns about the proposed FISA. Page's notes show the following:

- Lots of Qs re source's motivation re reliability/bias. Hired to do opp. Research, tasked network of subsources.
- Don't know who his sub-source is, who their sub-sources are.
- FISA bad idea from policy perspective.
- Email out the [unreadable] hacked email to [Steele] re talking to the FBI.[509]

FBI OGC Unit Chief-1's notes from the same meeting reflect that Evans was concerned that "[Steele] may have been hired by the Clinton campaign or the DNC. . . ."[510]

That same day, at 7:13 p.m., FBI OGC Unit Chief-1 emailed OGC attorneys Trisha Anderson and Clinesmith to advise them that, "We raised Stu's concerns to the D[irector] and D[eputy] D[irector] at the 130, and they are supportive if [sic] moving forward despite his

---

[506] OSC Report of Interview of OI Attorney-1 on July 1, 2020 at 5.

[507] *Id.*

[508] OIG Interview of Andrew McCabe on Aug. 15, 2019 at 208-09. McCabe, through his counsel, did not agree to be interviewed by the Office even after we offered to narrow the scope of subjects to be asked about.

[509] FBI-LP-00000111 (Handwritten notes of Lisa Page dated 10/12/16).

[510] E2018002-A-002016 (Handwritten notes of FBI OGC Unit Chief-1 dated 10/12/16).

concerns. I just talked to Lisa, and she had reached out to Stu and will inform the DD. We're close to losing our operational window."[511]

Over the next few days, Department and FBI personnel continued to exchange information on questions and needed clarifications in the draft application. On October 18th, Strzok emailed FBI OGC Unit Chief-1 and Clinesmith and asked, "How significant were Bakers [sic] changes back when he reviewed? If the DAG and we (investigative team) are good with the current draft, we need to ram this through. Thanks. I hate these cases."[512] FBI OGC Unit Chief-1 responded shortly thereafter:

> Just talked to Lisa. Baker had a bunch if [sic] comments, but they were not directed to issue Stu's now made a bug [sic] deal about. I think if the investigative team is good with the facts and the DAG is good with the PC, then Andy [McCabe] should push (regardless of Baker's comments.)[513]

The FISC approved the surveillance three days later, on October 21st.

NYFO Case Agent-1, the counterintelligence agent who led the NYFO investigation of Page, was never contacted by the Crossfire Hurricane investigators prior to the submission of the initial Page FISA application.[514] When interviewed by the Office, NYFO Case Agent-1 noted that the NYFO viewed Page as someone "we need[ed] to watch" due to the Russians contacting Page, but she and others were never overly concerned about Page being an intelligence officer for the Russians.[515] At no time during the course of her investigation did NYFO Case Agent-1 consider pursuing a FISA on Page.[516] NYFO Case Agent-1 later read the Page FISA applications and recalled seeing some aspects of her investigation referenced. NYFO Case Agent-1 felt the language used to link Page to the Russians was "a little strong."[517] Nevertheless, NYFO Case Agent-1 assumed the Crossfire Hurricane investigation had uncovered additional information linking Page to the Russians.[518] In fact, the additional information contained in the initial Page FISA application was largely taken from the Steele Reports and carefully selected portions of consensual recordings with an FBI CHS as described below. In retrospect, NYFO Case Agent-1 viewed the Page investigation as a "waste of money."[519]

---

[511] FBI-EMAIL-488872 (Email from FBI OGC Unit Chief-1 to Anderson & Clinesmith dated 10/12/16).

[512] FBI-EMAIL-483856 (Email from FBI OGC Unit Chief-1 to Strzok, Clinesmith dated 10/18/2016)

[513] *Id.* At the time, James Baker was the General Counsel of the FBI and FBI OGC Unit Chief-1's boss.

[514] OSC Report of Interview of NYFO Case Agent-1 on Sept. 5, 2019 at 3.

[515] *Id.* at 2.

[516] *Id.*

[517] *Id.* at 4.

[518] *See id.*

[519] *Id.*

ii. The Page FISA application renewals

In late January 2017, Supervisory Special Agent-1 transferred back to WFO.[520] Supervisory Special Agent-1 was replaced in that position by an experienced counterintelligence agent assigned to WFO ("Supervisory Special Agent-3").[521] In his interview with the Office, Supervisory Special Agent-3 stated that, upon arriving at FBI Headquarters, DAD Jennifer Boone informed him that his primary tasking was to renew the Page FISA application.[522] Despite this tasking, Supervisory Special Agent-3 stated that his investigators did not feel connected to the Page investigation and were excluded from the flow of information and decision-making process, an investigation that, according to Supervisory Special Agent-3, was still managed by the "Triumvirate of control" of the Crossfire Hurricane investigation, namely, Strzok, Auten, and Section Chief Moffa.[523] For example, during the course of their time on Crossfire Hurricane, neither Supervisory Special Agent-3 nor Special Agent-1, an investigator working for Supervisory Special Agent-3, knew that Page had previously served as a source for another government agency.[524] When Special Agent-1 eventually learned this information, he stated that he "felt like a fool."[525] Special Agent-1 also recalled that Supervisory Special Agent-3 would often rhetorically ask his investigators, "what are we even doing here."[526]

Moreover, based on their review of the case file and the lack of evidence obtained from the FISA surveillance, neither Supervisory Special Agent-3 nor his investigators believed that Page was a threat to national security or a witting agent of the Russian government.[527] Special Agent-1 and another agent working for Supervisory Special Agent-3, ("Supervisory Special Agent-2") shared Supervisory Special Agent-3's conclusion that Page was not a witting agent of the Russian government.[528] Special Agent-1 went as far to say that the surveillance on Page was a "dry hole."[529] Nonetheless, Special Agent-1 "assumed" that "somebody above them" possessed important information – unknown to the investigators – that guided the Crossfire Hurricane decision-making.[530] When Supervisory Special Agent-3 informed DAD Boone of his

---

[520] OSC Report of Interview of Supervisory Special Agent-3 on March 18, 2021 at 1.

[521] Id.

[522] Id. at 2.

[523] Id.

[524] OSC Report of Interview of Special Agent-1 on March 21, 2021 at 3; OSC Report of Interview of Supervisory Special Agent-3 on March 18, 2021 at 5.

[525] OSC Report of Interview of Special Agent-1 on March 21, 2021 at 3.

[526] Id. at 2.

[527] OSC Report of Interview of Supervisory Special Agent-3 on March 18, 2021 at 2, 5.

[528] OSC Report of Interview of Special Agent-1 on March 21, 2021 at 2; OSC Report of Interview of Supervisory Special Agent-2 on May 5, 2021 at 1.

[529] OSC Report of Interview of Special Agent-1 on March 21, 2021 at 2.

[530] Id.

team's assessment, he was largely ignored and directed to continue the FISA renewal process.[531] It was Supervisory Special Agent-3's opinion that Boone was being directed by FBI executive management to continue the FISA surveillance.[532] When interviewed by the Office, Boone did not recall Supervisory Special Agent-3 voicing concerns about the Page FISA, and stated that, if he had, she would have elevated those concerns to AD Bill Priestap.[533] Boone did state, however, that it was not the normal course of business to have the "7th floor" (FBI executive management) intimately involved in an investigation and very unusual to have an investigation run from FBI Headquarters.

Boone did not know why the 7th floor was so involved in this case nor did she know who from the 7th floor was the ultimate decision maker regarding Crossfire Hurricane.[534] Boone did not have direct communication with Deputy Director McCabe, but she understood that McCabe was heavily involved in all aspects of the investigation.[535] Her sense was that Priestap was not in charge and had to get approvals from the 7th floor.[536] On a few occasions, Boone "ran ideas" by Priestap and never heard back from him.[537] Boone recalled occasions when, during Crossfire Hurricane, Priestap would direct field offices to open cases on particular targets associated with the Trump campaign and the field offices would push back due to insufficient predication.[538] During one meeting, Boone and her investigators presented a "Russia Strategy" to Priestap. Boone could sense that Priestap was visibly upset by their strategy and walked out of the meeting.[539]

Supervisory Special Agent-2 signed all three renewals of the Page FISA application.[540] When interviewed by the Office, Supervisory Special Agent-2 stated that, after the initial FISA surveillance of Page, the investigators had "low confidence" that Page was a witting agent of the Russian government.[541] In fact, at the time of the third renewal, Supervisory Special Agent-2 stated that the probability of Page being a witting agent was "very low."[542] Nevertheless, Supervisory Special Agent-2 signed the final renewal because, in his opinion, it was incumbent

---

[531] Supervisory Special Agent-3 stated that he developed a sense of "helplessness" and was "powerless" to influence the course of the investigation. OSC Report of Interview of Supervisory Special Agent-3 on March 18, 2021 at 1-2, 4.

[532] *Id.* at 4.

[533] OSC Report of Interview of Jennifer Boone on July 9, 2021 at 2.

[534] *Id.*

[535] *Id.*

[536] *Id.*

[537] *Id.*

[538] *Id.*

[539] *Id.*

[540] OSC Report of Interview of Supervisory Special Agent-2 on May 5, 2021 at 1.

[541] *Id.*

[542] *Id.* at 2.

on the FBI to exhaust all resources to ensure that Page was not a Russian intelligence officer.[543] In essence, it appears that Supervisory Special Agent-2 saw the final renewal of the Page FISA as a "belt and suspenders" approach to confirm that Page was not a Russian agent. For his part, Supervisory Special Agent-3 told us that he would not have signed the renewal affidavits if he had been the agent responsible for certifying the accuracy of the government's assertions.[544] The approach taken by Supervisory Special Agent-2, an experienced agent, is concerning. A U.S. person is an agent of a foreign power if there is probable cause to believe that the person is knowingly engaged in clandestine intelligence activities on behalf of a foreign power, or knowingly helping another person in such activities.[545] That is an affirmative determination. FISA surveillance must be used for the purposes and in the ways specified in the statute rather than to prove that someone is not an agent of a foreign power.

iii. What the FBI knew from its intelligence collections as of early 2017

As the record reflects, as of early 2017, the FBI still did not possess any intelligence showing that anyone associated with the Trump campaign was in contact with Russian intelligence officers during the campaign. Indeed, based on declassified documents from early 2017, the FBI's own records show that reports published by *The New York Times* in February and March 2017 concerning what four unnamed current and former U.S. intelligence officials claimed about Trump campaign personnel being in touch with any Russian intelligence officers was untrue.[546] These unidentified sources reportedly stated that (i) U.S. law enforcement and intelligence agencies intercepted communications of members of Trump's campaign and other Trump associates that showed repeated contacts with senior Russian intelligence officials in the year before the election; (ii) former Trump campaign chairman Paul Manafort had been one of the individuals picked up on the intercepted "calls;" and (iii) the intercepted communications between Trump associates and Russians had been initially captured by the NSA.

However, official FBI documentation reflects that all three of these highly concerning claims of Trump-related contacts with Russian intelligence were untrue. Indeed, in a contemporaneous critique of the *Times* article prepared by Peter Strzok, who was steeped in the details of Crossfire Hurricane, all three of the above-referenced allegations were explicitly refuted.[547] Strzok's evaluation of the allegations included the following:

- The FBI had not seen any evidence of any individuals affiliated with the Trump team in contact with Russian intelligence officers. He characterized this allegation as misleading and inaccurate as written. He noted that there had been some individuals in contact with Russians, both governmental and non-governmental, but none of

---

[543] *Id.*

[544] OSC Report of Interview of Supervisory Special Agent-3 on March 18, 2021 at 3.

[545] *See* 50 U.S.C. § 1801(b)(2)(A), (b)(2)(B), & (b)(2)(E).

[546] SENATE-FISA2020-001163 to 001167 (Annotated version of Michael Schmidt, Mark Mazzetti & Matt Apuzzo, *Trump Campaign Aides Had Repeated Contacts With Russian Intelligence*, N.Y. Times (Feb. 14, 2017)).

[547] *Id.*

these individuals had an affiliation with Russian intelligence. He also noted previous contact between Carter Page and a Russian intelligence officer, but this contact did not occur during Page's association with the Trump campaign.

- The FBI had no information in its holdings, nor had it received any such information from other members of the Intelligence Community, that Paul Manafort had been a party to a call with any Russian government official. Strzok noted that the Intelligence Community had not provided the FBI with any such information even though the FBI had advised certain agencies of its interest in anything they might hold or collect regarding Manafort.[548]

- Regarding the allegation that the NSA initially captured these communications between Trump campaign officials and Trump associates and the Russians, Strzok repeated that if such communications had been collected by the NSA, the FBI was not aware of that fact.

In a second article published by the *Times* on March 1, 2017, bearing the headline, "Obama Administration Rushed to Preserve Intelligence of Russian Election Hacking," allegations were made that U.S. allies, including two named countries, had provided information describing meetings in European cities between Russian officials and other Russians close to Russian President Putin and associates of Trump. The article also repeated the assertions set forth in its February 14, 2017 article. Again, a review of official FBI documentation shows that Strzok had reviewed and refuted these additional allegations in a second critique.[549] With respect to the March 1, 2017 allegations, Strzok noted that no such information had been received from one of the named countries and that the only information received from the second named country, which was received in response to a specific request from the FBI, related to a woman of Russian descent purportedly having been in contact with former Trump National Security Advisor Michael Flynn. In this second critique, Strzok further noted that with respect to the information provided to the *Times* by the four unnamed former and current officials, the FBI (approximately three weeks after it was first reported) continued to be unaware of any information, other than that provided by Christopher Steele in his dossier reports, alleging contacts between Trump associates and senior Russian intelligence officials.

Thus, the FBI had no intelligence about Trump or others associated with the Trump campaign being in contact with Russian intelligence officers during the campaign at least as of early 2017.

Moreover, significant intelligence information that first became available for the FBI to review in 2018 showed that the Russians had access to sensitive U.S. government information years earlier that would have allowed them to identify Steele's subsources. Indeed, an experienced FBI analyst assessed that as a result of their access to the information, Steele's subsources could have been compromised by the Russians at a point in time prior to the date of

---

[548] *Id.* at 001164.

[549] FBI-EMAIL-428172 (Annotated version of article titled *Obama Administration Rushed to Preserve Intelligence of Russian Election Hacking*, N.Y. Times (Mar. 1, 2017)).

the first Steele dossier report.[550] The review team initially briefed Counterintelligence and Cyber executive management about their findings during a conference call. Following the call, while driving home, Headquarters Analyst-3 was called by Acting Section Chief-2. Acting Section Chief-2 told Headquarters Analyst-3 that they appreciated the team's work, but no more memorandums were to be written.[551] A meeting was then held with Assistant Director Priestap and others. During that meeting, the review team was told to be careful about what they were writing down because issues relating to Steele were under intense scrutiny.[552] Two weeks later, the Deputy Assistant Director for Counterintelligence, Dina Corsi, met with the review team and directed them not to document any recommendations, context, or analysis in the memorandum they were preparing. The instructions, which Headquarters Analyst-3 described as "highly unusual,"[553] concerned the team because analysis is what analysts do. Although the team did not fully adhere to that instruction because of the need to provide context to the team's findings, they did tone down their conclusions in the final memorandum.[554] Headquarters Analyst-3 recalled that a separate briefing on the review was eventually provided by the team in the Deputy Director's conference room, although Headquarters Analyst-3 could not recall if Deputy Director David Bowdich attended the briefing. Headquarters Analyst-3 did know that Bowdich was aware of the review itself.[555]

In this same regard, for a period of time, an FBI OGC attorney ("OGC Attorney-1") was part of the review team and was present for the meeting with Corsi. He confirmed that the team was told not to write any more memoranda or analytical pieces and to provide their findings orally.[556] OGC Attorney-1 remembered being shocked by the directive from Corsi.[557] OGC Attorney-1's recollection was that Corsi was speaking for FBI leadership, but that she did not say exactly who provided the directive. OGC Attorney-1 advised the Office that what Corsi said was not right in any circumstance, and it was the most inappropriate operational or professional statement he had ever heard at the FBI.[558] OGC Attorney-1 stated that the directive from Corsi was "really, really shocking" to him and that he was "appalled" by it. As a result of the incident,

---

[550] OSC Report of Interview of Headquarters Analyst-3 on Dec. 2, 2021 at 1; OSC Report of Interview of Headquarters Analyst-3 on Feb. 19, 2020 at 1.

[551] OSC Report of Interview of Headquarters Analyst-3 on Feb. 19, 2020 at 1.

[552] Id.

[553] OSC Report of Interview of Headquarters Analyst-3 on Dec. 2, 2021 at 1. Headquarters Analyst-3 was so concerned about the failure to fully exploit the materials involving Steele subsource information (and the possible need to bring information already exploited to the attention of the FISC) that she raised her concerns about the FBI's lack of action in an email to her supervisor in the hope of having the issues explored further. See FBI-0009265 (Email from Headquarters Analyst-3 to FBI employees dated 10/17/2018).

[554] OSC Report of Interview of Headquarters Analyst-3 on Dec. 2, 2021 at 1.

[555] Id. at 3.

[556] OSC Report of Interview of OGC Attorney-1 on June 30, 2021 at 3.

[557] Id.

[558] Id. at 3-4.

he ended up walking away from further participation in the review. OGC Attorney-1 said he felt guilty about leaving, but he felt he had to do it.[559] The record thus reflects that at the time the FBI opened Crossfire Hurricane on July 31, 2016, as noted above in the *SSCI Report*, the Russians already knew about Steele's election investigation,[560] and there is reason to believe that even earlier in time they had access to other highly sensitive information from which the identities of Steele's sources could have been compromised.[561]

Finally, in May 2017, about a month before the submission of the last Page FISA renewal application, Strzok was debating whether to join Special Counsel Mueller's investigation. He texted that he was hesitating about joining, "in part, because of my gut sense and concern there's no big there there."[562] Although the "there" does not appear to have been explicitly identified, it may well have been a reference to the Russia – Trump collusion investigation.[563] In any event, and more generally, the OIG found that, "as the investigation progressed and more information tended to undermine or weaken the assertions in the FISA applications," the FBI "did not reassess the information supporting probable cause."[564]

b. The "Steele dossier"

i. *Christopher Steele – FBI Confidential Human Source*

Beginning in 2010, Christopher Steele started providing information to the FBI on a range of subjects including, but not limited to, Russian oligarchs and corruption in international soccer competition. Steele had been introduced to his eventual FBI CHS handler ("Handling Agent-1") by former DOJ official Bruce Ohr.[565] In 2013, the FBI formally opened Steele as an FBI CHS,[566] and Handling Agent-1 would serve as Steele's primary handler over the course of his service as an FBI source. Steele would eventually be closed as an FBI source in November 2016 for disclosing his status as a CHS while providing information to the media regarding his work with Fusion GPS on behalf of the Clinton campaign and the DNC against Trump.[567]

---

[559] *Id.*; *see also* OSC Report of Interview of Headquarters Analyst-3 on Dec. 2, 2021 at 1.

[560] *See supra* footnotes 252 and 253.

[561] OSC Report of Interview of Headquarters Analyst-3 on Dec. 2, 2021 at 1-2; OSC Report of Interview of OGC Attorney-1 on June 30, 2021 at 2.

[562] U.S. House of Representatives Committee on the Judiciary Interview of Lisa Page on July 13, 2018 at 113.

[563] *See id.* at 113-16 (discussion between Lisa Page and Congressman Ratcliffe as to whether Strzok "had a concern that there was no big there there regarding any collusion . . . between the Trump campaign and Russia"); *see also id.* at 155-56 (discussion of same text from Strzok).

[564] *Redacted OIG Review* at 413.

[565] OSC Report of Interview of Handling Agent-1 on July 2, 2019 at 1.

[566] FBI-0000127 (Source Opening Communication dated 10/30/2013).

[567] FBI-0000237 (Source Closing Communication dated 11/17/2016).

Nevertheless, the FBI – using Department official Bruce Ohr as a conduit – continued to receive information from Steele despite his closure as a CHS.[568]

ii. The FBI first received the Steele Reports in July 2016

In July 2016, Handling Agent-1 was serving as the FBI's Assistant Legal Attaché ("ALAT") in Rome, Italy. In early July 2016, Steele contacted Handling Agent-1 and requested an urgent meeting at Steele's office in London.[569] On July 5, 2016, Handling Agent-1 met with Steele in London and Steele provided him with Report 2016/080 dated June 20, 2016.[570] This Report detailed, among other things, salacious information about Donald Trump's alleged sexual activities during trips to Moscow and details of how the Kremlin purportedly had been "feeding" information to Trump's campaign regarding his political rivals.[571] Steele informed Handling Agent-1 that he (Steele) had been hired by Fusion GPS to collect information on Trump, including Trump's relationship with the Kremlin and various business dealings with Russia.[572] Steele told Handling Agent-1 that Fusion GPS had been hired by a law firm and that his ultimate client was "senior Democrats" supporting Clinton.[573] Handling Agent-1's notes of this meeting reflect that "HC" was aware of his (Steele's) reporting.[574] During an interview with the Office, Handling Agent-1 was shown a copy of his notes from the July 5, 2016 meeting. As previously noted, while Handling Agent-1 did not have an independent recollection of Steele explicitly stating that "HC" referred to Hillary Clinton, he could think of no other individual – in that context – to whom "HC" could possibly refer.[575]

Steele claimed that prior to his July 5, 2016 meeting with Handling Agent-1, he and Chris Burrows, his co-principal at Orbis, had decided that the information collected by Steele had significant national security implications and therefore should be provided to the FBI and Fusion GPS principal Glenn Simpson agreed.[576] At the July 5, 2016 meeting, Steele informed Handling

---

[568] The Source Closing report indicates that Steele was closed as a CHS for disclosing his confidential relationship with the FBI. *Id.*

[569] OSC Report of Interview of Handling Agent-1 on July 2, 2019 at 2.

[570] Steele Source File at A-022 ("July 5 rpt"); OIG Interview of Handling Agent-1 on Aug. 30, 2018 at 152-158.

[571] SCO-105084 (Documents Known to the FBI Comprising the "Steele Dossier") at 2-4, (Company Intelligence Report 2016/080).

[572] OSC Report of Interview of Handling Agent-1 on July 2, 2019 at 2.

[573] U.S. House of Representatives Permanent Select Cmte. On Intelligence Interview of Handling Agent-1 on Dec. 20, 2017 at 24-25; OIG interview of Christopher Steele on June 5 and 6, 2019 at 26.

[574] Handwritten notes of Handling Agent-1 at 4 (July 5, 2016).

[575] OSC Report of Interview of Handling Agent-1 on Mar. 1, 2022 at 2.

[576] *OIG Review* at 95. Simpson told the HPSCI, however, that he did not approve of the disclosure beforehand. U.S. House of Representatives Permanent Select Cmte. On Intelligence Interview of Glenn Simpson on Nov. 14, 2017at 61-62.

Agent-1 that he was working on additional reports for Fusion GPS.[577] As discussed in detail below, following this meeting, Handling Agent-1 contacted NYFO ASAC-1 at the NYFO for guidance about the information Steele had provided.[578]

In his interviews with the Office, Handling Agent-1 stated his initial reaction to Steele's reporting was disbelief.[579] Handling Agent-1 knew that Steele possessed strong feelings against the Russians and their threat to the world, and Steele felt that the possibility of a Trump-compromised presidency would pose a global problem.[580] Furthermore, Steele explained to Handling Agent-1 that the information was gathered at the request of Simpson who was working with an unidentified law firm in the United States for the purpose of acquiring information on Trump and his activities in Russia.[581] In his HPSCI testimony, Handling Agent-1 told the committee that he assumed Steele's tasking was "politically motivated."[582] Notwithstanding his skepticism about the reporting, Handling Agent-1 deemed the allegations to be something he could not arbitrarily discount, particularly since Steele was his CHS and someone in whom he had faith.[583]

On July 19, 2016, Steele sent Handling Agent-1 an additional Report (2016/94) detailing, among other things, an alleged meeting that Trump campaign foreign policy advisor Carter Page had in July 2016 with Igor Sechin, Chairman of Russian energy conglomerate Rosneft, and another such meeting with Igor Divyekin, a senior official in the Russian Presidential Administration. This Report alleged details of (i) Page's conversations with Sechin regarding the lifting of U.S. sanctions, and (ii) Page's conversations with Divyekin about Russia being in possession of compromising information on both candidates Trump and Clinton.[584] On July 28, 2016, Handling Agent-1 forwarded Steele Reports 2016/080 and 2016/94 to NYFO ASAC-1.[585] These Reports – including four additional reports subsequently received by Handling Agent-1 from Steele – only reached the Crossfire Hurricane investigators at FBI Headquarters on September 19, 2016.[586]

---

[577] OIG Interview of Christopher Steele on June 5 and 6, 2019 at 7.

[578] OSC Report of Interview of Handling Agent-1 on July 2, 2019 at 2.

[579] *Id.*

[580] *Id.* at 1.

[581] *Id.* at 2.

[582] U.S. House of Representatives Permanent Select Cmte. On Intelligence Interview of Handling Agent-1 on Dec. 20, 2017 at 25.

[583] *Id.*

[584] SCO-105084 (Documents Known to the FBI Comprising the "Steele Dossier") at 8 (Company Intelligence Report 2016/94).

[585] FBI-EMAIL-130305 (Email from Handling Agent-1 to NYFO ASAC-1 dated 07/28/2016).

[586] FBI-EMAIL-129902 (Email from Handling Agent-1 to Supervisory Special Agent-1 on 09/19/2016); FBI-EMAIL-129908 (Email from Handling Agent-1 to Supervisory Special Agent-1 dated 09/19/2016).

iii. The delay in the FBI's transmission of the Steele Reports to the Crossfire Hurricane investigators

The Office endeavored to account for the nearly 75 days between when Handling Agent-1 received the initial report from Steele in London and when the reports ultimately were passed to the Crossfire Hurricane team at FBI Headquarters. As discussed more fully below, these issues remain unresolved, and the Office has not received a satisfactory explanation that would account for the unwarranted delay.

The FBI possessed the earliest Steele reporting claiming Russian efforts to assist the Trump campaign more than three weeks prior to the receipt of the information provided by the Australian diplomats concerning George Papadopoulos and the opening of the Crossfire Hurricane investigation on July 31, 2016. The Office's investigation has revealed that – taken in its most favorable light to the FBI – the initial reports provided by Steele to Handling Agent-1 in London on July 5, 2016, and then later in July 2016, met an inexplicable FBI bureaucratic delay. As a consequence, the Reports were not disseminated in a manner that would have allowed experienced FBI counterintelligence experts an early opportunity to examine the reports and subject them to appropriate analysis and scrutiny. The failure to act resulted in a gap in time of approximately 75 days from when Steele initially shared his first report with the FBI on July 5, 2016, and September 19, 2016, when the Crossfire Hurricane investigators appear to have first received six of the Steele Reports. Despite the lack of any corroboration of the Reports' sensational allegations, however, in short order portions of four of the Reports were included in the initial Carter Page FISA application without any further verification or corroboration of the allegations contained therein.

Due to conflicting recollections of those involved, significant gaps exist in our understanding of how and why this delay occurred in analyzing Steele's Reports. As discussed above, after meeting Steele in London on July 5, 2016, Handling Agent-1 returned to Rome with Steele's first report (Report 2016/080). Handling Agent-1 told the Office that he informed his immediate supervisor, ("Italy Legat-1"), about the Steele reporting, which led to a conversation about what to do with the Report.[587] Handling Agent-1 informed Italy Legat-1 that he intended to contact trusted colleagues in the NYFO for advice.[588]

In his interview with the OIG, Steele stated that he re-contacted Handling Agent-1 approximately one-week after their initial meeting on July 5, 2016, to inquire if Handling Agent-1 was interested in receiving additional reports that Steele had prepared.[589] Thereafter, Steele emailed Handling Agent-1 his second Report (2016/94).

On July 13, 2016, one week after receiving the initial Steele Report in London, Handling Agent-1 spoke with NYFO ASAC-1 to inform him of the reporting and to ask for guidance.[590]

---

[587] OSC Report of Interview of Handling Agent-1 on July 2, 2019 at 2.

[588] The NYFO was Handling Agent-1's former office of assignment.

[589] OIG Interview of Christopher Steele on June 5 and 6, 2019 at 8.

[590] FBI-AAA-EC-00001529 (Lync message exchange between Handling Agent-1 and NYFO ASAC-1 dated 07/13/2016).

During that call, Handling Agent-1 summarized his July 5ᵗʰ meeting with Steele and Report 2016/080.[591]

NYFO ASAC-1 told the Office that he was unsure of what to do about the Steele Report, but that he verbally informed both his NYFO Supervisor, Criminal SAC Michael Harpster, and NYFO Chief Division Counsel-1, of the Steele reporting and requested their guidance.[592] NYFO ASAC-1 believed that by informing SAC Harpster he was effectively placing the information in the right hands.[593] According to NYFO ASAC-1, NYFO Chief Division Counsel-1 assigned an Assistant Division Counsel ("NYFO Assistant Division Counsel-1") to handle the matter.[594]

No follow up activity appears to have occurred between the NYFO and Handling Agent-1 until NYFO ASAC-1 called Handling Agent-1 on July 28, 2016, at which time he asked Handling Agent-1 to send the Steele Reports to him.[595] NYFO ASAC-1 could not recall the reason for the two-week delay between his July 13th and July 28th calls with Handling Agent-1.[596] For his part, Handling Agent-1 recalled that in the July 28th call, NYFO ASAC-1 advised him that FBI leadership, including an FBI Headquarters official at the Executive Assistant Director ("EAD") level, was now aware of the existence of the reports.[597] That same day, Handling Agent-1 forwarded to NYFO ASAC-1 Steele Reports 2016/080 and 2016/94.

A few hours after receiving the reports, NYFO ASAC-1 forwarded them to SAC Michael Harpster.[598] Harpster initially told the Office that he recalled receiving the Reports from NYFO ASAC-1, but did not read them in order to avoid taint issues with respect to the Clinton Foundation matter that he was overseeing.[599] Harpster recalled, however, that he immediately forwarded the Reports to his supervisor, Assistant Director-in-Charge ("ADIC") Diego Rodriguez.[600] Harpster told the Office that he had no other involvement with the Steele Reports after he provided them to Rodriguez, and, further, that he could not recall speaking with anyone

---

[591] OSC Report of Interview of Handling Agent-1 on July 2, 2019 at 2.

[592] OSC Report of Interview of NYFO ASAC-1 on July 2, 2019 at 1-2.

[593] *Id.* at 1.

[594] *Id.*

[595] FBI-AAA-EC-00001529 (Lync message exchange between Handling Agent-1 and NYFO ASAC-1 dated 07/28/2016); OSC Report of Interview of Handling Agent-1 on July 2, 2019 at 2.

[596] OSC Report of Interview of NYFO ASAC-1 on July 2, 2019 at 2.

[597] OSC Report of Interview of Handling Agent-1 on July 2, 2019 at 2; U.S. House of Representatives Permanent Select Cmte. on Intelligence Interview of Handling Agent-1 on Dec. 20, 2017 at 31 (but in that interview Handling Agent-1 thought NYFO ASAC-1 told him this during a follow-up call on either July 31, 2016 or Aug. 1, 2016).

[598] FBI-EMAIL-135629 (Email from NYFO ASAC-1 to Harpster dated 07/28/2016).

[599] OSC Report of Interview of Michael Harpster on July 3, 2019.

[600] *Id.* Harpster noted that he did not believe the Steele Reports were appropriately sent to him, but rather that they should have been handled by the FBI's International Operations Division which has responsibility for the activities and intelligence involving the FBI's Legal Attaché offices.

else about the reporting.[601] According to Rodriguez, he recalled that there may have been a conversation with Harpster on this topic.[602] The Office has found no record in FBI files to indicate that the reports were emailed to Rodriguez.

A review of FBI records reflects that between July 27 and July 29, 2016, SAC Harpster was visiting FBI Headquarters "shadowing" Executive Management as part of a career development opportunity.[603] Records also reflect that, on the same day he received the Steele Reports from NYFO ASAC-1, Harpster met with several senior FBI officials at Headquarters.[604] Harpster, however, told the Office that he could not remember receiving the Steele Reports while at Headquarters on July 28, 2016.[605] Nevertheless, email records reflect that Harpster, in fact, received the Reports from NYFO ASAC-1 on July 28, 2016. The email sent by NYFO ASAC-1 contained the message, "As discussed."[606] FBI phone records also reflect multiple telephone calls between Harpster and NYFO ASAC-1 on July 28, 2016.[607] The first call occurred prior to transmission of the reports and the other calls occurred following NYFO ASAC-1's email to Harpster attaching the reports. FBI phone records also reflect a July 28, 2016 call between Harpster and Rodriguez after the reports were sent by NYFO ASAC-1 to Harpster. Thus, the records substantially corroborate NYFO ASAC-1's version of events.

In a second interview with the Office, Harpster recollected that he sent the initial Steele Reports to the Criminal Cyber Response and Services Branch Executive Assistant Director ("EAD") Randall ("Randy") Coleman and the Associate Executive Assistant Director ("AEAD") David ("DJ") Johnson.[608] Harpster also recalled that he met with Coleman and Johnson at Headquarters on July 28, 2016.[609] During these meetings, it appeared to Harpster that the FBI officials were already aware of the Steele Reports and that EAD Coleman appeared to have engaged in previous conversations with other FBI "higher ups" about the reports.[610] During their interviews with the Office, neither EAD Coleman nor AEAD Johnson could recall any conversation with Harpster about the Steele Reports and they did not recall receiving the reports from him.[611] In addition to his meetings with Coleman and Johnson, Harpster was scheduled to

---

[601] OSC Report of Interview of Michael Harpster on July 3, 2019.

[602] OSC Report of Interview of Diego Rodriguez on Aug. 12, 2019 at 1.

[603] FBI-EMAIL-137026 (Email to Harpster on 07/26/2016).

[604] Id.

[605] OSC Report of Interview of Michael Harpster on Apr. 23, 2020 at 2.

[606] FBI-EMAIL-135629 (Email from NYFO ASAC-1 to Harpster dated 07/28/2016).

[607] Phone Logs for Headquarters desk phone used by Harpster entry dated 07/28/2016.

[608] OSC Report of Interview of Michael Harpster on Apr. 23, 2020 at 2.

[609] Id.

[610] Id.

[611] OSC Report of Interview of Randall Coleman on Aug. 12, 2019; OSC Report of Interview of David Johnson on Jan. 6, 2020 at 1; OSC Report of Interview of David Johnson on May 6, 2020 at 1.

spend the entire next day (July 29th) in an executive management shadowing exercise with Deputy Director McCabe.[612]

While Harpster was at FBI Headquarters, others in the NYFO were conferring internally to determine what to do with the Steele Reports. On August 3, 2016, NYFO ASAC-1 held a meeting with NYFO Chief Division Counsel-1 and NYFO Assistant Division Counsel-1, as well as NYFO Clinton Foundation Case Agent-2, who at the time was overseeing the NYFO portion of the fraud and corruption allegations involving the Clinton Foundation.[613] When interviewed by the Office, NYFO Assistant Division Counsel-1 advised that he had been asked to provide legal advice on whether the Steele Reports, which he had not yet read, could be relevant to the Clinton Foundation investigation.[614] NYFO Assistant Division Counsel-1 told the Office that he was effectively serving as a "taint" attorney to avoid potential conflicts for the NYFO corruption team if it were to access Steele's reporting.[615] Shortly after this meeting, NYFO Assistant Division Counsel-1 had a discussion with Handling Agent-1 about the Reports.[616] On August 5, 2016, NYFO Assistant Division Counsel-1 received two Steele Reports from Handling Agent-1,[617] and on August 25, 2016, NYFO Assistant Division Counsel-1 had a discussion with Handling Agent-1 about Steele's role as an FBI CHS.[618]

NYFO Assistant Division Counsel-1 ultimately concluded that the Steele Reports appeared to be related exclusively to Trump and were not relevant to the Clinton Foundation investigation.[619] Moreover, NYFO Assistant Division Counsel-1 concluded that the Steele Reports should be examined by FBI counterintelligence personnel.[620] NYFO Assistant Division Counsel-1 subsequently met with the NYFO's ASAC for counterintelligence ("NYFO ASAC-2").[621] NYFO Assistant Division Counsel-1 told the Office that he did not provide copies

---

[612] FBI-EMAIL-137026 (Email to Harpster on 07/26/2016).

[613] OSC Report of Interview of NYFO ASAC-1 on July 2, 2019 at 2; OSC Report of Interview of NYFO Assistant Division Counsel-1 on Aug. 6, 2019 at 1.

[614] OSC Report of Interview of NYFO Assistant Division Counsel-1 on Aug. 6, 2019 at 1.

[615] Id.

[616] Handwritten notes of NYFO Assistant Division Counsel-1 dated 08/04/2016; FBI-AAA-EC-00001529 (Lync message exchange between Handling Agent-1 and NYFO Assistant Division Counsel-1 dated 08/05/2016); FBI-EMAIL-129083 (Email from Handling Agent-1 to NYFO Assistant Division Counsel-1 dated 08/05/2016).

[617] FBI-EMAIL-129199 (Email from Handling Agent-1 to NYFO Assistant Division Counsel-1 dated 08/05/2016).

[618] Handwritten notes of NYFO Assistant Division Counsel-1 dated 08/25/2016; FBI-AAA-EC-00001529 (Lync message exchange between Handling Agent-1 and NYFO Assistant Division Counsel-1 dated 08/25/2016).

[619] OSC Report of Interview of NYFO Assistant Division Counsel-1 on Aug. 6, 2019 at 2.

[620] Id.

[621] Id.

of the Steele Reports to NYFO ASAC-2 in this meeting, but that NYFO ASAC-2 appeared to already be familiar with the Reports.[622]

On August 29, 2016, NYFO ASAC-2 contacted Case Agent-1, one of the principal agents assigned to Crossfire Hurricane, stating, "We have a taint team in place up here. I am trying to get this reporting released to you so you guys can see it. Just debriefed today."[623] On September 1, 2016, NYFO ASAC-2 connected NYFO Assistant Division Counsel-1 with Case Agent-1 and Supervisory Special Agent-1.[624] In his email to Supervisory Special Agent-1, Case Agent-1, and NYFO Assistant Division Counsel-1, NYFO ASAC-2 explained, "[NYFO Assistant Division Counsel-1] has some information that I believe may directly impact your CROSSFIRE HURRICANE investigation. I would like [NYFO Assistant Divisional Counsel-1] to contact your team and deconflict the reporting."[625] On September 2, 2016, NYFO Assistant Division Counsel-1 emailed Handling Agent-1, NYFO ASAC-2, and NYFO ASAC-1 stating, "I spoke to [Supervisory Special Agent-1] briefly yesterday evening . . . [Supervisory Special Agent-1] has an open matter that touches upon what the CHS provided to you. We decided that he should create a subfile in the matter to serve as a repository for the information the CHS provided to you. It is my understanding that he did this last night."[626] However, Supervisory Special Agent-1 confirmed that Handling Agent-1 was unable to upload the reporting to the case file until September 13, 2016.[627] In his email of the same date to Handling Agent-1, NYFO Assistant Division Counsel-1 and Special Agent-2, Supervisory Special Agent-1 notified Handling Agent-1 in Rome that he (Handling Agent-1) has been added as a case participant to the restricted case file. Supervisory Special Agent-1 followed this with his apology "for not getting this to you earlier, but the initial email I sent almost 10 days ago had a hangfire and didn't go out!"[628]

Also of note is the fact that on August 22, 2016, Glenn Simpson of Fusion GPS asked DOJ official Bruce Ohr to call him.[629] Approximately one hour later, Ohr emailed Handling Agent-1 wanting to "check-in."[630] Ohr and Handling Agent-1 planned to speak by phone on

[622] Id.

[623] FBI-AAA-EC-00008439 (Lync message exchange between Case Agent-1 and NYFO ASAC-2 dated 08/29/2016).

[624] FBI-EMAIL-018184 (Email from NYFO ASAC-2 to Supervisory Special Agent-1, Case Agent-1, NYFO Assistant Division Counsel-1 dated 09/01/2016).

[625] Id.

[626] FBI-EMAIL-129523 (Email from NYFO Assistant Division Counsel-1 to Handling Agent-1, NYFO ASAC-2 and NYFO ASAC-1 dated 09/02/2016).

[627] FBI-EMAIL-018127 (Email from Supervisory Special Agent-1 to Handling Agent-1, Special Agent-2, NYFO Assistant Division Counsel-1 dated 09/13/2016).

[628] Id. "Hangfire" appears to refer to an email that gets stuck in a person's outbox and does not transmit.

[629] DocID 0.7.23326.122502 (Email from Simpson to Ohr dated 08/22/2016).

[630] DocID 0.7.23326.122508 (Email from Ohr to Handling Agent-1 dated 08/22/2016); OSC Report of Interview of Handling Agent-1 on July 2, 2019 at 2 (in which Handling Agent-1 informed the Office that he recalled receiving a mid-August 2016 call from Ohr.)

August 24, 2016.[631] During the call, Ohr inquired if the FBI was going to do anything with the information contained in the Steele Reports.[632] Handling Agent-1 told Ohr that a group at FBI Headquarters was working on them.[633]

In multiple interviews with both the Office and the OIG, Supervisory Special Agent-1 stated that he was instructed to call NYFO Assistant Division Counsel-1 by Deputy Director McCabe following a briefing at FBI Headquarters on August 25, 2016.[634] According to Supervisory Special Agent-1, McCabe directed him (Supervisory Special Agent-1) to reach out to the NYFO.[635] In context, McCabe had attended a retirement party in New York City for ADIC Rodriguez the night before.[636] When interviewed by the OIG, however, McCabe stated that he did not recall giving advice to Supervisory Special Agent-1 to call the NYFO.[637]

Ultimately, FBI records reflect that it was not until September 19, 2016, that the Crossfire Hurricane team at FBI Headquarters actually received the first six Steele Reports.[638] These Reports were sent to Supervisory Special Agent-1 by Handling Agent-1 – some 75 days after Handling Agent-1 first received the initial Report from Steele in London. The delayed dissemination within the FBI of the sensational information contained in the Steele Reports is both perplexing and troubling. Indeed, the failure of recollection by FBI personnel concerning the matter certainly raises the question of whether the FBI had misgivings from the start about the provenance and reliability of the Steele Reports. Nevertheless, within two days of their eventual receipt by the Crossfire Hurricane team, information from four of the Steele Reports were being used to support probable cause in the initial FISA application on Carter Page.[639]

---

[631] DocID 0.7.23326.122682 (Email from Ohr to Handling Agent-1 dated 08/24/2016).

[632] OSC Report of Interview of Handling Agent-1 on July 2, 2019 at 2.

[633] *Id.*

[634] OIG interview of Supervisory Special Agent-1 on Sept. 13, 2018 at 69-70; OIG interview of Supervisory Special Agent-1 on Jan. 24, 2019 at 89-97, 101-102; OIG interview of Supervisory Special Agent-1 on Feb. 1, 2019 at 86-88; OSC Report of Interview of Supervisory Special Agent-1 on June 17, 2019 at 3-4; Signed, Sworn Statement by Supervisory Special Agent-1 dated Mar. 3, 2021 at 14.

[635] OSC Report of Interview of Supervisory Special Agent-1 on July 22, 2020 at 3.

[636] FBI-EMAIL-624465 (McCabe calendar entry dated 08/24/2016); FBI-EMAIL-623520 (Email to McCabe dated 07/27/2016).

[637] OIG interview of Andrew McCabe on Aug. 15, 2019 at 191.

[638] FBI-EMAIL-129902 (Email from Handling Agent-1 to Supervisory Special Agent-1 dated 09/19/2016); FBI-EMAIL-129908 (Email from Handling Agent-1 to Supervisory Special Agent-1 dated 09/19/2016).

[639] As has been noted by several individuals, including Deputy Director McCabe, the FISA on Page would not have been authorized without the Steele reporting. Indeed, as discussed above, prior to receipt of the Steele Reports, the FBI had drafted a FISA application on Page that the FBI OGC determined lacked sufficient probable cause.

iv. The September 23, 2016 Yahoo! News article

On September 23, 2016, Michael Isikoff published his article in *Yahoo! News* titled "U.S. Intel Officials Probe Ties Between Trump Adviser and Kremlin."[640] The article detailed Carter Page's alleged meetings in July 2016 with Igor Sechin, Chairman of Russian energy conglomerate Rosneft, and Igor Divyekin, a senior official in the Russian Presidential Administration. The article contained information that was nearly identical to Steele Report 2016/94. The information in the article allegedly came from a "well-placed Western intelligence source" and had been confirmed by a "senior U.S. law enforcement official." A review of communications between and amongst Crossfire Hurricane personnel revealed that senior investigators, including Case Agent-1 and Supervisory Special Agent-1, believed the "Western intelligence source" was Steele. Further, a review of communications also revealed that members of the investigative team expressed disappointment that Steele had provided the information to the media, believing, justifiably,[641] that such an action would put the Page FISA application in jeopardy. As discussed in more detail below, until late in the process, several drafts of the Page FISA application contained a footnote that explicitly attributed the information in the *Yahoo! News* article to Steele.

v. The October meeting with Steele in Rome

On October 3, 2016, Special Agent-2, Acting Section Chief-1, and SIA Brian Auten traveled to Rome, Italy to meet with Handling Agent-1 and Steele.

During this meeting, the interviewers informed Steele, in sum, that the FBI might be willing to pay Steele in excess of $1,000,000 if he could provide corroborating evidence of the allegations contained in his reporting.[642] The FBI also admonished Steele about the need to have an exclusive reporting relationship with the FBI because, by this time, the FBI had been made aware of the fact that Steele had also been providing his Reports to the State Department through his acquaintance, State Department official Jonathan Winer.[643] In turn, Winer had been providing the Reports, to, among others, then-U.S. Assistant Secretary of State for European and Eurasian Affairs Victoria Nuland, a confidant of former-Secretary of State Clinton.[644] Notwithstanding these red flags, when interviewed by the Office, neither Auten nor Special Agent-2 had any recollection of addressing the *Yahoo! News* concerns with Steele.[645] Further, both Auten and Special Agent-2 drafted summaries of the October 3, 2016 meeting with Steele,

---

[640] Isikoff, *Officials Probe Ties*.

[641] Strzok told Auten, "Loking [sic] at the Yahoo article, i [sic] would definitely say at a minimum [Steele's] reports should be viewed as intended to influence as well as to inform." FBI-AAA-EC-00007359 (Lync message exchange between Strzok and Auten dated 09/26/2016).

[642] SCO-101648 (Email from Special Agent-2 to Supervisory Special Agent-1, Strzok, Auten, Case Agent-1, Acting Section Chief-1 & Handling Agent-1 dated 10/04/2016).

[643] *Id.*; OSC Report of Interview of Handling Agent-1 on July 2, 2019 at 4.

[644] OSC Report of Interview of Jonathan Winer on Nov. 9, 2021 at 2-3; OSC Report of Interview of Victoria Nuland on Nov. 30, 2021 at 8.

[645] OSC Report of Interview of Brian Auten on July 26, 2021 at 17; OSC Report of Interview of Special Agent-2 on June 25, 2020 at 4.

and neither summary addressed concerns about the *Yahoo! News* article or whether the issue had even been raised with Steele.[646]

Auten's summary provided, among others, the following pertinent facts:

- Steele had one primary sub-source who traveled frequently in Russia.

- Most of the primary sub-source's contacts appear to be unwitting of where their information was going.

- Steele's primary sub-source had personal contact with Sergei Millian. Millian appeared to be "Source E" referenced in Report 2016/095 and was possibly "Source D" in Report 2016/080.

- Steele provided the FBI with the names of four U.S. citizens who may have information regarding Russia and Trump: (i) Charles Dolan; (ii) U.S. Person-1; (iii) U.S. Person-2; and (iv) U.S. Person-3.

- Steele reiterated that Russian Presidential Administration Spokesman Dimitry Peskov was heavily involved in the Russia/Trump operation.[647]

vi. The draft Page FISA applications – Yahoo! News

In late September 2016, OI Attorney-1 received a draft copy of the initial Carter Page FISA application from FBI OGC attorney Kevin Clinesmith. This draft copy included information contained in the Steele Reports that first had been provided to Crossfire Hurricane team on September 19, 2016. On October 2, 2016, OI Attorney-1 emailed a revised draft FISA application to Case Agent-1, Auten, Supervisory Special Agent-1, OGC attorneys Clinesmith and FBI OGC Unit Chief-1, and OI Unit Chief-1.[648] Embedded in this draft FISA application was a question regarding the FBI's assessment of the *Yahoo! News* article, in particular, whether Steele had been the source for the article. OI Unit Chief-1 told the Office that, prior to that draft being sent, he was so certain that Steele was the source of the *Yahoo! News* leak that he included the information in a footnote of the draft application.[649] Case Agent-1 responded to OI Attorney-1's email, in sum, that it was the FBI's assessment that the *Yahoo! News* information had indeed come from Steele.[650]

---

[646] SCO-020139 (Email from Auten to Supervisory Special Agent-1, Moffa & Strzok dated 10/04/2016); SCO-101648 (Email from Special Agent-2 to Supervisory Special Agent-1, Strzok, Auten, Case Agent-1, Acting Section Chief-1 & Handling Agent-1 dated 10/04/2016).

[647] SCO-020139 (Email from Auten to Supervisory Special Agent-1, Moffa & Strzok dated 10/04/2016).

[648] FBI-EMAIL-557611 (Email from OI Attorney-1 to Case Agent-1, Clinesmith, FBI OGC Unit Chief-1, Auten, Support Operations Specialist-1, Moffa, Supervisory Special Agent-1 & OI Unit Chief-1 dated 10/02/2016).

[649] OSC Report of Interview of OI Unit Chief-1 on Oct. 27, 2020 at 1.

[650] FBI-EMAIL-381130 (Email from Case Agent-1 to OI Attorney-1 dated 10/03/2016).

Following the Rome trip, several additional drafts of the Page FISA application were circulated between the FBI and OI. Throughout these drafts, a footnote stated, in sum, that Source #1 (Steele) had been the "well-placed Western intelligence source" referenced in the *Yahoo! News* article, but that Steele had been admonished by the FBI and that going forward Source #1 would have an exclusive relationship with the FBI.[651] Notwithstanding this footnote, Deputy Assistant Attorney General Evans continued to have questions about Steele's decision to speak with the press about the same information that he had provided to the FBI.[652] Evans wanted further clarification on whether Steele's decision to speak with the press indicated a potential bias.[653]

On October 14, 2016, Special Agent-2 emailed OI Attorney-1 and stated that Steele had not previously mentioned the leak (to *Yahoo! News*) and "only acknowledged it when the FBI brought it up on October 4."[654] This email is directly contradictory to what both Auten and Special Agent-2 told the Office during their interviews, *i.e.*, that the *Yahoo! News* leak had not been raised with Steele. Despite being interviewed about this issue on two separate occasions by the Office, Special Agent-2 did not provide a satisfactory response to explain the contradiction between his memory of the October 3, 2016 meeting with Steele and his October 14, 2016 email to OI Attorney-1.

The confusing nature of Special Agent-2's email was not lost on OI Attorney-1. Indeed, later on October 14th, OI Attorney-1 sent an email to his supervisor, OI Unit Chief-1, which stated, in part:

> I am waiting to hear back from [first name of Case Agent-1], *but my super keen investigative skills tell me* (based on FBI's earlier comment that only mention of the leak is: "[Source #1] has not mentioned the leak and only acknowledges it when the FBI brought it up on October 4.") *they never asked and don't want to ask.*[655]

On October 14, 2016, OI Attorney-1 circulated a document titled "Source #1 footnote update v.2.docx," and informed the recipients that the document "lists the descriptions we

---

[651] *See, e.g.*, DOJ-NSD-00033886 (Email from Evans to Toscas & McCord dated 10/11/2016); DOJ-NSD-00028157 (Email from OI Unit Chief-1 to Case Agent-1, Clinesmith, FBI OGC Unit Chief-1, Auten, Support Operations Specialist-1, Moffa, Supervisory Special Agent-1 & OI Attorney-1 dated 10/11/2016).

[652] DOJ-NSD-00018909 (Email from Evans to OI Unit Chief-1, Sanz-Rexach, OI Deputy Section Chief-1 & OI Attorney-1 dated 10/11/2016).

[653] *Id.*

[654] DOJ-NSD-00024317 (Email from Special Agent-2 to Supervisory Special Agent-1, OI Attorney-1, Case Agent-1, Clinesmith, FBI OGC Unit Chief-1, OI Unit Chief-1, Strzok, Moffa & Page dated 10/14/2016).

[655] DOJ-NSD-00030201 (Email from OI Attorney-1 to OI Unit Chief-1 dated 10/14/2016) (emphasis added).

provide in the application about Source #1."[656] The last paragraph of the footnote provided the following:

> As discussed above, Source #1 was hired by a business associate [in context, Glenn Simpson] to conduct research into Candidate #1's ties to Russia. Source #1 provided the results of his research to the business associate, and the FBI assesses that the business associate likely provided this information to the law firm that hired the business associate in the first place. Given that the information contained in the September 23rd News Article generally matches the information about Page that Source #1 discovered during his/her research, the FBI assesses that Source #1's business associate or the law firm that hired the business associate likely provided this information to the press.[657]

Later that day, OI Attorney-1 circulated a new draft of the FISA application containing the Source #1 footnote he provided earlier. This version of the FISA application was then sent to the Office of the Deputy Attorney General ("ODAG") for review.

On October 17, 2016, OI Unit Chief-1 circulated follow-up questions to the FBI that had come from ODAG's review of the updated draft application. One question centered on reconciling the disparity between the current Source #1 footnote – now attributing the leak to Fusion GPS or the Clinton campaign's law firm – with the actual language of the article, *i.e.*, that the information in the article came *directly* from a "well-placed Western intelligence source."[658] Later that evening, Case Agent-1, Supervisory Special Agent-1 and others called OI Unit Chief-1 on the FBI's Top Secret Lync system (the FBI's voice chat platform). This call lasted approximately 16 minutes.[659] Following the call, Supervisory Special Agent-1 emailed OI Unit Chief-1 and stated, in sum, that the FBI had addressed all open questions.[660] OI Unit Chief-1 responded to Supervisory Special Agent-1's email and confirmed that all of the Department's questions had been answered.[661] In their interviews with the Office, however, Supervisory Special Agent-1 and OI Unit Chief-1 had no recollection of what was said in the conversation

---

[656] DOJ-NSD-00030255 (Email from OI Attorney-1 to Evans, Sanz-Rexach, OI Deputy Section Chief-1 & OI Unit Chief-1 dated 10/14/2016).

[657] *Id.* at 3.

[658] DOJ-NSD-00023245 (Email from OI Unit Chief-1to Case Agent-1, Supervisory Special Agent-1, Clinesmith, FBI OGC Unit Chief-1, OI Attorney-1 & Support Operations Specialist-1 dated 10/17/2016).

[659] FBI-SMS-0000106 (Outlook archive of Lync call dated 10/17/2016).

[660] DOJ-NSD-00023605 (Email from Supervisory Special Agent-1 to OI Unit Chief-1, Case Agent-1, Clinesmith, FBI OGC Unit Chief-1, OI Attorney-1 & Support Operations Specialist-1 dated 10/17/2016).

[661] DOJ-NSD-00023603 (Email from OI Unit Chief-1 to Supervisory Special Agent-1, Case Agent-1, Clinesmith, FBI OGC Unit Chief-1, OI Attorney-1 & Support Operations Specialist-1 dated 10/17/2016).

that changed the FBI's assessment that Steele was the source for the *Yahoo! News* article.[662] This failure of recollection on an important issue for ODAG is troubling and made the Office's potential prosecution of the matter untenable.

On October 18, 2016, OI Attorney-1 emailed Case Agent-1 and Clinesmith an updated draft of the Page FISA application. The Source #1 footnote now provided, in part, and with new language in italics, the following:

> As discussed above, Source #1 was hired by a business associate to conduct research into Candidate #1's ties to Russia. Source #1 provided the results of his research to the business associate, and the FBI assesses that the business associate likely provided this information to the law firm that hired the business associate in the first place. *Source #1 told the FBI that he/she only provided this information to the business associate and the FBI.* Given that the information contained in the September 23rd News Article generally matches the information about Page that Source #1 discovered during his/her research, the FBI assesses that Source #1's business associate or the law firm that hired the business associate likely provided this information to the press. *The FBI also assesses that whoever gave the information to the press stated that the information was provided by a "well-placed Western intelligence source." The FBI does not believe that Source #1 directly provided this information to the press.*[663]

In fact, by this time, the FBI knew that the statement "Source #1 told the FBI that he/she only provided this information to the business associate and the FBI" in itself was not accurate because the FBI was aware that Steele had already provided the Reports to the State Department.[664] Footnote 18 of the final signed October 2016 FISA application contained the identical language as included in the above October 18, 2016 draft.[665]

The Office did not receive a satisfactory answer as to the question of why the FBI initially believed that Steele provided the information *directly* to *Yahoo! News* and then subsequently came to believe that Fusion GPS and/or the Clinton campaign's law firm provided the information to *Yahoo! News*. The September 23, 2016 article itself says that "a well-placed Western intelligence source [told] *Yahoo! News*" about the intelligence reports,[666] and one would conclude (assuming that the article is accurate) that the information came directly from the source and not from a law firm, a business associate, or other person. And, in fact, Steele later admitted to the OIG that in September and October of 2016 he and others from Fusion GPS provided journalists, including *Yahoo! News*, with the allegations against Page. Why did the FBI's assessment change? No FBI or Department employee was able to provide the Office with

---

[662] OSC Report of Interview of Supervisory Special Agent-1 on July 21, 2021 at 1; OSC Report of Interview of OI Unit Chief-1 on Oct. 27, 2020 at 1-3.

[663] FBI-EMAIL-561795 (Email from OI Attorney-1 to Case Agent-1 & Clinesmith dated 10/18/2016) at 28.

[664] FBI-EMAIL-101535 (Email from Strzok to Moffa, Laycock, Supervisory Special Agent-1 and two other FBI employees dated 09/30/2016).

[665] *In re Carter W. Page*, No. 16-1182, at 23.

[666] Isikoff, *Officials Probe Ties*.

an explanation as to why the analysis changed, nor do any of the individuals interviewed recall discussions about it. In his interview with the Office, Auten had no recollection of who told him that Steele was not the source of the *Yahoo! News* article, but Auten said his "contemporaneous understanding" at the time of the Rome meeting was that Handling Agent-1 had provided that information.[667] Handling Agent-1, however, emphatically denied asking Steele about the *Yahoo! News* article and stated that his role in the October 2016 meeting was simply to make introductions.[668]

Given Steele's interactions with *Yahoo! News*, the questions about his potential bias raised by Evans and ODAG were completely justified. It seems reasonable to surmise that the FBI's assessment of the *Yahoo! News* article radically changed in order to protect the FISA application. Again, not a single FBI employee who participated in the October 3, 2016 meeting with Steele, no other employees with whom we spoke who assisted in drafting the initial FISA application, nor OI Unit Chief-1 had any recollection of why the FBI's assessment changed. For his part, OI Attorney-1 told the Office that he deferred to the FBI's assessment of the *Yahoo! News* issue because the FBI was the "owner of the facts."[669] OI Attorney-1 also recalled that the FBI was constantly pressuring OI to advance the FISA.[670] As mentioned above, OI Attorney-1 recalled Clinesmith informing him (OI Attorney-1) that Director Comey "wants to know what's going on," and that the Deputy Director asked who the FBI needed to speak with at the Department "to get this going."[671] OI Attorney-1 opined that in hindsight he should have been less deferential to the FBI given his concerns about the validity of the assessment.[672]

OI Unit Chief-1 told the Office that, in hindsight, the FBI's change in assessment regarding *Yahoo! News*, was "curious."[673] OI Unit Chief-1 stated that, at the time, the FBI's evolution on the assessment made sense to him.[674] Nonetheless, OI Unit Chief-1 told the Office that it would be "troubling" if the FBI never asked Steele about his role in the *Yahoo! News* leak, which no one apparently ever did.[675]

> vii.   *The Steele Reports are included in the Page FISA application*

As discussed in greater detail below, four Steele Reports (2016/080, 2016/94, 2016/095 and 2016/102) were relied on by the FBI to support probable cause in the initial Page FISA application and three renewals of that application. Before the receipt of the Steele Reports, the

---

[667] OSC Report of Interview of Brian Auten on July 26, 2021 at 17.

[668] OSC Report of Interview of Handling Agent-1 on Aug. 11, 2021 at 2.

[669] OSC Report of Interview of OI Attorney-1 on July 1, 2020 at 2.

[670] *Id.* at 7.

[671] *Id.* at 2.

[672] *Id.*

[673] OSC Report of Interview of OI Unit Chief-1 on Oct. 27, 2020 at 2.

[674] *Id.*

[675] *Id.* at 3.

FBI did not believe that there was sufficient probable cause to apply for a FISA warrant against Page.[676]

Although the FBI had reason to believe that the Steele Reports were opposition research documents commissioned by a law firm and that the candidate's campaign who hired the firm was aware of the Steele Reports, there is nothing in the FBI record to show that this was a consideration or subject of debate prior to the use of the Steele information in the initial FISA application targeting Page. Moreover, not a single substantive allegation pulled from the Steele Reports and used in the initial Page FISA application had been corroborated at the time of the FISA submission – or indeed, to our knowledge, has ever been corroborated by the FBI.[677]

The FBI obtained a total of four FISC orders targeting Page, which authorized intrusive electronic surveillance of Page and physical searches of certain items of his property from October 2016 through September 2017. Each of the FISA applications set forth the FBI's basis for believing that Page was knowingly engaged in clandestine intelligence activities on behalf of Russia, or knowingly helping others in such activities and alleged – based, in part, on the Steele Reports – that (i) Page was part of a "well-developed conspiracy of co-operation" between Trump's campaign and the Russian government (Steele Report 2016/095), (ii) Page allegedly met in July 2016 with Igor Sechin, Chairman of Russian energy conglomerate Rosneft, and Igor Divyekin, a senior official in the Russian Presidential Administration (Steele Report 2016/94), (iii) the Kremlin had for years gathered compromising information on Clinton (Steele Report 2016/080), and (iv) Russia had leaked DNC emails to Wikileaks, an idea concocted by Page and others (Steele Report 2016/102).

As discussed above, in late September 2016, OI Attorney-1 received a copy of a draft request to prepare a FISA application targeting Page from Clinesmith. OI Attorney-1 informed the Office that his subsequent primary responsibility was to "wordsmith" the application and to gather information regarding sources.[678] In this regard, OI Attorney-1 primarily worked with Case Agent-1 and Clinesmith.[679] OI Attorney-1 also told the Office that he was not aware of the fact that a previous draft application had been prepared by the FBI prior to the receipt of the Steele Reports which OGC determined lacked sufficient probable cause to move forward.[680] As discussed above, with respect to the initial application, FBI OGC Unit Chief-1 told the Office that she believed that the initial application was a "close call" but needed more information to meet the probable cause standard.[681] FBI OGC Unit Chief-1 stated that the inclusion of the Steele reporting allowed the FBI to clear the probable cause hurdle in the Page FISA

---

[676] See supra § IV.D.1.a.i.

[677] OSC Report of Interview of Brian Auten on July 26, 2021 at 24, 31; Danchenko Tr. 10/11/2022 PM at 75-76, 79-81, 87, 96-97, 111, 115-117, 154; Danchenko Tr. 10/12/2022 PM at 550-551; Danchenko Tr. 10/13/2022 AM at 671, 700. Notwithstanding this lack of corroboration, the three FISA renewal applications on Page continued to use the Steele reporting to support probable cause.

[678] OSC Report of Interview of OI Attorney-1 on July 1, 2020 at 1.

[679] Id.

[680] Id.

[681] OSC Report of Interview of FBI OGC Unit Chief-1 on Aug. 29, 2019 at 6.

application,[682] and, therefore, FBI OGC Unit Chief-1 approved the transmission of the request to OI.

FBI OGC Unit Chief-1 informed the Office, in sum, that she had no concerns with the inclusion of the Steele reporting in the Page FISA applications. FBI OGC Unit Chief-1, however, was not aware of what, if any, vetting had been done regarding the allegations prior to the submission of the initial application to the FISC.[683] FBI OGC Unit Chief-1 did have some recall that a lack of vetting of the Reports was a concern.[684] Finally, FBI OGC Unit Chief-1 told the Office that there was also some concern that Steele had been hired by a law firm on behalf of the Clinton campaign and the DNC to conduct opposition research on Trump.[685] Despite these concerns, the fact that Steele's information was being financed by the DNC and/or the Clinton campaign was not included in the affidavit's source description of Steele.[686] The failure to provide this information to the FISC was a major omission in that the information clearly had the potential to affect the analysis of any bias in Steele's reporting.

With respect to the Steele Report allegations in the initial FISA application, OI Attorney-1 told the Office that he did not think the FBI was initially concerned with corroborating Steele's reporting, although he recalled that at some point some unknown efforts had been made.[687] Rather than corroborating the allegations, OI Attorney-1 recalled that the FBI's primary focus was on Steele's past reliability as an FBI CHS.[688] In his interview with the Office, Case Agent-1 also noted the importance of Steele's past reliability as reason to include his (Steele's) reporting in the FISA application, but also stated, in sum, that it was essential for the FBI to corroborate the Steele reporting, to include verification of Steele's alleged sub-sources.[689] To that end, the Office directly asked Case Agent-1 whether *any* of Steele's allegations contained in the initial FISA application had been corroborated. Case Agent-1 stated that "he could not recall anything specific that was fully corroborated."[690] Shockingly, Case Agent-1 told the Office that the initial

---

[682] *Id.* at 6-7.

[683] OSC Report of Interview of FBI OGC Unit Chief-1 on July 23, 2020 at 7.

[684] *Id.*

[685] *Id.* at 9.

[686] A footnote in the FISA application did describe the person who hired Steele. It says this person "never advised [Steele] as to the motivation behind the research into [Trump's] ties to Russia." It went on to say that "[t]he FBI speculates that the . . . person was likely looking for information that could be used to discredit [Trump's] campaign." *In re Carter W. Page*, No. 16-1182, at 15-16 n.8. However, as noted above at page 111, prior to the submission of the initial Page FISA application, the FBI in fact knew Steele had told Handling Agent-1 that Fusion GPS had been hired by a law firm and that his ultimate client was "senior Democrats" supporting Clinton. Moreover, it knew that Handling Agent-1's notes of this meeting reflect that, according to Steele, "HC" (Hillary Clinton) was aware of his (Steele's) reporting.

[687] OSC Report of Interview of OI Attorney-1 on July 1, 2020 at 2.

[688] *Id.*

[689] OSC Report of Interview of Case Agent-1 on Aug. 21, 2019 at 3.

[690] *Id.* at 3-4.

FISA application targeting Page was being done in the hope that the returns would "self-corroborate."[691] In any event, over time, and as discussed in more detail below, the FBI did attempt to investigate, vet, and analyze the Steele Reports but ultimately was not able to confirm or corroborate any of the substantive allegations.

Notwithstanding these obvious infirmities, the FBI and the Department included these allegations in all four Page FISA applications, including in two applications *after* Steele's primary sub-source (Igor Danchenko) had been identified, interviewed by the FBI, and was not able to provide corroboration for any of the allegations he provided to Steele. To that end, as discussed more fully below, OI Unit Chief-1 was aware that the primary sub-source had been identified and interviewed by the FBI, but OI Unit Chief-1 only later learned that serious questions arose from those January 2017 interviews of Danchenko concerning the reliability of his information as well as apparent contradictions with Steele's reports. In OI Unit Chief-1's opinion, he doubted that NSD would have supported subsequent renewals of the Page surveillance had the FBI made it fully aware of the disconnect between Steele's reporting and the FBI's interviews of Danchenko.[692]

viii. The FBI identifies Steele's primary sub-source

During the October 3, 2016 Rome meeting, Steele informed FBI personnel that his reporting was primarily generated by a single sub-source, who in turn, relied on his own network of sub-sources to gather information.[693] Steele stated that this primary sub-source traveled freely in Russia and appeared to be well-connected.[694] Steele, however, would not provide the FBI with the name of his primary sub-source. In late December 2016, the FBI determined that Igor Danchenko, a U.S.-based Russian national living in Washington, D.C., was Steele's primary sub-source.[695] Notwithstanding this fact, the FBI and the Department did not correct in the final two FISA applications targeting Page the characterization of the primary sub-source as being "Russia-based."[696]

ix. Igor Danchenko

From 2005 through 2010, Igor Danchenko worked as an analyst at the Brookings Institution in Washington, D.C. where he focused primarily on Russian and Eurasian geo-political and economic matters.[697] Danchenko came to be employed at Brookings after writing to Brookings senior fellows ("Brookings Fellow-1" and "Brookings Fellow-2") while a student at the University of Louisville. Through that connection, Danchenko was hired as a research

---

[691] *Id.* at 4.

[692] OSC Report of Interview of OI Unit Chief-1 on Oct. 27, 2020 at 4.

[693] SCO-020139 (Email from Auten to Supervisory Special Agent-1, Moffa, & Strzok dated 10/04/2016).

[694] *Id.*

[695] OSC Report of Interview of Brian Auten dated July 26, 2021 at 24.

[696] SCO_105155 (Summary of FISA Applications Targeting Carter Page).

[697] SCID_00004743 (Curriculum Vitae of Igor Danchenko).

assistant to Brookings Fellow-2.[698] In approximately 2010, Brookings Fellow-1 introduced Danchenko to Christopher Steele.[699] In 2011, Steele retained Danchenko as a contractor for his London-based firm, Orbis Business Intelligence.[700] In his work for Orbis, Danchenko focused primarily on Russian and Eurasian business risk assessment and geopolitical analysis. As discussed above, beginning in June 2016, Steele – using information provided primarily by Danchenko[701] – began to compile and draft the Steele Reports containing unsubstantiated allegations of illicit ties between Trump and the Russian government.

As discussed in more detail below, from January 2017 through October 2020, and as part of its efforts to determine the truth or falsity of specific information in the Steele Reports, the FBI conducted multiple interviews of Danchenko regarding, among other things, the allegations that he provided to Steele that ultimately formed the core of the Steele Reports. During these extensive interviews, Danchenko was unable to provide the FBI with corroborating evidence for any of the substantive allegations contained in the Steele Reports. In fact, Danchenko claimed that the Ritz Carlton allegations he provided to Steele were nothing more than "rumor and speculation," and that most of the information he gathered for Steele was the product of casual conversation with people in his social circle, including those parts of the Steele Reports used in the Page FISA applications.[702]

> x. *Danchenko's employment at Danchenko Employer-1 and payments by Steele and others*

During the course of its investigation, the Office gathered evidence related to the unusual process through which Steele paid Danchenko over the course of his work for Orbis. A brief recitation of those facts is included below.

As discussed above, Danchenko informed the FBI during his January 2017 interviews that, in approximately 2011, he began conducting work for Steele's firm, Orbis Business Intelligence.[703] Danchenko described his work with Steele as a "side project []" in addition to his employment in the United States at a Virginia-based venture capital firm.[704]

---

[698] OSC Report of Interview of Brookings Fellow-2 dated Nov. 16, 2021 at 1.

[699] OSC Report of Interview of Brookings Fellow-1 on Sept. 17, 2021 at 4; SCO-005801 (Interview of Igor Danchenko Electronic Communication dated 02/09/2017) at 5.

[700] SCO-005801 (Interview of Igor Danchenko Electronic Communication dated 02/09/2017) at 6.

[701] According to Danchenko, he provided 80% of the intelligence and 50% of the analysis contained in the Steele Reports. *Danchenko* Government Exhibit 1502.

[702] SCO-005801 (Interview of Igor Danchenko Electronic Communication dated 02/09/2017) at 23, 39; SCO_105282 (CHS Reporting Document dated 06/01/2017).

[703] SCO-005801 (Interview of Igor Danchenko Electronic Communication dated 02/09/2017) at 6.

[704] *Id.*

In approximately 2014, Danchenko ceased working for the venture capital firm following the firm's declaration of bankruptcy.[705] According to Danchenko, at the time of its bankruptcy, the firm was in the process of sponsoring Danchenko's visa application to remain in the United States.[706] Following this development, Danchenko reached out to an acquaintance in the United States who operated Danchenko Employer-1, a Virginia-based information technology staffing firm.[707] Danchenko stated, in sum, that he was seeking employment at Danchenko Employer-1 in order to extend his visa and remain in the United States.[708] Orbis, due to its United Kingdom-based registration, was unable to sponsor Danchenko in furtherance of his work visa application.[709]

According to Danchenko, the principal of Danchenko Employer-1 informed Danchenko that he would hire him on the condition that Danchenko would be compensated by an outside source – in essence, Danchenko Employer-1 would hire Danchenko to assist with his immigration status, but not fund his salary.[710] Danchenko informed Steele about this arrangement and Steele agreed to pay Danchenko Employer-1 for the work that Danchenko was conducting on behalf of Orbis.[711] During his January 2017 interviews with the FBI, Danchenko described Danchenko Employer-1 as a "contract vehicle" through which Danchenko would be paid for his work on behalf of Orbis.[712] Put plainly, Danchenko Employer-1 was merely a front to allow Danchenko to continue his work on behalf of Orbis, while at the same time allowing him to secure a work visa through alleged employment with a U.S.-based company. As relevant to this investigation, Danchenko Employer-1 Executive-1, an ethnic Russian, described Danchenko as someone who was "boastful . . . having low credibility, *and a person who liked to embellish his purported contacts with the Kremlin.*"[713]

The Office's investigation discovered that Orbis, through a separate New Jersey-based company, paid Danchenko Employer-1 for the work Danchenko performed on behalf of Orbis.[714] In turn, Danchenko Employer-1 provided Danchenko with a salary funded by Orbis.[715] By any measure, this was an extremely odd arrangement given that Danchenko performed no work

---

[705] *Id.* at 4-5.

[706] *Id.* at 8.

[707] *Id.* at 9; OSC Report of Interview of Danchenko Employer-1 Executive-1 on June 30, 2021 at 1.

[708] SCO-005801 (Interview of Igor Danchenko Electronic Communication dated 02/09/2017) at 9.

[709] *Id.* at 8-9.

[710] *Id.* at 9.

[711] *Id.*

[712] *Id.*

[713] OSC Report of Interview of Danchenko Employer-1 Executive-1 on June 30, 2021 at 1 (emphasis added).

[714] OSC Report of Interview of New Jersey-Based Company Executive-1 on Aug. 9, 2021 at 1.

[715] *Id.*

related to Danchenko Employer-1's primary business purpose, *i.e.*, the staffing of information technology and engineering contractors.[716] Nevertheless, Danchenko Employer-1 ultimately sponsored Danchenko's work visa to remain in the United States.[717]

In sworn testimony that Steele provided in litigation in the United Kingdom concerning, among other things, the Steele Reports, Steele stated that he paid his sources an average retainer between $3,000 and $5,000 per month.[718]

Banking and other records also show that from January of 2016 through June 2021, Danchenko received over $436,000 in wire transfers from European businesses, including from Orbis and other entities affiliated with Orbis. These money transfers were in addition to the money that Orbis sent through Danchenko Employer-1 to fund Danchenko's salary.

c. The prior counterespionage investigation of Danchenko and the FBI's failure to account for his possible motivations and allegiance

Danchenko was a known entity to the FBI in December 2016 when he was identified as Steele's primary sub-source. As publicly reported, Danchenko was the subject of an FBI counterespionage investigation from 2009 to 2011.[719] In late 2008, while employed by the Brookings Institution in Washington, D.C., Danchenko engaged two fellow employees ("Brookings Researcher-1" and "Brookings Researcher-2") at a happy hour about whether one of the employees might be willing or able in the future to provide classified information in exchange for money.[720] Brookings Researcher-1 was a research fellow for an influential foreign policy advisor who was about to enter the Obama administration.[721] According to Brookings Researcher-1, Danchenko believed that he (Brookings Researcher-1) might also enter the Obama administration with the foreign policy advisor and have access to classified information. During this exchange, Danchenko informed Brookings Researcher-1 that he (Danchenko) had access to people who would be willing to pay money for classified information.[722] Rightly concerned, Brookings Researcher-1 informed a U.S. government contact at an appropriate government agency about this encounter, and the information was subsequently passed on to the FBI.[723]

---

[716] OSC Report of Interview of Danchenko Employer-1 Executive-1 on June 30, 2021 at 1-2.

[717] *Id.* at 1.

[718] *Steele Transcript* at 171.

[719] Andrew Desiderio & Kyle Cheney, *Steele Dossier Sub-Source Was Suspected of Spying for Russia, DOJ Reveals*, Politico, (Sept. 24, 2020); *Danchenko* Tr. 10/13/2022 PM at 876:3-877:18, 886:22-25; SCO_105161 (Summary of Final June 3, 2019 Significant Source Validation Report of Igor Danchenko); SCO-061528 (Letter from William Barr to Lindsey Graham dated Sept. 24, 2020); SCO-061530 (Overview of the Counterintelligence Investigation of Christopher Steele's Primary Sub-Source).

[720] SCO_105160 (Summary of Solicitation); OSC Report of Interview of Brookings Researcher-1 on Dec. 1, 2021 at 2.

[721] *Id.*

[722] *Id.*

[723] *Id.*

When interviewed by the FBI, Brookings Researcher-1 confirmed the details of the interaction with Danchenko.[724] With respect to his interactions with Danchenko at Brookings, Brookings Researcher-1 described Danchenko as "sketchy" and "suspicious."[725] The second Brookings employee, Brookings Researcher-2, was also interviewed by the FBI. While Brookings Researcher-2 did not specifically recollect the events in question, he did harbor suspicions that Danchenko was connected to Russian intelligence.[726] His suspicions were based, in part, on the fact that Danchenko held multiple advanced degrees but continued working as a low-level research assistant at Brookings – the implicit assumption being that Brookings unwittingly provided Danchenko access to information of high value to the Russians.[727]

Based on the information provided by Brookings Researcher-1, the FBI's Baltimore Field Office initiated a preliminary espionage investigation into Danchenko.[728] Two Baltimore Field Office Agents led the investigation into Danchenko ("Baltimore Case Agent-1" and "Baltimore Case Agent-2"). Brian Auten, who was at the time an Intelligence Analyst (IA) as opposed to a Supervisory IA, provided Headquarters analytical support to the investigation. The FBI converted its investigation of Danchenko into a "full investigation" after learning that Danchenko (i) had been identified as an associate of two other FBI espionage subjects, and (ii) had previous contact with the Russian Embassy and known Russian intelligence officers.[729] In particular, the FBI learned that in September 2006, Danchenko informed one Russian intelligence officer that he had an interest in entering the Russian diplomatic service.[730] Four days later, the intelligence officer contacted Danchenko and informed him that they could meet that day to work "on the documents and then think about future plans."[731] In October 2006, Danchenko contacted the intelligence officer "so the documents can be placed in [the following day's] diplomatic mail pouch."[732]

As part of its investigation into Danchenko, the FBI also interviewed several people at Georgetown University who knew Danchenko. At the time, Danchenko was attempting to obtain another advanced degree. One person, a U.S. citizen who had recently interned at an intelligence agency, recalled that Danchenko asked her about her knowledge of Russian matters

---

[724] SCO-061530 (Overview of the Counterintelligence Investigation of Christopher Steele's Primary Sub-source) at 1.

[725] OSC Report of Interview of Baltimore Case Agent-1 on Aug. 13, 2020 at 3.

[726] *Id.* at 2.

[727] *Id.*

[728] SCO-061530 (Overview of the Counterintelligence Investigation of Christopher Steele's Primary Sub-source) at 1.

[729] *Id.*

[730] *Id.* at 2.

[731] OSC Report of Interview of Baltimore Case Agent-1 on Aug. 13, 2020 at 3.

[732] SCO-061530 (Overview of the Counterintelligence Investigation of Christopher Steele's Primary Sub-source) at 2.

every time he encountered her.[733] On one occasion, Danchenko inquired about the person's knowledge of a specific Russian military matter.[734] That same person stated, in sum, that Danchenko informed her that he served in the Russian army and worked with rockets, but at the time worked on "special" matters.[735] Danchenko also told this person that his Russian passport listed him as GRU (the Russian military intelligence service) because of his language skills.[736] Based on these encounters, the individual believed that Danchenko was working for a Russian intelligence service.[737] Another Brookings colleague recalled that in 2008 Danchenko informed her that he (Danchenko) had been absent from work at Brookings because he had been in South Ossetia fighting Georgians.[738] Danchenko also bragged to this colleague about vandalizing the Georgian embassy in Belarus.[739]

Further, as part of its espionage investigation, the FBI determined that Danchenko was an associate of two FBI counterintelligence subjects.[740]

In July 2010, the FBI initiated a FISA request on Danchenko, which was subsequently routed to OI in August 2010.[741] However, the investigation into Danchenko was closed in March 2011 after the FBI incorrectly concluded that Danchenko had left the country.[742] Specifically, the FBI believed that Danchenko and his then-wife had traveled on a one-way ticket to London on September 26, 2010.[743] The Office's investigative efforts revealed that, in fact, Danchenko never boarded the flight to London but, unknown to the FBI, continued to reside in the Washington, D.C. area.[744]

In 2012, after the counterespionage investigation of Danchenko had been closed because he was thought to have left the country, Auten exchanged emails with Baltimore Special Agent-2 regarding Danchenko. Specifically, Auten advised Baltimore Special Agent-2 that Danchenko may not have left the United States as initially believed in September 2010.[745] FBI Baltimore

---

[733] SCO-101733 (Human Source Validation Report of Danchenko) at 5.

[734] *Id.*

[735] *Id.*

[736] *Id.*

[737] *Id.*

[738] *Id.*

[739] *Id.*

[740] SCO-061528 (Letter from William Barr to Lindsey Graham dated Sept. 24, 2020); SCO-061530 (Overview of the Counterintelligence Investigation of Christopher Steele's Primary Sub-Source); *see also* OSC Report of Interview of Brian Auten on July 26, 2021 at 1.

[741] SCO-061530 (Overview of the Counterintelligence Investigation of Christopher Steele's Primary Sub-source) at 2.

[742] *Id.* at 1; OSC Report of Interview of Baltimore Special Agent-1 on Aug. 13, 2020 at 2.

[743] OSC Report of Interview of Baltimore Case Agent-1 on Aug. 13, 2020 at 4.

[744] U.S. Customs and Border Protection Person Encounter List for Igor Danchenko at 5.

[745] OSC Report of Interview of Brian Auten on July 26, 2021 at 2.

apparently indicated that it would consider re-opening the investigation into Danchenko, but never did.[746] Thereafter, Auten contacted WFO about re-opening a case on Danchenko, or alternatively, attempting to recruit him as a CHS.[747] Auten, however, cautioned WFO to not "get played back," meaning the Russian intelligence services could be using Danchenko as a double-agent.[748] During his interview with the Office, Auten stated that he did not know what, if any, action WFO took with respect to this information.[749] Ultimately, the case against Danchenko was never reopened by the Baltimore Division and no recruitment effort was undertaken by WFO.

The Special Counsel interviewed both Baltimore Special Agent-1 and Baltimore Special Agent-2. Baltimore Special Agent-1 believed that, based on his review of the case file, Danchenko was connected in some manner to Russian intelligence.[750] Baltimore Special Agent-1 believed that Danchenko was "hiding in plain sight" in the United States while frequently traveling overseas to Europe to be debriefed by Russian intelligence.[751] Baltimore Special Agent-2 stated, in sum, that the counterintelligence case on Danchenko remained unresolved and, in her opinion, "certainly a lot more investigation" should have been conducted on Danchenko.[752]

i.   Danchenko becomes a paid FBI CHS despite the unresolved counterespionage investigation

Danchenko was interviewed by the FBI in January 2017 following his identification in December 2016 as Steele's primary sub-source. FBI materials reviewed by the Office revealed that the primary purpose for the FBI's initial engagement with Danchenko in January 2017 was to recruit him as a paid CHS.[753] If this recruitment was successful, the FBI planned to mine Danchenko for information that was corroborative of the damaging allegations about President-elect Trump in the Steele Reports.

The FBI initially interviewed Danchenko over the course of three days, January 24-26, 2017.[754] These interviews were conducted pursuant to a grant of letter immunity provided by the Department.[755] The interviews were conducted primarily by Case Agent-1 and Auten. Danchenko was represented by counsel during the entirety of the interviews. As Auten has

---

[746] *Id.*

[747] *Id.*

[748] *Id.*

[749] *Id.*

[750] OSC Report of Interview of Baltimore Case Agent-1 on Aug. 13, 2020 at 4.

[751] *Id.*

[752] OSC Report of Interview of Baltimore Special Agent-2 on July 28, 2020 at 5.

[753] *See, e.g.,* SCO_105244 (Email from Supervisory Special Agent-3 to Boone, Supervisory Special Agent-2, Special Agent-1, Case Agent-1, & Auten dated 01/12/2017).

[754] SCO-005801 (Interview of Igor Danchenko Electronic Communication dated 02/09/2017).

[755] Letter from David Laufman to Igor Danchenko dated Jan. 24, 2017.

stated both in interviews with the Office and as a trial witness in *United States v. Danchenko*, 21-CR-245 (E.D Va.), the game plan for the January 2017 interviews was to (i) have Danchenko identify his sources for the allegations contained in the Steele Reports and (ii) provide evidence to corroborate the allegations contained in the Steele Reports.[756] As Auten testified in *Danchenko*, during the January 2017 interviews, Danchenko was not able to provide *any* corroborative evidence related to *any* substantive allegation contained in the Steele Reports – and critically – was unable to corroborate *any* of the FBI's assertions contained in the Carter Page FISA applications.[757]

Nevertheless, following the January 2017 interviews, Crossfire Hurricane leadership reached out to WFO to begin the recruitment of Danchenko as an FBI CHS. SA Kevin Helson, assigned to a counterintelligence squad at WFO, was selected to serve as Danchenko's source handler.[758] According to Helson, he was selected because he was a senior agent with knowledge of Russian matters.[759] In early March 2017, Helson prepared the Danchenko source opening documentation. In preparing those documents, Helson incorrectly noted that there was no "derogatory" information associated with Danchenko and that Danchenko had not been a prior subject of an FBI investigation.[760] This was clearly not true as there had previously been the unresolved Baltimore FBI counterespionage investigation of Danchenko that was only closed because it was believed he had left the country and returned to Russia.

The Office was able to determine that Helson became aware of the counterespionage investigation shortly after completing the source opening documentation, but failed to revise the paperwork because of a purported belief that the prior case on Danchenko was based solely on hearsay.[761] In a November 24, 2020 interview with the Office, Helson was shown a spreadsheet listing Sentinel (the FBI's case management system) searches that he performed on March 7, 2017 – mere days after completing the CHS opening documentation – in which he specifically queried the counterespionage case file on Danchenko.[762] Helson stated that he had no recollection as to why he searched certain serials in that case file, and he advised that he would not have thought Danchenko should be the main subject of that type of espionage case since Danchenko, in Helson's view, was a foreign national without a security clearance.[763] Whatever the reason for not locating and documenting the serious derogatory information, the record is clear the FBI opened Danchenko as a CHS without ever resolving the Baltimore espionage matter or examining the file.

---

[756] OSC Report of Interview of Brian Auten on July 26, 2021 at 21; *Danchenko* Tr. 10/11/2022 PM at 125, 151.

[757] *Danchenko* Tr. 10/11/2022 PM at 154, *Danchenko* Tr. 10/12/2022 PM at 550-551.

[758] OSC Report of Interview of Brian Auten on July 26, 2021 at 21; *Danchenko* Tr.10/11/2022 PM at 152-153.

[759] OSC Report of Interview of Kevin Helson on Nov. 24, 2020 at 1.

[760] *Id.* at 7, 10; SCO-105224 (Source Opening Communication dated 03/07/2017).

[761] OSC Report of Interview of Kevin Helson on Nov. 24, 2020 at 10.

[762] *Id.* at 7.

[763] *Id.*

Despite having seen that Danchenko was identified in the opening serial of a counterespionage investigation in Baltimore, Helson informed investigators that he was surprised to learn from Auten on March 24, 2017 that Danchenko was indeed the main subject of that counterespionage case.[764] According to Helson, Auten informed him, in sum, that Danchenko had a long history with Russian intelligence officers, and that he had previously pitched someone for classified information. According to Helson, however, Auten advised him (Helson) that the case against Danchenko was "interesting, but was not a significant" matter.[765] Helson informed the Office that he had a clear recollection of this conversation with Auten. Notably, Auten did not inform Helson that he had previously assisted in the Baltimore investigation. Once Helson learned of the existence of the counterespionage case against Danchenko, he failed at the time to take even the basic step of conferring with the case agents previously assigned to the matter. In fact, and as discussed in more detail below, Helson did not reach out to Baltimore Special Agent-2 until May 2019 when Danchenko was being evaluated by the FBI's CHS Validation Management Unit ("VMU") and the VMU raised serious concerns about the prior counterespionage case.

When the Office asked Helson about his reaction to learning that Danchenko pitched a colleague for classified information, Helson stated "it sounds like something Danchenko would do, that's how Danchenko works."[766] Helson further stated, in sum, that the fact Danchenko comes off as a Russian spy is describing half the population of Washington, D.C. In his interviews with the Office, Helson was essentially dismissive of the prior counterespionage investigation on Danchenko.

Despite the unresolved counterespionage case against Danchenko and Helson's (and others) apparent lack of curiosity regarding the matter, the FBI began operating Danchenko as a paid CHS in March 2017.[767] As discussed further below, the FBI and Helson made no further efforts to examine the unresolved espionage case until the VMU exposed the security issues surrounding Danchenko in May 2019.

ii.   The VMU examines Danchenko's suitability as a source

The FBI's previous espionage investigation into Danchenko was raised in May 2019 in the context of a Human Source Validation Report ("HSVR") on Danchenko prepared by the FBI's VMU. The VMU raised several concerns related to Danchenko's past associations, behaviors, and travel history, including the prior and unresolved espionage case. In addition to the information contained in the prior espionage file, including Danchenko's fairly extensive contacts with known and suspected Russian intelligence officers, the HSVR detailed a February 2018 U.S. Customs and Border ("CBP") inspection of Danchenko when he re-entered the United States after being in the United Kingdom, in which a CBP officer discovered business cards for Russian diplomats residing in England.[768] The HSVR also detailed several falsehoods and

---

[764] Id. at 7-8.

[765] Id. at 7.

[766] Id. at 8.

[767] SCO-105224 (Source Opening Communication dated 03/07/2017).

[768] SCO-101733 (Human Source Validation Report) at 15-16.

inconsistencies found in Danchenko's visa applications and immigration documents. One member of the VMU with extensive prior service as an Army counterintelligence officer in Europe ("Headquarters Supervisory Analyst-1") expressed grave concerns about the counterespionage case and was strongly of the opinion that Danchenko was connected to Russian intelligence in some manner.[769]

In response to the concerns of Supervisory Analyst-1 and others in the VMU, Helson reached out to Baltimore Special Agent-2 for the *first* time – over two years after he initially learned of the counterespionage case against Danchenko. Helson informed the VMU (and later the Office), that Baltimore Special Agent-2 stated, in sum, that the investigation was premised on "hearsay at best."[770] However, when interviewed by the Office on July 28, 2020, Baltimore Special Agent-2 expressed disbelief when she first learned that Danchenko had been signed up as an FBI source because, among other things, the FBI had not resolved the prior counterespionage case.[771] When informed that Helson stated to the VMU that Baltimore Special Agent-2 had characterized the predication of the counterespionage case as "hearsay at best," Baltimore Special Agent-2 was adamant that she would never have characterized Danchenko's direct pitch to Brookings Researcher -1 for classified information as hearsay.[772] To the contrary, Baltimore Special Agent-2 stated that the information came directly from the individual who was the target of the pitch for classified information.[773] In two subsequent interviews with the Office, Baltimore Special Agent-2 again denied ever telling Helson that the counterespionage case against Danchenko was predicated on "hearsay at best."[774] Baltimore Special Agent-2 confirmed to the Office that the Danchenko counterespionage case would have continued if he had not left the country, as the FBI mistakenly believed he had.[775] When shown Helson's source opening documentation that contained the "no derog" entry, Baltimore Special Agent-2 agreed that the entry was clearly incorrect.[776]

iii. The VMU's recommendations to WFO and Helson

The HSVR on Danchenko recommended that he be allowed to remain open as a CHS but recommended that several steps be taken to help mitigate the VMU's substantial concerns about Danchenko. As an initial matter, when asked why the VMU recommended that Danchenko be allowed to remain open given the concerns noted above, several individuals who participated in the HSVR stated that the VMU lacked the institutional ability to do anything more than to make

---

[769] OSC Report of Interview of Headquarters Supervisory Analyst-1 on Dec. 8, 2020 at 1, 4; *Danchenko* Tr. 10/13/2022 PM at 890-91.

[770] SCO-105324 (Helson memo of May 24, 2019 conversation with Baltimore Special Agent-2 at 1).

[771] OSC Report of Interview of Baltimore Special Agent-2 on July 28, 2020 at 3.

[772] *Id.*

[773] *Id.*

[774] OSC Report of Interview of Baltimore Special Agent-2 on Aug. 13, 2020 at 1-2; OSC Report of Interview of Baltimore Special Agent-1 on Dec. 18, 2020 at 1.

[775] OSC Report of Interview of Baltimore Special Agent-2 on Aug. 13, 2020 at 1.

[776] *Id.* at 2.

recommendations to mitigate CHS issues. One supervisor in the VMU noted that it rarely recommended closure of sources out of a general fear that the field offices would largely be unreceptive to important recommendations designed to enhance source handling issues if the VMU recommended closure of a source.[777] In addition to the serious concern about the prior unresolved counterespionage investigation, the VMU also highlighted numerous problematic areas that warranted attention. For example, Danchenko's background and employment history had noted inconsistencies and omissions; his assessed motivation for providing information to the FBI had changed; his immigration applications omitted certain derogatory information and contained inconsistencies and falsehoods; and, despite his concerns for his personal safety, he traveled frequently to Russia before becoming a CHS. Danchenko also demonstrated knowledge of tradecraft and made contradictory statements, and much of the information he provided appeared to be hearsay that he was unable, despite requests, to validate. The VMU recommended several steps to mitigate these areas, such as administering a polygraph examination,[778] further controls on his reporting, and additional evaluation, but these did not occur. Instead, Helson and WFO ignored nearly all of the VMU's recommendations and continued to operate Danchenko as a CHS until WFO was ordered to close Danchenko in October 2020.[779] In total, the FBI paid Danchenko approximately $220,000 during the 3.5 years that Danchenko was a CHS.[780] FBI counterintelligence personnel at WFO and in the Counterintelligence Division at FBI Headquarters opposed efforts to close Danchenko and delayed doing so. Moreover, the Office learned that the FBI proposed making continued future payments to Danchenko, totaling more than $300,000, while the Office was actively

---

[777] At the time the evaluation was prepared on Danchenko, it was the practice of the VMU not to recommend that a CHS be closed, but rather to make recommendations of things to be done in continuing to operate a source. OSC Report of Interview of Headquarters Supervisory Special Agent-2 on March 2, 2021 at 6-7; OSC Report of Interview of Headquarters Supervisory Analyst-1 on Dec. 8, 2020 at 8. The *CHS Policy Guide*, issued in 2021, now includes requirements that:

- The VMU is to "manage[] the FBI's validation review processes" and "must determine what level of validation review is required for each CHS." *CHS Policy Guide* § 20.1.1.

- The Assistant Director for Intelligence is to approve or deny the reopening of a CHS closed for cause. *Id.* § 18.3.1.

- The Directorate of Intelligence manages the Senior Review Board, whose function is to ensure "comprehensive review by senior FBI officials of the FBI's highest-risk CHSs." *See id.* § 20.5.1.

[778] The FBI uses a polygraph examination as a straightforward and practical way to assess a source's motivations, allegiances, and vulnerabilities.

[779] OSC Report of Interview of Kevin Helson on Nov. 24, 2020 at 19; FBI-AAA-0019898 (Email from Headquarters Supervisory Special Agent-1 to Helson & others dated 10/29/2020).

[780] SCO-105237 (Source Closing Communication dated 10/29/2020).

investigating this matter, which would have been in addition to the $220,000 he had already received.[781]

It is extremely concerning that the FBI failed to deal with the prior *unresolved* counterespionage case on Danchenko. Given Danchenko's known contacts with Russian intelligence officers and his documented prior pitch for classified information, the Crossfire Hurricane team's failure to properly consider and address the espionage case prior to opening Danchenko as a CHS is difficult to explain, particularly given their awareness that Danchenko was the linchpin to the uncorroborated allegations contained in the Steele Reports.

Despite the FBI's awareness of (i) there being significant issues relating to conflicts between what Danchenko had reported to the FBI in January 2017 and thereafter as a paid CHS and what Steele, a long term paid CHS of the FBI, had stated in the "Company Intelligence" reports he provided to the FBI (and others), (ii) Danchenko's troubling history regarding a prior unresolved espionage matter, and (iii) a CHS validation report that raised various red flags concerning Danchenko, the counterintelligence executive managers at the WFO and FBI Headquarters resisted efforts to have Danchenko closed as a source. Instead, management supported continued payments to him, requiring FBI Headquarters approval, of sizable amounts of money and insisted that Danchenko was very valuable to the FBI's counterintelligence program. Interviews conducted by the Office revealed, however, that the Assistant Directors for Counterintelligence in WFO and FBI Headquarters, as well as the FBI's Executive Assistant Director for National Security, made clear that they were not even able to accurately describe the value or contributions of Danchenko that would justify keeping him open, much less making hundreds of thousands of dollars in payments to him. Indeed, the Assistant Director for Counterintelligence at FBI Headquarters thought Danchenko was being paid for information he was providing that corroborated the Steele Dossier reporting, which, of course, was not the case because Danchenko never produced any such evidence.

By (i) ignoring the significance of Danchenko's prior status as a subject of a counterespionage investigation, (ii) failing to resolve the conflict between that history and his role as primary sub-source for the Steele reporting, and (iii) failing to follow through on VMU's recommendations for continued operation of Danchenko as a CHS, Helson and the Counterintelligence Division missed another opportunity to make any needed course corrections to Crossfire Hurricane and in the use of Danchenko as a CHS.

d. Danchenko's relationship with Charles Dolan

When interviewed by the FBI in June 2017, Danchenko failed to disclose the role a U.S.-based individual named Charles Dolan played in the reporting Danchenko provided for inclusion in the Steele Reports. In particular, Danchenko denied that Dolan provided any specific information contained in the Steele Reports.[782] However, Dolan acknowledged to the Office that he provided information to Danchenko related to Paul Manafort's firing as Trump campaign

---

[781] SCO-105290 (Request for required expenses and lump sum payment Electronic Communication dated 10/21/2020).

[782] *Danchenko* Government Exhibit 171T.

manager.[783] Dolan further admitted to the Office that this allegation, which appears in Steele Report 2016/105, was fabricated.[784]

As discussed in a previous section, during the October 3, 2016 Rome meeting, Steele provided the FBI with the names of four U.S.-based individuals who might have information on Trump's connections to Russia. Three of the names provided by Steele were Washington, D.C.-based individuals Charles Dolan, U.S. Person-1 and U.S. Person-2.[785] An FBI report of a September 18th and 19th 2017 interview of Steele cryptically mentioned that Danchenko had drinks with Dolan, but the report included no further information on that topic.[786] In the same interview, however, Steele also stated that Dolan could have been the "American political figure associated with Donald Trump and his campaign"[787] referenced in the following paragraph of Steele Report 2016/105:

> Speaking separately, also in late August 2016, an American political figure associated with Donald TRUMP and his campaign outlined the reasons behind Paul Manafort's recent demise. S/he said it was true that the Ukraine corruption revelations had played a part in this, but also, several senior players close to TRUMP had wanted Manafort out, primarily to loosen his control on strategy and policy formulation. Of particular importance in this regard was Manafort's predecessor as campaign manager, Corey Lewandowski, who hated Manafort personally and remained close to TRUMP with whom he discussed the presidential campaign on a regular basis.[788]

The following section discusses in greater detail Dolan's role in the Steele reporting and his relationship with Danchenko.

i. Charles Dolan

Charles Dolan is a public relations professional who in 2016 was employed by a Washington, D.C.-based public relations firm called kglobal.[789] In addition to his work as a public relations professional, Dolan had previously served as (i) Executive Director of the Democratic Governors Association, (ii) Virginia Chairman of former President Clinton's 1992 and 1996 presidential campaigns, and (iii) an advisor to Hillary Clinton's 2008 presidential

---

[783] *Danchenko* Tr. 10/13/2022 AM at 616:3-621:22.

[784] *Danchenko* Tr. 10/13/2022 AM at 621:23-624:4.

[785] SCO-020139 (Email from Auten to Supervisory Special Agent-1, Moffa, & Strzok dated 10/04/2016) at 2.

[786] SCO-006313 (Interview of Christopher Steele on Sept. 18, 2017) at 3.

[787] *Id.* at 17.

[788] SCO-105084 (Documents Known to the FBI Comprising the "Steele Dossier") at 18-19, (Company Intelligence Report 2016/105) (capitalization in original).

[789] *Danchenko* Tr. 10/13/2022 AM at 596:22-597:1; OSC Report of Interview of Charles Dolan on Aug. 31, 2021 at 1.

campaign.[790] Moreover, beginning in 1997, President Clinton appointed Dolan to two four-year terms on the State Department's U.S. Advisory Commission on Public Diplomacy.[791] With respect to the 2016 Clinton campaign, Dolan described himself as a "door to door" guy in New Hampshire who did not hold any significant position.[792]

ii. Dolan's connections to the Kremlin

In his role as a public relations professional, Dolan spent much of his career interacting with Eurasian clients with a particular focus on Russia. For example, from approximately 1999 through 2004-2005, Dolan was employed by global public relations firm Ketchum Inc. where he assisted with Ketchum's representation of the Russian Federation.[793] Part of Dolan's responsibility on the Russian Federation account consisted of, among other things, monitoring current policy discussions of U.S.-based think tanks and reporting back to the Russian government.[794] Dolan also assisted in media consulting and press operations for the 2006 G8 Summit held in St. Petersburg, Russia.[795] As a senior member of Ketchum's Russian Federation team, Dolan frequently interacted with Russian government officials, including, most importantly, Dimitry Peskov, Press Secretary of the Russian Presidential Administration, and Alex Pavlov, Deputy Press Secretary of the Presidential Administration.[796] Peskov has often been described in media reports as Russian President Putin's "right-hand man."[797] As discussed more below, both Peskov and Pavlov would subsequently feature prominently in the Steele Reports.[798] Additionally, Dolan maintained relationships with Sergei Kislyak, who served as Russian Ambassador to the United States from 2008-2017, and Mikhail Kalugin, the head of the Russian Embassy's Economic Section in Washington, D.C. from 2010-2016. Both Kislyak and Kalugin would also feature prominently in the Steele Reports.[799]

---

[790] *Danchenko* Tr. 10/13/2022 AM at 590:6-592:12; OSC Report of Interview of Charles Dolan on Aug. 31, 2021 at 1.

[791] SCID_00013647 (Charles Dolan kglobal biography).

[792] OSC Report of Interview of Charles Dolan on Nov. 1, 2021 at 1.

[793] OSC Report of Interview of Charles Dolan on Aug. 31, 2021 at 1-2; *Danchenko* Tr. 10/13/2022 AM at 592:14-593:14.

[794] OSC Report of Interview of Charles Dolan on Aug. 31, 2021 at 1-2.

[795] *Id.*

[796] OSC Report of Interview of Charles Dolan on Aug. 31, 2021 at 2; *Danchenko* Tr. 10/13/2022 AM at 593:18-594:21.

[797] Mick Krever, *Putin Aide Predicts Relations 'Renaissance' . . . If Russian 'National Interests' Respected*, CNN (Feb. 27, 2015).

[798] Annotated Steele Dossier at 3, 4, 8, 9, 19, 20.

[799] *Id.* at 15, 19.

In March 2016, Brookings Fellow-1 introduced Dolan to Danchenko in connection with a potential business opportunity.[800] Specifically, Danchenko had reached out to Brookings Fellow-1 in an attempt to broker business between a U.S.-based public relations firm and his longtime friend, Olga Galkina, an executive at a Cyprus-based computer firm named Servers.com.[801] Danchenko would later inform the FBI that Galkina served as a source of information for allegations contained in the Steele Reports.[802] Brookings Fellow-1 subsequently connected Danchenko and Dolan to discuss a possible business venture between Dolan and Servers.com. In March 2016, Danchenko brokered a meeting between Dolan (and his firm kglobal) and Galkina to discuss a potential business arrangement between kglobal and Servers.com, the latter of which was attempting to enter the U.S. marketplace.[803] Dolan was joined at this meeting by a Washington-based lobbyist ("U.S. Person-2") with whom Dolan had previously worked[804] – and who Steele would later name along with Dolan as a possible source for information on Trump/Russia connections.

Dolan and kglobal would ultimately enter a contractual relationship with Servers.com.[805] As discussed in detail below, Dolan traveled to Cyprus on two occasions in the summer of 2016 to meet with Galkina, Aleksej Gubarev (the principal of Servers.com) and other executives at Servers.com.[806] As a result of this collaboration, Dolan and Danchenko continued to communicate through the Spring of 2016.

In late April 2016, Dolan and Danchenko engaged in separate discussions regarding a potential business collaboration between kglobal and Orbis. For example, on April 29, 2016, Danchenko sent an email to Dolan indicating that Danchenko had passed a letter to Christopher Steele on behalf of Dolan.[807] Specifically, the email sent to Dolan stated that Danchenko had "forwarded your letter" to Steele and Steele's business partner, Christopher Burrows. The email continued, "I'll make sure you gentlemen meet when they are in Washington, or when you are in London." That same day, Danchenko sent an email to Dolan outlining certain work that

---

[800] OSC Report of Interview of Charles Dolan on Aug. 31, 2021 at 2; SCID_00007741 (Email from Danchenko to Dolan dated 03/08/2016).

[801] SCID_00007741 (Email from Danchenko to Dolan dated 03/10/2016). According to their website, Servers.com provides access to computer servers in data centers throughout the world.

[802] SCO-005801 (Interview of Igor Danchenko Electronic Communication dated 02/09/2017) at 16.

[803] SCID_00007741 (Email from Danchenko to Dolan dated 03/10/2016); SCID_00017834 (Email from Galkina to Dolan, U.S. Person-2 on 03/24/2016).

[804] OSC Report of Interview of Charles Dolan on Aug. 31, 2021 at 3

[805] *Id.*

[806] *Id.*

[807] SCID_00006415 (Email from Danchenko to Dolan dated 04/29/2016).

Danchenko was conducting for Orbis. The email attached an Orbis report titled "Intelligence Briefing Note, 'Kompromat' and 'Nadzor' in the Russian Banking Sector."[808]

Beginning in early 2015, a Washington, D.C.-based lawyer and acquaintance of Dolan, ("U.S. Person-1") informed Dolan that he was planning a business conference for October 2016 in Moscow.[809] The conference, titled "Inside the Kremlin," was being sponsored by the Young President's Organization, and was designed to introduce senior international business executives to potential investment opportunities in Russia (the "YPO Conference").[810] To that end, the YPO Conference was to include individuals who could provide insight into the economic, political, diplomatic and cultural aspects of the Russian Federation. The YPO Conference was to be held at the Ritz Carlton hotel in Moscow.[811] U.S. Person-1 enlisted Dolan to participate in the YPO conference because of Dolan's access to senior Russian government officials and his ability to provide analysis of the approaching 2016 U.S. presidential election.[812]

In April 2016, Dolan asked Danchenko to assist Dolan and U.S. Person-1 with the YPO conference, which Danchenko agreed to do.[813] Dolan believed that Danchenko's language skills and his supposed contacts in the Russian government would be of assistance to the conference.[814] Dolan subsequently asked and received permission from U.S. Person-1 to enlist Danchenko to assist with logistics, provide translation services, and present on various relevant topics at the YPO Conference.[815] In preparation for the YPO Conference, Dolan and U.S. Person-1 planned to travel to Moscow in June 2016 to view the Ritz Carlton and other potential sites for the conference (the "June Planning Trip").[816] At the same time, Danchenko informed Dolan that he (Danchenko) would be present in Moscow in June on other business.[817]

On April 30, 2016, Dolan sent an email to a U.S.-based acquaintance and stated, in part, the following:

> Waiting on confirmation for meetings with the Kremlin. If all goes well I will probably leave on the 9th [June] and stop in London to meet with these intelligence guys (another potential project but nothing certain) and leave on the 10th for Moscow and stay for the week.[818]

---

[808] SCID_00016038 (Email from Danchenko to Dolan, U.S. Person-2 dated 04/29/2016).

[809] SCID_00017536 (Email from U.S. Person-1 to Dolan, others dated 02/11/2015).

[810] SCID_00014254 (Email from Dolan to U.S. Person-1 dated 02/12/2015).

[811] SCID_00017536 (Email from U.S. Person-1 to Dolan, others dated 02/11/2015) at 2.

[812] OSC Report of Interview of U.S. Person-1 on Apr. 13, 2021 at 1-2.

[813] SCID_00014427 (Email from Dolan to Danchenko dated 04/11/2016); SCID_00015922 (Email from Danchenko to Dolan dated 04/22/2016).

[814] *Danchenko* Tr. 10/13/2022 AM at 610:23 – 611:3.

[815] *Danchenko* Tr. 10/13/2022 AM at 611:4-8; 640:1-641:15.

[816] SCID_00016172 (Email from U.S. Person-1 to Dolan, others dated 05/21/2016).

[817] SCID_00006540 (Email from Danchenko to Dolan dated 06/03/2016).

[818] SCID_00004759 (Email from Dolan dated 04/30/2016).

In his interviews with the Office, Dolan denied meeting with Steele.[819] Travel records confirm that Dolan did not travel to London prior to the June Planning Trip.[820] In fact, the Office was not able to find any definitive evidence to indicate that Dolan ever met with Steele.

To further prepare for the YPO Conference, in May, July, and October 2016, Dolan and U.S. Person-1 attended at least three meetings at the Russian Embassy in Washington, D.C., and communicated with Russian Embassy staff, including Ambassador Sergei Kislyak and the Head of the Economic Section, Mikhail Kalugin.[821] As noted above, both Kislyak and Kalugin would feature prominently in the Steele Reports. Danchenko was not present at any of these meetings.

In anticipation of the June Planning Trip to Moscow, Dolan attempted to communicate with Press Secretary Peskov and Deputy Press Secretary Pavlov, as well as former Russian President and then-Prime Minister Dimitry Medvedev.[822] Dolan had previously attended several lunches with Medvedev when he (Dolan) served as an advisor to the Valdai Club in connection with his work at Ketchum.[823] (The Valdai Club is a Moscow-based think tank that is closely associated with Russian President Putin and is viewed by many in the West as a vehicle for Russian propaganda). In May 2016, Dolan reached out to Medvedev's Press Secretary to have Medvedev speak at the YPO Conference.[824]

When interviewed by the FBI in September 2017, Steele noted that his primary sub-source (Danchenko) has sub-sources who had access to Dimitry Peskov.[825] In particular, Steele stated that information in the Reports involving Peskov stemmed from a "friend of a friend" of his primary sub-source (Danchenko).[826] Later in the interview, Steele informed the FBI that his primary sub-source had a sub-source who had contact with Alexey Pavlov and had conversations with Pavlov about Peskov.[827] Steele told the FBI that this unidentified source was close to then-Russian Prime Minister Dimitry Medvedev.[828] (As discussed above, Dolan claimed to have met Medvedev on several occasions.) Steele also stated that his primary sub-source (Danchenko)

---

[819] OSC Report of Interview of Charles Dolan on Aug. 31, 2021 at 6.

[820] U.S. Customs and Border Protection Person Encounter List for Charles Dolan at 1.

[821] SCID_00016319 (Email from U.S. Person-1 to Dolan, Kalugin, others dated 05/31/2016); SCID_00016626 (Email from U.S. Person-1 to Dolan, others dated 07/15/2016); SCID_00017124 (Email to Kalugin, U.S. Person-1, Dolan, others dated 10/14/2016).

[822] SCO-005678 (Email from Dolan dated 06-03-2016); OSC Report of Interview of Charles Dolan on Sept. 7, 2021 at 2; SCID_00001127 (Email from Dolan to U.S. Person-1 dated 09/30/2016); SCID_00000633 (Email from Dolan to U.S. Person-1 dated 06/03/2016); SCID_00014550 (Letter from Dolan dated May 19, 2016).

[823] KG_0002092 (Email from Dolan dated 12/28/2017).

[824] SCID_00014550 (Letter from Dolan dated 05/19/2016).

[825] SCO-006313 (Interview of Christopher Steele on Sept. 18, 2017) at 6.

[826] Id. at 7.

[827] Id. at 15.

[828] Id.

would meet Pavlov for drinks when he (the primary sub-source) traveled to Russia.[829] However, as discussed more fully below, the Office found no information to indicate that Danchenko maintained a relationship with Pavlov.

On June 10, 2016, before traveling abroad, Dolan sent an email to a U.S.-based acquaintance reflecting that Dolan and Danchenko had become colleagues. Dolan stated in part:

> On Monday night I fly to Moscow and will meet with a Russian guy [Danchenko] who is working with me on a couple of projects. He also works for a group of former MI 6 guys in London who do intelligence for businesses. Send me your questions and I'll pass them on to Igor. He owes me as his Visa is being held up and I am having a word with the Ambassador.[830]

Shortly thereafter, Dolan sent another email to the U.S.-based acquaintance. In describing Danchenko, Dolan stated: "He is too young for KGB. But I think he worked for FSB. Since he told me he spent two years in Iran. And when I first met him he knew more about me than I did. [winking emoticon]."[831] (The Federal Security Service of the Russian Federation, or "FSB" is the principal security agency of Russia and principal successor agency to the KGB.) When interviewed by the Office, Dolan stated that he was "speculating" about Danchenko's connections to Russian intelligence, and that he was "half joking and half serious."[832]

Dolan was scheduled to be in Moscow for the June Planning Trip from June 13-18, 2016. In connection with the June Planning Trip, Dolan decided to first travel to Cyprus to meet with executives from Servers.com.[833] Dolan departed Washington, D.C. on June 9th, arrived in Moscow on the morning of June 10th, and departed for Cyprus later that afternoon.[834] While in Cyprus, Dolan met with Galkina, Gubarev and the other executives at Servers.com's offices.[835] Dolan then left Cyprus on June 13th and flew to Moscow to attend the June Planning trip.[836]

During the June Planning Trip, Dolan and U.S. Person-1 stayed at the Ritz Carlton in Moscow.[837] On June 14th, Danchenko, who as noted above was already present in Moscow, met Dolan for lunch at a restaurant in Moscow.[838] Dolan and Danchenko took a photograph together in front of the Kremlin, which was later posted by Danchenko on Facebook.[839] According to Dolan, this was the only time he encountered Danchenko on the June Planning Trip, and

---

[829] *Id.* at 14.

[830] SCID_00000732 (Email from Dolan dated 06/10/2016).

[831] SCID_00000735 (Email from Dolan dated 06/10/2016).

[832] OSC Report of Interview of Charles Dolan on Sept. 7, 2021 at 1.

[833] SCID_00000653 (Email from Dolan to Galkina dated 06/01/2016).

[834] SCID_00000726 (Email from Dolan to U.S. Person-1 dated 06/08/2016).

[835] SCID_00008141 (Email from Galkina to Dolan dated 06/13/2016).

[836] SCID_00000653 (Email from Dolan to Galkina dated 06/01/2016).

[837] SCID_00041378 (Email to Dolan dated 06/09/2016).

[838] SCID_00000787 (Email from Dolan to U.S. Person-1 dated 06/14/2016).

[839] *Danchenko* Government Exhibit 605.

Danchenko did not stay at the Ritz Carlton during the June Planning Trip – a fact that was confirmed by hotel records.[840]

While in Moscow, Dolan and U.S. Person-1 participated in, among other things, (i) a meeting with the German-national general manager of the Ritz Carlton, and at least one female hotel staff member to discuss the logistics of the YPO Conference, (ii) a lunch with the general manager and three hotel staff members who assisted in the preparations for the YPO conference, and (iii) a tour of the hotel.[841]

Dolan told the Office that during the June Planning Trip he met with two deputies from the Russian Presidential Administration Press Office (Dimitry Peskov's Office).[842] According to Dolan, Danchenko was not present for any events at the Ritz Carlton during the June Planning Trip and was not present for his meeting with the deputies from the Press Office.[843] As discussed in detail below, the general manager and other hotel staff members would later appear in the Steele Reports.

On June 15, 2016, Dolan emailed an acquaintance from Moscow: "I'm in Russia making plans to be adopted in the event this mad man [Trump] gets elected."[844] On June 18, 2016, Dolan returned to Washington, D.C.[845]

> iv.   *Trump's alleged salacious sexual activity at the Ritz Carlton Moscow appears in a Steele Report*

On June 17, 2016, Danchenko flew from Moscow to London and met with Christopher Steele on the following day.[846] Three days later, in Steele Report 2016/080 dated June 20, 2016, an allegation appeared that described salacious sexual activity that Trump allegedly had participated in while a guest at the Ritz Carlton Moscow. The allegation stated, in part:

> According to Source D, where s/he had been present, TRUMP's (perverted) conduct in Moscow included hiring the presidential suite of the Ritz Carlton, where he knew President and Mrs OBAMA (whom he hated) had stayed on one of their official trips to Russia, and defiling the bed where they had slept by employing a number of prostitutes to perform 'golden showers' (urination) shows in front of him. The hotel was known to be under FSB control with microphones and concealed cameras in all the main rooms to record anything they wanted to.

---

[840] OSC Report of Interview of Charles Dolan on Aug. 31, 2021 at 5.

[841] OSC Report of Interview of U.S. Person-1 on Apr. 13, 2021 at 3; OSC Report of Interview of Charles Dolan on Aug. 31, 2021 at 5-6.

[842] OSC Report of Interview of Charles Dolan on Nov. 1, 2021 at 2.

[843] *Id.* at 2.

[844] KG_0003739 (Email from Dolan dated 06/15/2016).

[845] SCID_00000726 (Email from Dolan to U.S. Person-1 dated 06/08/2016).

[846] SCO-007286 (Danchenko Facebook messages dated 06/16 to 06/17/2016); SCO-016761 (Facebook message from Danchenko to Galkina dated 06/18/2016); OIG interview of Christopher Steele on June 5 & 6, 2019 at 45.

The Ritz Carlton episode involving TRUMP reported above was confirmed by Source E, a senior (western) member of staff at the hotel, who said that s/he and several of the staff were aware of it at the time and subsequently. S/he believed it had happened in 2013. Source E provided an introduction for a company ethnic Russian operative to Source F, a female staffer at the hotel when TRUMP had stayed there, who also confirmed the story.[847]

Certain of the information in the June 20, 2016 Steele Report reflected facts that Dolan learned during the June Planning Trip to Moscow. For example, while at the Ritz Carlton, Dolan (1) received a tour of the hotel and (according to Dolan) possibly the Presidential Suite, and (2) met with the senior Western member of staff – in context the general manager – and other staff of the Ritz Carlton. As noted, Danchenko did not stay at the Ritz Carlton in June 2016, but had lunch with Dolan during the June Planning Trip at some other location.

Notably, when interviewed by the Office, U.S. Person-1 recalled he and Dolan took a tour of the Presidential Suite.[848] Following his initial interview with the Office, Dolan called U.S. Person-1 and U.S. Person-1 confirmed that he (U.S. Person-1) and Dolan had in fact taken a tour of the Presidential Suite.[849] During that tour, a hotel staff member told the participants that Trump had previously been a guest in the Presidential Suite.[850] According to U.S. Person-1, the staff member informed them that Donald Trump had stayed in the Suite, but did not mention any sexual or salacious activity.[851] When interviewed by the Office, Dolan's recollection about taking a tour of the Presidential suite at the Ritz Carlton was inconsistent and his recollection vacillated over the course of several interviews. Dolan stated, in sum, that it was possible that he (Dolan) told Danchenko about the Presidential Suite and Trump, but he had no specific recollection of doing so.[852] Dolan was adamant that he never told Danchenko about any salacious sexual activity that occurred in the suite.[853]

The Office also interviewed the then-general Manager of the Ritz-Carlton Moscow. The general manager, a German citizen who does not speak Russian, was described in the Steele Report as a "senior (western) member of staff at the hotel and identified as "Source E."[854] The general manager did not recognize the photograph of Danchenko he was shown by the Office.[855]

---

[847] SCO-105084 (Documents Known to the FBI Comprising the "Steele Dossier") at 3, (Company Intelligence Report 2016/080).

[848] OSC Report of Interview of U.S. Person-1 on Apr. 13, 2021 at 3.

[849] OSC Report of Interview of Charles Dolan on Nov. 1, 2021 at 1.

[850] OSC Report of Interview of U.S. Person-1 on Apr. 13, 2021 at 3.

[851] Id. at 3.

[852] OSC Report of Interview of Charles Dolan on Nov. 1, 2021 at 1.

[853] Id.

[854] SCO-105084 (Documents Known to the FBI Comprising the "Steele Dossier") at 3, (Company Intelligence Report 2016/080).

[855] OSC Report of Interview of general manager of the Moscow Ritz Carlton on Aug. 9, 2022 at 4.

He also denied having knowledge of the Ritz-Carlton allegations concerning Trump at any time prior to their being reported in the media.[856] As such, the general manager adamantly denied discussing such allegations with, or hearing them from, Danchenko, or anyone else.[857] Further, the Office obtained records from the Ritz Carlton Moscow that reveal that Trump was a guest at the hotel in 2013, but did not stay in the Presidential Suite then or at any other time.[858]

When interviewed by the FBI in January 2017, Danchenko claimed that he had sourced this information, in part, while staying at the Ritz-Carlton Moscow during the June Planning Trip.[859] While Danchenko initially told the FBI that he had been a guest at the Ritz-Carlton Moscow during the June Planning Trip, in a later interview, he acknowledged that he had visited, but not stayed at, the hotel during that June Planning Trip.[860] Danchenko also claimed that he inquired about the Ritz-Carlton allegations with hotel staff who did not deny their validity.[861] Finally, Danchenko told the FBI that he reported the names of these hotel staff members to Christopher Steele.[862] In his September 2017 interview, Steele also told the FBI that "Source E" and "Source F" were employees at the Ritz Carlton Moscow with whom his primary sub-source [Danchenko] personally met.[863] Thus, it seems apparent that Danchenko provided the general manager's information to Steele. Danchenko also told the FBI that "Source D" – another purported source of the Ritz Carlton allegations – could be referring to Sergei Millian.[864]

In a subsequent May 2017 FBI interview (while serving as an FBI CHS), Danchenko again confirmed that he had spoken with hotel management about the Ritz-Carlton allegations.[865] In that interview, Danchenko also stated that "Source E" was probably one of the hotel managers.[866]

---

[856] *Id.* at 6-7.

[857] *Id.*

[858] SCO-101769 (Moscow Ritz Carlton Records).

[859] SCO-005801 (Interview of Igor Danchenko Electronic Communication dated 02/09/2017) at 38-39.

[860] Transcript of meeting with Danchenko on May 18, 2017 at 27-29.

[861] SCO-005801 (Interview of Igor Danchenko Electronic Communication dated 02/09/2017) at 39.

[862] *Id.*

[863] SCO-006313 (Interview of Christopher Steele on Sept. 18, 2017) at 14.

[864] However, as discussed in more detail below, Danchenko told the FBI that his purported first contact with Millian was July 21, 2016. Since Danchenko was the only Orbis person who reported had contact with Millian, his contention that Millian could be a source for the Steele Report dated June 20, 2016 was an impossibility. SCO_105282 (CHS Reporting Document dated May 18, 2017).

[865] Transcript of meeting with Danchenko on May 18, 2017 at 25-27.

[866] *Id.* at 28.

When interviewed by the FBI in September 2017, Christopher Steele stated that "Source D" was in fact Sergei Millian, an individual who was in direct contact with his primary sub-source [Danchenko].[867] However, given that Danchenko repeatedly told the FBI that the *first* and *only* time he allegedly communicated with someone he thought was Millian was late July 2016 when he received an anonymous call from a male with a Russian accent, it would have been impossible for Millian to have been a source of the Ritz Carlton allegations (and other information) to Danchenko in June 2016. Thus, Danchenko's statements to the FBI about having no previous contact with Millian were false, or Danchenko's statements to Steele about Source D were false, or Steele gave knowingly false information to the FBI.[868]

The Office found the general manager's statement that he never met with Danchenko to be credible, especially in light of his well-spoken, thoughtful demeanor, and his confidence in his recollections.

Based on the above analysis, the only person who met with both Danchenko and the Ritz Carlton general manager (and the other managers) during the June Planning Trip was Dolan.

The same Steele Report (2016/080) that contained the Ritz Carlton allegations also contained the following allegation:

> Continuing on this theme, Source G, a senior Kremlin official, confided that the CLINTON dossier was controlled exclusively by senior Kremlin spokesman, Dimitry PESKOV, on the direct instructions of Putin himself. The dossier had not been made available, as yet, inter alia, to any foreigners, including TRUMP and his inner circle. However, PUTIN's intentions with regard to the dossier and future dissemination remained unclear.[869]

When interviewed by the FBI in September 2017, Steele identified "Source G" as Alexey Pavlov[870] – the Deputy Press Secretary for the Russian Presidential Administration. Steele stated, in sum, that this information was collected by his primary sub-source (Danchenko) during a trip to Russia, which, given the date of the Report, would coincide with his June 2016 trip and Dolan's June Planning Trip.

The FBI appears to have never addressed this particular allegation with Danchenko or explored whether Danchenko maintained a relationship with Alexey Pavlov. The Office has not seen any independent evidence to indicate that Danchenko had a relationship with Pavlov. As discussed above, Dolan, however, did have a relationship with Pavlov. Leading up to the June Planning Trip, Dolan attempted to contact Pavlov on several occasions.[871] Dolan, however, stated that he could not recall if he connected with Pavlov prior to or during the June Planning

---

[867] SCO-006313 (Interview of Christopher Steele on Sept. 18, 2017 at 14).

[868] As discussed below, the Crossfire Hurricane team appears to have never endeavored to resolve this question.

[869] SCO-105084 (Documents Known to the FBI Comprising the "Steele Dossier") at 4, (Company Intelligence Report 2016/080).

[870] SCO-006313 (Interview of Christopher Steele on Sept. 18, 2017) at 14.

[871] SCO-005678 (Email from Dolan dated 06/03/2016); SCID_00000790 (Email from Dolan to Galkina dated 06/14/2016).

Trip.[872] In light of these facts, there appears to be a real likelihood that Dolan was the actual source of much of the Ritz Carlton and Pavlov information contained in the Steele Reports.

v. *Dolan returns to Cyprus in July 2016*

Following the June Planning Trip, Dolan returned to Washington, D.C. where he continued to communicate with both Danchenko and Galkina. In July 2016, Dolan returned to Cyprus to meet with Galkina, Gubarev and other executives at Servers.com.[873] Curiously, Steele was in Cyprus at the same time Dolan was meeting with Galkina and others in Cyprus.[874]

During this July trip and continuing through the fall of 2016, Dolan and Galkina communicated regularly via telephone, email and social media. In several of these communications, Dolan and Galkina discussed their political views, support for Clinton, and Galkina's future employment. For example, during the July 2016 meetings in Cyprus, Dolan gave Galkina an autobiography of Clinton, which he signed and inscribed with the handwritten message, "To my good friend Olga, A Great Democrat."[875] On July 13, 2016, Galkina sent a message to a Russia-based associate and stated that Dolan had written a letter to Dimitry Peskov, the Russian Press Secretary, in support of Galkina's candidacy for a position in the Russian Presidential Administration.[876] In his interviews with the Office, Dolan did not recall the specific position Galkina was referring to, and noted that it was "possible" that he reached out to Peskov on behalf of Galkina, but had no specific recollection of doing so.[877]

On July 22, 2016, Dolan sent an email to Galkina and informed her that he would be attending a reception for Hillary Clinton. Shortly thereafter, Galkina responded: "[T]ell her please she [Clinton] has a big fan in [city name], Cyprus. Can I please ask you to sign for me her (anything)."[878] In August 2016, Galkina sent a message to a Russia-based associate describing Dolan as an "advisor" to Hillary Clinton.[879] Galkina further commented regarding what might happen if Clinton were to win the U.S. presidential election, stating in Russian, "[W]hen Dolan takes me off to the State Department [to handle] issues of the former USSR, then we'll see who is looking good and who is not."[880] In September 2016, Galkina made a similar comment in a

---

[872] OSC Report of Interview of Charles Dolan on Aug. 31, 2021 at 4; OSC Report of Interview of Charles Dolan on Sept. 7, 2021 at 2.

[873] OSC Report of Interview of Charles Dolan on Aug. 31, 2021 at 3; *Danchenko* Tr. 10/13/2022 AM at 614:3-17.

[874] Doc. ID 0.7.23326.102657 (Email from Steele to Bruce Ohr dated 07/01/2016). As discussed more below, SA Kevin Helson speculated that Charles Dolan may have directly communicated with Christopher Steele. The Office, however, uncovered no evidence to support this speculation.

[875] SCO-002223 (Galkina Facebook messages dated 07/21/2016).

[876] SCO-002228 (Galkina Facebook messages dated 07/13/2016).

[877] OSC Report of Interview of Charles Dolan on Nov. 1, 2021 at 2.

[878] SCO_002190 (Email from Galkina to Dolan dated July 22, 2016)

[879] SCO_002235 (Galkina Facebook messages dated Aug. 21, 2016).

[880] *Id.*

message to the same associate, stating in Russian that Dolan would "take me to the State Department if Hillary wins."[881]

On October 15, 2016, Galkina communicated with a Russia-based journalist and stated that because of her [Galkina] "acquaintance with Chuck Dolan and several citizens from the Russian presidential administration," Galkina knew "something and can tell a little about it by voice."[882]

On November 7, 2016 (the day before the 2016 U.S. Presidential election), Galkina emailed Dolan in English and stated, in part:

> I am preparing you some information on former USSR/UIC countries, Igor [Danchenko] possibly told you about that . . . . Tomorrow your country is having a great day, so, as a big Hillary fan, I wish her and all her supporters to have a Victory day. Hope, that someday her book will have one more autograph on it).
>
> Thank you for your help and support,
>
> Best regards,
>
> Olga[883]

When initially interviewed by the Office, Dolan stated that Galkina was the "last person" with whom he would ever discuss U.S. politics.[884] However, in a subsequent interview when confronted with emails and social media messages with Galkina evincing communications about Clinton and the 2016 U.S. presidential election, Dolan admitted that he had some discussions with Galkina about the 2016 election and her support for Clinton.[885] However, in an August 2017 FBI interview, Galkina stated, in sum, that she discussed some of the information contained in the Steele Reports with Dolan.[886] Despite Galkina's identification of Dolan as someone with whom she discussed the Steele Reports, and the fact that Dolan resided in the Washington, D.C. area, the FBI failed to interview Dolan about Galkina's statements concerning the Steele Reports.

vi.   Dolan is a source for certain information in a Steele Report

At least one allegation contained in a Steele Report dated August 22, 2016 (2016/105), reflected information that Danchenko collected directly from Charles Dolan. In particular, that Report detailed the August 2016 resignation of Trump's campaign manager Manafort and his allegedly strained relationship with Corey Lewandowski. The allegation in the Steele Report stated:

---

[881] SCO_002238 (Galkina Facebook messages dated Sept. 2, 2016).

[882] SCO_076721 (Galkina Facebook messages dated Oct. 15, 2016).

[883] SCID_00001417 (Email from Galkina to Dolan dated 11/07/2016).

[884] OSC Report of Interview of Charles Dolan on Aug. 31, 2021 at 3.

[885] OSC Report of Interview of Charles Dolan on Nov. 1, 2021 at 2.

[886] *Danchenko* Tr. 10/14/2022 AM at 977:3-13.

Close associate of TRUMP explains reasoning behind MANAFORT's recent resignation. Ukraine revelations played part but others wanted MANAFORT out for various reasons, especially LEWANDOWSKI who remains influential . . . . Speaking separately, also in late August 2016, an American political figure associated with Donald TRUMP and his campaign outlined the reasons behind MANAFORT's recent demise. S/he said it was true that the Ukraine corruption revelations had played a part in this, but also, several senior players close to TRUMP had wanted MANAFORT out, primarily to loosen his control on strategy and policy formulation. Of particular importance in this regard was MANAFORT's predecessor as campaign manager, Corey LEWANDOWSKI, who hated MANAFORT personally and remained close to TRUMP with whom he discussed the presidential campaign on a regular basis.[887]

This Steele Report contained information that Danchenko had gathered directly from Dolan in response to a specific request. In particular, on August 19, 2016, Danchenko emailed Dolan to solicit any "thought, rumor, or allegation" about Paul Manafort. In the email, Danchenko also informed Dolan that he (Danchenko) was working on a "project against Trump":

Could you please ask someone to comment on Paul Manafort's resignation and anything on Trump campaign? Off the record of course! Any thought, rumor, allegation. I am working on a related project against Trump. I asked [U.S. Person-2]] three months ago but he didn't say much although shared a couple of valuable insights.

Thanks a lot!

Best,

Igor[888]

Danchenko referenced U.S. Person-2, a Republican lobbyist and acquaintance of Dolan, who was present at the meeting between Dolan and Galkina in March 2016 regarding the proposed business venture between kglobal and Servers.com. In connection with a voluntary interview by the Office, U.S. Person-2 provided an email which appears to be referenced by Danchenko above, which stated, in part:

I have a question about Viktor Yanukovich and Dmitry Firtash, former Ukrainian president and former gas oligarch respectively, and some Russian oligarchs. The relationship is mentioned, for example here [internet address].

My question is:

My friends in England [in context, Steele] have heard that a number of oligarchs, including Oleg Deripaska, Suleiman Kerimov and Dmitry Firtash made certain investments in the U.S. real estate, maybe other sectors . . . And that then they made various "loans," "good will payments" etc., coincidently in the summer of 2008, just in the run up to the presidential election, where Mr. Manafort and also

---

[887] SCO-105084 (Documents Known to the FBI Comprising the "Steele Dossier") at 18-19, (Company Intelligence Report 2016/105) (capitalization in original).

[888] SCID_00006671 (Email from Danchenko to Dolan dated 08/19/2016).

Richard Davis were working for the Republican candidate. Was that the case? What were they trying to achieve? Can these payments- if existed – be viewed as political contributions? I understand it is a sensitive question. I'll be happy to discuss it or other perhaps more general things over a coffee at any time. At my end, I'll be happy to share insights on Russia/FSU.

Thanks a lot!

Kind Regards,

Igor[889]

When interviewed by the FBI in September 2017, Steele stated that his initial entrée into U.S. election-related material dealt with Paul Manafort's connections to Russian and Ukrainian oligarchs. In particular, Steele told the FBI that Manafort owed significant money to these oligarchs and several other Russians.[890] At this time, Steele was working for a different client, Russian oligarch Oleg Deripaska, often referred to as "Putin's Oligarch" in media reporting, on a separate litigation-related issue.[891] This information comports with Danchenko's inquiries to U.S. Person-2 in April 2016. As mentioned above, U.S. Person-2's name was provided by Steele during his October 2016 interview with the FBI as an individual who would have information regarding Trump's connections to Russia.

In any event, on August 19th, Dolan replied to Danchenko, stating in part:

Let me dig around on Manafort. Pretty sure the new team wanted him gone asap and used today's NYT story to drive a stake in his heart.[892]

On August 20, 2016, Dolan emailed Danchenko the following:

Hi Igor:

I had a drink with a GOP friend of mine who knows some of the players and got some of what is in this article, which provides even more detail. She also told me that Corey Lewandowski, who hates Manafort and still speaks to Trump regularly played a role. He is said to be doing a happy dance over it. I think the bottom line is that in addition to the Ukraine revelations, a number of people wanted Manafort gone. It is a very sharp elbows crowd.[893]

Dolan attached to the email a link to a *Politico* news article that discussed Manafort's resignation as Trump's campaign manager.[894] Later that day, Danchenko replied to Dolan

---

[889] SCO-061675 (Email from Danchenko to U.S. Person-2 dated 04/18/2016).

[890] SCO-006313 (Interview of Christopher Steele on Sept. 18, 2017) at 6.

[891] Kenneth P. Vogel & Matthew Rosenberg, *Agents Tried to Flip Russian Oligarchs. The Fallout Spread to Trump*, N.Y. Times (Sept. 1, 2018).

[892] SCID_00000936 (Email from Dolan to Danchenko dated 08/19/2016).

[893] SCID_00000941 (Email from Dolan to Danchenko dated 08/20/2016).

[894] Kenneth P. Vogel & Marc Caputo, *Inside the fall of Paul Manafort*, Politico (Aug. 19, 2016).

expressing his appreciation for the information, and stating that their "goals clearly coincide[d]" with regard to Danchenko's efforts to gather derogatory information about Trump.

> Dear Chuck,
>
> Thank you for this. Any additional insights will be much appreciated. It is an important project for me, and our goals clearly coincide. I've been following the Russia trail in Trump's campaign. It is there so what you read in the news is hardly an exaggeration. Some things are less dramatic while others are more than they seem.[895]

Dolan replied to Danchenko with the following: "Thanks! I'll let you know if I hear anything else."[896]

Dolan provided this information regarding Manafort to Danchenko two days before it appeared in the August 22, 2016 Steele Report (2016/105). As reflected above, the information provided by Dolan was substantially the same as the information contained in that Steele Report. In particular: (i) Dolan claimed to have received the information from a "GOP friend," whom the Steele Report describes as a "close associate of Trump"; (ii) in his email, Dolan referred to "Ukraine revelations" about Manafort, which the Steele Report also refers to as the "Ukraine corruption revelations"; (iii) Dolan's email stated that "a number of people wanted Manafort gone," and the Steele Report similarly stated that "several senior players close to TRUMP had wanted Manafort out"; and (iv) Dolan's email stated that "Corey Lewandowski, who hates Manafort and still speaks to Trump regularly played a role" in Manafort's departure, and the Steele Report similarly stated that Manafort's departure was due to "Corey Lewandowski, who hated Manafort personally and remained close to TRUMP."

When interviewed by the Office, Dolan later acknowledged that he never met with a "GOP friend" in relation to the information that he passed to Danchenko but, rather, fabricated the fact of the meeting in his communications with Danchenko.[897] Dolan instead obtained the information about Manafort from public news sources.[898]

According to Dolan, he was not aware at the time of the specifics of Danchenko's "project against Trump," or that Danchenko's reporting would later appear in the Steele Reports.[899] Dolan agreed that the information about Manafort contained in Steele Report 2016/105 appeared to be based on the information he provided to Danchenko.[900] Dolan, however, denied that he had knowingly provided any additional information to Danchenko that appeared in the Steele Reports, but acknowledged that it was possible that he could have been an

---

[895] SCID_00006677 (Email from Danchenko to Dolan dated 08/20/2016).

[896] SCID_00000938 (Email from Dolan to Danchenko dated 08/20/2016).

[897] OSC Report of Interview of Charles Dolan on Nov. 1, 2021 at 3.

[898] *Id.*

[899] OSC Report of Interview of Charles Dolan on Nov. 1, 2021 at 1; OSC Report of Interview of Charles Dolan on Aug. 31, 2021 at 7; *Danchenko* Tr. 10/13/2022 AM at 641.

[900] OSC Report of Interview of Charles Dolan on Sept. 7, 2021 at 2.

unwitting source for the Reports.[901] Nevertheless, as discussed below, Dolan appears to have had access to substantially similar information to that which would later appear in other Steele Reports as well.

vii. The Kalugin allegation in Steele Report 2016/111

For example, in connection with the YPO Conference, Dolan and U.S. Person-1 met with Russian Ambassador Sergei Kislyak and Russian diplomat Kalugin, the head of the Russian Embassy's Economic Section in Washington. These meetings took place in May, July, and October 2016.[902] According to Dolan, Danchenko was not present at these meetings.[903] Following the meeting on May 31, 2016, a member of Kalugin's staff, Maria Antonova, sent an email to Dolan and U.S. Person-1 telling them that, among other things, Kalugin would be returning to Moscow in September 2016 and would be replaced by another diplomat, Andrey Bondarev. Specifically, Antonova wrote:

> Mikhail [Kalugin] assumes that the right contact point at the MFA could be Mr. Andrey Bondarev who is the Deputy Head of Economic Section at the Ministry's Department of North America. Andrey will be replacing Mikhail here as the Head of Economic Office this September so it may be useful to start working with him now. Though, we need to double-check first whether he will be in Moscow during your visit. We will get back to you when we have a reply.[904]

Danchenko was not a recipient of the email. On August 19, 2016, Kalugin sent an email to Dolan and others. The email stated, in part:

> Dear Colleagues and Friends,
>
> After six years of Foreign Service in Washington, it feels very timely now to bid farewell and go back home to Moscow for embarking on my new endeavors.
>
> [...]
>
> Let me also take this opportunity and introduce you [to] the new Head of Economic Office, Counselor Mr. Andrey Bondarev. Many of you may remember that Mr. Bondarev since his previous appointment at the Embassy a couple of years ago. Andrey is a talented diplomat and economist with impressive experience in American studies. I'm glad to leave you in a such a good company and have no doubts that you will find common ground very soon.[905]

Again, Danchenko was not a recipient of this email.

---

[901] OSC Report of Interview of Charles Dolan on Nov. 1, 2021 at 3.

[902] SCID_00016319 (Email from U.S. Person-1 to Dolan, Kalugin, others dated 05/31/2016); SCID_00016626 (Email from U.S. Person-1 to Dolan, others dated 07/15/2016); SCID_00017124 (Email to Kalugin, U.S. Person-1, Dolan, others dated 10/14/2016).

[903] OSC Report of Interview of Charles Dolan on Nov. 1, 2021 at 1-2.

[904] SCID_00016319 (Email from U.S. Person-1 to Dolan, Kalugin, others dated 05/31/2016).

[905] SCO-002194 (Email from Kalugin to various recipients dated 08/19/2016).

A Steele Report dated September 14, 2016 (2016/111) contained the following allegation:

[S]peaking separately to the same compatriot, a senior Russian MFA official reported that as a prophylactic measure, a leading Russia diplomat, Mikhail Kalugin, had been withdrawn from Washington on short notice because Moscow feared his heavy involvement in the US presidential election operation, including the so-called veterans' pensions ruse (reported previously), would be exposed in the media there. His replacement, Andrei Bondarev however was clean in this regard.[906]

This allegation bore substantial similarities to information that Dolan received in May and August 2016 from Russian Embassy staffer Maria Antonova and Kalugin himself, insofar as Dolan was aware that Kalugin was being replaced by Bondarev. Further, records obtained by the Office revealed that Dolan reached out to Danchenko on September 13, 2016 – the day prior to the date of the Steele Report.[907] On the day of the call, Danchenko was initially in Russia but later traveled to London.[908]

When interviewed by the FBI in January 2017, Danchenko stated that he had known Kalugin since 2014.[909] Danchenko purported to learn the information about Kalugin's departure from Kalugin himself when the diplomat was allegedly assisting Danchenko in obtaining a new Russian passport. Danchenko further stated that Kalugin described his replacement, Andrey Bondarev, as a "bright young guy."[910] Danchenko also stated that his conversation with Kalugin took place in late spring 2016 – which also happened to be the same time in which Dolan received the email from Embassy staffer Maria Antonova, indicating that Kalugin was being replaced in the ordinary course.[911]

A review of Danchenko's phone records, emails and social media accounts do not indicate that Danchenko maintained a relationship with Kalugin. Moreover, during the January 2017 interviews, Danchenko provided the FBI with a business card for Kalugin.[912] The business card contained a handwritten cell phone number on the card. When interviewed by the Office, Dolan identified the handwriting on the business card as his own.[913]

When Steele was interviewed by the FBI in September 2017, he stated, in sum, that Danchenko told him that he (Danchenko) had learned of the Kalugin information after bumping

---

[906] SCO-105084 (Documents known to the FBI comprising the "Steele Dossier") at 20-22, (Company Intelligence Report 2016/111).

[907] AT&T Record dated 09/13/2016. (The records reflect a duration of only 16 seconds).

[908] SCO-007308 (Danchenko Facebook entry dated 09/13/2016).

[909] SCO-005801 (Interview of Igor Danchenko Electronic Communication dated 02/09/2017) at 25.

[910] Id. at 27-28.

[911] Id. at 26.

[912] SCO-005860 (Interview of Igor Danchenko Electronic Communication dated 02/09/2017 1A) at 4.

[913] OSC Report of Interview of Charles Dolan on Nov. 1, 2021 at 2.

154

into Kalugin on a Moscow street in August 2016 – which was the same time that Dolan received the email from Kalugin indicating that he was leaving for Moscow and being replaced by Andrey Bondarev.[914] However, the Office's investigation has revealed that Danchenko was present in the United States during the entire month of August 2016.[915]

Steele further told the FBI that the information contained in Report 2016/111 was derived from his primary sub-source's [Danchenko's] direct contact with multiple sub-sources.[916] These sub-sources included Alexey Pavlov [Deputy Press Secretary of the Russian Presidential Administration], senior Ministry of Foreign Affairs personnel, and two other unidentified individuals.[917] Steele did not identify the two other individuals. However, as noted above, (i) Charles Dolan maintained a relationship with Alexey Pavlov; (ii) had attempted to reach out to Pavlov in connection with the YPO Conference; and (iii) had met with two deputies from the Press Office during the June Planning Trip. Again, the Office found no evidence showing that Danchenko met directly with Pavlov or had previously maintained a relationship with Pavlov. Indeed, in the months leading up to the YPO conference, it was Dolan – not Danchenko – who had reached out to Pavlov on behalf of both YPO and Olga Galkina.[918] Dolan informed the Office that he would be surprised if Galkina had any contacts in the Kremlin.[919]

When initially interviewed by the Office, Dolan stated, in sum, that he was unsure if he told Danchenko about Kalugin being replaced by Bondarev, but that he had no specific recollection of doing so.[920] In a later interview, Dolan stated, in sum, that he believed there was a low probability that he mentioned the Kalugin departure to Danchenko, but that he could not completely rule out the possibility.[921]

Nevertheless, on February 9, 2018, Dolan sent the following email to three U.S.-based acquaintances:

> Dear boy – you must pay attention. Unlike your pal the short lived National Security Advisor General Flynn, I can remember meeting with Mr. Mikhail KULAGIN [sic][922] several times and would be happy to come forward with details to the FBI and others. There are several other

---

[914] SCO-006313 (Interview of Christopher Steele on Sept. 18, 2017) at 11, 16; SCO-002194 (Email from Kalugin dated 08/19/2016).

[915] U.S. Customs and Border Protection Person Encounter List for Igor Danchenko at 3.

[916] SCO-006313 (Interview of Christopher Steele on Sept. 18, 2017) at 17.

[917] Id.

[918] SCO-005678 (Email from Dolan dated 06/03/2016); SCID_00000776 (Email from Dolan to Galkina on 06/13/2016).

[919] OSC Report of Interview of Charles Dolan on Nov. 1, 2021 at 2.

[920] OSC Report of Interview of Charles Dolan on Sept. 7, 2021 at 2.

[921] OSC Report of Interview of Charles Dolan on Nov. 1, 2021 at 1-2.

[922] In Steele Report 2016/111 Mikhail Kalugin's name is misspelled as "Kulagin."

points in the dossier that are true! Let me know if you need additional clarification.[923]

Dolan attached to the email a BBC News article titled "Trump Russia dossier key claim 'verified.'" In the article, BBC journalist Paul Wood stated that "sources I know and trust have told me the US government identified Kalugin as a spy while he was still at the embassy."[924] In this email, Dolan appears to volunteer that he possesses inside information on the Steele Report allegations concerning Kalugin as well as other information pertaining to the veracity of additional Steele Report allegations.

viii.   *The Ivanov allegation contained in Steele Report 2016/111*

An additional allegation appearing in the same Steele Report as the Kalugin allegation (2016/111) concerned the firing of Sergei Ivanov, the then-chief of staff of the Russian Presidential Administration. The allegation stated, in part:

> PUTIN had been receiving conflicting advice on interfering from three separate and expert groups. On one side had been the Russian ambassador to the US, Sergei KISLYAK, and the Ministry of Foreign Affairs, together with an independent and informal network run by presidential foreign policy advisor, Yuri USHAKOV (KISLYAK's predecessor in Washington) who had urged caution and the potential negative impact on Russia from the operation/s. On the other side was former PA Head, Sergei IVANOV, backed by Russian Foreign Intelligence (SVR), who had advised PUTIN that the pro-TRUMP, anti-CLINTON operation/s would be both effective and plausibly deniable with little blowback. The first group/s had been proven right and this had been the catalyst in PUTIN's decision to sack IVANOV (unexpectedly) as PA Head in August. His successor, Anton VAINO, had been selected for the job partly because he had not been involved in the US presidential election operation/s.[925]

This allegation coincided with information that Dolan had received from Galkina regarding changes in the Russian Presidential Administration in the weeks prior to the issuance of Steele Report 2016/111. In particular, on August 12, 2016, the same day that Ivanov was reportedly fired, Galkina sent a Facebook message to Dolan stating, "Russian presidential administration is making significant changes right now."[926] Danchenko was not copied on this message. Minutes later, Dolan and Galkina spoke for approximately 10 minutes.[927] On September 13, 2016 – the

---

[923] KG_0002357 (Email from Dolan dated 02/09/2018).

[924] Paul Wood, *Trump Russia Dossier key claim 'Verified,'* BBC News (Mar. 30, 2017). https://www.bbc.com/news/world-us-canada-39435786.

[925] SCO-105084 (Documents Known to the FBI Comprising the "Steele Dossier") at 20-21, (Company Intelligence Report 2016/111) (capitalization in original).

[926] SCO-002232 (Facebook exchange between Dolan and Galkina dated 08/12/2016).

[927] SCO-101564 (Dolan Facebook entry dated 08/12/2016).

day prior to the date of the Steele Report containing the Ivanov allegation – Dolan called Danchenko.[928] As discussed above, at the time of this call, Danchenko was in Russia.

When interviewed by the FBI in January 2017, the FBI asked Danchenko about the sourcing of this allegation. Danchenko stated that he learned about the allegation involving Ivanov from Galkina and "two other friends."[929] According to the FBI's interview report, Danchenko did not identify the two other "friends," nor did he mention Dolan in connection with the allegation.[930] The FBI interview report does not state whether Danchenko was asked to provide the names of the "two other friends."

When interviewed by the FBI in September 2017, Steele stated that the information in this Report was derived from Danchenko's direct contact with multiple sub-sources, including Alexey Pavlov.[931]

When interviewed by the Office, Dolan initially stated that he never discussed Russian politics with Galkina.[932] When confronted with the Facebook exchange regarding the shakeup in the Russian Presidential Administration, Dolan stated that it was "possible" that he had spoken with Galkina about Ivanov being fired, but, again, had no specific recollection of doing so.[933]

ix. The YPO Conference – October 2016

On September 30, 2016, U.S. Person-1 sent Dolan the final draft agenda for the YPO Conference.[934] Dolan replied "Thanks – will send to Peskov."[935] Thereafter, in early October 2016, Dolan and Danchenko made their way separately to Moscow for the YPO Conference. During the January 2017 interviews, Danchenko informed the FBI that he did not collect any information for Steele during the YPO conference.[936] Steele, however, told the FBI that, in fact, two reports (2016/130 and 2016/132) were comprised of information that Danchenko purported to gather during the YPO Conference.[937]

In any event, the YPO Conference featured several Russian government officials including Konstantin Kosachev, a senior member of the Russian Duma (parliament) and Mikhail Kalugin, a member of the Russian Ministry of Foreign Affairs (and, as discussed above, formerly

---

[928] AT&T Record dated 09/13/2016. (The records reflect a duration of only 16 seconds).

[929] SCO-005801 (Interview of Igor Danchenko Electronic Communication dated 02/09/17) at 45.

[930] Id.

[931] SCO-006313 (Interview of Christopher Steele on Sept. 18, 2017) at 17.

[932] OSC Report of Interview of Charles Dolan on Aug. 31, 2021 at 3.

[933] OSC Report of Interview of Charles Dolan on Nov. 1, 2021 at 2.

[934] SCID_00007020 (Email from U.S. Person-1 to Dolan dated 09/30/2016).

[935] SCID_00001127 (Email from Dolan to U.S. Person-1 dated 09/30/2016).

[936] SCO-005801 (Interview of Igor Danchenko Electronic Communication dated 02/09/2017) at 49-50.

[937] SCO-006313 (Interview of Christopher Steele on Sept. 18, 2017) at 18-19.

assigned to the Russian Embassy in Washington).[938] Andrei Bondarev, another member of the Russian Ministry of Foreign Affairs (and, as discussed above, the diplomat who replaced Kalugin in Washington), was listed as a point of contact for the conference.[939] Dolan informed the Office that during the conference he sat next to Kosachev.[940] A Steele Report dated October 20, 2016 (2016/136) – less than two weeks after the YPO Conference – contained the following allegation:

> The Kremlin insider went on to identify leading pro-PUTIN Duma figure, Konstantin KOSACHEV (Head of the Foreign Relations Committee) as an important figure in the TRUMP campaign-Kremlin liaison operation. KOSACHEV, also "plausibly deniable" being part of the Russian legislature rather than executive, had facilitated the contact in Prague and by implication, may have attended the meeting/s with COHEN there in August.[941]

During the January 2017 interviews, Danchenko stated the information in the Steele Reports related to Cohen and Prague came from Galkina.[942] This is consistent with what Steele informed the FBI during his September 2017 interview.[943] However, as discussed more below, when interviewed by the FBI in August 2017, Galkina denied knowing anything about a Cohen meeting in Prague.[944] Indeed, the FBI found no evidence that Cohen had met Russian officials in Prague.[945]

x. Dolan's contact with Danchenko following the YPO Conference

Upon returning from the YPO Conference in early October 2016, Dolan and Danchenko continued to communicate. On October 8, 2016, Danchenko traveled from Moscow to London to meet with Christopher Steele.[946] On October 9, 2016, Danchenko asked Dolan – who was still in Moscow – to purchase medication for him from a Russian pharmacy.[947] Dolan agreed that he would collect the medicine and deliver it to Danchenko when he (Dolan) returned to

---

[938] SCID_00007020 (Email from U.S. Person-1 to Dolan dated 09/30/2016) at 4.

[939] SCID_00016533 (Email from U.S. Person-1 dated 07/09/2016) at 11.

[940] OSC Report of Interview of Charles Dolan on Sept. 7, 2021 at 2.

[941] SCO-105084 (Documents Known to the FBI Comprising the "Steele Dossier") at 33, (Company Intelligence Report 2016/136).

[942] SCO-005801 (Interview of Igor Danchenko Electronic Communication dated 02/09/2017) at 30-33.

[943] SCO-006313 (Interview of Christopher Steele on Sept. 18, 2017) at 19-20.

[944] SCO-FBIPROD_022241 (Debriefing of Olga Galkina dated 08/26/2017) at 3.

[945] *See Redacted OIG Review* at 196.

[946] SCO-007318 (Danchenko Facebook entries dated 10/08/2016); SCO-005801 (Interview of Igor Danchenko Electronic Communication dated 02/09/2017) at 49-50.

[947] SCO-101469 (Facebook exchange between Dolan and Danchenko dated 10/09/2016).

Washington, D.C.[948] Thereafter, on October 18, 2016, Danchenko and Dolan met at kglobal's office in Washington, ostensibly for Danchenko to secure the medication from Dolan.[949]

The day following this meeting at kglobal, two Steele Reports were generated (2016/135 and 2016/136). These reports alleged, among other things, that Cohen was heavily engaged in covering up Trump's ties to Russia, and specifically, to contain further scandals involving Manafort and Page. As discussed above, this Report 2016/136 also contains reference to Konstatin Kosachev. In the January 2017 interviews, Danchenko attributed this information to Galkina. Again, Galkina told the FBI that she was not aware of Cohen's alleged meeting in Prague.

Later, on November 3, 2016, Dolan and Danchenko met for lunch in Washington, D.C.[950] After that, on New Year's Day 2017, Danchenko and Dolan met in a park in Arlington, Virginia.[951] When asked about the circumstances of this meeting, Dolan informed the Office, in sum, that he was looking at Facebook and he noticed that Danchenko had posted a picture with his daughter in the park.[952] Dolan stated that since the park was close to his house, he decided to drive over to meet Danchenko.[953]

On the evening of January 10, 2017, Buzzfeed became the first media outlet to publish the Steele Reports.[954] On the morning of January 11, 2017, Dolan called Danchenko.[955] Dolan stated that he called Danchenko because he had suspicions that Danchenko was behind the Steele Reports based on the fact that, among other things, he learned "it was a London operation" and he knew that Danchenko did due diligence work for Orbis, which was based in London.[956] Dolan also thought Galkina might have been a source for Danchenko given her employment at Servers.com.[957] During the call, Danchenko told Dolan, in sum, that he did not know who was behind the reports, but that he would let Dolan know if he came across any information.[958]

---

[948] *Id.* at 1.

[949] *Id.* at 3.

[950] SCO-101471 (Facebook exchange between Dolan and Danchenko dated 11/02/2016).

[951] SCO-101472 (Facebook exchange between Dolan and Danchenko dated 01/01/2017).

[952] OSC Report of Interview of Charles Dolan on Nov. 1, 2021 at 3.

[953] *Id.*

[954] Ken Bensinger, Miriam Elder & Mark Schoofs, *These Reports Allege Trump Has Deep Ties to Russia*, Buzzfeed (Jan. 10, 2017).

[955] AT&T Record dated 01/11/2017.

[956] *Danchenko* Tr. 10/13/2022 AM at 635; OSC Report of Interview of Charles Dolan on Sept. 7, 2021 at 1.

[957] *Danchenko* Tr. 10/13/2022 AM at 635; OSC Report of Interview of Charles Dolan on Sept. 7, 2021 at 2.

[958] *Danchenko* Tr. 10/13/2022 AM at 635; OSC Report of Interview of Charles Dolan on Sept. 7, 2021 at 1.

According to Dolan, the January 11, 2017 call was the last time he had contact with Danchenko.[959]

On January 13, 2017, Dolan emailed a U.S.-based acquaintance the following:

> I've been interviewed by the Washington Post and the London Times - three times over the last two days over the MI-6 Dossier on Trump and I know the Russian agent who made the report (He used to work for me). My client in Cyprus has been accused of being the party that organized the hacking. Presently speaking with the barrister in London who is filing a brief against Former British intelligence officer Christopher Steele has been unmasked as <u>the man behind an explosive</u> dossier about <u>US president-elect</u> <u>Donald Trump</u>. Also, in conversation with former British Ambassador who knows Steele. Quite right- Oh what a boring life.[960]

At the time the email was sent, Danchenko was not publicly known to be a source for Steele. When asked by the Office why he referred to Danchenko as a "Russian agent," Dolan initially said that he was being facetious, but then also elaborated that he had suspicions about Danchenko's ties to Russian intelligence.[961]

e. The FBI's failure to investigate Charles Dolan's role as a possible source for the Steele Reports

Information from four Steele Reports (2016/080, 2016/94, 2016/095 and 2016/102) was included in the four FISA applications targeting Page. As discussed above, the FBI was not able to corroborate a single substantive allegation in the Steele Reports. Nevertheless, the Steele Reports would form the foundation for the narrative that a U.S. presidential campaign was actively engaged in "a well-developed conspiracy of co-operation" with a foreign adversary. Danchenko was the primary source of information for this narrative that was weaved throughout the Steele Reports. Indeed, as noted earlier,[962] in his own words to an acquaintance, Danchenko stated that he "collected some 80% of [the] raw intel and [performed] half the analysis for the Chris Steele Dossier."[963] Accordingly, Danchenko's relationship with Dolan and Dolan's proximity to key figures and events that appear in the Steele Reports should have been an ample basis to, at a minimum, interview Dolan. However, as discussed below, Dolan was never interviewed, despite the suggestion from both Steele and Galkina that Dolan could have information related to the Steele Reports and the detailed analysis undertaken by two FBI personnel assigned to the Mueller team.

i. Danchenko's hesitancy to speak to the FBI about Charles Dolan

Danchenko did not mention Dolan to the FBI during the January 2017 interviews, despite revealing his (Danchenko's) participation in the YPO Conference in October 2016. Further, in a

---

[959] *Danchenko* Tr. 10/13/2022 AM at 636, 653.

[960] SCO-002217 (Email from Dolan dated 01/13/2017) (underline in original).

[961] OSC Report of Interview of Charles Dolan on Sept. 7, 2021 at 1-2.

[962] *See* footnote 701.

[963] *Danchenko* Government Exhibit 1502.

June 15, 2017 interview with Helson – which in part focused on Dolan – Danchenko only revealed that he was present with Dolan during the YPO Conference in October 2016.[964] Notably, Danchenko did not inform the FBI that he met with Dolan in Moscow during the June Planning Trip; a material omission given the fact that, according to Steele, Danchenko was collecting information for Steele during that trip.

In a June 2017 interview, Danchenko was also asked if he had spoken to Dolan regarding any allegations contained in the Steele Reports. Danchenko denied that Dolan provided any specific information related to the Steele Reports. In particular, when Helson mentioned Dolan's name during a conversation about individuals who may have contributed to the Steele Reports, the following exchange, in part, occurred:

Helson: Um, because obviously I don't think you're the only . . .

Danchenko: Mm-hmm.

Helson: Person that has been contributing. You may have said one - and this is the other thing we are trying to figure out. [...]

Helson: Do you know a Chuck Dolan?

Danchenko: Do I know Chuck Dolan? Yeah.

Helson: How long have you known him?

     [laughing]

     [approximately 15 second pause]

Danchenko: I've known Chuck for [pause] I don't know, a couple years maybe.

Helson: Couple years?

Danchenko: But but but but but but but I've known of him for like 12 years.

Helson: Okay.

Danchenko: Uh, 11 years. Because he'd always come to Russia and Ru-Russian – Russian [UI] when he worked for Ketchum.

Helson: Okay.

Danchenko: In like 2006, 2007.

Helson: So that was how far back?

Danchenko: Yeah, when . . .

Helson: And that was with Ketchum?

Danchenko: when – you know – well . . .

Helson: Okay.

Danchenko: uh, Russia organized the G20 and he was on – he worked with Ketchum on the – on the – on Russia power.

---

[964] Transcript of June 15, 2017 interview of Danchenko at 42-44.

Helson:	That would make sense.
Danchenko:	But he's a very nice guy.
Helson:	Yes.
Danchenko:	Yeah. Yeah he likes Russia. I don't think he is uh – would be any way be involved. But-but-uh-b-but he's uh [UI] what I would think would be easily played. Maybe. Uh, he's a bit naïve in his, um liking of Russia.
Helson:	Okay, so you've had . . . was there any . . . but you had never talked to Chuck about anything that showed up in the dossier right?
Danchenko:	No.
Helson:	You don't think so?
Danchenko:	No. We talked about, you know, related issues perhaps but no, no, no, nothing specific.[965]

In a later part of the conversation, Danchenko informed Helson that Dolan had conducted business with Olga Galkina and Servers.com and that Dolan maintained a professional friendship with Dimitry Peskov, the Russian PA Press Secretary.[966] In his FBI reporting document detailing this interview, Helson observed that Danchenko was "hesitant" about acknowledging his association with Dolan.[967] Indeed, when interviewed by the OIG in October 2018, Helson stated that in the course of his meetings with Danchenko, "When I brought up Charles [Dolan] it was very gray, not complete."[968]

Following the June 15, 2017 interview, Helson raised Dolan's name on several other occasions. For example, in an interview on October 23, 2017, Danchenko provided the names of several individuals, including Dolan, who concerned Danchenko because of their relationship with the Russian government.[969] Danchenko characterized Dolan as having too many dubious connections to Russian government officials, including Dimitry Peskov and Alexey Pavlov.[970] Additionally, in a December 20, 2018 interview, Danchenko stated that Dolan had shared emails about Manafort's ties to Russia and Ukraine. Danchenko also stated that U.S. Person-2 was someone who may have known about his (Danchenko's) work on the Steele Reports, because Dolan would have confided in U.S. Person-2 about Danchenko.[971] Helson documented the content of this meeting in an FBI reporting document; however, Danchenko provided no further information or context about Dolan or U.S. Person-2.

---

[965] *Id.* at 40-42.

[966] *Id.* at 43-45.

[967] SCO_105284 (CHS Reporting Document dated 06/15/2017).

[968] OIG Report of Interview of Kevin Helson on Oct. 31, 2018 at 147-48.

[969] SCO_105285 (CHS Reporting Document dated 10/23/2017).

[970] S-00081750-R-026 (CHS Reporting Document dated 10-23-2017) at 1.

[971] S-00081750-R-059 (CHS Reporting Document dated 01/04/2019) at 2.

ii. The FBI's failure to interview Charles Dolan

As discussed above, Dolan first came to the attention of Crossfire Hurricane investigators during Steele's October 2016 interview in Rome.[972] Following that meeting, the Crossfire Hurricane personnel prepared a background report on Dolan.[973] Steele again raised Dolan during a September 2017 interview with the FBI when he indicated that at least one allegation in his reporting was sourced to Dolan.[974] Notwithstanding Steele's October 2016 statements about Dolan, the FBI did not question Danchenko during the January 2017 interviews about Dolan or any of the other U.S. citizens that Steele suggested might have information about Trump and Russia.

iii. The FBI learns of Dolan's relationship with Olga Galkina

In the January 2017 interviews, Danchenko informed the FBI that Galkina was a source for several of the allegations contained in the Steele Reports.[975] As testimony in the *Danchenko* trial detailed, following this revelation, in the Spring of 2017, the FBI began to review its databases for information related to Galkina. From its review, the FBI learned, among other things, that (i) Galkina maintained a relationship with Charles Dolan, and (ii) Galkina had met with Dolan, Danchenko and others in Washington, D.C. in March 2016 to discuss a business relationship between Servers.com and kglobal.[976] As discussed more fully below, beginning in the fall of 2017, Mueller Analyst-1, whose assignment was to find corroborating information for the Steele reporting, drafted a lengthy memorandum outlining the FBI's holdings on Galkina as they related to the Steele Reports. Dolan featured prominently in this memorandum because of his connections to, among others, Galkina, Danchenko, and Dimitry Peskov and his work for Servers.com.

Based on the information detailed above, in the late spring and early summer 2017, the FBI began to investigate what, if any, role Dolan played vis-à-vis the Steele Reports. To that end, on June 12, 2017, Auten, who at that time was a member of the Mueller Special Counsel team, sent an email to Helson, another Mueller team member ("Mueller Supervisory Special Agent-1") and others, stating, in part:

Some thoughts –

1. I'm not sure [Danchenko] has ever mentioned his connections with Dolan.

2. I'm positive Danchenko never mentioned that he'd done limiting [*sic*] consulting for Servers.com (i.e. putting Dolan in touch)

---

[972] SCO-020139 (Email from Auten to Supervisory Special Agent-1, Moffa, Strzok & others dated 10/04/2016).

[973] FBI-0040963 (Intelligence Memo dated 10/06/2016).

[974] SCO-006313 (Interview of Christopher Steele on Sept. 18, 2017) at 3, 16-17.

[975] SCO-005801 (Interview of Igor Danchenko Electronic Communication dated 02/09/2017) at 13-16.

[976] *Danchenko* Tr. 10/14/2022 AM at 946, 948-49.

3. As Dolan is tied to Peskov and Presidential Administration press/communications, who is to say that he vs. Galkina is the "true" subsource for Peskov and PA-related reporting in [Steele].

4. Can we run Dolan through unattrib open source to see if he's done any oppositional political research, etc?

The path of information could have been:

Kremlin → Galkina →[Danchenko] →[Steele]; or,

Kremlin → Dolan → Galkina → [Danchenko] → [Steele]; or,

Kremlin → Dolan → [Danchenko] → [Steele][977]

Three days later, on June 15, 2017, Helson became the first FBI employee to ask Danchenko about his relationship with Dolan – despite the fact that the Crossfire Hurricane team was aware of Dolan's potential connections to the Steele Reports as far back as October 2016 and their direct interactions with Danchenko since January 2017.[978]

iv. Helson requests to interview Charles Dolan

Given Danchenko's reluctance to speak about Dolan and information learned from the Mueller Special Counsel team, Helson concluded that an interview of Dolan was a logical investigative step. However, when Helson raised this prospect with the Mueller Special Counsel team, he was explicitly told not to interview Dolan. Helson expressed confidence that Auten was the individual who told Helson to "hold off" on interviewing Dolan.[979] When interviewed by the Office, Auten did not have a recollection of telling Helson not to interview Dolan.[980]

During a July 27, 2021 interview with the Office, Helson stated he aggressively "pushed" the Dolan information to the Mueller Special Counsel team but received very little feedback.[981] Helson believed that Mueller Special Counsel attorney Andrew Weissman and a female attorney he was unfamiliar with were present for at least one briefing Helson provided to the Mueller team in which he shared information regarding Dolan.[982] Helson also stated, in sum, that Dolan should have been further investigated in connection with the Steele Reports, or at a minimum, interviewed, based on the information that was available to the FBI at that time.[983]

In December 2017, Helson shared his concerns about Dolan with Mueller Supervisory Special Agent-1 and Mueller Analyst-1, both part of the Mueller Special Counsel team. For

---

[977] FBI-AAA-02-0032414 (Email from Auten to WFO Analyst-1, Helson, Mueller Supervisory Special Agent-1 & Analyst-2 dated 06/12/2017).

[978] Transcript of June 15, 2017 interview of Danchenko at 42.

[979] OSC Report of Interview of Kevin Helson on July 27, 2021 at 3.

[980] OSC Report of Interview of Brian Auten on July 26, 2021 at 20, 22, 25.

[981] OSC Report of Interview of Kevin Helson on July 27, 2021 at 3.

[982] *Id.* at 1.

[983] *Id.* at 1-7.

example, on December 21, 2017, in an FBI Lync chat with Mueller Analyst-1, Helson wrote "I really don't like that guy [Dolan]" and that he (Helson) was "fighting to get them [Mueller Team] interested in what I have here," referring to Dolan.[984] In the same chat, Helson informed Mueller Analyst-1 that he would "keep talking to him [Danchenko] about CD [Charles Dolan]."[985] On January 9, 2018, Helson sent a Lync message to Mueller Analyst-1 stating, "What a little triangle the three of them have [Danchenko], [Galkina] and Dolan."[986] Finally, on January 17, 2018, after reviewing Mueller Analyst-1's memorandum on Galkina, Helson wrote to Mueller Analyst-1, "It really makes CD [Dolan] look like he should be investigated."[987] Indeed, as Helson would later state to the OIG:

> There is an individual we kind of [were] watching pop up a lot and that's Chuck Dolan, formerly with Ketchum Group. He's in the same circles. I'm like, are you sure that, I mean, because it would be classic potential tradecraft [to be] like, if you can get information corroborated by one, you can attribute to one, and mask exactly where you got it, is it because, and I don't think anyone's interviewed [him], because I, at the time I had suggested interviewing Dolan, Special's [Mueller Special Counsel] like no, no, don't, don't go talk to him yet. So, and I never, when they said, stay away, I was like, okay, I don't want to. Because I was concerned, I was like, is Dolan [the source], because, and think there's actual, like when I talked with [Danchenko] about him, he initially was reluctant to bring Dolan up. Then he seemed fond of him in a way.[988]

> [. . . .]

> So he [Dolan] was in the same, he was in the same events [YPO Conference]. And we're, like, does he [Dolan] go to London, does he talk to, I mean, does Chris Steele got him too? I'm like, and that is a question I have flagged, it's like, when it gets quiet and Dolan is, from what I understand, Dolan doesn't want to be talking at this point. So I want to strike that at some point and, say, cross that off my list of, here's what I would really like to talk about. Or at least interview him [Dolan]. That would be the only one that, I would think, would be a source that could have contributed to the dossier and have attributed it to [Galkina]. And thinks it is too, because he's there too. And it would be, there's more sources to it [Steele Reports] than actually there are. Chris [Steele] hasn't come off of any of them at this point. I mean, I don't want to, that's just a theory that I . . .[989]

---

[984] SCO_FBIPROD_026627 (Lync message from Helson to Mueller Analyst-1 dated 12/21/2017).

[985] Id.

[986] SCO_FBIPROD_026631 (Lync message from Helson to Mueller Analyst-1 dated 01/09/2018).

[987] SCO_FBIPROD_026632 (Lync message from Helson to Mueller Analyst-1 dated 01/17/2018).

[988] OIG Interview of Kevin Helson on Oct. 31, 2018 at 54-55.

[989] Id. at 56.

Nevertheless, as discussed below, a case was never opened on Dolan and Dolan was never interviewed by the FBI.

  v. Mueller Supervisory Special Agent-1 and Mueller Analyst-1 investigate the relationship between Dolan, Danchenko and Galkina

  Mueller Supervisory Special Agent-1 was assigned to the Crossfire Hurricane investigation in April 2017.[990] Shortly thereafter, Mueller Supervisory Special Agent-1 transitioned to the Mueller Special Counsel team. Mueller Supervisory Special Agent-1 was assigned, in part, the task of validating the Steele Reports, *i.e.*, to verify the reporting or, alternatively, to determine that the reporting was not accurate.[991] Beginning in July 2017, Mueller Supervisory Special Agent-1 worked closely with, among others, Mueller Analyst-1. As discussed above, Mueller Analyst-1, who joined the Mueller investigation in July 2017, was responsible for reviewing the FBI's databases for information related to Galkina.[992] During that process, Mueller Supervisory Special Agent-1 and Mueller Analyst-1 discovered, as described in testimony in the *Danchenko* trial, that (i) Dolan was connected to both Danchenko and Galkina, and (ii) had extensive ties to the Kremlin and Russian government officials, including Dimitry Peskov.[993] Mueller Supervisory Special Agent-1 and Mueller Analyst-1 also conducted open-source searches which corroborated certain information contained in the FBI's databases.

  vi. The FBI interviews Olga Galkina

  In August 2017, Mueller Supervisory Special Agent-1, Auten and a Russian speaking agent, ("WFO Special Agent-1") traveled to Cyprus to interview Galkina.[994] Mueller Supervisory Special Agent-1 testified during the *Danchenko* trial that the purpose of the interview was to determine if Galkina provided Danchenko with information contained in the Steele Reports and, if so, her motivation for doing so.[995] During the Cyprus interview, which was conducted over the course of two days, Mueller Supervisory Special Agent-1 stated that Galkina appeared to be forthcoming on most questions posed, except when she was asked about Dolan. Galkina informed Mueller Supervisory Special Agent-1 that she did not want to speak about Dolan.[996] On the second day of the interview, Galkina stated, in sum, that she had spoken with two individuals about information that would later appear in the Steele Reports. One of the individuals Galkina passed information to was Danchenko, but Galkina initially refused to identify the other individual.[997] Later in the interview, Mueller Supervisory Special Agent-1

---

[990] OSC Report of Interview of Mueller Supervisory Special Agent-1 on May 1, 2020 at 1.

[991] OSC Report of Interview of Mueller Supervisory Special Agent-1 on May 1, 2020 at 1.

[992] *Danchenko* Tr. 10/14/2022 AM at 945-946.

[993] *Id.* at 946, 947-48.

[994] OSC Report of Interview of Mueller Supervisory Special Agent-1 on Aug. 31, 2021 at 1; *Danchenko* Tr. 10/14/2022 AM at 975.

[995] *Danchenko* Tr. 10/14/2022 AM at 975-976.

[996] OSC Report of Interview of Mueller Supervisory Special Agent-1 on Aug. 31, 2021 at 2; *Danchenko* Tr. 10/14/2022 AM at 976.

[997] OSC Report of Interview of Mueller Analyst-1 on Oct. 29, 2021 at 1.

again pressed Galkina about Dolan.[998] This time, Mueller Supervisory Special Agent-1 directly asked Galkina if Dolan had a connection to the information contained in the Steele Reports and whether Dolan was the second unidentified individual with whom she had discussed Steele Report related information.[999] Before answering, Galkina asked Mueller Supervisory Special Agent-1 to remove her (Mueller Supervisory Special Agent-1's) sunglasses from her face so that Galkina could look Mueller Supervisory Special Agent-1 in the eyes.[1000] Galkina then confirmed to Mueller Supervisory Special Agent-1 that Dolan was the second unidentified individual with whom she had discussed Steele Report information.[1001] Galkina also stated that Dolan was a "big democratic supporter."[1002] As discussed above, in October 2016, Galkina would later inform a friend that because of her [Galkina's] "acquaintance with Chuck Dolan and several citizens from the Russian presidential administration," Galkina knew" something and can tell a little about it by voice."[1003]

      vii.   Mueller Supervisory Special Agent-1 and Mueller Analyst-1 push to open a case on Charles Dolan

Armed with the information provided by Galkina, Mueller Supervisory Special Agent-1 returned to the United States and began to further investigate Galkina and Dolan's involvement, if any, with the Steele Reports. As discussed above, beginning in July 2017, Mueller Analyst-1 assisted Mueller Supervisory Special Agent-1 in vetting the Steele Reports.[1004] As part of that work, Mueller Analyst-1 began researching Galkina's relationships with various individuals possibly connected to the Steele Reports, including Danchenko and Dolan.[1005] In connection with that research, Mueller Analyst-1 began drafting a memorandum to memorialize her findings.[1006]

In or about late August 2017, Mueller Supervisory Special Agent-1 and Mueller Analyst-1 briefed various members of the Mueller Special Counsel investigation about Dolan's relationship with Danchenko and Galkina. Those present for this briefing included Auten, Supervisory Special Agent-2 (Mueller Supervisory Special Agent-1's supervisor), and Jeannie Rhee, a prosecutor on the Mueller Special Counsel team, who, at the time, was leading the Special Counsel's investigation into Russian efforts to influence the 2016 presidential election

---

[998] OSC Report of Interview of Mueller Supervisory Special Agent-1 on Aug. 31, 2021 at 1-2.

[999] *Id.*; *Danchenko* Tr. 10/14/2022 AM at 977:3-13.

[1000] OSC Report of Interview of Mueller Supervisory Special Agent-1 on Aug. 31, 2021 at 1-2; *Danchenko* Tr. 10/14/2022 AM at 977:3-13.

[1001] *Danchenko* Tr. 10/14/2022 AM at 977:3-13.

[1002] SCO-FBIPROD_022274 (Opening Communication dated 12/14/2017) at 4.

[1003] SCO_076721 (Facebook exchange with Galkina dated 10/15/2016).

[1004] *Danchenko* Tr. 10/14/2022 AM at 944:11-22.

[1005] *Id.* at 945:12-947:16.

[1006] *Id.* at 954:12-956:3.

(colloquially known as "Team R").[1007] Following the meeting, Mueller Supervisory Special Agent-1 believed that the team was supportive of continuing to investigate Charles Dolan and what connection, if any, he had to the Steele Reports.[1008]

On September 1, 2017, Mueller Supervisory Special Agent-1 drafted a case opening document for Dolan. The opening document detailed, among other things, (i) Dolan's connections to Danchenko and Galkina, (ii) Dolan's connections to the Democratic party, and (iii) Dolan's connections to the Kremlin.[1009] The document also summarized Danchenko's June 15, 2017 conversation with Helson about Dolan.

Nevertheless, on September 7, 2017, Auten instructed Mueller Analyst-1 to cease all research and analysis related to Dolan.[1010] Later that day, Supervisory Special Agent-2 informed Mueller Analyst-1 that she was being transferred from "Team R" to the Mueller team investigating Paul Manafort (colloquially known as "Team M").[1011] In her interview with the Office, Mueller Analyst-1 recalled that she asked Supervisory Special Agent-2 for permission to continue researching Dolan before moving to "Team M," but that her request was denied.[1012] Nevertheless, as discussed more below, following her transfer, Mueller Analyst-1 continued to refine her memorandum regarding Galkina's connections to, among others, Danchenko and Dolan.[1013]

As noted above, in September 2017, Mueller Supervisory Special Agent-1 participated in the two-day interview of Christopher Steele in which Steele admitted that Dolan "had drinks" with Danchenko and was responsible for at least one allegation in the Steele Reports (regarding

---

[1007] OSC Report of Interview of Mueller Analyst-1 on Aug. 16, 2021 at 2, 3; OSC Report of Interview of Mueller Supervisory Special Agent-1 on Aug. 31, 2021 at 4.

[1008] OSC Report of Interview of Mueller Supervisory Special Agent-1 on Aug. 31, 2021 at 4.

[1009] SCO-FBIPROD_022274 (Opening Communication dated 12/14/2017).

[1010] It should be noted that this information provided by Mueller Analyst-1 is corroborated by a contemporaneous timeline she kept of the events at issue during her time with the Mueller Special Counsel team. In her interview with the Office, Mueller Analyst-1 stated that she prepared the contemporaneous timeline in the event she were later interviewed about her role on the Mueller Special Counsel investigation. *See* OSC Report of Interview of Mueller Analyst-1 on Oct. 29, 2021 at 2-3.

[1011] OSC Report of Interview of Mueller Analyst-1 on Oct. 29, 2021 at 2.

[1012] *Id.* at 2

[1013] In her interview with the Special Counsel, Mueller Analyst-1 stated that Auten had made edits to her memorandum, some of which removed information regarding Dolan. Mueller Analyst-1 recalled being frustrated by many of these edits and wondered if the edits were being made by individuals other than Auten and with a political motive. However, Mueller Analyst-1 was unable to provide any evidence to support this speculation. *See* OSC Report of Interview of Mueller Analyst-1 on Aug. 16, 2021 at 5. When interviewed by the Office, Auten recalled that his edits were reflective of his belief that some of the information regarding Dolan was too speculative. *See* OSC Report of Interview of Brian Auten on July 26, 2021.

Manafort's resignation as Trump campaign manager.)[1014] Mueller Supervisory Special Agent-1 stated that they did not probe Steele further about Charles Dolan because the FBI did not want to "show their hand" to Steele.[1015]

On September 22, 2017, Mueller Supervisory Special Agent-1 and Mueller Analyst-1 attended a meeting with Supervisory Special Agent-2, Auten, and attorney Rhee to discuss, among other things, the recently completed interview of Steele.[1016] At various times in September 2017, Mueller Analyst-1 recalled that Rhee opined, in sum, that there was no longer a need to investigate the Steele Reports, because the Reports were not within the scope of the Mueller Special Counsel mandate.[1017] Similarly, Auten told the Office he recalled that in September 2017 Deputy Assistant Director David Archey informed the team that they should cease work on attempting to corroborate the Steele Reports.[1018] This directive given by the Mueller investigation leadership is somewhat surprising given that Director Mueller's broad mandate was to investigate, among other things, Russian election interference in the 2016 presidential election – parameters that clearly would seem to include the Steele Reports. Indeed, as Mueller Analyst-1 noted in her interview with the Office, the Mueller Special Counsel team continued to investigate cases involving non-Russian persons and entities. Thus, Mueller Analyst-1 disagreed with the contention that Dolan fell outside of the Mueller mandate.[1019] In her interview with the Office, Mueller Supervisory Special Agent-1 stated that while she did not recall the "outside the mandate" justification for the denial of the Dolan case opening, it would "surprise" her if that was the reason provided by Mueller team leadership.[1020] This purported position also is curious given that the Steele Reports underpinned, in a significant way, the probable cause contained in the Page FISA applications.

Mueller Supervisory Special Agent-1 also recalled that attorney Rhee, while initially favorable to investigating Dolan, gradually soured on the idea.[1021] In that same vein, in a meeting on October 17, 2017, Supervisory Special Agent-2 informed Mueller Supervisory Special Agent-1, Mueller Analyst-1, and Auten that (i) Dolan fell outside of the Mueller investigation's mandate, (ii) the investigators had too much work and too few resources to focus on Dolan, and (iii) WFO could task Danchenko regarding Dolan.[1022] In fact, Mueller Analyst-1's contemporaneous notes explicitly state that Mueller investigation leadership directed Mueller Analyst-1 and Mueller Supervisory Special Agent-1 to "dedicate no resources to CD

[1014] SCO-006313 (Interview of Christopher Steele on Sept. 18, 2017) at 3, 16-17.

[1015] OSC Report of Interview of Mueller Supervisory Special Agent-1 on Aug. 31, 2021 at 2.

[1016] OSC Report of Interview of Mueller Analyst-1 on Oct. 29, 2021 at 3.

[1017] Id. at 3-4; Timeline prepared by Mueller Analyst-1.

[1018] OSC Report of Interview of Brian Auten on July 26, 2021 at 19.

[1019] OSC Report of Interview of Mueller Analyst-1 on Oct. 29, 2021 at 7.

[1020] OSC Report of Interview of Mueller Supervisory Special Agent-1 on Aug. 31, 2021 at 5.

[1021] Id. at 4.

[1022] OSC Report of Interview of Mueller Analyst-1 on Oct. 29, 2021 at 4; Timeline prepared by Mueller Analyst-1, entry dated Oct. 17, 2017.

[Dolan]."[1023] Nevertheless, Supervisory Special Agent-2 stated that tangential work on Dolan could be continued, although it was unlikely that a case opening on Dolan would be approved.[1024]

Ultimately, Supervisory Special Agent-2 informed Mueller Supervisory Special Agent-1 that her request to open a case on Dolan had been denied and that it was a "higher level decision."[1025] Supervisory Special Agent-2 directed Mueller Supervisory Special Agent-1 to delete the case opening from Sentinel.[1026] Despite repeated inquiries, neither Mueller Supervisory Special Agent-1 nor Mueller Analyst-1 was ever provided a specific rationale for the denial of the case opening.[1027] Similarly, Mueller Supervisory Special Agent-1 never learned who ultimately denied the case opening.[1028] In a December 21, 2017 Lync message exchange, Mueller Analyst-1 and Helson discussed the case opening on Dolan. In one message, Mueller Analyst-1 stated, "yeah . . . it isn't good what EM [FBI Executive Management] decides to do with it, is beyond my pay-grade, I've made arguments in person – and that's all I can do . . . and serialize the relationship."[1029]

During an interview with the Office, Supervisory Special Agent-2 opined in retrospect that it was an "oversight" not to open on Dolan, and that Dolan should have been, at a minimum, interviewed.[1030] It should also be noted that in his interviews with the Office, Auten stated that he was supportive of opening an investigation of Dolan.[1031] This recollection was corroborated by both Mueller Supervisory Special Agent-1 and Mueller Analyst-1.[1032]

> viii.   *Mueller Supervisory Special Agent-1 and Mueller Analyst-1 expressed concerns about the appearance of political bias in the decision not to open on Charles Dolan*

In her interview with the Office, Mueller Supervisory Special Agent-1 recalled that she and Mueller Analyst-1 discussed whether the decision not to open on Dolan was politically motivated, given Dolan's extensive connections to the Democratic party.[1033] Mueller Supervisory Special Agent-1 stated that she did not believe the decision not to open on Dolan

---

[1023] Timeline prepared by Mueller Analyst-1, entry dated Oct. 17, 2017.

[1024] OSC Report of Interview of Mueller Analyst-1 on Oct. 29, 2021 at 4.

[1025] OSC Report of Interview of Mueller Supervisory Special Agent-1 on Aug. 31, 2021 at 5.

[1026] *Id.* at 3.

[1027] *Id.* at 5.

[1028] *Id.*

[1029] SCO_FBIPROD_026627 (Lync message from Mueller Analyst-1 to Helson dated 12/21/2017).

[1030] OSC Report of Interview of Supervisory Special Agent-2 on May 5, 2021 at 7.

[1031] OSC Report of Interview of Brian Auten on July 26, 2021 at 19.

[1032] OSC Report of Interview of Mueller Supervisory Special Agent-1 on Aug. 31, 2021 at 3; OSC Report of Interview of Mueller Analyst-1 on Aug. 16, 2021 at 6.

[1033] OSC Report of Interview of Mueller Supervisory Special Agent-1 on Aug. 31, 2021 at 4-5.

was political, but that she did worry about the optics of the decision, given that Dolan was a prominent Democrat.[1034] Mueller Supervisory Special Agent-1 further stated that she did not witness any explicit political bias during her work with the Mueller Special Counsel team.[1035] Nonetheless, at the time, Mueller Supervisory Special Agent-1 believed that the decision not to open on Dolan would eventually be reviewed by the OIG.[1036]

When interviewed by the Office, Mueller Analyst-1 did speculate that the decision not to open on Dolan was politically motivated. Mueller Analyst-1 speculated that the information on Dolan ran counter to the narrative that the Mueller Special Counsel investigators were cultivating given that Dolan was a former Democratic political operative.[1037] However, Mueller Analyst-1 was unable to provide the Office with definitive evidence to support her belief. Like Mueller Supervisory Special Agent-1, Mueller Analyst-1 believed that the decision not to investigate Dolan would eventually be reviewed by the OIG.[1038] In fact, Mueller Analyst-1 informed the Office that she uploaded her Galkina memorandum to three separate case files on the FBI Sentinel system to ensure that the OIG would have access to the document.[1039]

ix. The FBI's failure to investigate Dolan

In sum, save for efforts by Auten, Helson, Mueller Supervisory Special Agent-1, and Mueller Analyst-1, the FBI's failure to complete logical investigative steps concerning what, if any, role Dolan played in the Steele Reports was troubling. As discussed above, the Office has determined that Dolan was a source for at least one allegation in the Steele Reports, and was one of only three U.S. persons named by Steele (in both his October 2016 and September 2017 interviews) who had more information about the reports. If the FBI had learned nothing more about Dolan, Steele's statements alone would have been an ample basis to interview Dolan. Moreover, Mueller Supervisory Special Agent-1, Mueller Analyst-1, and others had uncovered significant information about Dolan – independent from what the Office subsequently unearthed – that potentially connected him to the Steele Reports; this was information that plainly warranted further investigation. In summary, the evidence possessed by the FBI and later elicited during the *Danchenko* trial showed that:

- Dolan maintained a relationship with Danchenko, Steele's primary sub-source for the Steele Reports;

- Dolan maintained relationships with various Russian government officials, including Dimitry Peskov and Alexey Pavlov, both of whom feature prominently in the Steele Reports;

[1034] *Id.*; OSC Report of Interview of Mueller Analyst-1 on Aug. 16, 2021 at 7.

[1035] OSC Report of Interview of Mueller Supervisory Special Agent-1 on Aug. 31, 2021 at 4-5.

[1036] *Id.*

[1037] OSC Report of Interview of Mueller Analyst-1 on Aug. 16, 2021 at 7.

[1038] *Danchenko* Tr. 10/14/2022 AM at 956:1-957:23.

[1039] *Id.*

- Dolan was present in Moscow in June 2016, met with the General Manager of the Moscow Ritz Carlton, toured the premises, including the Presidential Suite, and had at least one meeting with Danchenko who also was in Moscow;

- Dolan was present in Moscow with Danchenko in October 2016 – during the time frame Danchenko was gathering information for the Steele Reports;

- Dolan maintained a relationship with Galkina, allegedly a sub-source for Danchenko, and met with Galkina in Cyprus on two occasions in the summer of 2016;

- Dolan performed work for Galkina's former employer, who would later appear in the Steele Reports;

- Galkina admitted to the FBI that she provided Dolan with information that would eventually be in the Steele Reports; and

- Dolan was a prominent and longtime Democratic political operative who vocally supported candidate Clinton;

The FBI interviewed hundreds of individuals through the course of the Crossfire Hurricane and Mueller Special Counsel investigations, and yet, they did not interview Dolan or the other two U.S. persons identified by Steele as early as October 2016. The Office interviewed Dolan on several occasions and he denied being a source of information for the Steele Reports, save for the Manafort campaign-related allegation he provided to Danchenko in August 2016 – an allegation he acknowledged to the Office that he fabricated. Although both Steele and Galkina suggested that Dolan may have information related to the Steele Reports, our investigation was not able to definitively prove that Dolan was the actual source for any additional allegations set forth in the Steele Reports. That said, in light of the foregoing, there does not appear to be an objectively sound reason for the decision that was made not to interview him.

f. Sergei Millian

A particularly disturbing example of the unsupported narratives regarding Trump and Russia – created and pressed by Fusion GPS and Steele – involved a Belarussian-American named Sergei Millian. At the time of his purported involvement in Trump-related matters, Millian was a New York-based real estate broker who from 2006-2016 served as president of the Russian-American Chamber of Commerce. In the course of his employment, Millian had occasion to be involved in some relatively minor listings of Trump Organization properties.

As discussed more fully below, Danchenko claimed to have sourced several of the most serious allegations in the Steele Reports to Millian, including allegations of an ongoing conspiracy between the Trump campaign and Russian officials. Several of these allegations were included in the Page FISA applications. In particular, and perhaps most importantly, Steele Report 2016/095 stated, in part:

Speaking in confidence to a compatriot *in late July 2016, Source E, an ethnic Russian close associate of Republican US presidential candidate Donald TRUMP,* admitted that there was a well-developed conspiracy of co-operation between them and the Russian leadership. This was managed on the TRUMP side by the Republican candidate's campaign manager, Paul MANAFORT, who was using foreign policy advisor, Carter PAGE, and others as intermediaries. The two sides had a mutual interest in defeating Democratic presidential candidate Hillary CLINTON, whom President PUTIN apparently both hated and feared.[1040]

During several interviews with the FBI, Danchenko said that he believed "Source E" in Report 2016/095 referred, at least in part, to Millian. According to Steele, Danchenko was the only one communicating with Millian, and Steele stated that Danchenko had had direct contacts with Millian in New York City and Charleston, South Carolina. On the other hand, Danchenko told the FBI that, although Steele believed that he (Danchenko) had met with Millian, he never did.[1041] Further, Danchenko did not correct Steele in his mistaken belief that Danchenko had met directly with Millian.[1042]

As explained in greater detail below, the spectacular claim contained in Steele Report Number 2016/095 of a "well-developed conspiracy of co-operation" between the Trump campaign and Russian leadership is based entirely on a purported anonymous telephone call Danchenko said he received from someone he had never spoken to before. In particular, the information about the conspiracy was conveyed to him by an anonymous caller who Danchenko told Crossfire Hurricane investigators he believed might have been Millian based on Danchenko's claimed comparison of the caller's voice to a known *YouTube* video featuring Millian.[1043] Yet this unvetted, completely uncorroborated allegation was included in the Page FISA applications, both before and after the FBI learned its provenance from Danchenko himself.

     i.   Danchenko's statements to the FBI regarding Millian

When interviewed by the FBI in January 2017, Danchenko was twice asked to review Steele Report Number 2016/095 and explain where the information came from concerning a well-developed conspiracy between the Trump campaign and Russian leadership and the roles allegedly being played by Manafort and Page. Danchenko told the FBI that the "Source E" information sounded as though it were from a call he had received in late July 2016 from an anonymous caller who Danchenko believed was Sergei Millian. In particular, Danchenko described the following "strange" event:

Danchenko told the FBI that in June or July 2016, he communicated with Alexey Bogdanovsky, a U.S.-based Russian national employee of RIA Novosti (a Russian state-run media outlet) about reaching out to Millian, who Danchenko had never met or spoken with.[1044] Bogdanovsky indicated that his colleague at RIA Novosti, Dimitry Zlodorev, had a relationship

---

[1040] SCO-105084 (Documents Known to the FBI Comprising the "Steele Dossier") at 9 (Company Intelligence Report 2016-095) (capitalization in original; emphasis added).

[1041] SCO_105287 (CHS Reporting Document dated 11/14/2017).

[1042] *Id.*

[1043] *Id.*

[1044] SCO-005801 (Interview of Igor Danchenko Electronic Communication dated 02/09/2017 at 35-36).

with Millian and had previously interviewed Millian about Trump.[1045] Bogdanovsky ultimately provided Danchenko with Millian's contact information.[1046] Thereafter, Danchenko told the FBI that he reached out to Millian via email twice, but did not receive a response back from him.[1047] Danchenko did not provide the FBI with copies of these emails, despite explicit requests to provide any records of communication with Millian.[1048]

Danchenko next told the FBI that, in late July 2016, after receiving no email response from Millian, he (Danchenko) received a 10-15 minute phone call from an anonymous individual who he believed to be Sergei Millian.[1049] During this purported phone call, the caller, who did not identify himself, reportedly informed Danchenko about (i) Trump and the Kremlin, (ii) "communications" and an ongoing relationship between the parties, and (iii) Manafort and Page.[1050] The unidentified caller also supposedly said that while there was nothing bad about the "exchange of information" between Trump and the Kremlin, the information could be good for Russia and damaging to Trump, although deniable.[1051] Danchenko said that he and the person he believed to be Millian agreed to meet at a bar in New York City in late July 2016.[1052] Danchenko also told the FBI that he traveled to New York in late July 2016, but that Millian, or the person he believed to be Millian, never showed up for the meeting.[1053] As discussed in detail below, Danchenko's versions of events regarding his trip to New York conflict with the relevant record. Nevertheless, Danchenko did admit to the FBI that he had, in fact, never met with Millian in person,[1054]although, as noted above, Danchenko knew that Steele mistakenly thought that they had met on several occasions and Danchenko intentionally did not correct him on that point.[1055]

[1045] *Id.* at 35-36.

[1046] *Id.* at 36.

[1047] *Id.* at 20. In the January 2017 interviews with the FBI, Danchenko first told the FBI that he received the late-July 2016 anonymous call from the individual he believed to be Millian following his initial email to Millian. Danchenko later told the FBI that he received the anonymous call after his second email to Millian. As discussed below, given the date of his second email to Millian, Danchenko's shifting version of events is inconsistent with the documentary evidence obtained during the investigation.

[1048] *Danchenko* Tr. 10/13/2022 AM at 700:23-701:09.

[1049] SCO-005801 (Interview of Igor Danchenko Electronic Communication dated 02/09/2017 at 36-37).

[1050] *Id.* at 20, 37.

[1051] *Id.* at 37.

[1052] *Id.*; SCO_105287 (CHS Reporting Document dated 11/14/2017).

[1053] SCO-005801 (Interview of Igor Danchenko Electronic Communication dated 02/09/2017 at 36).

[1054] SCO_105286 (CHS Reporting Document dated 11/13/2017).

[1055] SCO_105287 (CHS Reporting Document dated 11/14/2017).

Instead, Danchenko told the FBI that the damaging allegations contained in Steele Report 2016/095 stemmed from the single telephone call from the anonymous individual he believed to be Millian.[1056] The Office did not find any evidence, or uncover any motive, that would explain why Millian, a vocal Trump supporter,[1057] would call a complete stranger and provide damaging information about Trump.

In any event, Danchenko was not able to produce phone records or other evidence to corroborate this alleged call, despite explicit requests by the FBI to do so.[1058] Nor does it appear from FBI records that Crossfire Hurricane personnel pulled and reviewed Danchenko's toll records in an attempt to corroborate his statements regarding an anonymous call. Danchenko surmised during one interview that the purported call may have been received on an encrypted phone "app,"[1059] although a review of his email messages to Millian reflect that he made no mention of having or using any phone apps. Consistent with his inability to keep his narrative straight, Danchenko also later told the FBI that he had a "couple" of calls with Millian.[1060]

Danchenko also told the FBI that "Source D" in Steele Report 2016/080, relating in part to the scandalous Moscow Ritz Carlton allegations against Trump, "could be" referring to Millian.[1061] Danchenko's efforts to partially attribute the Ritz Carlton allegations to Millian support the notion that he fabricated his interaction with Millian. Indeed, as noted above, Danchenko told the FBI that the information he obtained from Millian came from a single, 10-15-minute anonymous phone call that took place in late-July 2016 and was the only time that Danchenko allegedly communicated with Millian. Given that the Steele Report containing those sexual allegations was dated June 20, 2016 – *over a month prior* to Danchenko's alleged call with Millian, the above-described "Source D" (Millian) allegation concerning the Ritz Carlton is highly probative of the fact that there was never such a phone call between Danchenko and Millian.[1062] It would have been impossible for Millian to confirm the Ritz Carlton allegations (and other information) to Danchenko in June 2016 because, as Danchenko repeatedly informed the FBI, the *first* time he allegedly communicated with Millian was late July 2016.

  ii. *Steele's statements to the FBI about Millian*

On September 18 and 19, 2017, FBI personnel from the Mueller Special Counsel investigation interviewed Steele. Steele stated, in part, that Danchenko had collected election-

---

[1056] SCO-005801 (Interview of Igor Danchenko Electronic Communication dated 02/09/2017) at 37.

[1057] *E.g., Sergei Millian: Donald Trump will improve relations with Russia*, RIA Novosti (Apr. 13, 2016).

[1058] SCO_105282 (CHS Reporting Document dated 06/01/2017).

[1059] Transcript of March 16, 2017 interview of Danchenko at 106-107.

[1060] SCO_105286 (CHS Reporting Document dated 11/13/2017).

[1061] SCO_105282 (CHS Reporting Document dated 06/01/2017).

[1062] SCO-105084 (Documents Known to the FBI Comprising the "Steele Dossier") at 2-4, (Company Intelligence Report 2016/080).

related material in the United States for Orbis.[1063] As part of that undertaking, Danchenko informed Steele that he met in person with Millian on two or three occasions – in New York and "perhaps" in Charleston, South Carolina.[1064] However, as noted, Danchenko informed the FBI that he had not in fact met with Millian on any occasion and did not correct Steele in that misimpression.[1065]

iii.   The evidence obtained by the Office

The evidence obtained by the Office shows that Danchenko, in fact, never received a phone call or any information from Millian, and Danchenko never made arrangements to meet with Millian in New York. Rather, the evidence demonstrates that Danchenko fabricated these facts regarding Millian. Indeed, a review of the emails sent by Danchenko to Millian in the summer of 2016 support this conclusion – the same emails Danchenko failed to provide the FBI when interviewed regarding Millian. Those emails are described below.

Danchenko first came to the attention of Millian on May 26, 2016 when Russian journalist Dimitry Zlodorev emailed Millian the following:

Sergey, hello.

I hope all is well with you and your [sic] are once again in America. It is my recollection you told me that you either have or will have news. Will it be convenient if I call sometime next week?

In addition, my colleagues have an acquaintance, Igor Danchenko, who works here in consulting. Through them, he requested I find out if it is okay to get in touch with you? If I understood correctly, it is about Trump and Russia.

Can I give him your contact information—e-mail, phone, or just e-mail?[1066]

Later that day, Millian replied to Zlodorev that he was leaving for Asia on June 10, 2016 and would call him soon.[1067] Millian's reply does not mention Danchenko.

On July 21, 2016, Danchenko, who appears to have acquired Millian's email address from Zlodorev, sent Millian the following message:

Colleagues from RIA Novosti gave me your contact information. You spoke to Dimitry Zlodorev about Donald Trump and his trips to Russia. I wanted to ask you: what projects was he looking into or were these just image-building trips for beauty contests? There has been a lot of speculation for months now on this topic. It would be interesting to chat about this topic. It's confidential of course – I don't have any relationship to media, though of course I do have acquaintances here. In any case, it would be interesting if and when possible to chat with you by phone or meet for coffee/beer in Washington or in New York where I will be next

---

[1063] SCO-006313 (Interview of Christopher Steele on Sept. 18, 2017) at 7.

[1064] *Id.*

[1065] SCO_105287 (CHS Reporting Document dated 11/14/2017).

[1066] SC_IDC_0042618 (Email from Zlodorev to Millian dated 05/26/2016).

[1067] SC_IDC_0044205 (Email from Millian to Zlodorev dated 05/26/2016).

week. I myself am in Washington. It is also possible by e-mail in Russian or in English. I sent to you a request to LinkedIn – there my work is clearer.[1068]

Millian did not respond to Danchenko's July 21, 2016 email. In fact, Millian was traveling in Asia at the time Danchenko sent this email and did not return to New York until the night of July 27, 2016.[1069] Notably, Millian had suspended his cellular phone service effective July 14, 2016 (prior to his travel) and his service was only reconnected effective August 8, 2016.[1070]

On July 26, 2016, Millian emailed Zlodorev the following:

Dimitry, on Friday I'm returning from Asia. An email came from Igor. Who is that? What sort of person?[1071]

That same day, Zlodorev responded:

Sergey, hello! Do you remember I said that a friend of my colleague wanted to get acquainted with you? You gave permission to give your email. The way I understand it, this is who this is. He and I are not personally acquainted, though he is, it seems, in my LinkedIn. And I didn't know what he wanted to talk about. If I remember correctly, he works at some think tank in Washington.[1072]

Millian did not respond to Danchenko's July 21, 2016 email.

On August 18, 2016 – more than two weeks *after* Danchenko purportedly received the aforementioned anonymous call and allegedly agreed to meet with Millian in New York – Danchenko again emailed Millian, stating in part: "Hello, Sergey! I wrote you several weeks ago. We are contacts on LinkedIn."[1073] Danchenko then described a real estate deal in Russia and inquired about Millian's interest in the transaction. Danchenko closed the email by stating, "Write, call. My contact information is below."[1074] This email – which post-dated the alleged "late July" call from Millian, clearly reflected that Danchenko had not, in fact, spoken with Millian and did not believe he had done so. Specifically, Danchenko's email did not mention a possible call from Millian and did not discuss plans to meet in New York with Millian.

On August 24, 2016, Danchenko emailed Zlodorev, stating in part:

Aleksey Bogdanovsky recommended that I get in touch with Sergey Millian. I've read your interviews with him. *But for some reason Sergey doesn't respond.* I already both asked him about TRUMP and also proposed a project in Russia.

[1068] SC_IDC_0042660 (Email from Danchenko to Millian dated 07/21/2016).

[1069] SCO-101428 (U.S. Customs and Border Protection Person Encounter List for Sergei Millian at 1).

[1070] SCO-101860 (Verizon Notes on Account 404-667-9319); Verizon Subscriber Records for 404-667-9319.

[1071] SC_IDC_0042661 (Email from Millian to Zlodorev dated 07/26/2016).

[1072] SC_IDC_0042663 (Email from Zlodorev to Millian dated 07/26/2016).

[1073] SC_IDC_0042676 (Email from Danchenko to Millian dated 08/18/2016).

[1074] *Id.*

What is your relationship with him like? *Would you be able to ask him to reply to me? I could call or write on LinkedIn, but until he responds I would not like to pester him.* By the way, you and I are also contacts there.[1075]

This August 24, 2016 email to Zlodorev again made it clear that Danchenko had not, in fact, spoken with Millian in "late July." Again, Danchenko's email did not mention a possible call from Millian, did not discuss plans to meet in New York with Millian, and did not inform Zlodorev that Millian did not show up to the alleged meeting in New York.

Later that day, Zlodorev responded in part:

> Igor, hello, Sergey Millian asked me a couple of weeks ago who Igor Danchenko is. I had told him earlier, but he apparently forgot. At that time, he wrote to me from South Korea. The thing is that he, based on his own words, now spends more time in Asia than in America. Try to write to him once again. I simply know that he is constantly travelling and could actually have forgotten.[1076]

The emails quoted above are further evidence that between July 21, 2016 and August 24, 2016, Millian did not call, email or meet with Danchenko, and Danchenko knew he had not received a call from someone who he believed to be Millian.

In addition, in July 2020, the Senate Judiciary Committee released a heavily redacted report of Danchenko's January 2017 interview with the FBI.[1077] In the report, Danchenko is only identified as Steele's "primary subsource." When the redacted interview was released, Millian had been publicly reported to be a source for certain information in the Steele Reports, including the information purportedly collected in "late July" 2016 alleging that Trump and his campaign were engaged in a "well-developed conspiracy of co-operation" with Russian officials. The redacted and anonymized interview also indicated that the "primary subsource" (Danchenko) had received contact information for "Source 6," *i.e.*, Millian, from a journalist who had previously interviewed Millian, *i.e.*, Zlodorev.[1078] Following the release of the interview, Millian began to email Zlodorev attempting to uncover the identity of Steele's primary subsource.[1079] In late July 2020, Danchenko was identified by name in press reporting as Steele's primary subsource. On July 19, 2020, Millian emailed Zlodorev, stating in part:

> "I believe they've already found Steele's source: [internet address]. Do you remember such a person? Igor Danchenko?"[1080]

On July 20, 2020, Millian again emailed Zlodorev the following:

[1075] SCO-005860 (Interview of Igor Danchenko Electronic Communication dated 02/09/2017 1A) at 2 (emphasis added; capitalization in original).

[1076] *Id.*

[1077] U.S. Senate Committee on the Judiciary, Judiciary Committee Releases Declassified Documents that Substantially Undercut Steele Dossier, Page FISA Warrants (July 17, 2020).

[1078] SENATE-FISA2020-001106 at 20, 35-36.

[1079] SC_IDC_0043005 (Email from Millian to Zlodorev dated 07/17/2020).

[1080] SC_IDC_0043065 (Email from Millian to Zlodorev dated 07/19/2020).

I've been informed that Bogdanovsky travelled to New York with Danchenko at the end of July 2016; Danchenko, supposedly to meet with me (but the meeting didn't take place). Can you inquire with Bogdanovsky whether he remembers something from that trip and whether they touched upon my name in conversation, as well as for what reason Danchenko was travelling to NY? Steele, it seems, made Danchenko the fall guy, but Danchenko himself made several statements that were difficult to understand, for example, about the call with me. Did he tell Bogdanovsky that he communicated with me by phone and on what topic? Thank you! This will clarify a lot for me personally. It's a convoluted story![1081]

These 2020 emails between Millian and Zlodorev again point to the fact that Danchenko did not receive a call from Millian in late-July 2016.

The Office also reviewed phone records for both Danchenko and Millian from 2016 and 2017. Those records reveal no communication between Millian and Danchenko. In fact, the Office was able to identify nearly every call received by Danchenko during the relevant timeframe. Of the small number of calls that could not be identified, none had a duration approaching 10-15 minutes.[1082] Moreover, as noted above, service to Millian's primary cellular telephone number was suspended at the time Danchenko allegedly received the anonymous call. Further, the contention that Danchenko may have received an "anonymous call" from someone he believed to be Millian on an internet-based application was not supported by the evidence obtained by the Office. Indeed, at no time did Danchenko inform Millian that he could be contacted on an internet-based application, to say nothing of the particular application Millian should use. Rather, the evidence did show that when Danchenko wanted to communicate on an internet-based application, he explicitly communicated that to his contacts and identified the application to use.[1083]

With respect to the purported meeting with Millian in New York, the evidence obtained by the Office revealed that Danchenko had planned to travel to New York during the week of July 24, 2016, *prior* to even reaching out to Millian for the first time.[1084] Indeed, the evidence revealed that Danchenko's trip to New York was a sightseeing excursion with his young daughter. In order to credit Danchenko's version of events, one would have to accept that Danchenko, with his young daughter, planned to meet an *unidentified* individual at an *unidentified* bar – in a city of 8 million people – at night.

Finally, the Office interviewed Millian. Millian unequivocally stated that he never met with or spoke with Danchenko.[1085] When asked if he provided the information reflected in the Steele Reports to Danchenko, Millian stated "[t]hat did not happen. One-hundred percent did not

---

[1081] SC_IDC_0043181 (Email from Millian to Zlodorev dated 07/20/2020).

[1082] *Danchenko* Government Exhibit 1603.

[1083] *See, e.g., Danchenko* Government Exhibits 610, 610T, 611, 612, 612T.

[1084] SC_IDC_0003641 (Email from Danchenko dated 07/18/2016).

[1085] OSC Report of Interview of Sergei Millian on Feb. 5, 2022 at 1.

happen."[1086] Millian stated he has received threats to his and his family's safety because of his alleged role in the Steele Reports.[1087]

iv. *Fusion GPS implicates Sergei Millian*

As discussed above, the Office found no evidence that Millian was a source for any of the allegations in the Steele Reports. Given this fact, the Office endeavored to determine the genesis of Millian's implication in the Steele Reports. In particular, what caused Danchenko to first reach out to Millian in late July 2016. To that end, the Office reviewed, among other things, records obtained from Fusion GPS and the public statements of Fusion GPS principals Glenn Simpson and Peter Fritsch.[1088]

Specifically, Fusion GPS records demonstrate that Nellie Ohr first identified Millian as having connections to Trump. Ohr was a Russian-language contractor employed by Fusion GPS and the wife of Department official Bruce Ohr. On April 22, 2016, Nellie Ohr prepared a report for Fusion GPS that set forth, in part, Millian's connections to Trump.[1089] This report was prepared just ten days after Fusion GPS was retained by Perkins Coie to conduct opposition research on Trump, and prior to Steele being retained by Fusion GPS.[1090] Notably, on April 13, 2016 – approximately one week prior to Ohr's report – RIA Novosti published an interview with Millian that was conducted by Dimitry Zlodorev.[1091] In that interview, Millian described his alleged real estate connections to Trump and spoke positively about Trump's candidacy.[1092] Millian was interviewed by RIA Novosti several more times over the course of the summer and

---

[1086] *Id.*

[1087] *Id.* at 4.

[1088] The Office collected various records and statements from Fusion GPS and Fusion GPS employees over the course of its investigation. No one at Fusion GPS, however, would agree to voluntarily speak with the Office. In addition, the DNC and the Clinton campaign asserted attorney-client privilege over a substantial number of Fusion GPS's emails.

[1089] *See* Nellie Ohr, *Report 22 April 2016* at 29.

[1090] Consulting Agreement between Fusion GPS and Perkins Coie was signed on Apr. 11, 2016. SC-00004920 (Consulting Agreement dated Apr. 1, 2016). Steele was approached by Simpson to research Trump in May, 2016. OIG Interview of Christopher Steele on June 5 and 6, 2019 at 11; *Crime in Progress* at 69.

[1091] RIA Novosti, *Sergei Millian: Donald Trump Will Improve Relations with Russia* (translated) (Apr. 13, 2016).

[1092] *Id.*

all of 2016.[1093] On May 7, 2016, Nellie Ohr compiled another report discussing, among other things, Millian.[1094] All told, Ohr prepared at least 12 reports that discussed Sergei Millian.[1095]

Nellie Ohr's reports included Millian's views on how a potential "Trump presidency might affect US-Russia relations."[1096] Notably, Ohr included internet links in the reports to several *YouTube* videos from 2012 featuring Millian.[1097] As discussed above, Danchenko told the FBI that the anonymous caller from late-July 2016 "sounded like Millian" based on a *YouTube* video that Danchenko had previously watched.[1098] The reports prepared by Ohr and others at Fusion GPS were ultimately provided to Crossfire Hurricane investigators by Ohr's husband, Bruce Ohr.[1099]

As discussed above, Fusion GPS approached Steele in May 2016. Prior to his retention, Glenn Simpson met with Steele at Heathrow Airport in London and pitched Steele on the opposition research project.[1100] Approximately one week later, Danchenko contacted RIA Novosti journalists seeking Millian's contact information.[1101] The timing of Danchenko's request to RIA Novosti on the heels of Steele's meeting with Simpson in London strongly supports the inference that Fusion GPS directed Steele to pursue Millian.[1102] Indeed, by the time of Steele's meeting with Simpson, Nellie Ohr had already identified Millian's alleged connections to Trump.

In addition to Ohr, other Fusion GPS employees also appear to have worked on research pertaining to Millian. While the vast majority of the internal Fusion GPS emails were withheld from the Office based on privilege claims by the Clinton campaign or the DNC, the privilege log provided revealed that Fusion GPS employees regularly emailed about Millian, often attaching what appear to be draft memoranda about Millian or forwarding news articles concerning Millian.[1103] For example, on July 1, 2016, Fusion GPS employee Jake Berkowitz emailed a draft

---

[1093] *E.g.* Dmitry Zlodorev, *Political scientist: Trump's reform will be based on the principle of Americanism*, RIA Novosti (Aug. 09, 2016); Dmitry Zlodorev, *RATP President: Trump will choose a businessman or military man as vice president of the United States*, RIA Novosti (June 10, 2016).

[1094] Nellie Ohr, Weekly Writeup 7 May 2016.

[1095] *See, e.g.*, Nellie Ohr, Sergei Millian Compendium Updated 24 September 2016.

[1096] Nellie Ohr, *Report 22 April 2016* at 29-34.

[1097] *Id.* at 32.

[1098] SCO_105287 (CHS Reporting Document dated 11/14/2017)

[1099] U.S. House of Representatives Executive Session, Cmte. on the Judiciary Joint with the Cmte. on Government Reform and Oversight, Interview of Bruce Ohr on Aug. 28, 2018 at 7-9.

[1100] *Crime in Progress* at 69.

[1101] SC_IDC_0042618 (Email from Zlodorev to Millian dated 05/26/2016).

[1102] In their book, Simpson and Fritsch state that Steele identified Millian as "one of the key intermediaries between Trump and the Russians." *Crime in Progress* at 97.

[1103] Bean LLC/Fusion GPS Privilege Log dated Mar. 11, 2022.

memo entitled "Sergei Millian 6.30.16docx.[1104] Several weeks later, on July 13, 2016, Berkowitz forwarded the same document to Glenn Simpson.[1105]

At the same time the research on Millian was being conducted, Fusion GPS was promoting Millian to the press as a key intermediary between Trump and Russia. For example, on June 27, 2016, Fusion GPS principal Peter Fritsch sent an email to Franklin Foer, a reporter at *Slate* magazine, with subject line "we think."[1106] The email stated:

> this dude is key:
>
> https.//nestseekers.com/agent/sergei-millian
>
> he is clearly kgb. That minsk [*sic.*] state linguistic university is something of a giveaway.
>
> If you are downtown, come by....[1107]

Fusion GPS's research on Millian appeared to increase substantially in late-July 2016. In fact, between July 25, 2016, and July 28, 2016, Fusion GPS employees exchanged several dozen internal emails pertaining to Millian.[1108] During this time, Glenn Simpson was in contact with ABC News producer Matthew Mosk about Millian.[1109] Notably, emails showed that Mosk had been communicating with Millian since at least July 13, 2016.[1110] During the course of this correspondence, Mosk learned that Millian was abroad, but planned to return to the United States in late July.[1111]

On July 26, 2016, Mosk emailed Millian the following:

> Hello Sergei-
>
> I am writing to see if you might have any photographs of Donald Trump or Don Jr. visiting Russia from your firm's work with the Trump Organization? We would very much like to be able to illustrate his past travels to, and business interests in Russia.[1112]

Later that day, Millian replied that he only had a single photograph with Trump that had been taken in Miami. In reply, Mosk asked Millian if he would be willing to do an interview with ABC News about his experiences with Trump and proposed to conduct the interview in New

---

[1104] *Id.* at 13.

[1105] *Id.*

[1106] SC-00100874 (Email from Fritsch to Foer dated 06/27/2016).

[1107] *Id.*

[1108] Bean LLC/Fusion GPS Privilege Log dated Mar. 11, 2022 at 17-23.

[1109] *See, e.g.,* SC_00083448 (Email from Simpson to Mosk dated 07/27/2016); SC_00082580 (Email from Simpson to Mosk & Berkowitz dated 07/28/2016).

[1110] SC_IDC_0044254 (Emails between Millian, Mosk dated 07/13-27/2016) at 2-3.

[1111] 0.7.8516.58233 (Email from Millian to Mosk dated 07/26/2016).

[1112] SC_IDC_0044254 (Emails between Millian and Mosk dated 07/13-27/2016) at 1-2.

York. Millian indicated that he would be available to conduct an interview in New York on the "Week-end or next week I can."[1113] While making arrangements with Millian, Mosk emailed Simpson and informed Simpson that he (Mosk) was "making arrangements to interview Millian on camera" and that he and Simpson "should chat."[1114] Millian ultimately was interviewed by Brian Ross of ABC News on July 29, 2016.[1115]

For reasons unknown to the Office, ABC News did not air the Millian interview in its entirety until January 2017, after the Steele Reports became public.[1116] Nevertheless, Fusion GPS continued to send Mosk information about Millian,[1117] including Fusion GPS's comprehensive report on Millian dated June 30, 2016.[1118] On September 13, 2016, Mosk emailed Simpson and Berkowitz and asked "What's the most official thing we have showing Millian tied to Trump? That would make it hard for the Trump org to disavow Millian?"[1119] Berkowitz responded with a screenshot of Millian's Trump Gold Donor card that Millian had posted on his Instagram page.[1120] Throughout the fall of 2016, Fusion GPS continued to communicate with the media about Millian and Trump.[1121]

v. Fusion GPS attempts to tie Millian to Alfa Bank

As discussed in detail below, throughout the summer and fall of 2016, Fusion GPS was promoting to the media an allegation of secret computer server communications between the Trump campaign and Russian-based Alfa Bank. In an attempt to tie Millian to the Alfa Bank allegations, Fusion GPS sought the assistance of Perkins Coie attorney Michael Sussmann. In turn, Sussmann contacted technology executive Rodney Joffe to determine if Millian had any ties to Alfa Bank.

On August 20, 2016, Joffe emailed a fellow technology executive ("Tech Company-2 Executive-1") and two academic researchers ("University-1 Researcher-1" and "University-1 Researcher-2") a document titled "birdsnest-1.pdf" that contained "known associates" of

[1113] *Id.*

[1114] SC-00083448 (Email from Simpson to Mosk dated 07/27/2016).

[1115] SC_IDC_0044296 (Email from Mosk to Millian, others dated 07/28/2016).

[1116] *US-Russia Businessman Claimed Ties to Donald Trump (July 2016)*, ABC News (Jan. 24, 2017). https://abcnews.go.com/Politics/video/us-russia-businessman-claimed-ties-donald-trump-july-45022871

[1117] SC-00082251 (Email from Berkowitz to Mosk, Simpson dated 09/19/2016).

[1118] SC-00082580 (Email from Simpson to Mosk, Berkowitz dated 07/28/2016).

[1119] SC-00082257 (Email from Mosk to Berkowitz, Simpson dated 09/13/2016).

[1120] SC-00083205 (Email from Simpson to Mosk, Berkowitz dated 09/13/2016).

[1121] *See, e.g.*, SC-00083036 (Email from Simpson to Catherine Belton, Financial Times, dated 09/23/2016); SC-00099806 (Email from Simpson to Belton dated 09/22/2016); SC-00027869 (Email from Mark Hosenball, Reuters to Fritsch, Berkowitz & Simpson dated 11/23/2016); SC-00100363 (Email from Eric Lichtblau, N.Y. Times, to Fritsch & Simpson dated 09/27/2016); SC-00088073 (Email from Simpson to David Corn, Mother Jones dated 11/01/2016); SC-00028499 (Email from Peter H. Stone to Berkowitz dated 11/16/2016).

Trump.[1122] Included in the attached "birdnest-1" document was a description of Millian along with (i) his past mailing addresses, (ii) various email addresses, (iii) websites, and (iv) IP addresses that were associated with Millian.[1123] Joffe described the document as "the result of significant investigative effort of Eyore's[1124] professional team," and informed Tech Company-2 Executive-1, University-1 Researcher-1 and University-1 Researcher-2 that other than Paul Manafort, Millian is "seen as the most likely intermediary" between Trump and Russia. Joffe also specifically called the group's attention to the "Russianamericanchamber.com" website.

On September 22, 2016, Sussman emailed Joffe and attached a document containing IP location information for "Russianamericanchamber.com."[1125] The body of the email was redacted by Perkins Coie based on privilege claims by the Clinton campaign.[1126] On the evening of September 26, 2016, Joffe emailed Sussman a message containing the subject line "As requested."[1127] The body of the email was also redacted by Perkins Coie based on privilege claims by the Clinton campaign.[1128] Sussmann and Joffe exchanged additional emails (withheld for privilege) later that night and into the early morning hours of September 27, 2016.[1129]

Further, on September 27, 2016,[1130] Fritsch and Simpson emailed Millian's website (the Russian-American Chamber of Commerce) IP look-up information to Eric Lichtblau at the New York Times.[1131] As discussed below, during the fall of 2016, Fusion GPS was pressuring Lichtblau to write a story about the Trump/Alfa Bank allegations. In the email, Fritsch pointed out that "Alfa" was the website service provider for Millian's website. However, the Office determined that the relevant IP information does not indicate that "Alfa Bank" is the service provider, but rather Alfa Telecom, a Lebanese-based telecom company, which appears to have no affiliation with Alfa Bank whatsoever.[1132]

[1122] SC-00000578 (Email from Joffe to Tech Company-2 Executive-1, University-1 Researcher-1, University-1 Researcher-2 dated 08/20/2016).

[1123] *Id.* at 5.

[1124] The Office was not able to identify the individual referred to as "Eyore."

[1125] SC_00109377 (Email from Sussmann to Joffe dated 09/22/2016).

[1126] Perkins Coie Privilege Log dated 09/07/2021 at Worksheet 2 row 41.

[1127] SC_00109375 (Emails between Joffe and Sussmann dated 09/26-27/2016).

[1128] Perkins Coie Privilege Log dated 09/07/2021 at Worksheet 2 rows 45-48.

[1129] SC_00109375 (Emails between Joffe and Sussmann dated 09/26-27/2016).

[1130] Coincidentally – or not – the day following Sussmann and Joffe's exchange of emails concerning the same information.

[1131] SC-00100359 (Email from Fritsch to Lichtblau, Simpson dated 09/27/2016).

[1132] *Id.*

vi.   *The FBI's conduct concerning Millian*

From September 2007 to March 2011, Sergei Millian served as an FBI CHS.[1133] During that time, Millian reported on matters related to Belarus and Russia.[1134] Following, among other things, Danchenko's revelations concerning Millian, in August 2017, FBI agents attached to the Mueller Special Counsel team began investigating Millian to determine what, if any, involvement Millian had in relation to the Russian Government's efforts to influence the 2016 Presidential Election. On January 17, 2019 the FBI closed its case on Millian noting that "the investigation found no confirmation that [Millian] was directed to engage in activities related to Russian Government efforts to interfere with the 2016 U.S. Presidential Election."[1135]

In their interviews with the Office, both Auten and Helson expressed skepticism about Danchenko's alleged interaction with Millian.[1136] It does not appear, however, that the Crossfire Hurricane investigators made any effort to corroborate Danchenko's version of events. For example, it does not appear that the FBI examined either Danchenko or Millian's phone records. Nor does it appear that the FBI questioned Danchenko about the implausibility of the meeting he supposedly planned with Millian in New York. Lastly, and perhaps most importantly, nobody from the FBI questioned Danchenko about the incongruity between Millian's vocal support for Trump and his alleged statements to Danchenko. Again, in order to credit Danchenko's narrative, one would have to accept that Millian called Danchenko, an individual he did not know, and provided him with damaging information on Trump during a 10-15-minute phone call. In sum, the evidence obtained by the Office simply does not support Danchenko's version of events. Nevertheless, despite the obvious infirmities in Danchenko's narrative, the information allegedly provided by Millian remained in the Page FISA applications through the final renewal in June 2017.

g.   The FBI's failure to disclose to OI and include in the Page FISA applications Page's role as a source for another government agency

In addition to the inclusion of highly questionable information in the Page FISA applications, the FBI also failed to include highly relevant information in those applications. As disclosed in the *OIG Review*, one of the serious errors in the four Page FISA applications was the failure to report that Page had been approved as an "operational contact" for at least one other government agency ("OGA") during the period from 2008 to 2013.[1137] The record reflects that the Crossfire Hurricane investigators had been made aware of this relationship months prior to the submission of the initial Page FISA application in October 2016.

In the course of its investigation, the OIG also discovered evidence that, prior to the submission of the fourth and final Page FISA application, the issue of Page's relationship with the OGA was raised with the FBI's OGC by the FBI affiant on that application. In particular, the

---

[1133] *Danchenko* Tr. 10/11/2022 PM at 99-100.

[1134] SCO_105159 (Summary re Sergei Millian).

[1135] SCO_105145 (Case Closing Electronic Communication dated 01/17/2019) at 5.

[1136] OSC Report of Interview of Brian Auten on July 26, 2021 at 21; OSC Report of Interview of Kevin Helson on July 27, 2021 at 3-4.

[1137] *See Redacted OIG Review* at xi, 157-58.

affiant, Supervisory Special Agent-2, sought clarification from Kevin Clinesmith, the OGC attorney who was working with the Crossfire Hurricane investigators, on what, if any, relationship Page had with the OGA.[1138] Clinesmith (i) inquired of the other agency, (ii) received a response stating that Page did in fact have a relationship with it during a relevant time period, (iii) altered that response to reflect the opposite, and (iv) sent the altered document to the affiant, which the affiant then relied on in making representations to the FISC. After discovering this misconduct, OIG timely informed the Attorney General and the Director of the FBI of the matter pursuant to the Inspector General Act of 1978.[1139] Further information about Clinesmith's activities is set forth below:

i.   *FBI attorney Kevin Clinesmith*

From July 2015 until September 2019, Clinesmith was employed by the FBI's OGC as an Assistant General Counsel in the National Security and Cyber Law Branch.[1140] Among other duties, Clinesmith assisted FBI agents in preparing FISA applications and worked directly with attorneys in OI.[1141]

In the late summer and fall of 2016, Clinesmith was assigned to provide legal support to FBI personnel working on the Crossfire Hurricane investigation. In this role, Clinesmith interacted with an OGA on issues of importance to the Crossfire Hurricane effort. In addition, Clinesmith provided support to the Crossfire Hurricane investigators who worked with OI to prepare the FISA applications seeking authority to conduct surveillance of Page.[1142]

On August 17, 2016, months prior to the October 21, 2016, approval of the initial FISA application targeting Page, the OGA provided the Crossfire Hurricane investigators a memorandum (the "August 17 Memorandum") advising that Page had been approved as an "operational contact" for the OGA for the period 2008 to 2013. The Memorandum described the reporting Page had provided to the OGA, including detailing his prior contacts with certain Russian intelligence officers.[1143] As discussed in greater detail below, Clinesmith would later claim to the OIG that he did not recall reviewing the August 17th Memorandum and that he did not have access to it in FBI OGC office space.[1144] Although technically true that the document

---

[1138] *Id.* at 157-58, 248; OSC Report of Interview of Supervisory Special Agent-2 on May 5, 2021 at 3.

[1139] *See Redacted OIG Review* at 256.

[1140] *United States v. Kevin Clinesmith*, Crim. No. 20-cr-165 (JEB), (D.D.C.), Doc. 9 (Statement of Offense) at 2. As part of his plea agreement, Clinesmith agreed "to be personally debriefed" by the FBI regarding the FBI's review of FISA matters and "any information he possesses . . . that should be brought to the attention" of the FISC. Letter from John Durham to attorney Justin Shur, *Re: United States v. Kevin Clinesmith*, at 7 (Aug. 14, 2020). Clinesmith otherwise declined to be interviewed by the Office or cooperate with our investigation.

[1141] *Id.*

[1142] *United States v. Kevin Clinesmith*, Crim. No. 20-cr-165(JEB) (D.D.C.), Doc. 1 (Information) at 1-2.

[1143] *Id.* at 2.

[1144] OIG Report of Interview of Kevin Clinesmith on Aug. 29, 2019 at 19.

was not located in OGC space, the document was located at FBI Headquarters and available upon request to Crossfire Hurricane personnel, including Clinesmith.[1145]

The first three Page FISA applications made no reference to Page's prior relationship with the OGA. However, before the FBI's submission of the final FISA application, Page himself publicly stated that he had assisted named government entities in the past.[1146] During the preparation of the final FISA application, the affiant on the proposed application, Supervisory Special Agent-2, asked Clinesmith to ask whether Page had ever been a source for the OGA.[1147]

On June 15, 2017, Clinesmith sent an email to a liaison from the OGA ("OGA Liaison-1") stating:

> We need some clarification on Page. There is an indication that he may be a '[digraph]'[1148] source. This is a fact we would need to disclose in our next FISA renewal . . . To that end, can we get two items from you? 1) Source Check/Is [Page] a source in any capacity? 2) If he is, what is a [digraph] source (or whatever type of source he is)?[1149]

OGA Liaison-1 responded by email that same day and provided Clinesmith with a list (but not copies) of pertinent OGA documents. That list included a reference to the August 17 Memorandum the OGA had previously provided to the Crossfire Hurricane team. The liaison also wrote that the OGA uses

> the [digraph] to show that the encrypted individual . . . is a [U.S. person]. We encrypt the [U.S. persons] when they provide reporting to us. My recollection is that Page was or is . . . [digraph] but the [documents] will explain the details. If you need a formal definition for the FISA, please let me know and we'll work up some language and get it cleared for use.[1150]

Clinesmith responded that same day to OGA Liaison-1 stating, "Thanks so much for the information. We're digging into the [documents] now, but I think the definition of the [digraph] answers our questions."[1151]

At the time of the exchange between Clinesmith and OGA Liaison-1, Supervisory Special Agent-2 was on leave, so Clinesmith forwarded the liaison's email to two other Crossfire Hurricane investigators ("Special Agent-3" and "Supervisory Special Agent-4"). Notably, before forwarding the email, Clinesmith removed his initial email to OGA Liaison-1 that

---

[1145] OSC Report of Interview of Supervisory Special Agent-4 on Nov. 20, 2019 at 4.

[1146] Letter from Carter Page to FBI Director Comey (Sept. 25, 2016).

[1147] *See* OSC interview of Supervisory Special Agent-2 on Oct 17, 2019 at 4.

[1148] The digraph was redacted for classification reasons.

[1149] FBI-EMAIL-444179 (Email from Clinesmith to OGA Liason-1 dated 06/15/2017).

[1150] FBI-EMAIL-444164 (Email from Clinesmith to OGA Liason-1 dated 06/15/2017).

[1151] *Id.*

inquired about Page's status as a source.[1152] That same day, Supervisory Special Agent-4 emailed Clinesmith and OI Unit Chief-1, informing OI Unit Chief-1 that she (Supervisory Special Agent-4) would "pull these [documents] for you tomorrow[.]"[1153] In a subsequent reply to Clinesmith, Supervisory Special Agent-4 suggested that OI Unit Chief-1 may have previously been aware of Page's relationship with the OGA.[1154]

Later that evening, notwithstanding the information he received from OGA Liaison-1, Clinesmith told FBI OGC Unit Chief-1 that Page was not a source, but rather a "U.S. subsource of a source."[1155] Clinesmith also sent an email to OI Attorney-1, the OI attorney working on the Page FISA renewal, and requested a time to talk the following day.[1156]

The next day, Clinesmith and OI Attorney-1 spoke for approximately 30 minutes.[1157] Following the call, Clinesmith forwarded to OI Attorney-1 the June 15, 2017, email from OGA Liaison-1.[1158] Once again, Clinesmith omitted the initial email he sent to the liaison that inquired about Page's status as a source.[1159] When interviewed by the OIG, OI Attorney-1 did not recall the substance of his telephone call with Clinesmith.[1160] However, documents reviewed by the Office reflect that OI Attorney-1 replied to Clinesmith's forward of OGA Liaison-1's email and stated, "thanks I think we are good and no need to carry it any further."[1161] Copying Case Agent-1, Clinesmith replied, "Music to my ears."[1162] The Office has found no evidence to indicate that Case Agent-1 went back to look at the OGA documents after he received OI Attorney-1's guidance on the issue from Clinesmith.

On June 19, 2017, Supervisory Special Agent-2, who had returned from leave, exchanged a series of Lync messages with Clinesmith regarding Page:

> Supervisory Special Agent-2: Do we have any update on the [OGA] CHS [that is, Page] request? Also, [Case Agent-1]

[1152] FBI-EMAIL-444176 (Email from Clinesmith to OI Unit Chief-1 & Supervisory Special Agent-4 dated 06-15-2017).

[1153] FBI-EMAIL-441659 (Email from Supervisory Special Agent-4 to Clinesmith, OI Unit Chief-1 dated 06/15/2017).

[1154] FBI-EMAIL-441647 (Email from Supervisory Special Agent-4 to Clinesmith & OI Unit Chief-1 dated 06/19/2017).

[1155] FBI-AAA-EC-00006440 (Lync exchange between Clinesmith and FBI OGC Unit Chief-1 dated 06/15/2017).

[1156] FBI-EMAIL-441654 (Email from Clinesmith to OI Attorney-1 dated 06/15/2017).

[1157] FBI-EMAIL-447802 (Lync archive dated 06/16/2017).

[1158] FBI-EMAIL-444161 (Email from Clinesmith to OI Attorney-1 dated 06/16/2017).

[1159] Id.

[1160] OIG interview of OI Attorney-1 on Sept. 11, 2019 at 5-9.

[1161] FBI-EMAIL-444159 (Emails between Clinesmith and OI Attorney-1 dated 06/16/2017).

[1162] Id.

	said [OI Attorney-1] is not so optimistic.
Clinesmith:	[OGA] CHS: You are referring to Page?
Supervisory Special Agent-2:	Yes.
Clinesmith:	He is cleared.
Supervisory Special Agent-2:	Cleared to fly?
Clinesmith:	[digraph]=Masked USPER.[1163]
Supervisory Special Agent-2:	So, he was, and the relationship officially ended?
Clinesmith:	So, essentially, the real . . . source was using Page as a [Steele]-like subsource.[1164]
Clinesmith:	[Carter Page] was never a source.
Supervisory Special Agent-2:	You mean the [OGA] officer?
Clinesmith:	Right. Whomever generated the reporting from the [documents].
Clinesmith:	It was just liaison with Page which resulted in reporting, eventually they closed it out as unhelpful.
Clinesmith:	So, in discussing with [OI Attorney-1], he agreed we do not need to address it in the FISA.
Clinesmith:	[OI Attorney-1] is always Eeyore in drafting these special FISA applications.
Supervisory Special Agent-2:	So, Page was a [digraph] or Page was a subsource of the [digraph].

[1163] "USPER" is short for "U.S. Person."

[1164] Steele is a reference to Christopher Steele, who prepared certain reports, based on information from subsources. The FISA applications on Page relied, in part, on information taken from those reports.

Clinesmith:	It's [sic] sounds like a subsource of the [digraph].
Clinesmith:	And yes, [the OGA] confirmed explicitly he was never a source.
Supervisory Special Agent-2:	Interesting.
Clinesmith:	But like, interesting good, right?
Clinesmith:	*I mean, at least we don't have to have a terrible footnote.*
Supervisory Special Agent-2:	Sure. Just interesting they say not a source. We thought otherwise based on the writing . . . I will re-read.
Clinesmith:	At most, it's [another person] being the CHS, and you talking to [the other person].
Supervisory Special Agent-2:	Got it. Thank you. Do we have that in writing.
Clinesmith:	On TS. I'll forward.[1165]

As reflected above, Clinesmith told Supervisory Special Agent-2 that Page "was never a source" and that "[the OGA] confirmed explicitly he was never a source." When Supervisory Special Agent-2 asked if Clinesmith had that in writing, Clinesmith responded he did and that he would forward the email that the OGA had provided.

Immediately after the Lync messages between Clinesmith and Supervisory Special Agent-2, Clinesmith forwarded to Supervisory Special Agent-2 a version of OGA Liaison-1's June 15, 2017 email containing alterations that Clinesmith had made. The altered email from the liaison read as follows:

My recollection is that Page was or is "[digraph]" *and not a "source"* but the [documents] will explain the details. If you need a formal definition for the FISA,

---

[1165] FBI-AAA-EC-00006440 (Lync exchange between Clinesmith and Supervisory Special Agent-2 dated 06/19/2017) (emphasis added); *see also* OSC Report of Interview of Supervisory Special Agent-2 on May 5, 2021 at 3. (Supervisory Special Agent-2 believes Clinesmith lied to him about Page's history with the OGA).

please let me know and we'll work up some language and get it cleared for use.[1166]

Clinesmith had altered the original June 15, 2017 email from the liaison by adding the words "and not a source" to the email, thus making it appear that OGA Liaison-1 had written in the email that Page was "not a source" for the OGA. Relying on the altered email, Supervisory Special Agent-2 signed the application that was submitted to the FISC on June 29, 2017.[1167] This final FISA application did not include Page's history or status with the OGA.

The Office's investigators, like the OIG investigators, confirmed with OGA Liaison-1 that she had no recollection of ever having told Clinesmith that Page was not a source for the OGA.[1168]

h. CHS meetings with Papadopoulos, Page, and a third Trump campaign member, the *Yahoo! News* article about Page, and Page's offer to be interviewed

In addition to opening Crossfire Hurricane, the FBI opened or had open investigations of four individuals associated with the Trump campaign.[1169] FBI CHSs or undercover employees ("UCEs") met with two of those individuals (Papadopoulos and Page), as well as with a senior Trump campaign foreign policy official, and recorded many of these meetings.[1170] Many of the omissions and much of the misleading information found in the Page FISA applications, described by the OIG, deserve additional emphasis in this report based on the Office's review of the transcripts and careful review of the actual recorded conversations themselves. Indeed, listening to the recordings and reviewing the transcripts was especially important when considered against the backdrop of an unauthorized disclosure made to *Yahoo! News* about the federal investigation into Page, and Page's subsequent offer to be interviewed by the FBI.

i. The FBI's engagement with CHS-1 and first consensual recording of Carter Page on August 20, 2016

Approximately ten days after the Crossfire Hurricane investigation was opened on Page, Case Agent-1 worked to arrange a meeting with CHS-1, a long-term counterintelligence source who the FBI had paid a substantial amount of money over many years. WFO closed CHS-1 for cause in January 2011 for "displaying aggressiveness toward handling Agents as a result of what he/she perceived as not enough compensation . . . and for exhibiting questionable allegiance to

---

[1166] FBI-EMAIL-444157 (Email from Clinesmith to Supervisory Special Agent-2 dated 06/19/2017) (emphasis added).

[1167] *See* OSC Report of Interview of Supervisory Special Agent-2 on May 5, 2021 at 3-4.

[1168] OSC Report of Interview of OGA Liaison-1 on Oct. 3, 2019 at 2.

[1169] *See supra* § IV.A.3.c.

[1170] The *AGG-Dom* lists consensual monitoring as an authorized investigative method that requires legal review. *AGG-Dom* § V.A.4. It defines consensual monitoring as "monitoring of communications for which a court order or warrant is not legally required because of the consent of a party to the communication." *Id.* § VII.A. The party consenting to the monitoring may be an FBI CHS or UCE.

the [intelligence] targets with which CHS-1 maintained contact."[1171] Nevertheless, Case Agent-1 reopened CHS-1 within two months of the CHS's closing and continued to serve as his/her handling agent through the Crossfire Hurricane investigation.[1172] (Case Agent-1 had served as CHS-1's handling agent for most of the five-year period before the opening of Crossfire Hurricane).[1173]

When the FBI approached CHS-1 in August 2016 to determine whether he/she knew Papadopoulos, CHS-1 said that he/she was not familiar with Papadopoulos. However, CHS-1 asked Case Agent-1 and two other FBI employees who were present if the FBI had any interest in Carter Page, with whom CHS-1 had met a month earlier in July 2016.[1174] [1175] The FBI learned that Page had been invited to attend a July 2016 meeting focused on intelligence and global security affairs. Page's attendance at the overseas event occurred just days after his visit to Russia, where he had delivered a commencement address at the New Economic School in Moscow. Given the circumstances and familiarity that CHS-1 had with Page from their recent meeting together at the overseas seminar, the FBI believed CHS-1 could initiate contact with Page without arousing any suspicions.[1176] CHS-1 contacted Page at the behest of the FBI and a meeting was arranged for August 20, 2016, which CHS-1 recorded.[1177] The primary purpose of

---

[1171] FBI-0000812 (Source Closing Communication dated 01/25/2011).

[1172] FBI-0000814 (Source Reopening Communication dated 03/23/2011).

[1173] CHS-1 also maintained relationships with other government agencies, and had likewise been paid for his/her services.

[1174] One individual interviewed by the Office advised that CHS-1 was directly involved in deciding which individuals would be invited to that earlier meeting and had authorized an invitation being sent to Page. OSC Report of Interview of U.S. Person-4 on 06/04/2020 at 1.

[1175] It does not appear that, at that time, CHS-1 disclosed to the Crossfire Hurricane investigators that on May 3, 2016, CHS-1 sent an email to Trump Policy Director-1 that contained his/her resume, spoke of her/his prior political experience regarding foreign policy matters, offered to help Trump in the foreign policy area, and, although stating that he/she was not seeking a position in a Trump administration, said he/she believed it was important to see Trump elected. When the Office asked about the email, CHS-1 said that Page had asked him/her to send it. However, when reminded that he/she had not even met Page until nearly two months later, CHS-1 said he/she probably sent it because he/she thought he/she could be helpful to the campaign regarding a particular country (which was not Russia). OSC Report of Interview of CHS-1 on April 6, 2021 at 3.

Relatedly, shortly after Trump's election in November 2016, CHS-1, while still an FBI CHS, sent a senior Trump transition team member an email offering his/her congratulations on Trump's victory and expressing an interest in assisting the new Administration. See Email from CHS-1 to Trump Senior Foreign Policy Advisor-1 dated 11/14/ 2016. We have no information to suggest that the FBI requested CHS-1 to send this email.

[1176] FBI-0016044 (EC "Meeting with CHS to discuss CROSSFIRE HURRICANE" dated Aug. 11, 2016).

[1177] FBI-0002721 (EC "Meeting with CHS-1 to discuss CROSSFIRE HURRICANE" dated 08/12/2016).

the meeting (and three additional consensually recorded meetings with Page made by CHS-1) was to assist in determining whether Page had information relevant to the allegation that predicated the opening of the Crossfire Hurricane investigation.

The first meeting between Page and CHS-1 took place as scheduled on August 20, 2016. Before the meeting, the FBI briefed CHS-1 on the information received from Foreign Government-1 that predicated the opening of Crossfire Hurricane. Because Page and CHS-1 were acquainted from their July meeting, they discussed a number of topics during the August 20th engagement. CHS-1 said that he had once known Manafort, the Trump campaign manager who had resigned the previous day.[1178] Page told CHS-1 that he (Page) had "actually literally never met Manafort . . . never said one word to him."[1179] When Page added that he had sent Manafort a couple of emails, the CHS interrupted him and said, "And he [Manafort] never responded probably." Page then replied, "Never, never responded one word."[1180] Since that time, Page has repeatedly stated that, despite allegations to the contrary, he never met or corresponded with Manafort while they worked on the campaign.[1181] Later in the conversation, Page told CHS-1 that, "I was never from the beginning a Manafort fan . . . ."[1182] Page also said that he believed Manafort might be in some trouble, but he provided no further information regarding the source of the trouble.[1183] Page's statements about Manafort, especially about their having no relationship, seriously undercut the reports from Steele subsequently received by the Crossfire Hurricane investigators that alleged that Page was engaged in a conspiracy with Manafort, the Trump campaign and the Russians.[1184]

Importantly, FBI records reflect that the Crossfire Hurricane investigators apparently failed to determine at that time whether Page's statements to CHS-1 had a basis in fact. Had they done so, investigators would have found that Page had previously sent Manafort one direct email message and copied him on two other messages, none of which Manafort appears to have answered.[1185] This documentary evidence provides significant corroboration of Page's

---

[1178] Transcript of Aug. 20, 2016 conversation between Carter Page and CHS-1 at 40.

[1179] Id. at 39.

[1180] Id.

[1181] See U.S. House of Representatives Permanent Select Cmte. on Intelligence Testimony of Carter Page on Nov. 02, 2017 at 21-22.

[1182] Transcript of conversation between Carter Page and CHS-1 on 08/20/2016 at 136.

[1183] Id. at 137-38.

[1184] As noted previously, the first Steele Reports were provided to the FBI by Steele beginning on July 5, 2016. Steele Source File at A-022 ("July 5 rpt"); OIG Interview of Handling Agent-1 on Aug. 30, 2018 at 152-158. For some still unexplained reason, however, members of the Crossfire Hurricane team working on drafting the Page FISA did not receive them until September 19, 2016. FBI-EMAIL-129902 (Email from Handling Agent-1 to Supervisory Special Agent-1 dated 09/19/2016); FBI-EMAIL-129908 (Email from Handling Agent-1 to Supervisory Special Agent-1 dated 09/19/2016).

[1185] Email from Carter Page to Paul Manafort, Sam Clovis & J.D. Gordon dated 07/25/2016; Email from Page to Hope Hicks & Manafort dated 08/15/2016; Email from Page to Hicks & Manafort dated 08/16/2016. Our investigation found no evidence that Manafort responded to

statements about Manafort and should have raised, at the time when the FBI was assessing the Steele reporting, serious concerns about the reliability of an important piece of that reporting.

In addition to discussing Manafort, Page and CHS-1 also discussed three other topics:

First, at several points in the conversation, Page was asked about a possible "October surprise" being planned by the Trump campaign.[1186] In one place CHS-1 referenced an October surprise from an earlier Presidential election, and Page responded that he wanted to know the definition of an October surprise "because there's a different October surprise in, uh, this year, but you know . . . [a]lthough maybe some similarities."[1187] Toward the end of their meeting, Page was bluntly asked, "[w]hat is the October surprise you are planning?" The recording reflects that this was followed by someone laughing. Page responded "[W]ell I want to have the conspiracy theory about the, uh, Ru- the next email dump with these 33 thousand, you know." In reply, CHS-1 asked, "Well the Russians have all that don't they?" and Page stated, "I don't, I-I don't know."[1188]

Second, Page discussed with and confirmed for CHS-1 certain recent media reports regarding his (Page's) business relationships in Russia.[1189] Nevertheless, during this meeting and all other subsequent recorded meetings with CHS-1, Page either implicitly or explicitly denied that those relationships were with the Russian government.[1190] Additionally, during all of his meetings with CHS-1, Page never provided any information, evidence, or documentation indicating knowledge of any relationship between the Trump campaign and the Russian government. Rather, in this meeting and on several occasions during their subsequent meetings, Page told CHS-1 that Trump wanted improved relations between the United States and Russia and Russian President Putin.[1191] At no time did Page discuss anything about the campaign working in concert with the Russian government.

Third, CHS-1 initiated a discussion with Page about Papadopoulos, asserting that, "someone in [redacted] said there's a guy in London [Papadopoulos] who's talking about the Trump campaign relations with the Russians,"[1192] alluding to the information passed to the FBI by Australia that FBI officials stated formed the basis for the Crossfire Hurricane investigation. Page, however, did not confirm or even address CHS-1's insinuation of a relationship between

---

any of these emails sent by Page. The three emails were contained on a **thumb drive** voluntarily provided to the FBI in August, 2017 by an attorney representing then-President Trump.

[1186] Transcript of conversation between Carter Page and CHS-1 on 08/20/2016 at 52-53, 71-74, 159-160.

[1187] *Id.* at 53.

[1188] *Id.* at 159-160.

[1189] *Id.* at 64-66.

[1190] *Id.* at 66; Transcript of conversation between Carter Page and CHS-1 on 10/17/2016 at 17; Transcript of conversation between Carter Page and CHS-1 on 12/15/2016 at 19-20; Transcript of conversation between Carter Page and CHS-1 on 01/25/2017 at 7, 38, 42-43.

[1191] Transcript of conversation between Carter Page and CHS-1 on 08/20/2016 at 92-93.

[1192] *Id.* at 95.

the Trump campaign and Russia.[1193] Rather, Page was somewhat dismissive of Papadopoulos's youth and described him as "[having gotten] in some hot water" over comments he (Papadopoulos) made about British Prime Minister David Cameron owing Trump an apology. Again, Page did not display any knowledge of an illicit relationship between the Trump campaign and Russia. Finally, when CHS-1 again tried to elicit information on this subject by stating, "So this fellow Papadopoulos is just, um, a young guy who's . . . [s]aying things that he shouldn't say or what," Page responded by simply stating, "No, he's a fine guy." Again, Page did not state or display any knowledge of an existing relationship between the campaign and Russia despite CHS-1's baited statements designed to elicit such information from Page. Page's recorded statements were significant because this was the first time Crossfire Hurricane investigators had an opportunity to obtain direct evidence that might corroborate or, alternatively, raise questions about the allegations passed on by Australia. In this first recorded conversation, Page did not corroborate this information.

Five days later, a briefing concerning this first recording of Page was held at FBI Headquarters for Deputy Director McCabe, Assistant Director Priestap, General Counsel Baker, Section Chief Strzok, Deputy General Counsel Anderson, and other FBI personnel. In addition to a discussion of the meeting between CHS-1 and Page, excerpts from the recorded meeting were played at the briefing.[1194]

> ii.   *The receipt of the first Steele Reports, publication of the Yahoo! News article naming Page, and Page's expressed willingness to be interviewed by the FBI*

There were no additional meetings between Page and CHS-1 until almost two months later. In the interim, on September 19, 2016, FBI personnel conducting the Crossfire Hurricane investigation received documents that were represented to be intelligence-type products authored by former British intelligence official Christopher Steele. These documents were part of what has become known collectively as the "Steele Dossier." While other sections of this report discuss in detail Steele and his reporting, two allegations relating to Page are relevant to this section. In particular, one allegation stated that "there was a well-developed conspiracy of co-operation between them [the Trump campaign] and the Russian leadership . . . [that] was managed on the Trump side by . . . Paul MANAFORT, who was using foreign policy advisor Carter PAGE and others as intermediaries."[1195] In that role, Page purportedly served as the liaison or "go between" for Trump campaign Chairman Manafort and Russian officials working with the Trump campaign. This allegation was in stark contrast to, and in direct conflict with, what CHS-1 had recorded Page saying in August. Somewhat inexplicably, in subsequent meetings between CHS-1 and Page, CHS-1 never attempted to re-engage Page on the subject of

---

[1193] *Id.* at 94-97.

[1194] OSC Report of Interview of James Baker on Feb. 7, 2020, at 12; *see also Redacted OIG Review* at 319-320.

[1195] SCO-105084 (Documents Known to the FBI Comprising the "Steele Dossier") at 9 (Company Intelligence Report 2016/095) (capitalization in original). Interestingly, CHS-1 had met Page in a different country on or about July 12, 2016, approximately one month prior to being approached by the FBI about Page, and Company Intelligence Report 2016/094 implicating Page was dated July 19, 2016.

his relationship with Manafort. Moreover, prior to submitting the initial FISA application to the FISC in October 2016, the Crossfire Hurricane investigators apparently never sought to obtain Page's email or phone records (whether from Page himself or otherwise) to verify or disprove Page's statement about his lack of a relationship with Manafort. As a result, at no time either before or during the electronic surveillance of Page did the FBI resolve the glaring conflict between Page's unequivocal statement regarding Manafort and the critical assertion in the Steele reports that Page served as one of Manafort's liaisons to the Russians.

The second Page-related allegation in the Steele reporting was a claim that, in July 2016, while in Moscow to deliver a speech to the New Economic School, Page had met secretly with Vladimir Putin's ally and Chief Executive Officer of Rosneft, Igor Sechin,[1196] and also with Kremlin Internal Affairs official Igor Divyekin.[1197] In late September, the allegations concerning Page's meetings with Sechin and Divyekin first made their way into the public domain with the publication of an article in *Yahoo! News* authored by Michael Isikoff.[1198] In the article, Mr. Isikoff wrote that Page, an American businessman who had been identified as a foreign policy adviser to then-Presidential candidate Trump, was the subject of an investigation being conducted by U.S. intelligence officials. The officials reportedly were trying to determine if Page was having private communications with senior Russian officials. The article went on to refer to a congressional source and said that "[Page's] talks with senior Russian officials close to President Vladimir Putin were being 'actively monitored and investigated' and that a senior U.S. law enforcement official did not dispute that characterization, stating, 'It's on our radar screen'. . . . It's being looked at.'"[1199] The article credited a "well-placed Western intelligence source" as identifying Sechin and Divyekin, both of whom were alleged to be close to Putin, as individuals with whom Page had met while in Moscow[1200]

Two days after publication of the *Yahoo! News* article, Page sent a letter to FBI Director Comey.[1201] In that letter, Page requested that the FBI promptly end its inquiry into his recent trip to Russia. Page alluded to the fact that he had previously been interviewed by the FBI and

---

[1196] At the time, Rosneft was Russia's largest oil and gas producer. *See* Isikoff, *Officials Probe Ties*.

[1197] SCO-105084 (Documents Known to the FBI Comprising the "Steele Dossier") at 8 (Company Intelligence Report 2016/94).

[1198] Isikoff, *Officials Probe Ties*.

[1199] So far as we were able to determine, the FBI did not refer for investigation this leak of highly sensitive information by a "senior U.S. law enforcement official" relating to an ongoing investigation of a presidential campaign.

[1200] As discussed in greater detail in Section IV.D.1.b.vi, the initial consensus of the FBI's Crossfire Hurricane investigators was that Steele, who himself was an FBI CHS, was the unnamed "Western intelligence source" referenced in the article. However, that consensus, which was set out in footnotes of drafts of the initial Page FISA application, changed for unexplained reasons shortly before the final version of the application was submitted to the FISC. That final version of the application attributed the leak of information not to Steele, but rather to Steele's employer, Fusion GPS.

[1201] Letter from Carter Page to FBI Director Comey (Sept. 25, 2016).

specifically volunteered to speak to any member of the FBI "in the interest of helping them put these outrageous allegations [about him] to rest."[1202] Page denied what he termed "completely false media reports . . . [stating] for the record, I have not met this year with any sanctioned official in Russia." Page also publicly stated that he had "interacted with members of the U.S. intelligence community including the FBI and CIA for many decades."[1203] The FBI, however, did not take Page up on his offer to be interviewed, and, indeed, the Crossfire Hurricane investigators were prohibited by FBI senior executives from approaching Page until former Director Comey finally authorized an interview in March 2017, almost six months after Page's written offer. In this regard, FBI records reflect the following relevant Lync messages:

On October 13, 2016, one week *before* the initial Page FISA application was submitted to the FISC, two Crossfire Hurricane investigators, Case Agent-1 (a principal source of information for the Page FISA application) and Special Agent-2, had the following exchange:

Case Agent-1:   It looks like Mgmt doesn't want us to do an interview, right now.

Special Agent-2:   of course not, that would make too much sense...

Case Agent-1:   Yeah, exactly. We... were told by [Supervisory Special Agent-1] that *mgmt wants to see what we get from his meeting with [CHS][1204] (Monday) and what we see in the FISA.*[1205]

Shortly thereafter, the following exchange occurred between Special Agent-2 and Supervisory Special Agent-1:

Special Agent-2:   Yeah [Case Agent-1] says no appetite to interview [P]age either. thats [sic] stupid.

Supervisory Special Agent-1: yeah- dude i dont [sic] know why we are even here.[1206]

[1202] Other parts of this report discuss the fact that Page had been interviewed several times previously by the FBI, most recently in March 2016, when he was interviewed as a potential trial witness for the government in the prosecution of three Russian nationals in the case known as *U.S. v. Buryakov, et al.*, 1:15-CR-00073 (S.D.N.Y.); *see supra* § IV.A.1.a.

[1203] Letter from Carter Page to FBI Director Comey (Sept. 25, 2016).

[1204] As discussed below, four days after this exchange, on October 17, 2016, Page met with FBI CHS-1, who recorded their conversation. During the meeting, Page explicitly stated that he had not met with Sechin and that he did not even know who Divyekin was. *See* Section IV.D.1.h.iii.

[1205] FBI-AAA-EC-00008439 (Lync message exchange between Case Agent-1 and Special Agent-2 dated 10/13/2016) (emphasis added).

[1206] FBI-AAA-EC-00000365 (Lync message exchange between Special Agent-2 and Supervisory Special Agent-1 on 10/13/2016). FBI records make clear that the decision not to interview Page was being driven by the top-echelon of the FBI, including Comey and McCabe. Six months later, the following exchanges occurred between Crossfire Hurricane personnel:

Special Agent-3 to Supervisory Special Agent-3: What's the over/under on getting the approval today from the DD [Deputy Director]?

It is clear from the Lync message exchanges that there was frustration on the part of Crossfire Hurricane investigators over their inability to conduct a timely interview of Page. It is

> Supervisory Special Agent-3 to Special Agent-3: I bet you one cocktail of choice the approval does NOT come today.
>
> Case Agent-1 to Supervisory Special Agent-3: . . . Do you think this happens today?
>
> Supervisory Special Agent-3 to Case Agent-1: I already bet [Special Agent-3's first name] one cocktail of choice the DD sits on it.
>
> Case Agent-1 to Supervisory Special Agent-3: Question, what's the hold up with the DD?
>
> Supervisory Special Agent-3 to Case Agent-1: It's the political sensitivities and the whole timing of everything.

FBI-AAA-EC-00008079 (Lync message exchange between Supervisory Special Agent-3, Special Agent-3 & Case Agent-1 dated 03/08/2017).

> Case Agent-1 to Chicago Agent-1: ...We were all set to interview [Page] this morning, but apparently, we need DD to do it now
>
> Chicago Agent-1 to Case Agent-1: oh great

FBI-AAA-EC-00008439 (Lync message exchange between Case Agent-1 and Chicago Agent-1 dated 03/08/2017).

> Support Operations Specialist-1 to Case Agent-1: Who is the hold up? McCabe?
>
> Case Agent-1 to Support Operations Specialist-1: I'm wondering if it's McCabe or if it's Priestap holding off telling McCabe
>
> Case Agent-1 to Support Operations Specialist-1: DD is good with it, waiting to hear from the big guy and we're going to head out.
>
> Case Agent-1 to Support Operations Specialist-1: We've been told to follow the letter that he sent to Comey. We can't mention any names today, etc.
>
> Case Agent-1 to Support Operations Specialist-1: Just waiting for the Director to approve, they're in Boston together, so we anticipate it to be within the hour
>
> Support Operations Specialist-1 to Case Agent-1: So there's just been no word from the director? Is that literally all you guys are waiting on?

FBI-AAA-EC-00008439 (Lync message exchange between Case Agent-1 and Support Operations Specialist-1 dated 03/08/2017).

> Support Operations Specialist-1 to Case Agent-1: It's a normal investigative step. Who cares what the politics are.
>
> Support Operations Specialist-1 to Case Agent-1: If thy [sic] don't want to look political, stop trying not to look political.

FBI-AAA-EC-00008439 (Lync message exchange between Case Agent-1 and Support Operations Specialist-1 dated 03/09/2017).

also clear from the messages sent by Case Agent-1, Special Agent-2, and their supervisor on the investigation, Supervisory Special Agent-1, that the timing and circumstances of the interview were not left to the individuals conducting and supervising the investigation, but rather the decisions on those issues were effectively being made by the Director and Deputy Director of the FBI. In this regard, according to McCabe, "Director Comey was getting daily briefings on this stuff, regularly" and the Director was intimately involved with the team that was working the case.[1207]

We observed that Page's letter to Director Comey was received by the FBI less than one week following the Crossfire Hurricane investigative team's receipt of some of the startling, but uncorroborated, Steele Reports. As noted above, those reports included, among a number of other allegations, specific claims that Page was serving as an intermediary between Manafort and Russian leadership, and that Page had met with both Sechin and Divyekin while travelling to Russia in July 2016.[1208] As to the former, as detailed above, Page had already been recorded on August 20, 2016, informing CHS-1 that he had no relationship with Manafort and, indeed, had never even spoken with him. As to the latter claim, Page would be recorded on October 17, 2016 informing CHS-1 that he had not met with Sechin as reported by Steele and was completely unfamiliar with Divyekin. During this same timeframe, and as set forth in greater detail below, the Crossfire Hurricane investigative team was working with OI to secure authorization from the FISC for a FISA warrant on Page.

An interview of Page at that time, for which he had volunteered, would have undoubtedly been beneficial to the nascent Crossfire Hurricane investigation. As noted, Page had previously been interviewed by the FBI on multiple occasions, unrelated to his work on the Trump campaign,[1209] and there was no indication of any reticence on his part to speak openly and at length with the FBI. Indeed, an interview with Page would have enabled the FBI to explore whatever topics were deemed relevant to the investigation, including, but not limited to, the following:

- Page's assessment of Papadopoulos, whose statement to the Australian diplomats had served as the predication for the Crossfire Hurricane investigation. (At the time Page volunteered to be interviewed, he had already discussed Papadopoulos with CHS-1).

- Page's relationship, if any, with Manafort, Sechin, Divyekin and other persons of interest to the investigators.

- An evaluation of any in-person denials made by Page of the allegations contained in the Isikoff *Yahoo! News* article, which would have served the dual purpose of enabling the FBI to better assess the credibility of the Steele Dossier reporting by obtaining more detailed information about the allegations directly from Page.

- Explore with Page any contact(s) that he knew of or suspected between individuals working on the campaign and any Russian officials. Because he was familiar with

---

[1207] OIG Interview of Andrew McCabe dated Aug. 15, 2019 at 33.

[1208] SCO-105084 (Documents Known to the FBI Comprising the "Steele Dossier") at 8-10 (Company Intelligence Reports 2016/94 and 2016/095).

[1209] *See supra* § IV.A.1.a.

Russia, the FBI might have been better able to assess the credibility of the media reporting on Trump's alleged relationship with Russian officials.

An interview with Page also would have enabled the FBI to better assess the reliability of CHS-1. Finally, if the Crossfire Hurricane investigators believed that Page was not being candid, they could have asked Page to submit to a voluntary polygraph exam and to produce relevant records.

Although there may have been a concern that interviewing Page would adversely affect the FBI's ability to secure a FISA warrant, Page had already denied the allegations in the Isikoff article (and the Steele Reports, which he was not even aware at the time) in his letter to Director Comey. Page again denied the allegations in a September 26, 2016 *Washington Post* article, calling them "garbage."[1210] As previously noted, and discussed in more detail below, in a recorded conversation with CHS-1 on October 17, 2016, four days before the FISA surveillance application was approved, Page explicitly denied meeting with Sechin and Divyekin. All of Page's denials were characterized by the FBI in the initial FISA application, as discussed below, as not credible.[1211] If Page had further denied the allegations in an interview, those denials, too, could have been included in the application. Moreover, again, they also may have succeeded in getting Page to agree to take a voluntary polygraph examination on unresolved issues and areas of concern.

Nevertheless, senior FBI management made the decision not to interview Page and, instead, continued to move forward on the FISA surveillance targeting Page.

Notably, once Comey authorized an interview of Page to go forward in March 2017, Page sat for five voluntary interviews and fully cooperated with the FBI, even going so far as to bring his own PowerPoint presentation to one of the interviews.[1212] In those interviews, consistent with representations he had made to CHS-1 in recorded conversations, Page denied meeting with Sechin and Divyekin. Additionally, and also consistent with what he said to CHS-1, Page denied ever meeting with or speaking to Manafort.

Although the Office recognizes the benefit of hindsight in reviewing investigative decision-making, the failure to promptly conduct a voluntary interview of Page, contemporaneous with his request for such an interview, was a missed opportunity to further assess, on a timely basis and in a different light, the actual value of the Papadopoulos information provided by Australia. It also was a missed opportunity to test the reliability of claims about Page contained in the Steele Reports. Other investigative deficiencies with respect to Page – in the Office's assessment – are discussed further below.

[1210] Josh Rogin, *Trump's Russia Adviser Speaks Out, Calls Accusations 'Complete Garbage'*, Wash. Post (Sept. 26, 2016).

[1211] *In re Carter W. Page*, No. 16-1182, at 25-27. The first two denials by Page, in the letter to the Director and the *Washington Post* article, were described as "self-serving" in the FISA affidavit. The latter denial was described as vague statements that minimized his activities.

[1212] FBI Interviews of Carter Page on March 9, 2017, March 10, 2017, March 16, 2017, March 30, 2017 and March 31, 2017.

iii. The second recording of Page made by CHS-1

On October 17, 2016, CHS-1 and Page had a second meeting, which was also recorded by CHS-1. Regarding the allegation in the Steele reporting that Page had met with Sechin and Divyekin, Page expressly denied that he met with either one and described the reporting on the matter as lies planted in the media by "[Senator] Harry Reid . . . and the Clinton [campaign] team in Brooklyn."[1213] Additionally, Page stated, "the core lie is that I met with these sanctioned Russian officials . . . several of which I never even met in my entire life."[1214] Later in the conversation, Page also advised CHS-1 that Rosneft (Sechin's company) had denied that a meeting between Page and Sechin had taken place.[1215] Finally, Page referred to a story regarding an interview Trump campaign manager Kellyanne Conway conducted with CNN during which, according to Page, she said that "[Page] is not allowed to talk to the Russians, we-he was never authorized."[1216] In relating this story, Page told CHS-1, "I told everyone in the campaign . . . you know I never actually talked to these people. So, it's just kind of . . . you know, complete lies."[1217]

CHS-1 and Page also discussed Page's alleged meeting with Divyekin. Early in the meeting, neither Page nor CHS-1 could even recall Divyekin's name, with Page wondering whether he may have shaken the hand of some unknown person -- who may have been Divyekin -- after his speech at the New Economic School in Moscow in July 2016. With respect to Divyekin, the following exchange occurred:

CHS-1:   And there's another one who worked for, uh--

Page: There's another guy—

CHS-1:   --Putin

Page: I have never even heard of, you know, he's like in the inner circle.

CHS-1:   What's his name again?

Page: I—I can't even remember. It's so outrageous.

CHS-1:   Yeah. Right, he's in the inner circle. He-he works in the Kremlin or something.

[1213] Transcript of conversation between Carter Page and CHS-1 on 10/17/2016 at 16. Case Agent-1 told the OIG that the Crossfire Hurricane team never fully transcribed the October 17, 2016, recording, but rather only transcribed certain excerpts taken from the recording. *See Redacted OIG Review* at 321. Our investigation made use of the fully transcribed recording.

[1214] Transcript of conversation between Carter Page and CHS-1 on 10/17/2016 at 17.

[1215] *Id.* at 45 (quoting a Rosneft spokesman's statement in Julia Ioffe, *Who is Carter Page? The Mystery of Trump's Man in Moscow*, Politico (Sept. 23, 2016)).

[1216] David Cohen, *Conway Denies Trump Campaign Ties to Russia Figure*, Politico (Sept. 25, 2106) (quoting Trump campaign manager Kellyanne Conway's statement on CNN's "State of the Union").

[1217] Transcript of conversation between Carter Page and CHS-1 on 10/17/2016 at 107.

Page: But he's, you know, he's not someone—Again, I—I was asking –I wanted to double check, you know, I wanted to make sure that it—the graduation, I—you know, I called up, the, uh, people that were, you know, when I was a Commencement Speaker, you know. Did I happen to shake hands with this guy? Like—this guy is just completely, you know--they didn't even know of him because he's like—I mean is like for example, uh, a Senior Director on the NSC. Right? I mean they're not household names where, you know . . .[1218]

Later in the meeting, CHS-1 (not Page) recalled Divyekin's name and the following exchange took place in which Page denied even having heard of Divyekin:

CHS-1: The guy...that we were trying to think of earlier is Devianken [sic].

Page: Oh yeah, yeah, Right, right, right, yeah. *Never heard of him until-*

CHS-1: I never- I never heard of him either.

Page: . . . the Russian guys at the University who are kind of ins and outs- . . . live in Moscow, right?

CHS-1: They don't know him either, no?

Page: *Hadn't heard of him, you know.* He's kind of again Senior Director on NSC.[1219]

Later in the conversation, in response to an inquiry as to whether Page would be attending the upcoming Presidential debate in Nevada, Page advised that he was taking a break from the campaign. When CHS-1 asked, "Oh, you're not in touch with the campaign . . . ?" Page responded "[I] told them I-I need to fight out- fight against these FBI investigations and, you know it . . . it's not appropriate for me to be making statements if I'm still officially affiliated with the campaign . . . ."[1220]

At the end of the meeting, CHS-1 and Page discussed the possible establishment of a think tank to be located in London focused on Russia's relations with the West, a topic they had briefly discussed in their first meeting. After telling CHS-1 that he liked the idea, Page said, "[T]he only big question obviously like most things is, you know, funding for it . . . ." In response, CHS-1 stated that, "[I] would imagine that you could probably find funds . . . ."[1221] Returning to the topic a little later, Page said, "[W]ell the only interesting question [CHS-1's name deleted], on your point is, I don't wanna say they'd be an open check book, but the Russians would definitely . . ." at which time CHS-1 interrupted saying," [T]hey would fund it." Page then responded "uh-hum."[1222]

[1218] *Id.* at 18-19.

[1219] *Id.* at 99 (emphasis added).

[1220] *Id.* at 78.

[1221] *Id.* at 111.

[1222] *Id.* at 112.

A few hours after this meeting, Supervisory Special Agent-1 contacted Strzok to provide a summary of it (which Supervisory Special Agent-1 had received from Case Agent-1). In that exchange, Supervisory Special Agent-1 informed Strzok that Page "did not deny knowing Sechin," and "*outright denied knowing Divyekin.*"[1223] As an initial matter, Page denied *meeting* with either Sechin or Divyekin, the actual allegation set forth in the Steele Report and contained in the initial Page FISA. Supervisory Special Agent-1, however, accurately relayed Page's "outright" denial that he knew Divyekin. Minutes later, Supervisory Special Agent-1 cut-and-pasted his message to Strzok and sent it to both Brian Auten and Section Chief Moffa. Thus, as of October 17, 2016, a principal source of information for the FISA, Case Agent-1, the two most senior analysts on Crossfire Hurricane, Moffa and Auten, and the Deputy Assistant Director of the Counterintelligence Division, Strzok, were all made aware of the fact that Page explicitly denied knowing Divyekin, and should have been made aware that Page denied meeting with either individual. Nevertheless, Page's exculpatory statements were not included in the initial FISA application signed just four days later.

iv. *Crossfire Hurricane investigators submit the initial FISA application on October 21, 2016*

On October 21, 2016, four days after the second recorded meeting with Page, the Department submitted its initial Page FISA application to the FISC, which the Court granted that same day. (Unbeknownst to the Court at the time, the application contained numerous significant defects, many of which were identified by the OIG).[1224] In support of the application, the FBI made several assertions that directly conflicted with explicit statements made by Page in the two recorded conversations with CHS-1. One such assertion was the FBI's assessment that Page was still likely involved with the Trump campaign despite the facts that (i) Page told CHS-1 that he was taking a break from the campaign;[1225] (ii) campaign officials by then had publicly distanced themselves from Page and his purported contacts with the Russians;[1226] and (iii) the campaign manager had publicly stated that Page was not part of the campaign she was running.[1227] The FISA application attributed this assessment to the fact that because Page was one of the campaign's first foreign policy advisors and had established relationships with other members of the campaign, this would enable him to have continued access to these advisors and he would attempt to exert influence on foreign policy matters, regardless of any formal role he

---

[1223] FBI-AAA-EC-00006182 (Lync message exchange between Strzok and Supervisory Special Agent-1 dated 10-17-2016) (emphasis added).

[1224] *See Redacted OIG Review* at viii-ix; 413.

[1225] Transcript of conversation between Carter Page and CHS-1 on 10/17/2016 at 77-78.

[1226] Isikoff, *Officials Probe Ties* (quoting Trump campaign advisers Hope Hicks and Jason Miller).

[1227] David Cohen, *Conway Denies Trump Campaign Ties to Russian Figure*, Politico, (Sept. 25, 2016) (quoting Trump Campaign Manager Kellyanne Conway's statement on CNN's "State of the Union").

played in the campaign.[1228] This assertion was unsupported by actual evidence that such continued involvement in the campaign was occurring.[1229]

Additionally, notwithstanding Page's explicit denials to CHS-1 and Director Comey of meeting with either Sechin or Divyekin in July 2016, an uncorroborated claim that had been included in the Steele Reports and publicized in the *Yahoo! News* article,[1230] the FISA application mischaracterized and misrepresented Page's words and actions regarding this subject matter. In particular, the FISA application stated that during his meeting with CHS-1, "Page did not provide any specific details to refute, dispel, or clarify the media reporting [and] he made vague statements that minimized his activities."[1231] This assertion, however, seriously misrepresents Page's recorded statements set forth above.

Finally, even though Page told CHS-1 that he was taking a break from the Trump campaign, the FISA application implies that the opposite was true. It said of Page's discussion on October 17th:

> During this meeting with [CHS-1], Page said that he was no longer officially affiliated with [Trump's] campaign, but added that he may be appearing in a television interview within the next week when he travels to the United Kingdom. According to Page, the interview will be discussing the potential change in U.S. foreign policy as it pertains to Russia and Syria if [Trump] wins the election. Accordingly, although Page claimed that he is no longer officially affiliated with the campaign, the FBI assesses that Page continues to coordinate with the Russian Government, and perhaps others, in efforts to influence the U.S. Presidential election.[1232]

[1228] *In re Carter W, Page*, No. 16-1182, at 26-27.

[1229] The initial FISA application on Page contained numerous "assessments" similar to the aforementioned statement which, whether correct or incorrect, conflicted with Page's explicit statements.

[1230] In *Crime in Progress*, authors Glenn Simpson and Peter Fritsch (owners of the investigative firm Fusion GPS that hired Christopher Steele to investigate Trump's relationships in Russia) write about a series of background interviews they arranged with selected journalists, including Michael Isikoff, for Steele to share the results of his research. Simpson and Fritsch wrote that the information provided by Steele was only to be attributed to a "former senior Western intelligence official." *See Crime in Progress*, at 108-112. The Isikoff article, however, identified the person providing the information as a "Western intelligence source." *See* Isikoff, *Officials Probe Ties*. Steele also admitted in an interview with Special Counsel Mueller's Office that he had provided information to the American media, specifically to *Mother Jones*. *See* SCO-006313 (Interview of Christopher Steele on Sept. 18, 2017) at 8. Finally, Steele admitted in testimony given in a civil suit filed in the United Kingdom that in September he and Glenn Simpson had meetings in Washington, D.C. with a number of journalists and shared his information with them. *See Steele Transcript* (Mar. 17, 2020) at 163:14-167:9.

[1231] *In re Carter W, Page*, No. 16-1182, at 27.

[1232] *Id.* at 28.

The Crossfire Hurricane personnel assessed, without citing any particular fact or explaining the basis for the assessment, that this discussion of a possible television interview was somehow evidence that Page was continuing to coordinate with the Russian government, and perhaps others, in an effort to influence the U.S. Presidential election. In support, the application asserted that Page's discussion with CHS-1 during their October 17, 2016 meeting about the possibility of him (Page) doing an interview with a British television personality on the implications of a Trump campaign victory on the relationship of the United States with Russia and Syria belied his statement to CHS-1 that he was taking a break from the campaign.

     v.   The third recording of Page

Approximately two months after the initial Page FISA surveillance warrant was authorized, Page and CHS-1 had a third meeting on December 15, 2016. The meeting covered a number of topics. At the outset of the meeting, CHS-1 initiated a general discussion of the potential Russian think tank in London. After CHS-1 discussed a possible partnership with a particular UK-based entity in establishing the think tank, Page advised CHS-1 that he had been "kind of talking with the New Economic School a little bit . . . and they were actually quite, uh, quite positive." Page went on to note that "they've got a lot of support internally, you know."[1233] When CHS-1 asked whether the "support was from the faculty or from the government or what?" Page responded "[F]rom the government, yeah. High level."[1234] Later Page and CHS-1 had a more general discussion regarding logistics of such a think tank, discussing issues such as funding and location. When CHS-1 noted that "you [Page] said last time we met that, um, can I, you got to, you thought you had the funding lined up . . . you said the Russians are giving you a blank check," Page responded, "Well I, I don't know that I went that far. I-I-I thought there was some support of, you know, certainly, uh, this trip proved it, but I think you know, having an institutional base . . . they said well come back to us with a proposal so you know . . . and they, again, very high level people [Russians] were quite supportive of a [particular type of entity]."[1235] Nevertheless, Page later noted during the conversation that, "some people have warned me, be careful with having too much Russian connection for obvious reasons."[1236] Finally, Page and CHS-1 discussed logistical information about possibly setting up the think tank in London, potentially to be sponsored by a UK entity.[1237]

During this meeting, Page also told CHS-1 that, according to the press, he (Page) was under FBI investigation. Page made this statement in response to an inquiry regarding Page's next trip to Moscow. Page said that he had been invited to Christmas parties at Russian energy companies Gazprom and Rosneft,[1238] but had told them, "I said I-I got enough investigation [Unintelligible] going along . . . ." CHS-1 then asked Page who was investigating him and in

---

[1233] Transcript of conversation between Carter Page and CHS-1 on 12/15/2016 at 8-9.

[1234] *Id.* at 9.

[1235] *Id.* at 24-25.

[1236] *Id.* at 25.

[1237] *Id.* at 25, 59-61.

[1238] *Id.* at 44.

response Page said, "Oh the FBI the whole [Unintelligible] . . . well that's what the press says, you know, no one has contacted me . . . ."[1239]

      vi.   *CHS-1's misrepresentation to Crossfire Hurricane investigators of his/her*
             conversation with Page regarding Page's alleged meeting with Sechin

Approximately one week after the December 15th meeting between Page and CHS-1, Case Agent-1 had a Lync message exchange with Supervisory Special Agent-1. Case Agent-1 advised Supervisory Special Agent-1 that CHS-1 had reached out to him (Case Agent-1) that day and had advised Case Agent-1 that CHS-1 had just remembered that Page had told CHS-1 that he (Page) had met with Sechin on Page's most recent trip to Russia. When Supervisory Special Agent-1 expressed what appeared to be skepticism about CHS-1's claim, Case Agent-1 responded that CHS-1 stated that he/she had remembered Page's statements after reading Sechin's name in the paper.[1240] In a Lync exchange two days later with a Crossfire Hurricane analyst ("Analyst-1"), Case Agent-1 advised Analyst-1 that he was trying to determine when Page advised CHS-1 of this purported meeting, while also expressing skepticism that such a meeting had occurred. Case Agent-1 speculated with Analyst-1 that Page may exaggerate things about his meetings. Analyst-1 concurred with Case Agent-1, additionally speculating that there would be no benefit for Sechin in meeting with Page.[1241] Nonetheless, neither Case Agent-1 nor Analyst-1 appear to have considered the possibility that exaggeration regarding the purported Page/Sechin meeting may have come not from Page but rather from CHS-1, whose account of the statement by Page, at least according to Case Agent-1, easily could have been corroborated or disproven by simply listening to the December 15, 2016, recording of the conversation. This was an especially important point for investigators to resolve since, as mentioned above, during his October 17, 2016 meeting with CHS-1, Page had explicitly denied having met with Sechin in July 2016. If it were true that Page had now told CHS-1 that he (Page) had met with Sechin during his most recent trip to Moscow, such information would have been significant in bolstering suspicions about Page and his relationship with the Russians, and also arguably would have given more credibility to the earlier Steele Report assertion that Page had met with Sechin in July 2016. A review of the December 15th recorded meeting clearly shows, however, that

---

[1239] As noted, at the time of this third recording made on December 15, 2016, the FBI and Crossfire Hurricane personnel still had not taken Page up on his offer to be interviewed which he had made back on September 25, 2016.

[1240] Case Agent-1: "CHS reached out to me today, remembered that [Page] told [CHS] that he met with Sechin this past trip." Supervisory Special Agent-1: "Come on." Case Agent-1: "yup, said [CHS] just remembered it yesterday after reading Sechin's name in the paper. Supervisory Special Agent-1: "We need that audio then." FBI-AAA-EC-00008439 (Lync message exchange between Case Agent-1 and Supervisory Special Agent-1 dated 12/22/2016).

[1241] Case Agent-1: "I'm trying to find out when he told [CHS] he met with Sechin." Analyst-1: "man, yeah, I just don't get him or Cohen at all man... it's like they are living in a dream world... that would be pretty interesting if he really did meet with him." Analyst-1: "what possible reason would Sechin have to meet with him now, serves no benefit to him." Case Agent-1: "I really believe he exaggerates his meetings. He may have been in a meeting where he was 1 of 200 people." FBI-AAA-EC-00008439 (Lync Message exchange between Case Agent-1 and Analyst-1 dated 12/23/2016).

Page made no such statement to CHS-1. Although there was brief discussion by the two about Secretary of State nominee Rex Tillerson's relationship with Sechin,[1242] and the accusation made by Senator Harry Reid that Page had purportedly met with Sechin, which was referenced in a recent *Washington Post* column by Josh Rogin,[1243] Page never advised CHS-1 that he had met with Sechin on a recent post-election trip to Russia. As noted above, Supervisory Special Agent-1 told Case Agent-1 that they needed to listen to the audio of the recording. If, in fact, the Crossfire Hurricane investigators listened to the recording, they either missed this fact or elected not to make it known to the OI lawyers with whom they were working on the Page FISA applications.[1244] In either event, CHS-1's misstatement of an important fact was significant in that information provided to the FBI by CHS-1, again according to Case Agent-1, regarding his conversations with Page was used in all four of the Page FISA applications.

vii.   The first renewal of the Page FISA Warrant surveillance order

Less than a month after the third recorded meeting between Page and CHS-1, the FBI received authorization from the FISC to continue its surveillance of Page for an additional 90 days. The renewal application, like the application to initiate the surveillance, included misrepresentations and mischaracterizations of the recorded conversations. Additionally, the same errors that were contained in the first FISA application were repeated in the renewal application. As noted in the *OIG Review*, the failure to correct these errors in the first FISA renewal application was repeated in the second and third renewal applications.[1245] Specifically, the OIG noted that the first renewal application omitted information the FBI had received from persons who previously had professional interactions with Steele and who in part questioned both his judgment and his pursuit of individuals with political risk, but no intelligence value.[1246] Moreover, as noted later in the *OIG Review*, another significant error in the renewal applications was the omission of a recorded statement made to a second FBI CHS ("CHS-2") by Papadopoulos. In that recorded conversation, Papadopoulos expressly denied any knowledge of the Trump campaign's involvement in the circumstances surrounding the hack of the DNC computers.[1247]

In addition to those defects, the first renewal application included mischaracterizations about the details of the December 15, 2016, meeting between Page and CHS-1. In particular, it mischaracterized the nature of their discussions concerning the creation of a potential think tank

---

[1242] Transcript of conversation between Carter Page and CHS-1 on 12/15/2016 at 17-18.

[1243] *Id.* at 44-45. This is the allegation that had been referenced in a recent *Washington Post* column by Josh Rogin.

[1244] No records were provided to the Office by the FBI which reflect that the recording had been reviewed and its specific contents were shared with the Department of Justice lawyers working on the Page FISA; *see also FBI Inspection Division Report* at 217 (reflecting that the recording was not reviewed and the investigating agents relied on the CHS's erroneous report of the conversation).

[1245] *See Redacted OIG Review* at xi, 413.

[1246] *See id.* at 182.

[1247] *Id.* at xi-xii.

focusing on Russian relations with the West. An objective reading of the transcript and review of the recordings of the two conversations between Page and CHS-1 on this subject in both the October 17, 2016 meeting and the December 15, 2016 meeting reflect that, although the two engaged in a general discussion about the possibility of establishing such an entity, neither discussed the specific details that would be required for such a project to move forward.[1248] Further, although they generally discussed the possible location of the think tank and possible sources of funding, the renewal application asserted that, "[A]ccording to more recent reporting from [CHS-1] . . ." in the December meeting, "[CHS-1] asked Page for additional information regarding the financials for the proposed think tank. According to [CHS-1], Page initially attempted to distance the think tank from Russian funding. When [CHS-1] reminded Page of his previous statement regarding the 'open checkbook,' Page did not refute his previous comment and provided some reassurance to [CHS-1] about the likelihood of Russian financial support."[1249] That assertion, based on the language in the application, perhaps was premised on information provided to the Crossfire Hurricane investigators by CHS-1, rather than the actual words spoken by Page as captured in CHS-1's recordings of the meetings. As provided to the FISC, however, the assertion is an inaccurate representation of the conversation. As noted above, when CHS-1 stated to Page, "[y]ou said the Russians are giving you a blank check," Page immediately responded, "[W]ell I, I don't know that I went that far. I-I-I thought there was some support . . . ."[1250] The actual language used by Page is inconsistent with CHS-1's assertion to Page that Page had been promised a "blank check" by the Russians. The assertion in the FISA application was, at a minimum, incomplete.

The first renewal application also stated that the FBI assessed that Page's attempts to downplay Russian funding may have been an attempt by him to soften his connection to Russia or, alternatively, may have been the result of an instruction from the Russians not to discuss any possible Russian financial involvement.[1251] There is nothing in the actual conversation between the two men, however, that would give rise to such an assessment. A fair and objective reading of the actual conversation indicates that the source of funding, if any, by the Russians was undetermined, and as also noted above,[1252] according to Page, subject to Page submitting a written proposal. And as previously noted, during this discussion with CHS-1, Page also mentioned that "some people have warned me, be careful with having too much Russian connection for obvious reasons."[1253] Instead of including Page's verbatim statements regarding Russian funding in the application, the FISA application makes assertions about funding that are at odds with what Page actually told CHS-1 as reflected in the recording of the meeting.

Moreover, the renewal application was submitted to the FISC only three weeks after Case Agent-1's conversations with Supervisory Special Agent-1 and Analyst-1 regarding CHS-

---

[1248] *See supra* footnotes 1221, 1222 re 10/17/2016 transcript and footnotes 1233 - 1237 re 12/15/2016 transcript.

[1249] *In re Carter W. Page*, Docket No. 17-52, at 35 (FISC Jan. 12, 2017).

[1250] *See supra* footnote 1235.

[1251] *In re Carter W. Page*, No. 17-52, at 35-36.

[1252] *See supra* footnote 1235.

[1253] *See supra* footnote 1236.

1's misstatement that Page had advised CHS-1 that he (Page) had met with Sechin during a post-election trip to Russia. Because of their apparent skepticism about this claim by CHS-1, this issue should have been brought to the attention of the OI attorneys working on the application, as well as the FISC. However, the Office found no evidence that it was appropriately addressed.[1254]

In a number of instances, the Page FISA applications relied on "assessments" to address what otherwise appeared to be plainly exculpatory statements by Page. Because of the sensitive and classified nature of those portions of one or more of the FISA applications, review of those assessments is set forth in the Classified Appendix to this report.

> viii.   The fourth recording of Page made by CHS-1 January 25, 2017

On January 25, 2017, less than two weeks after the first renewal of the Page FISA surveillance order was granted, CHS-1 met with and recorded Page for the fourth and final time. Importantly, on January 10, 2017, *Buzzfeed News* had published the contents of the Steele Reports. The next day, the *Wall Street Journal* identified "former British MI-6 Intelligence Officer Christopher Steele" as the author of the Reports.[1255] Unsurprisingly, the Reports were a topic of conversation as Page and CHS-1 began their fourth meeting. In response to Page's inquiry as to whether CHS-1 knew "[S]teele . . . the MI-6 guy," CHS-1 responded, "No, I never did. I never met him."[1256] Page then speculated that former MI-6 Director Richard Dearlove, who had attended the same July 2016 gathering that Page and CHS-1 had attended,[1257] must have known Steele. CHS-1 responded, "[Y]eah, Dearlove would know him. I mean Dearlove knew any-everybody in Six, and Six is a small organization."[1258] CHS-1 went on to state that, "[h]e [Steele] certainly produced [laughing] electrifying memoranda, didn't he?" Page responded, "[W]ell, you know. I mean, it's-it's just so false that where [Background Noise] do you begin [Unintelligible]?"[1259] This exchange contained yet another denial by Page of the allegations made about him in the Steele Reports, but this specific denial was never brought to the attention of the FISC in the second and third renewal applications for the Page FISA surveillances.[1260]

During this fourth recorded conversation, Page complained to CHS-1 about being under surveillance by the FBI, comparing his plight to that faced by Martin Luther King, Jr. who had

---

[1254] A review conducted by the Office of various documents, including the first FISA renewal application, the *OIG Review*, and documented interviews of FBI and OI personnel conducted by the Office, do not indicate that the information provided by CHS-1, as allegedly related to him by Page, regarding an alleged Page-Sechin meeting, was discussed beyond the two Lync message exchanges involving FBI employees Case Agent-1, Supervisory Special Agent-1, and Analyst-1 discussed above.

[1255] Bradley Hoe, Michael Rothfeld, and Alan Cullison, *Christopher Steele, Ex- British Intelligence Officer, Said to Have Prepared Dossier on Trump*, Wall St. Journal, (Jan. 11, 2017).

[1256] Transcript of conversation between Carter Page and CHS-1 on 01/25/2017 at 6.

[1257] *Id.* at 7.

[1258] *Id.*

[1259] *Id.*

[1260] *In re Carter W. Page*, Docket No.17-375 (FISC April 7, 2017); *In re Carter W. Page*, No.17-679 (FISC June 29, 2017).

been under FBI surveillance during the time that J. Edgar Hoover served as FBI Director. Page informed CHS-1 that both he and King were under surveillance for exercising their constitutional rights of freedom of speech and freedom of expression.[1261]

Later, CHS-1 again turned the conversation to a discussion of the establishment of the possible think tank focused on relations between Russia and the West and the finances related to such an endeavor.[1262] CHS-1 told Page:

> CHS-1:   [A]nd I think that if you could bring some Russian money to the table, uh, I might be able to help you get some U.S. money.
>
> Page: Uhm-hum.
>
> CHS-1:   That could be useful. You know?[1263]

Shortly thereafter, CHS-1 raised the think tank issue again, and the following exchange occurred:

> CHS-1:   [I] think the real issue you have to deal with is the decision whether you want to create a think tank, and, you know, once you make that decision then we could talk about money and personnel, but you should take your time and-and think carefully...
>
> Page: ...[h]ere's the problem with taking the time. And this is why I'm kind of anxious and this is my conversation last month in Moscow. The momentum is building, you know. The Cold War sort of—you know like [UI] it's people trying to show that they're not un-American.[1264]

Later in the conversation, Page indicated to CHS-1 that he believed the Russians were "[f]ully on board. But the question is, you know, the who, whats, whys, when and hows, you know?"[1265]

CHS-1 and Page then discussed possible dollar amounts for starting the think tank, with each discussing finding sponsors to share in the cost. Page initially suggested $1 million, and CHS-1 suggested he/she did not think that he/or she (CHS-1) could raise even a million "bucks," but said to Page:

> CHS-1:   [U]h, if they [referring to the Russians] could come up with a million and you could tell them that you could keep the doors open for a year with that, and then I could try to find whatever I can get to add to it.[1266]

[1261] Transcript of conversation between Carter Page and CHS-1 on 01/25/2017 at 21-22.

[1262] *Id.* at 25.

[1263] *Id.*

[1264] *Id.* at 29-30.

[1265] *Id.* at 30.

[1266] *Id.* at 33.

A short time later, not hearing any firm commitment from Page regarding the establishment of the think tank, CHS-1 stated, "[I]'m just sort of blue skying here. I'm not trying to, you know, persuade you really to do this."[1267]

The various discussions between Page and CHS-1 regarding the possible creation of the think tank occurred over the course of their four conversations. The first occurred, albeit briefly, in their first meeting on August 20, 2016, with more extensive discussions occurring in their three follow up meetings on October 17, 2016, December 15, 2016, and January 25. However, none of the conversations advanced the establishment of the think tank from the aspirational to the concrete. The FBI's original language referring to the initial discussions between Page and CHS-1 regarding the think tank and the possibility of Russian funding did not change in the first three FISA applications (the original plus two renewal applications).[1268] However, some additional language regarding this issue was added in the final renewal application. In that application, the FBI wrote, "[B]ased on more recent information developed through its ongoing investigation of Page, the FBI now assesses that Page is no longer interested in establishing a think tank, likely due to lack of funding."[1269]

Later in their January 25, 2017 conversation, Page again advised CHS-1 that the stories about him and Russia were false. Page stated that the "[f]alse evidence isn't the fault of the Bureau . . . there's been lots of reports the Bureau sort of pushed back on this. And the fact that they never contacted me says something as well."[1270] Finally, Page told CHS-1 the following regarding the allegations against him:

Page: [Y]ou know, what a complete lie, what a complete sham.

CHS-1:   But, you know—

Page: And this is the big fraud. . . . If you look at the narrative that was defined all around using government resources based on completely false evidence... and again false evidence is a crime.[1271]

Page subsequently told CHS-1, "Let's see where this all started. This all started based on complete utter lies. Right?"[1272]

    ix.   The second and third renewals of the Page FISA surveillance

The Crossfire Hurricane investigators sought a second renewal of the FISA authorization, which was granted by the FISC in April 2017.[1273] While there was only one additional recorded conversation between Page and CHS-1 during the time between the first renewal of the FISA

[1267] *Id.* at 34.

[1268] *In re Carter W. Page*, No. 16-1182, at 28; *In re Carter W. Page*, No. 17-52, at 30; *In re Carter W. Page*, No. 17-375, at 31.

[1269] *In re Carter W. Page*, No. 17-679, at 45.

[1270] Transcript of conversation between Carter Page and CHS-1 on 01/25/2017 at 41.

[1271] *Id.* at 42.

[1272] *Id.* at 43.

[1273] *In re Carter W. Page*, No. 17-375.

warrant and the second application for a renewal, there were several significant events that occurred in the Crossfire Hurricane investigation during that time. These included the five interviews that the FBI eventually conducted with Page in March 2017. As noted above, these interviews occurred nearly six months after Page wrote to Director Comey volunteering to be interviewed.[1274] Additionally, in late January 2017, the FBI conducted a three-day interview of Steele's primary sub-source, Igor Danchenko, who Steele relied heavily upon to gather information for inclusion in the Steele Reports.[1275] Finally, as discussed below, during that same approximate time period, the FBI made a series of recordings of conversations between a second CHS ("CHS-2") and Papadopoulos. The recordings were made in an effort to capture relevant information about the Australian communication that was the basis for opening Crossfire Hurricane.

At the expiration of the second FISA renewal authority, the Crossfire Hurricane investigators sought, and were granted, a third renewal of authority to conduct additional FISA surveillance of Page.[1276]

As noted previously, however, the Crossfire Hurricane investigators did not correct the errors, omissions, and misrepresentations that were contained in both the original FISA application and the first renewal application at the time they submitted the second and third renewal applications to the FISC.[1277] Moreover, additional significant problems were identified by the OIG (and also in a later investigation conducted by the FBI's Inspection Division)[1278] in the second and third renewal applications.[1279] One of the most significant problems relates to Page's recorded statements telling CHS-1 that he never met with Sechin or Divyekin, his public statements to the same effect, and his statements to the FBI during his five interviews, when compared to information provided to the FISC in the three renewal applications. Because of the sensitive and classified nature of those portions of one or more of the FISA renewal applications, review of this issue is necessarily contained in the Classified Appendix to this report.

> x. *Recording of a high-level Trump campaign foreign policy advisor by CHS-1 on September 1, 2016*

In addition to the four recordings CHS-1 made of meetings with Page, CHS-1 also recorded a breakfast meeting he/she had in early September 2016 with a high-level Trump campaign foreign policy advisor ("Trump Senior Foreign Policy Advisor-1") who was not a

---

[1274] Again, Page had volunteered to be interviewed by the FBI just two days after the publication of the *Yahoo! News* article in September 2016 identifying him as the subject of an FBI investigation.

[1275] According to Danchenko himself, he was responsible for gathering approximately 80% of the "intel" in the Steele reporting and producing approximately 50% of the analysis in those reports. *Danchenko* Government Exhibit 1502.

[1276] *In re Carter W. Page*, No. 17-679.

[1277] *See supra* footnotes 1228, 1231 and 1232.

[1278] *See FBI Inspection Division Report* at 367.

[1279] *See supra* footnotes 1249 and 1251 for errors specific to the first renewal application; *see also Redacted OIG Review* at xi-xii, 413

subject of the FBI's investigation. As CHS-1 had a background in policy development through his/her work in several Presidential administrations and campaigns, it was not unusual for CHS-1 to request a meeting with Trump Senior Foreign Policy Advisor-1. A prospective meeting between the two had been discussed beforehand during CHS-1's first meeting with Page, who encouraged CHS-1 to have such a meeting, [1280] and this meeting occurred approximately ten days after CHS-1 first met with Page.

FBI records reflect that, prior to the meeting, there had been discussions among FBI personnel about the sensitivities surrounding meeting with a high-level campaign figure and the need to ensure the conversation would remain focused on topics relevant to the main purpose of the Crossfire Hurricane investigation, namely whether there was evidence of collusion between Russian officials and persons associated with the Trump campaign. Those discussions also covered the possibility that the conversation between CHS-1 and the foreign policy advisor might digress into campaign strategy and tactics, with the FBI personnel involved in the discussions expressing concern that such topics were to be avoided if at all possible.[1281] (We note that Crossfire Hurricane investigators properly recognized that other sensitive topics unrelated to the Crossfire Hurricane investigation might come up in the conversation given CHS-1's background and Trump Senior Foreign Policy Advisor-1's position in the Trump campaign).[1282]

Although there were a number of topics covered by CHS-1 and Trump Senior Foreign Policy Advisor-1 that were unrelated to Crossfire Hurricane, they also discussed several matters that were directly relevant to the investigation.[1283] At one point during the conversation, CHS-1, while referencing his/her prior experience in Presidential campaigns, stated:

CHS-1:	[W]e were accused of having an October surprise. What do you guys got going? You have WikiLeaks out there.
Advisor:	We have a lot hanging over our head. September 13, State [Department] has to produce those emails, that's a big deal.
CHS-1:	You can do something with that?
Advisor:	Absolutely.[1284]

[1280] Transcript of conversation between Carter Page and CHS-1 on 08/20/2016 at 98.

[1281] *See Redacted OIG Review* at 326-328.

[1282] *Id.* at 327 (wherein former AD Priestap told the OIG that "the team discussed the objectives of having the [CHS] engage with members of the Trump campaign... and the 'need to steer clear' of collecting campaign information 'dealing with policies, plans, staffing decisions, [or] anything related.' Priestap also said that 'it's not always possible...once people start talking' to a source to stay on point because the target of the operation may tell a source about the topic as well as a lot of additional information.")

[1283] The FBI did not transcribe the recording of this meeting so the references to the excerpts of the conversation that follow are identified by timestamp.

[1284] Audio recording of CHS-1 and Trump Senior Foreign Policy Advisor-1's conversation on 09/01/2016 at 09:14:15.

This portion of the conversation appears to have been intended to elicit information from Trump Senior Foreign Policy Advisor-1 about any knowledge the advisor had regarding WikiLeaks' disclosures of DNC-related emails and the Russians. Trump Senior Foreign Policy Advisor-1, however, did not touch on WikiLeaks in their response to CHS-1's question, instead focusing on a then-upcoming public release of former Secretary Clinton's emails by the State Department. Trump Senior Foreign Policy Advisor-1 told CHS-1 that the campaign could "absolutely" make use of those soon-to-be released documents. Trump Senior Foreign Policy Advisor-1's response to CHS-1's question about the WikiLeaks issue was not mentioned in any of the FISA applications even though the WikiLeaks disclosures, believed to have been facilitated by Russian intelligence services' intrusions into the DNC computers, were mentioned in all four FISA applications.[1285]

Later in their conversation, CHS-1 and Trump Senior Foreign Policy Advisor-1 briefly discussed WikiLeaks founder Julian Assange and then discussed possible Russian influence on the election. The following exchanges took place:

CHS-1:   The front page of the New York Times is about Julian Assange. What can you do to offset their worry about Russian influence in the Trump campaign?

Advisor: To the average voter, it's a non-starter; in this city it's a big deal, New York big deal. From the perspective of the average voter, there is no connection.[1286]

                          *   *   *

Advisor: ... about Russian influence, we need to raise the level of abstraction to discuss the security of a voter interaction. It is up to each state to provide security. Make sure every state has secured its system.[1287]

CHS-1:   What I am concerned with is the impression that Russia has a hand in what we are doing. Carter [Page], for example, he made a speech in Moscow, I know you are familiar with, and there was a tilt in the speech that was alarming.[1288]

Advisor: It's important to you and me, but not the campaign, except to say no interference in our electoral process.[1289]

Although this portion of the recorded conversation covered topics which were of interest to the Crossfire Hurricane investigators, *i.e.*, Julian Assange; Russian influence; and Page's speech at

---

[1285] *In re Carter W. Page*, No. 16-1182, at 6-7; *In re Carter W. Page*, No. 17-52, at 7-8; *In re Carter W. Page*, No. 17-375, at 7-8; *In re Carter W. Page*, No. 17-679, at 7-8.

[1286] Audio recording of CHS-1 and Trump Senior Foreign Policy Advisor-1's conversation on 09/01/2016 09:46:50.

[1287] *Id.* at 09:48:21.

[1288] *Id.* at 09:50:46.

[1289] *Id.* at 09:51:25.

the New Economic School, there was nothing said or discussed by Trump Senior Foreign Policy Advisor-1 regarding any of these issues that would evidence any type of assistance being provided by the Russians to the Trump campaign. In fact, even though these issues were raised by CHS-1, the advisor did not engage on the prompts or baited statements advanced by CHS-1 to spark confirmation of Russian assistance to the Trump campaign. Again, however, even though this recorded conversation was with a senior foreign policy advisor to the campaign and the tenor of the conversation between CHS-1 and the advisor provided no indication of assistance being provided to the campaign by the Russians, there is no mention of this meeting, nor of anything said by Trump Senior Foreign Policy Advisor-1 at the meeting, in any of the Page FISA applications. Indeed, based on our collection of pertinent FBI records, the actual results of this meeting do not appear to have been memorialized by the FBI in an FBI FD-302 or other substantive report.[1290]

xi. Recordings of George Papadopoulos by FBI UCEs and CHS-1

In addition to its recordings of meetings between CHS-1 and Page and CHS-1 and the Trump senior campaign foreign policy advisor, the Crossfire Hurricane investigators also used CHS-1 to record two meetings with Trump campaign foreign policy advisor Papadopoulos (whose statements to the Australian diplomats formed the predication cited in the FBI opening communication for the Crossfire Hurricane investigation).[1291] Papadopoulos had been announced as a Trump campaign foreign policy advisor at the same time as Page in late March 2016. Subsequent to his/her initial meeting with Page on August 20, 2016, CHS-1, whose experience and credentials regarding foreign policy and Presidential campaigns are noted above, arranged for Papadopoulos to visit him/her in September 2016 to discuss the possibility of Papadopoulos writing a research paper on oil, gas and energy-related issues, these fields having been noted as areas of Papadopoulos's expertise when he was announced as one of the Trump campaign's foreign policy advisors.[1292]

Additionally, in connection with CHS-1's two meetings with Papadopoulos, two FBI Undercover Employees ("UCE-1" and "UCE-2") also met and had a total of three conversations with Papadopoulos in September 2016, two of which were recorded. Two of these meetings occurred in a foreign country and the other occurred while Papadopoulos was going to meet with CHS-1.[1293]

When interviewed by the Office, UCE-1 was certain that nothing of substantive value was said to him/her by Papadopoulos.[1294] According to UCE-1, unprompted, Papadopoulos

---

[1290] *See Redacted OIG Review* at 327-329 (indicating that the FBI did not do anything with this recorded meeting; it was not transcribed; and there was no evidence that the recording was put to any use. The FBI produced no documents regarding this recording to our Office.)

[1291] *Crossfire Hurricane Opening EC.*

[1292] Alan Rappeport, *Top Experts Confounded by Advisers to Donald Trump*, N.Y. Times (Mar. 22, 2016); Jeremy Diamond & Nicole Gaouette, *Donald Trump Unveils Foreign Policy Advisers*, CNN (Mar. 21, 2016).

[1293] OSC Report of Interview of FBI UCE-1 on October 21, 2021.

[1294] The conversation was not recorded by UCE-1.

identified himself as a Trump campaign advisor almost immediately after they began talking and showed him/her a picture of Trump and himself. Papadopoulos also told UCE-1 that he was traveling to meet an individual who UCE-1 subsequently learned was CHS-1. UCE-1 and Papadopoulos had a general conversation about the media reports involving Trump and Russia, with UCE-1 recalling that Papadopoulos laughed off such reports. UCE-1 recalled that Papadopoulos made no mention of Russian election interference efforts during their conversation.[1295] UCE-1 met later with the Crossfire Hurricane investigators and briefed them on the conversation he/she had had with Papadopoulos. He/she did not write a report regarding the encounter with Papadopoulos, explaining that it was common in UCE-1's experience that a case Agent would be briefed on the details of meetings and the case Agent was then responsible for writing the report of the meeting. UCE-1 advised that he/she had never seen any write-up or report of his/her meeting with Papadopoulos.[1296]

On September 14, 2016, Papadopoulos first met with UCE-2, who was posing as an assistant to CHS-1. During their conversation, which UCE-2 recorded, Papadopoulos provided UCE-2 with biographical-type information as well as background information concerning his role in the Trump campaign.[1297] Papadopoulos also bragged to UCE-2 that since his initial selection as a campaign advisor (1) his position in the campaign shifted higher due to campaign management changes,[1298] (2) he was with Trump all the time;[1299] (3) he was famous,[1300] and (4) his name now was global.[1301] One exchange between Papadopoulos and UCE-2 was of particular significance regarding Russia:

GP:	The only thing I can't do is any business in Russia, right now, … Russia has become like a hectic country with the campaign and all the other things.
UCE-2:	What [UI] on campaign?
GP:	Putin says he likes Trump, Trump says he likes Putin.
UCE-2:	Oh yeah, yeah. And that's a problem?
GP:	It shouldn't be. But if I do business…I will give you an example. I was supposed to speak at the largest energy conference in Russia later this

---

[1295] OSC Report of Interview of FBI UCE-1 on October 21, 2021 at 2-3.

[1296] *Id.* at 3. No such report was produced to our investigators by the FBI and one does not appear to have been written.

[1297] The Crossfire Hurricane investigators did not prepare a transcript of this conversation so references to excerpts that follow are to the recording timestamps.

[1298] Audio recording of UCE-2 and George Papadopoulos conversation on 09/14/2016 at 19:06:20.

[1299] *Id.* at 19:10:44

[1300] *Id.* at 19:32:26

[1301] *Id.* at 19:57:46.

	month... It is so difficult in the U.S. politically right now. So, I can do any country except Russia.
UCE-2:	Why is it a problem if you want to build bridges to Russia... why give him [Trump] a hard time about it?
GP:	As you said, he wants to build bridges. The media is saying he's bad. What's important is to deal with Russia.
UCE-2:	Have you ever been to Russia?
GP:	No.[1302]

The following day, September 15, 2016, Papadopoulos met twice with CHS-1. During the first part of their first conversation, which CHS-1 recorded at the direction of the Crossfire Hurricane investigators, they discussed a variety of topics, including a proposal that CHS-1 made to pay Papadopoulos $3,000 to write a research paper on oil and energy involving Cyprus, Turkey, Greece, Russia and Syria.[1303] After advising Papadopoulos that he/she had met with the Trump campaign's senior foreign policy advisor,[1304] CHS-1 discussed his/her admiration for Trump's realistic view of Russia.[1305] The two then discussed other world affairs involving China, North Korea and Japan.[1306]

Following those discussions, the conversation moved to the campaign when, in an apparent reference to the WikiLeaks disclosures of DNC emails, CHS-1 asked Papadopoulos, "do they have more?" In response, Papadopoulos said, "Public statements of Assange has stated that get ready for October. Whatever that means no one knows but..."[1307] Later in the conversation, in an apparent reference to an "October surprise," the following exchange occurred:

CHS-1:	We were frightened to death about those surprises in 1980.
GP:	[Laughing] Hillary is not that bad but hope-hopefully for her it is a catastrophe along those lines and ah, it-it likely will...
CHS-1:	Yeah.
GP:	...you know a lot of dirt has come out on the Clinton Foundation.
CHS-1:	Do you think that's when it will happen?

[1302] *Id.* at 19:58:52 - 20:01:57

[1303] Transcript of conversation between Papadopoulos and CHS-1 on 09-15-2016 AM at 15. In testimony to the House Judiciary Committee, Papadopoulos confirmed that he had been paid $3,000 for writing the paper. *See* U.S. House Committee on the Judiciary, Interview of George Papadopoulos on 10/25/2018 at 101, 109-110.

[1304] Transcript of conversation between Papadopoulos and CHS-1 on 09-15-2016 AM at 15.

[1305] *Id.* at 14-15.

[1306] *Id.* at 19-31.

[1307] *Id.* at 35-36.

GP:	It could be that, it could be about her health.
CHS-1:	Yeah, that's right. It could be about her health.
GP:	It could be about her health.
CHS-1:	Release that story so [UI].
GP:	But it, yeah, it could be, you know, she falsified information, her doctors they colluded with the campaign, who knows when it may be. But the CEO of the Clinton Foundation just yesterday released a statement that yes, we did provide access for high bidders to the State Department...she's just digging a grave for herself.
CHS-1:	Her grave?
GP:	Yeah. That's why I think [UI] and the CEO of the Clinton Foundation came out with a statement that yes, we're indirectly guilty of providing access to the State Department for the high-level donors to our foundation...[1308]

Later in the conversation, CHS-1 and Papadopoulos discussed what Papadopoulos described as an invitation from the Russian Ministry of Foreign Affairs to speak in Russia, which he turned down because "[i]t's just too sensitive, ah, advisor on the campaign trail...especially with what is going on with Paul Manafort . . . so I mean the man lost his job essentially over media allegations, whether they were warranted or unwarranted...."[1309]

Papadopoulos also mentioned another reason for him not going to Russia and discussed Page:

GP:	So, the last thing they needed at that time was oh now he's going, Carter Page, I think, was in Russia though.
GP:	The entire Trump campaign is in Moscow within two weeks of each other. And now Mr. Trump is talking about how he adores his relationship with Putin so, ah, that's the last thing we want to have happen. [chuckles]
CHS-1:	Carter is still maintaining relations with the Russians.
GP:	I don't know and to be, ah, honest. I don't know what Carter has told you or what [another Trump foreign policy advisor] has told you but Carter has never actually met Trump. I know he hasn't actually advised him on Russia. He might be advising him indirectly through [another Trump foreign policy advisor] or...
CHS-1:	Yeah [UI]
GP:	But the media made a whole fuss about... That's not the reality....[1310]

[1308] *Id.* at 36.

[1309] *Id.* at 42.

[1310] *Id.* at 42-43.

A short time later, Papadopoulos described Page as "[A] very nice guy, you know, very smart."[1311]

At no time during this conversation did Papadopoulos mention anything about any support being provided by Russia to the Trump campaign, even when the discussion turned to Julian Assange and WikiLeaks. None of the statements made by Papadopoulos during this first meeting, including the aforementioned subjects of Assange, WikiLeaks, Page, and the prospect of some October surprise, were referenced in the FISA applications.

Later that day, however, in the second meeting between CHS-1 and Papadopoulos, there was an explicit discussion about the allegation which predicated the opening of the Crossfire Hurricane investigation. The Crossfire Hurricane investigative team's interpretation of that conversation, as included in the initial and subsequent Page FISA applications, is unsettling.

Shortly after the meeting began, the two engaged in a discussion about the recent publication of DNC emails by WikiLeaks:

CHS-1:   I was going to ask you, did you guys have any idea that, um...you know that the, that the, ah, about the DNC leaks?

GP: Oh no.

CHS-1:   Because I thought that was a really significant thing....

GP: And no one has proven that the Russians actually did the hacking....[1312]

After briefly discussing the possibility of other countries being involved in the DNC computer intrusion, the discussion continued:

CHS-1:   ...[s]o actually what you're saying to me is that you didn't feel like the campaign was able to benefit at all from what the Russians could help with.

GP: What do you mean by [Unintelligible]?

CHS-1:   Well, you know, I mean I-I think this is a time when given Hillary's weakness and given her strengths that help from the, from a third party like WikiLeaks for example or some other third party like the Russians, could be incredibly helpful. I mean it makes all the difference.

GP: Well as a campaign, of course, we don't advocate for this type of activity because at the end of the day, it's, ah, illegal. First and foremost, it compromises the U.S. national security and third it sets a very bad precedence.

CHS-1:   Yeah.

GP: So, the campaign does not advocate for this, does not support what is happening. The indirect consequences are out of our hands.

CHS-1:   Yep. Yep.

[1311] *Id.* at 43-44.

[1312] Transcript of conversation between Papadopoulos and CHS-1 on 09-15-2016 PM at 12-13.

GP:	That's how, that's the best way I can, ah…
CHS-1:	But…
GP:	For example, our campaign is not [chuckling] engage or reaching out to WikiLeaks or to the whoever it is to tell them please work with us, collaborate because we don't, no one does that.
CHS-1:	Yeah.
GP:	Unless there's something going on that I don't know which I don't because I don't think anybody would risk their, their life, ah, potentially going to prison over doing something like that. Um … because at the end of the day, you know, it's an illegal activity. Espionage is, ah, treason.
CHS-1:	Yeah. Well particularly involvement with American elections.
GP:	Especially if somebody is collaborating with x-group that no one yet knows who they are…
CHS-1:	Yeah.
GP:	…Then… I mean that's why, you know, it became a very big issue when Mr. Trump said, "Russia if you're listening…" Do you remember?
CHS-1:	Yeah, I remember that comment. Yeah.
GP:	And you know we had to retract it because, of course, he didn't mean for them to actively [chuckles] engage in espionage but the media then took and ran with it.[1313]

Finally, toward the end of their conversation, CHS-1 broached the subject one more time with Papadopoulos:

CHS-1:	[W]ell you know I'm-I'm happy to hear from you that, um, you know that there has been no interference in the campaign from outside groups like WikiLeaks or any of these people.
GP:	No. And, and, and to run a shop like that, you know, of course it's illegal. No one's looking to, um, obviously get into trouble like that and, you know, as far as I understand that's, no one's collaborating, there's been no collusion and it's going to remain that way.[1314]

In this conversation, Papadopoulos clearly stated at several points that he was not aware of the Trump campaign working or collaborating with the Russians in any manner. In fact, he stated three times that such activity by the campaign would be illegal. These statements directly contradicted the underlying premise of the Crossfire Hurricane investigation, namely that a member or members of the Trump campaign might be or were colluding with the Russians regarding the release of information detrimental to the Clinton campaign. These were direct, explicit denials by Papadopoulos of his otherwise vague statements to the Australian diplomats about Russian assistance to the campaign – statements that Australia conveyed may have come

---

[1313] *Id.* at 17-18

[1314] *Id.* at 27.

from public sources.[1315] As previously discussed, these statements were used to predicate Crossfire Hurricane, the active investigation of unknown members of a Presidential campaign.

Significantly, these explicit, recorded denials of Trump campaign involvement with the Russians came *after* the initial meeting between Page and CHS-1 on August 20, 2016, and *after* the September 1, 2016, meeting between CHS-1 and the Trump campaign senior foreign policy advisor, both of which were recorded at the direction of the FBI and were in the possession of the Crossfire Hurricane investigators. In his conversation with CHS-1, Papadopoulos clearly said that such assistance from the Russians would be illegal. This was arguably the most significant information the FBI had gathered after approximately six weeks of investigative effort to evaluate the information it had received from Australia. Yet the FBI chose to discount the information and assessed it to mean the opposite of what was explicitly said.

As reflected in the *OIG Review*, the FBI chose to adopt an interpretation of Papadopoulos's denials of any knowledge of the Trump campaign's involvement with the Russians in connection with the DNC computer intrusion and subsequent publication of certain DNC emails as being "weird," "rote," "canned," and "rehearsed."[1316] They described Papadopoulos as having "a free flowing conversation" with the CHS that changed "to almost a canned response."[1317] Other comments made to the OIG by Crossfire Hurricane investigators included that the perceived change in tone of the conversation may have been an indication that Papadopoulos had been coached by legal advisors to provide certain responses to CHS-1, notwithstanding the lack of any actual evidence to support such a conclusion.[1318]

In interviews conducted by the Office, two Crossfire Hurricane investigators gave similar responses to what they previously told the OIG. One Agent stated that Papadopoulos's emphatic response to CHS-1's statement of a possible connection between the Trump campaign and the Russians was "curious," so much so that there was a consensus view that Papadopoulos's response may have been rehearsed and was, therefore, not authentic.[1319] Another Crossfire Hurricane investigator briefed several FBI Executives regarding this issue, including Deputy Director McCabe, Assistant Director Priestap, General Counsel Baker, Section Chief Moffa, and the Deputy Director's Special Counsel, Lisa Page, noting that the general consensus of the group after the briefing was that one of the statements made by Papadopoulos in his meeting with CHS-1, which would normally be considered exculpatory, was instead assessed as an outlier and intentionally scripted by him to give a false impression.[1320]

Our investigators listened very carefully to this recording and did not detect any change in Papadopoulos's tone of voice when he made these statements to CHS-1. As the Crossfire Hurricane investigators' interpretation of Papadopoulos's actual words was the exact opposite of what was said, and given how critical those words were to an objective assessment of the

---

[1315] *See supra* footnote 214.

[1316] *See Redacted OIG Review* at 332-333.

[1317] *Id.* at 332.

[1318] *Id.*

[1319] OSC Report of Interview of Case Agent-1 on June 19, 2019 at 3.

[1320] OSC Report of Interview of Supervisory Special Agent-1 on June 17, 2019 at 3.

relationship between the Trump campaign and Russia, the entire exchange between Papadopoulos and CHS-1 should have been brought to the attention of the OI attorneys working with the Crossfire Hurricane personnel on the Page FISA application. The FBI, however, failed to do so at the time (and, as a consequence, the FISC also was not advised of the exculpatory statements). Indeed, these statements were only brought to the attention of the FISC more than two years later, on July 12, 2018, when the Department submitted a filing with the Court pursuant to the requirements of Rule 13, Rules of Procedure for the United States Foreign Intelligence Surveillance Court, as promulgated under Title 50, United States Code, Section 1803(g).[1321]

Importantly, these exculpatory statements were made by Papadopoulos more than a month *before* the initial Page FISA application was submitted to the FISC.[1322] Thus, at the time Papadopoulos made the recorded statements, the Crossfire Hurricane investigators were actively involved, or were soon to be involved, in drafting an updated application asserting that there was probable cause to believe that Page was an agent of a foreign power.[1323] Further, one Crossfire Hurricane investigator told the OIG that discussion of the September 15, 2016 meeting between CHS-1 and Papadopoulos and the interpretation of Papadopoulos's denials of cooperation with the Russians remained a topic of conversation for days afterward.[1324] Yet the FBI failed to apprise OI,[1325] and therefore the FISC, of these significant statements.

Finally, with respect to Papadopoulos's denial of any knowledge of a relationship between the Russians and the Trump campaign, it does not appear that the FBI gave any serious thought to simply interviewing him to resolve the discrepancy between his unambiguous statements to CHS-1 and what the Australian officials had reported concerning a "suggestion" regarding possible Russian assistance to the Trump campaign.[1326] [1327] Thus, an opportunity to potentially resolve any underlying national security concern early on was missed.

[1321] *See Redacted OIG Review* at 230-231.

[1322] As noted previously, the initial FISA warrant issued on October 21, 2016.

[1323] The effort took on additional vigor when four days after the CHS-1/Papadopoulos meetings, Crossfire Hurricane team members first received copies of some of the unvetted and uncorroborated Steele Dossier reporting.

[1324] *See Redacted OIG Review* at 332.

[1325] OSC Report of Interview of OI Attorney-1 on July 1, 2020 at 6.

[1326] According to Case Agent-1, the idea of a direct subject interview of Papadopoulos was "kicked around", as was the notional idea of going directly to the Trump campaign leadership with a briefing about the intelligence threats. Neither of these approaches were taken and the Crossfire Hurricane team pressed forward with its investigation. *See* OSC Interview of Case Agent-1 dated June 19, 2019 at 3.

[1327] As related in the opening EC for the Crossfire Hurricane investigation, quoting the text exactly as it had been received from Australia, "[P]apadopoulos suggested [to the Australian diplomats] that the Trump team had received some kind of suggestion from Russia that it could assist this process with the anonymous release of information during the campaign that would be damaging to Mrs. Clinton (and President Obama)."

xii.   Recordings of Papadopoulos by CHS-2

In addition to the recorded meetings Papadopoulos had with CHS-1 and the FBI UCEs during his trip to meet with CHS-1, he also had numerous conversations which were recorded at the FBI's direction with a second CHS ("CHS-2"). CHS-2 was a longtime acquaintance of Papadopoulos. From the first recorded conversation with CHS-2, which occurred on October 23, 2016, until their last recorded conversation, which occurred on May 6, 2017, CHS-2 made a total of 23 separate recordings for the FBI. CHS-2 challenged Papadopoulos with approximately 200 prompts or baited statements which elicited approximately 174 clearly exculpatory statements from Papadopoulos. While their recorded conversations totaled 120 hours and 17 minutes, covering a wide variety of topics, many of which did not relate to the Crossfire Hurricane investigation, there were a number of conversations that were particularly relevant. Indeed, over the course of their recorded meetings, Papadopoulos repeatedly denied that he, the Trump campaign, and Russia had some type of cooperative relationship. However, as with the statements Papadopoulos made in his monitored conversations with CHS-1, none of Papadopoulos's exculpatory statements to CHS-2 regarding his lack of knowledge of assistance from the Russians to the Trump campaign were included in the succeeding Page FISA renewal applications.[1328]

[1328] *See Redacted OIG Review* at 233. The OIG report notes that similar denials made by Papadopoulos in interviews he conducted with the FBI were included in the second and third FISA renewals. However, these denials, submitted as footnote 4 to the two renewals, contained qualifying language regarding the denials. While noting that during his interviews with the FBI Papadopoulos had denied discussing anything related to Russia during his meetings with the Australian officials, the footnote also contains the FBI's belief that the interview responses to FBI questions by Papadopoulos regarding these denials were misleading and incomplete. *See In re Carter W. Page*, No. 17-375, at 11 n.4; *In re Carter W. Page*, No. 17- 679, at 11 n. 4.

With regard to misleading and incomplete information being provided to the FBI, Papadopoulos was subsequently charged in a one-count Information with and convicted of making false statements in violation of 18 U.S.C. § 1001(a)(2). *United States v. George Papadopoulos*, Crim. No. 17-cr-182 (RMD) (D.D.C.), Document 8 (Information). Specifically, during his first interview with the Crossfire Hurricane Agents on January 27, 2017, Papadopoulos told the Agents about an individual associated with a London-based entity who had told him about the Russians having "dirt" on Clinton. Although Papadopoulos provided the FBI with the name of the individual and where he could be contacted, Papadopoulos lied to the Agents about when he had received the information (it was received after not before he was named as a foreign policy advisor to the Trump campaign) and he downplayed his understanding of the individual's connections to Russian government officials. *U.S. v. Papadopoulos* Document 19 (Statement of the Offense) at 1-2. In addition, Papadopoulos misled the Agents about his attempts to use the individual and a female associated with that person to arrange a meeting between the Trump campaign and Russian government officials. *Id.* at 2-3. Ultimately, Papadopoulos pleaded guilty to making false statements. On multiple occasions he then met with, answered questions for, and provided information to the Government, *id.* at 13, and eventually was sentenced to 14 days incarceration. *U.S. v. Papadopoulos* Document 50.

On October 29, 2016, in a conversation with CHS-2 that occurred approximately one week after the initiation of the FISA surveillance on Carter Page and ten days before the election, Papadopoulos and the CHS had the following exchanges:

CHS-2:	You think Russia is playing a big game in this election?
GP:	No.
CHS-2:	Why not?
GP:	Why would they?
CHS-2:	Don't you think they have special interest?
GP:	I do not think so, that's all [expletive].

***

CHS-2:	You don't think they hacked the DNC?
CHS-2:	Who hacked the [expletive] DNC then?
GP:	It could be the Chinese, could be the... Iranians, it could be some Bernie supporters...Could be Anonymous[1329]

***

CHS-2:	You don't think anyone from the Trump campaign hacked her emails.
GP:	No, no.
CHS-2:	You don't think anyone from the Trump campaign had anything to do with [expletive] over at the DNC?
GP:	No, I know that for a fact.
CHS-2:	How do you know that for a fact?
GP:	Because I have been working for them the last nine months that's how I know. And all of this stuff has been happening, what, over the last four months?
CHS-2:	But you don't think anyone would have done it like undercover or anything like that?
GP:	You know when I was in [Redacted] this [Redacted] and he was like a big advisor...asked me the same question. I told him absolutely not. And he actually was probably going in and tell the CIA or something if I'd have told him something else. I assume that's why he was asking. And I told him absolutely not. There's absolutely no reason... First of all, it is illegal, you know, to do that [expletive] ... No one would put their [expletive] life at risk or

---

[1329] Transcript of conversation between Papadopoulos and CHS-2 on 10-29-2016 at 157-158.

going to jail for the next 50 years to hack some [expletive] that may mean nothing.[1330]

Later in the conversation, Papadopoulos addressed the topic again, in response to CHS-2's inquiries:

GP: First of all, it is illegal to do that. So, no one in their right mind would, right?[1331]

Finally, the two discussed it one more time:

CHS-2: Do you think maybe Russia would have done... it because they could get away with it?

GP: Any foreign government.

CHS-2: They can get away with it?

GP: Yeah, Yeah, any foreign government.[1332]

The language used by Papadopoulos in his conversation with CHS-2 is consistent with the language he used in his conversation with CHS-1 almost six weeks earlier. Indeed, as noted above, Papadopoulos told CHS-2 that he told CHS-1 (whom he did not identify to CHS-2) the same thing as he was telling CHS-2 regarding allegations about the Trump campaign and Russia. Despite these denials by Papadopoulos to two different CHSs at two different times and places, as captured and memorialized on recordings made at the direction of the FBI, no information from either recorded conversation was brought to the attention of the FISC in the applications for the Page FISA renewals. Notably, these statements were made by Papadopoulos not just to an individual who he was meeting for the first time (CHS-1), but also, as the Crossfire Hurricane investigators well knew, to an individual with whom he had been well-acquainted over a long period of time (CHS-2).

In yet another conversation between CHS-2 and Papadopoulos, which occurred on January 25, 2017 (two weeks after publication of the Steele Reports by *BuzzFeed*, and amid media speculation that Sergei Millian, a person Papadopoulos had met and with whom he corresponded, was the source for some of the allegations in the Steele Reports), Papadopoulos expressed concerns about Millian to CHS-2. In this regard, the following relevant comments were recorded by CHS-2:

16:11:25

GP: I think he [Millian] was trying to get me to say a Trump person was trying to do business on the side with the Russians, that is what I think.

16:58:48

[1330] *Id.* at 159-160 (redaction in original).

[1331] *Id.* at 163.

[1332] *Id.* at 164 (redaction in original).

GP:	I am not part of the government. I have never been to Russia in my life.

17:02:50

CHS-2:	Have you done anything to like help [expletive]?
GP:	I'm telling you I done nothing.[1333]

Papadopoulos's denial to CHS-2 of working with the Russians was not mentioned in the FBI's second or third renewal applications for FISA warrants on Page.[1334] As noted above, certain denials made by Papadopoulos in FBI interviews were mentioned in a footnote, but the Crossfire Hurricane team reported that it believed Papadopoulos was misleading in those interviews. This denial from Papadopoulos in this conversation with CHS-2, which occurred prior to those two renewal applications being submitted to the FISC, was also omitted from any discussion in that referenced footnote.

In a third conversation, which took place on March 20, 2017, Papadopoulos and CHS-2 briefly discussed media reporting regarding an FBI investigation of the Trump campaign and possible contacts with Russia during the 2016 presidential campaign. The fact of the investigation had been publicly reported that day in Congressional testimony given by then-FBI Director Comey.[1335] This March 20, 2017, conversation included the following relevant exchanges:

11:38:35

GP:	They are doing an investigation, huh?
CHS-2:	Did you see Comey's press?

11:39:30

GP:	If they are trying to prove that people in the campaign were like sitting with Russians like colluding…
	What [expletive] are they even talking about, you know? What does that even mean colluding?
	That means they were sitting in a room together plotting [expletive]. Which is the craziest thing I ever heard of in my life.

11:39:58

CHS-2:	Is it though?
GP:	I think so. I highly doubt someone would be doing that. First of all, it would be suicide …You know what I think's going to end up

---

[1333] Audio recording of Papadopoulos and CHS-2 conversation on 01/25/2017. References are to timestamps of recording.

[1334] The second FISA Renewal application, Docket 17-375 was submitted to the FISC on April 7, 2017, and the third, Docket 17-679 was submitted to the FISC on June 29, 2017.

[1335] Matt Apuzzo, Matthew Rosenberg & Emmarie Huetteman, *F.B.I Is Investigating Trump's Russia Ties, Comey Confirms*, N.Y. Times (March 20, 2017).

happening.... I think that it will be like oh some of these guys were talking about but... you know some [expletive] like that. I do not know. What do you think?

CHS-2   I think everyone's [expletive].

11:40:53

GP: No-Even the guy the Congressman who's like focusing the Committee today.... Adam Schiff 'cuz I was watching him after breakfast and he's like if people met with them or are doing business in Russia that's not a crime. The crime that we are looking into is if there was like collusion. Which like I said that would be [expletive] nuts. But, I don't believe it.

CHS-2   You think anyone involved would have been dumb enough to leave a paper trail?

GP: Well, like I said, I don't.... I think it would just be insane. I just don't think anybody would be that psychotic unless they have like medical problems.[1336]

As with previous statements made by Papadopoulos to CHS-1 and CHS-2 which were relevant to the predicating information for the Crossfire Hurricane investigation, none of this additional dialogue, wherein Papadopoulos expressed absolutely no knowledge about Trump campaign/Russia collusion, was mentioned in either the second or third Page renewal applications submitted to the FISC. The omission of these March 20, 2017 statements of Papadopoulos is even more concerning in that he made them the very same day the FBI Director publicly confirmed the Crossfire Hurricane investigation which brought heightened attention to these matters.

Finally, in a fourth conversation between Papadopoulos and CHS-2 on March 31, 2017, they once again briefly discussed possible Russian interference in the 2016 election. The following exchange took place:

14:03:45

CHS-2:   Do you think the Russians would come and kill you if you said something? The Russian Mafia?

GP: I have nothing to do with the Russians.

14:14:30

CHS-2:   If Russia [expletive] meddled in our elections, what else are they controlling about us? That just makes America look weak.

GP: I still don't believe that [they did].[1337]

[1336] Audio recording of Papadopoulos and CHS-2 conversation on 03/20/2017. References are to timestamps of recording.

[1337] Audio recording of Papadopoulos and CHS-2 conversation on 03/31/2017. References are to timestamps of recording.

As in the earlier instances, these exchanges between Papadopoulos and CHS-2 were not mentioned in the second or third FISA renewal applications targeting Page. Nevertheless, it illustrates a consistency in Papadopoulos's denials that either he individually or, to his knowledge, others in the Trump campaign, colluded or worked in collaboration with the Russians during the 2016 presidential campaign.

These statements of Papadopoulos to two individuals with whom he talked openly and believed he could trust, statements which undercut the legitimate concerns raised by the Australian reporting and which resulted in the opening of the Crossfire Hurricane investigation, along with Page's statements in meetings with CHS-1 on multiple occasions, were deliberately ignored or dismissed by the FBI, preventing other entities, such as the OI and the FISC, from being able to adequately scrutinize the FBI's FISA submissions.

i. Other aspects of the Page FISA applications

i. *Multiple levels of subsources*

Much of the probable cause in the Page applications is based on multiple layers of sub-source reporting. The first surveillance application said of a key informant (Steele) that:

> Source #1 maintains a network of sub-sources, who, in many cases, utilize their own sub-sources. The source reporting in this application, which was provided to the FBI by Source #1, is derived primarily from a [redacted], who uses a network of sub-sources. Thus, *neither Source #1 nor the [redacted] had direct access* to the information being reported by the sub-sources identified herein . . . .[1338]

In other words, much of the information came through at least three people before it reached the FBI.

Referring to Steele's sub-sources, Supervisory Intelligence Analyst Brian Auten stated that he "did not have a good handle on how the sub-sources worked or who had what access to whom." He went on to say that "[b]y late January 2017 . . . [w]e knew we had a three-layer problem regarding Steele's sub-sources."[1339] Moreover, once Danchenko had been interviewed, Crossfire Hurricane investigators knew that Danchenko was not operating a "network of subsources," but rather would talk with people in his social circle about issues and then would report what he learned to Christopher Steele.[1340]

ii. *Reliability of subsources*

One of Source #1's sub-sources reported that there was "a well-developed conspiracy of co-operation." This was quoted twice in the initiation as it was at the heart of the factual

---

[1338] *In re Carter W. Page*, Order No. 16-1182, at 16 n.8 (emphasis added) (bolding in original omitted).

[1339] *FBI Inspection Division Report* at 365-66.

[1340] SCO-005801 (Interview of Igor Danchenko Electronic Communication dated 02-09-2017) at 23, 39.

information.[1341] The sub-source said the conspiracy was "between them [assessed to be individuals involved in Candidate #1's campaign] and the Russian leadership."[1342] This was "managed by Candidate #1's then campaign manager, who was using . . . foreign policy advisor Carter Page as an intermediary."[1343] There is no discussion in the FISA application of the reliability of the sub-source who provided this important information,[1344] and the FBI has secured no evidence that corroborated the allegations.

iii.   Role of campaign manager

Although the campaign manager was reported to be managing the cooperation with Russia, the application included no other information – such as information about suspicious Russian contacts with the manager – to support that statement. Based on our review, the FBI had no substantive evidence that corroborated this allegation.

iv.   Involvement in criminal activity

The Page FISA initiation approaches the issue of Page's involvement in criminal activity in a manner consistent with FISA's legislative history:[1345]

> As the activities discussed herein involve Page aiding, abetting, or conspiring with Russian Government officials and elements of the [Russian Intelligence Service] in clandestine intelligence activities, the FBI submits that there is probable cause to believe that such activities *involve or are about to involve* violations of the criminal statutes of the United States, including 18 U.S.C. § 371 (Conspiracy), 18 U.S.C. § 951 (Agents of Foreign Governments) and 22 U.S.C. §§ 612, et seq. (Foreign Agents Registration Act).[1346]

In applying the higher standard of criminal involvement to Page, the application did not discuss the standard, or explain how it was met, beyond what is stated above.

2. Prosecution decisions

In light of the foregoing, the Special Counsel carefully reviewed and analyzed the evidence related to (i) Clinesmith and the altered email; (ii) statements made to the FBI regarding the Steele Reports; (iii) the receipt and dissemination of the Steele Reports; (iv) the *Yahoo! News* article; (v) the use of the Steele Reports in the FISA applications targeting Page; (vi) Igor Danchenko, including the legality of Danchenko's visa arrangement and the FBI's handling of the prior counterespionage investigation of Danchenko; (vii) the recordings of Page,

---

[1341] *In re Carter W. Page*, Order No. 16-1182, at 10, 20. For a discussion of this and other parts of the information used to support probable cause, *see supra* § IV.C.1.

[1342] *Id.* at 20 (brackets in original).

[1343] *Id.*

[1344] *In re Carter W. Page*, Order No. 16-1182, at 19 n.17. Like this footnote, other footnotes describe sub-sources and state that they did not know that their reporting would be directed to the FBI, but the footnotes do not provide any information about the reliability of the sub-sources.

[1345] *See supra* § III.C.1.

[1346] *In re Carter W. Page*, Order No. 16-1182, at 32-33 (emphasis added).

Papadopoulos, and others; and (viii) the certification of the Page FISA applications. In determining whether the actions of individuals or entities warranted criminal prosecution, the Special Counsel adhered to the *Principles of Federal Prosecution*.

a. Kevin Clinesmith

Not only was the altered email itself a falsified document, the statement Clinesmith made in the altered email and in the instant messages to Supervisory Special Agent-2 — that Page was not a source — was also false. In fact, Page had been a source for the OGA and had provided direct reporting to the OGA in the past.[1347] When interviewed by the OIG, and as later confirmed when interviewed by our investigators, OGA Liaison-1 described Page as a "source" under the FBI's terminology and said that the reason she offered in the email to assist in providing language for the FISA application was because she was telling Clinesmith that, using the FBI's terminology, Page had been a source for the OGA.[1348] As the liaison told the OIG, it was incorrect to describe Page as a subsource.[1349] The liaison also stated that she saw no basis for Clinesmith to have concluded, based on their communications and the August 17th Memorandum, that Page never had a direct relationship with the OGA.[1350] In addition, the liaison said that she did not recall having any telephone discussions with Clinesmith on this issue.[1351] When interviewed by the Office, the liaison confirmed the accuracy of the information that she provided to the OIG.

The alteration made by Clinesmith also was unquestionably material to the final Page FISA application.[1352] As several individuals involved in the application process explained in interviews with the Office, Page's status as should have been disclosed to the FISC because it bore on whether there was probable cause to believe that Page was acting as an agent of a foreign power. OI Attorney-1 stated that it would have been a significant fact if Page had a relationship with the OGA that overlapped in time with his interactions with known Russian intelligence officers that were described in the FISA applications, as was the case here, because it would raise the issue of whether Page had those interactions with the intent to assist the U.S. government.[1353] Deputy Assistant Attorney General Stuart Evans stated that a FISA target's relationship with an OGA is typically included in an application,[1354] and he believed the information about Page's prior relationship with the OGA should have been disclosed because it "goes to the question of where the person's loyalties lie[.]"[1355]

[1347] *See Redacted OIG Review* at 251.

[1348] *Id.*

[1349] *Id.* at 251, 254-256.

[1350] *Id.* at 251.

[1351] *Id.*

[1352] *United States v. Kevin Clinesmith*, Crim. No. 20-cr-165(JEB) (D.D.C.), Doc. 1 (Statement of Offense) at 6.

[1353] *See Redacted OIG Review* at 157.

[1354] *Id.*

[1355] *Id.* at 159.

Indeed, Clinesmith himself knew that, if Page had been a source with the OGA, that information would need to be disclosed in the FISA application.[1356] Clinesmith acknowledged as much in his original email to OGA Liaison-1, stating "This is a fact we would need to disclose in our next FISA renewal."[1357] Later, when interviewed by the OIG, Clinesmith stated there was "a big, big concern from both [NSD OI] and from the FBI that we had been targeting a source, because that should never happen without us knowing about it."[1358] Clinesmith added that, if it were true, they would "need to provide [the information] to the court" because such information would "drastically change the way that we would handle . . . [the] FISA application."[1359]

Supervisory Special Agent-2 also described the importance of knowing Page's prior relationship with the OGA. According to Supervisory Special Agent-2, "if [Page] was being tasked by another agency, especially if he was being tasked to engage Russians, then it would absolutely be relevant for the Court to know . . . [and] could also seriously impact the predication of our entire investigation which focused on [Page's] close and continuous contact with Russian/Russia-linked individuals."[1360] When interviewed by our Office, Supervisory Special Agent-2 echoed the information he provided to the OIG.[1361]

To that end, Clinesmith was the person that Supervisory Special Agent-2 relied on to resolve the issue of whether Page had been a source for the OGA in the past.[1362] Clinesmith's statement to Supervisory Special Agent-2 that the OGA had said "explicitly" that Page had never been a source was "the confirmation that [he] need[ed]."[1363] According to Supervisory Special Agent-2, the language that Clinesmith inserted into the liaison's email — that Page was "not a source" — was the most important part of the email for him.[1364] Supervisory Special Agent-2 stated, "if they say [Page is] not a source, then you know we're good."[1365] Supervisory Special Agent-2 further stated that if the email from the liaison had not contained the words "not a source" then, for him, the issue would have remained unresolved, and he would have had to seek further clarification. As Supervisory Special Agent-2 told the OIG, "If you take out 'and not a

---

[1356] *United States v. Kevin Clinesmith*, Crim. No. 20-cr-165(JEB), (D.D.C.), Doc. 1 (Statement of Offense) at 4.

[1357] *Id.* at 4-5.

[1358] *Id.* at 4.

[1359] *Id.*

[1360] *See Redacted OIG Review* at 249.

[1361] OSC Report of Interview of Supervisory Special Agent-2 on May 5, 2021 at 3; OSC Report of Interview of Supervisory Special Agent-2 on Oct. 17, 2019 at 3-5.

[1362] *See Redacted OIG Review* at 255; OSC Report of Interview of Supervisory Special Agent-2 on Oct. 17, 2019 at 4.

[1363] *See Redacted OIG Review* at 253; OSC Report of Interview of Supervisory Special Agent-2 on May 5, 2021 at 3.

[1364] *Id.* at 255.

[1365] *Id.*

source,' . . . it doesn't really answer the question." Supervisory Special Agent-2 also stated that even a verbal statement from OGA liaison-1 would not have resolved the issue for him.[1366]

As discussed above, the OIG subsequently conducted a review of the FISA applications targeting Page and discovered Clinesmith's conduct in altering the email. When confronted with the altered email by the OIG, Clinesmith initially stated that he was not certain how the alteration occurred, but subsequently acknowledged that he made the change.

The seriousness of the Clinesmith's conduct is highlighted by the FISC's reiteration of the fact that "the government . . . has a heightened duty of candor to the [FISC] in *ex parte* proceedings," and "[t]he FISC 'expects the government to comply with its heightened duty of candor in ex parte proceedings at all times. Candor is fundamental to this Court's effective operation . . .'"[1367] In submissions dated October 25, 2019, and November 27, 2019, the Department provided the FISC with notice of Clinesmith's conduct and the failure to disclose Page's prior relationship with the OGA.[1368]

On August 19, 2020, the Office charged Clinesmith in the United States District Court for the District of Columbia with the felony offense of Making False Statements, in violation of 18 U.S.C. § 1001(a)(3). On that same date, in the case known as *United States v. Kevin Clinesmith*, Crim. No. 20-cr-165(JEB) (D.D.C.), Clinesmith waived indictment and pleaded guilty to a one-count Criminal Information.[1369] On January 29, 2021, Clinesmith was sentenced to a term of 12-months' probation.

Finally, it appears likely that political or personal bias contributed at least to some extent to Clinesmith's conduct in this matter.[1370] As mentioned in the *OIG Review*, Clinesmith had also been investigated by the FBI's Office of Professional Responsibility, and ultimately suspended, for sending improper political messages to other FBI employees.[1371] On the day after the 2016 presidential election, Clinesmith wrote, "I am so stressed about what I could have done differently."[1372] In a later exchange with another FBI colleague, Clinesmith was asked "[i]s it

---

[1366] *Id.*

[1367] *In Re Accuracy Concerns Regarding FBI Matters Submitted to the FISC*, Docket No. Misc. 19-02, at 2 (FISC Dec. 17, 2019) (citing Docket No. BR 14-01, Op. and Order issued on Mar. 21, 2014, at 8, *available at* http://repository.library.georgetown.edu/bitstream/handle/10822/1052715/gidc00098.pdf?seque nce=1&isAllowed=y, and Docket No. [Redacted], Mem. Op. and Order issued on Nov. 6, 2015, at 59, *available at* https://repository.library.georgetown.edu/bitstream/handle/10822/1052707/gid_c_00121.pdf?se quence=1&isAllowed=y).

[1368] *Id.* at 1, n.1.

[1369] *United States v. Kevin Clinesmith*, Crim. No. 20-cr-165(JEB) (D.D.C.), Doc. 1 (Information).

[1370] *United States v. Kevin Clinesmith*, Crim. No. 20-cr-165(JEB) (D.D.C.), Doc. 22 (Government's Sentencing Memorandum at 14).

[1371] *See Redacted OIG Review* at 256, n. 400.

[1372] FBI, Office of Professional Responsibility, *Report of Investigation* [of Kevin Clinesmith] at 7 (July 17, 2018).

making you rethink your commitment to the Trump administration[,]" and Clinesmith replied, "Hell no," and then added "Viva le resistance."[1373]

b. Statements made to the FBI regarding the Steele reporting

As an initial matter, despite multiple requests to his counsel, Christopher Steele refused to be voluntarily interviewed by the Office. Steele was hired by Fusion GPS to essentially conduct opposition research against then-candidate Trump in the midst of a U.S. presidential election. While many may find this practice unseemly, political opposition research is a firmly entrenched feature of U.S. electoral politics and existed, in one form or another, since the founding of the nation.

Nonetheless, the Office examined evidence to determine if anyone knowingly passed materially false information to the government, including to the FBI, State Department, or to members of Congress. In his two interviews with the FBI's Crossfire Hurricane investigators and the Mueller investigators (October 2016 and September 2017), Steele provided the FBI with his understanding of how the allegations contained in his reporting were gathered, which, according to Steele, was almost exclusively through the efforts of Igor Danchenko. During those interviews, Steele told the FBI about, among other things, his understanding of Danchenko's sub-sources, the location of those sub-sources, and the time period in which Danchenko purported to collect the information. As discussed above, a significant amount of the information Steele provided to the FBI conflicts with what Danchenko would later tell the FBI in the January 2017 interviews and beyond.

For instance, with respect to the Mikhail Kalugin allegations in Report 2016/111, Steele told the FBI that Danchenko learned of Kalugin being recalled to Moscow after he (Danchenko) randomly bumped into Kalugin on a street in Moscow. For his part, Danchenko informed the FBI that he learned of the Kalugin allegations while Kalugin assisted him with renewing his Russian passport. Danchenko also told the FBI that he (Danchenko) did not provide Steele with the Kremlin's rationale for the recall, *i.e.*, Kalugin's involvement in Russia's efforts to interfere with the U.S. presidential election. By way of another example, Steele told the FBI that Danchenko had personally met with alleged Steele Report source Sergei Millian on at least two occasions. During his interviews with the FBI, Danchenko denied telling Steele that he had met with Millian in person (although he acknowledged knowing that this was Steele's belief and Danchenko did not correct Steele on the matter). Danchenko was adamant about only receiving an anonymous call from a Russian male whom Danchenko believed to be Millian. These are just two examples in which Steele's recollection of events differed significantly from those of Danchenko.

The Office attempted to reconcile these conflicting versions of events but was largely unsuccessful. Indeed, untangling the web of allegations proved difficult given that (i) the Office was unable to interview either Steele or Danchenko, (ii) both Danchenko and Steele said that they destroyed all notes reflecting the content of their meetings and communications, (iii) Danchenko deleted most, if not all, of his emails during the relevant timeframe, and (iv) Danchenko's alleged sub-sources, with the notable exception of Charles Dolan, were all domiciled overseas. Thus, while the Office examined the feasibility of false statements charges

---

[1373] *Id.* at 8.

against any participants in the creation of the Steele Dossier, there was insufficient definitive evidence to warrant bringing such charges.

c. The FBI's receipt and dissemination of the Steele Reports

The winding and disjointed path the Steele Reports traveled to arrive at FBI Headquarters on September 19, 2016 is certainly concerning. Indeed, the Office was never provided a satisfactory explanation of why the Steele Reports took 75 days to reach the Crossfire Hurricane investigators. Even more basic, FBI records were insufficient to establish who came into contact with the Reports before September 19th, to say nothing of the motivations of those individuals in deciding to advance or hold the Reports. Despite repeated interviews and good-faith attempts to refresh recollections, the path of the Steele Reports is littered with failed memories and inconsistent versions of events. The evidence gathered was not sufficient to prove at trial that any FBI personnel intentionally violated any criminal statutes in relation to the transmittal of the Steele Reports. Nor was there sufficient evidence to establish that any FBI personnel intentionally lied during their interviews.

d. The *Yahoo! News* article

As noted, on September 23, 2016, Michael Isikoff published an article in *Yahoo! News* titled "U.S. Intel Officials Probe Ties Between Trump Adviser and Kremlin."[1374] The article detailed Page's alleged meetings with Sechin and Divyekin and contained information that was nearly identical to Steele Report 2016/94. The information in the article allegedly came from a "well-placed Western intelligence source" and had been confirmed by a "senior U.S. law enforcement official." The FBI's initial assessment of the article – an assessment ultimately confirmed by Steele – was that Steele had leaked the information to *Yahoo! News*. Understandably, following a review of the initial draft FISA application targeting Page, senior personnel in OI and ODAG raised concerns that the *Yahoo! News* leak revealed a potential significant bias on Steele's part. OI was initially told that the FBI's assessment was that the information in *Yahoo! News* had come from Steele.

Again, as discussed in detail above, part of the FBI's work during its October 2016 interview of Steele in Rome was to determine if Steele had been the source of the leak to *Yahoo! News*. Following the October 2016 Rome trip, several drafts of the Page FISA application were circulated that contained a footnote reflecting that Steele had, in fact, been the source of information in the *Yahoo! News* article. Upon review of these drafts, Department and OI leadership continued to press the FBI on whether Steele harbored a bias given his willingness to speak with the press. Thereafter, on October 14, 2016, a Crossfire Hurricane investigator emailed an OI attorney stating that Steele had not previously mentioned the leak (to *Yahoo! News*) and "only acknowledged it when the FBI brought it up on October 4." This is despite the fact that when interviewed by the Special Counsel *every* FBI participant in the Rome meeting could not recall the issue of the *Yahoo! News* leak being discussed with Steele. Auten, for his part, had a vague recollection that one participant in the meeting may have spoken with Steele about the issue *prior* to the meeting with Crossfire Hurricane personnel – a contention that participant adamantly denied. Nevertheless, the next draft of the Page FISA application contained a footnote stating that the FBI assessed that Steele provided the *Yahoo! News*

[1374] *See supra* § IV.D.1.b.iv.

information to his business associate who, in turn, passed it on to the law firm that hired the business associate.

Understandably, Department leadership had trouble squaring this assessment with the plain reading of the *Yahoo! News* article which stated that a "well-placed Western intelligence source" (in context, Steele) had provided the information directly to *Yahoo! News*. On October 17, 2016, the FBI conducted a Lync call over Top Secret servers with OI to discuss this issue, and the FBI purported to resolve all the questions raised by Department leadership. During their respective interviews with the Special Counsel, not a single participant in that call could recollect the rationale for the changed assessment. Ultimately, the footnote in the final application submitted to the FISC reflected that Steele had not been responsible for the leak to *Yahoo! News*.

The Office was left to answer the obvious question: How did the FBI's assessment change from the rational assessment that Steele leaked the information to *Yahoo! News* to the unfounded assessment that Steele was not responsible for the leak? Unfortunately, this question remains unanswered. Despite repeated interviews and attempts to refresh recollections, we were left with what investigators and analysts stated were failed memories and, as a consequence, inconsistent versions of events. The Office, however, struggles to credit the failed recollections of those whom the Office interviewed given the import of the information to the ODAG and senior officials in NSD.

In any event, given the dearth of contemporaneous documentary evidence reflecting the events in question, the available evidence was insufficient to definitively establish that any of the participants intentionally (i) submitted false information to the FISC, in violation of 18 U.S.C. §1621(2) (perjury), (ii) provided false statements to the Special Counsel, in violation of 18 U.S.C. §1001(a)(2) (false statements), or (iii) violated the civil rights of Page, in violation of 18 U.S.C. §242 (civil rights violations). Again, the Office was unable to establish that any government officials acted with a criminal intent to violate the law, as opposed to mere negligence or recklessness.

Nevertheless, the FBI's conduct concerning the *Yahoo! News* issue is extremely troubling. Again, the Office is left to speculate that the FBI's unfounded assessment of the *Yahoo! News* information was driven by the pressure emanating from FBI Headquarters executives to commence FISA surveillance of Page. Indeed, OI Attorney-1's contemporaneous email to OI Unit Chief-1 noting that Crossfire Hurricane investigators "never asked and [didn't] want to ask" about the *Yahoo! News* leak encapsulates the Office's findings in this matter.[1375]

   e.   The use of the Steele Reports in the Page FISA applications

The pressure on Crossfire Hurricane investigators to commence FISA surveillance coverage of Page was palpable in the late summer and early fall of 2016. Indeed, as discussed above in Section IV.D.1.a.i, multiple FBI and Department employees described the unusual interest of high-level FBI executives in the Page FISA application. The inclusion of the unvetted Steele Reports in the Page FISA applications is problematic for the FBI, but the issue for the Special Counsel was whether it constituted a provable federal crime.

At the time of the initial application, not a single substantive allegation contained in Reports 2016/080, 2016/094, 2016/095/ and 2016/102 had been corroborated in any meaningful

---

[1375] *See supra* footnote 655.

way by the FBI. The allegations in those Reports and used in the initial FISA application were not mere ancillary facts that supported substantiated allegations. Rather, they contained extremely serious and indeed shocking allegations to the effect that (i) the Kremlin was supplying the Trump campaign with compromising information on Hillary Clinton (2016/080), (ii) Page, an advisor to the Trump campaign, was actively engaging with Russian officials to discuss the lifting of sanctions against Russia as well as the sharing of compromising information on Hillary Clinton (2016/094), (iii) Page was serving as an intermediary between Trump campaign manager Manafort and Russian officials in what the Steele Reports described as a "well-developed conspiracy" of cooperation (2016/095), and (iv) Russia had released hacked DNC emails to Wikileaks – an idea allegedly conceived of by Page. Again, at the time these serious allegations were put into the Page FISA application, the FBI had not corroborated any of these claims.

As discussed above, the Crossfire Hurricane team received the Steele Reports on September 19, 2016. Approximately two days after receipt, the uncorroborated information from the Steele Reports was inserted into the request for FISA surveillance of Page. The Special Counsel's interviews of the relevant players in the drafting of the Page FISA have all acknowledged that minimal efforts had been undertaken at that point to corroborate the Steele reporting. Rather, to a person, the FBI and Department personnel have all stated that the Steele reporting was deemed reliable based on Steele's prior history as an FBI CHS as well as his past employment with the British intelligence services. While undoubtedly the past performance of a source is an important factor in determining the reliability of information, surely establishing probable cause to accuse a U.S. person, to say nothing of a U.S. presidential campaign advisor, with colluding with a foreign adversary requires, at minimum, some degree of independent corroboration.

Notably, not one of the damning allegations contained in the Steele reporting was ever corroborated: not the salacious allegations of events at the Ritz Carlton in Moscow,[1376] not the allegation of there being a "well-developed conspiracy of co-operation" between Trump and the Russians,[1377] not the allegations of secret meetings involving Page and certain sanctioned Russians (namely, Igor Sechin and Igor Divyekin),[1378] and not the allegation of Page serving as Manafort's conduit for information between the Russians and the Trump campaign.[1379] This is true even after the FBI had offered Steele $1 million or more for such corroboration and after Danchenko was signed up as an FBI CHS and paid more than $220,000 for information on other matters.[1380] In addition, Helson told the Office that, as reflected in reports he had written on

---

[1376] SCO-105084 (Documents Known to the FBI Comprising the "Steele Dossier") at 2-4 (Company Intelligence Report 2016/080).

[1377] *Id.* at 9-10 (Company Intelligence Report 2016/095).

[1378] *Id.* at 8 (Company Intelligence Report 2016/094).

[1379] *Id.* at 9-10 (Company Intelligence Report 2016/095).

[1380] OSC Report of Interview of Brian Auten on July 26, 2021 at 18, 24, 31(When asked if there was any substantive information corroborated from the Steele Reports, Auten advised that there were facts that checked out such as names and positions, but that they were not able to corroborate any of the discrete allegations in the dossier); OSC Report of Interview of Kevin Helson on July 14, 2020 at 5, 14 (Helson remembered asking Danchenko if there were any

March 1, 2017 and March 16, 2017, there had been no corroboration of what Danchenko alleged about the Steele reporting during his three-day interview with the FBI.[1381]

Moreover, Auten told the Office that to the best of his recollection, when they checked with another U.S. intelligence agency on matters relating to the Steele reporting, they received no corroborating information back.[1382] As one long-time counterintelligence expert at that agency told the Office, the Dossier contained unverified allegations from sub-sources who allegedly provided the information, information that the government could not obtain despite its vast intelligence resources and paying millions of dollars for intelligence. Indeed, after the Steele Dossier was leaked and became public, that expert's reaction was to ask the FBI, "You didn't use that, right?"[1383]

One Crossfire Hurricane investigator said out loud what others may have been thinking: The initial FISA application targeting Page was being done in the hope that the returns would "self-corroborate." Here, the pressure from FBI leadership to commence surveillance of Page coupled with the FBI's previous unsuccessful attempt to advance the application against Page provided the Crossfire Hurricane investigators with ample motive to include the unvetted Steele Reports in the FISA application.

Although the evidence assembled by the Office may have been sufficient to meet a negligence standard, in order to prove a criminal violation of Page's civil rights, the government would be required to prove, beyond a reasonable doubt, that one or more persons acted *intentionally* to violate his rights. What in our judgement would be the admissible evidence in such a prosecution did not meet that standard.

In addition, in order to prove a false statement charge under 18 U.S.C. S 1001, such a prosecution would have to rest largely on not what was a provable, affirmative false statement, but rather on material omissions (*e.g.*, Page's relationship with another government agency, Page's exculpatory statements to a long-term FBI CHS, and the like). Given the claimed inability of the principal actors to recall the details of critical conversations, and the lack of evidence as to who was responsible for information that was included or withheld in the FISA applications, the standard of proof beyond a reasonable doubt could not be met. Accordingly, the Office did not seek criminal charges against any FBI or Department personnel in relation to the inclusion of the Steele Reports in the four Page FISA applications presented to the FISC.

f. Igor Danchenko

In November 2021, a grand jury sitting in the Eastern District of Virginia returned an indictment ("Indictment") charging Igor Danchenko with five counts of making false statements

---

statements [in the dossier] that could be proven by emails or other documentation. Danchenko, however, could not provide any corroborating information to support this information because, according to Danchenko, the information stemmed from casual conversations); OSC Report of Interview of Analyst-1 on July 14, 2020 at 19 ("the dossier could not be corroborated" and "no substantive facts in the dossier were corroborated").

[1381] OSC Report of Interview of Kevin Helson on July 14, 2020 at 5.

[1382] OSC Report of Interview of Brian Auten on July 26, 2021 at 26.

[1383] OSC Report of Interview of CIA Employee-1 on July 17, 2019 at 3.

to the FBI. The false statements, which were made during Danchenko's time as an FBI CHS, related to his role as Steele's primary sub-source for the Reports.

First, the Indictment alleged that Danchenko stated falsely that he had never communicated with Charles Dolan about any allegations contained in the Steele Reports. As discussed above, the documentary evidence clearly showed that Dolan was the source for at least one allegation in the Steele Reports. Specifically, that information concerned Manafort's resignation as Trump's campaign manager, an allegation Dolan told Danchenko that he sourced from a "GOP friend" but that he told our investigators was something he made up.[1384] The allegations regarding Dolan formed the basis of Count One of the Indictment.

Second, the Indictment alleged that Danchenko falsely stated that, in or about late July 2016, he received an anonymous phone call from an individual whom Danchenko believed to be Sergei Millian. Danchenko also falsely stated that, during this phone call, (i) the person he believed to be Millian informed him, in part, about information that the Steele Reports later described as demonstrating a well-developed "conspiracy of cooperation" between the Trump campaign and Russian officials, and (ii) Danchenko and Millian agreed to meet in New York. The available evidence was sufficient to prove beyond a reasonable doubt that Danchenko fabricated these facts regarding Millian. The allegations regarding Millian formed the bases for Counts Two through Five of the Indictment.

Following a one-week trial, and before the case went to the jury, the Court dismissed Count One of the Indictment pursuant to Federal Rule of Criminal Procedure 29. The Court held that Danchenko's statement to the FBI regarding Dolan, *i.e.*, that he [Danchenko] never "talked to [Dolan] about anything that showed up in the dossier" was "literally true" because, in fact, the information about Manafort was exchanged over email rather than in an actual verbal conversation. The Court denied Danchenko's Rule 29 motion to dismiss related to the remaining counts of the Indictment. Following two days of deliberations, the jury concluded that the case had not been proven beyond a reasonable doubt.

In determining whether to bring criminal charges against Danchenko, the Office expected to be able to introduce additional evidence against Danchenko that supported the charged crimes. Thus, prior to trial, the Office moved *in limine* to introduce certain evidence as direct evidence of the charged crimes. Alternatively, the Office moved to admit the evidence as "other act" evidence pursuant to Federal Rule of Evidence 404(b) to prove Danchenko's motive, intent, plan and absence of mistake or accident. In particular, the Office sought permission to introduce evidence of:

> (1) Danchenko's uncharged false statements to the FBI regarding his purported receipt of information reflecting Trump's alleged salacious sexual activity at the Ritz Carlton Hotel in Moscow. In particular, the Office planned to call as a witness the German-national general manager of the Ritz Carlton, identified in the Steele Report 2016/080 as "Source E." The Office expected the general manager would testify that he (i) had no recollection of speaking with Danchenko in June 2016 or at any time, (ii) had no knowledge of the allegations set forth in the Steele Report before their appearance in

---

[1384] OSC Report of Interview of Charles Dolan on September 7, 2021 at 1.

the media, and (iii) never discussed such allegations with Danchenko or any staff member at the hotel;

(2) Danchenko's uncharged false statements to the FBI reflecting the fact that he never informed friends, associates, and/or sources that he worked for Orbis or Steele and that "you [the FBI] are the first people he's told." In fact, the evidence revealed that Danchenko on multiple occasions communicated and emailed with, among others, Dolan regarding his work for Steele and Orbis, thus potentially opening the door to the receipt and dissemination of Russian disinformation; and

(3) Danchenko's email to a former employer in which Danchenko advised the employer, when necessary, to fabricate sources of information. Specifically, on February 24, 2016, just months before Danchenko began collecting information for the Steele Reports, the employer asked Danchenko to review a report that the employer's company had prepared. Danchenko emailed the employer with certain recommendations to improve the report. One of those recommendations was the following:

> Emphasize sources. Make them bold of CAPITALISED [*sic*]. The more sources the better. If you lack them, use oneself as a source ("[Location redacted]-Washington-based businessman" or whatever) to save the situation and make it look a bit better.[1385]

Danchenko's advice that he attach multiple sources to information and obscure one's own role as a source for information was consistent with Danchenko's alleged false statements in which he denied or fabricated the roles of sources in the Steele Reports.

The Court ruled, however, that the evidence described above was inadmissible at trial. The prosecution was forced to then proceed without the benefit of what it believed in good faith was powerful, admissible evidence under Rule 404(b) of the Federal Rules of Evidence.

g. The legality of Danchenko's visa arrangement

The Office consulted with attorneys and investigators from the Department of Homeland Security, United States Citizenship and Immigration Services ("USCIS") to determine if Danchenko's U.S. visa was obtained through fraudulent pretenses, given, in the Office's view, the unusual circumstances in which an individual lists a U.S.-based employer as the sponsor of the visa application (Danchenko Employer-1), but is in actuality employed by a foreign entity (Orbis) and merely paid by the sponsoring entity for work done on behalf of the foreign employer. The USCIS informed the Office that this arrangement was legal.

The Office also reviewed the evidence of Danchenko's circuitous payment stream to determine if Orbis, Danchenko Employer-1, or other entities engaged in money laundering in violation of 18 U.S.C. § 1956. Given the apparent legality of Danchenko's visa arrangement, however, the Office determined that no specified unlawful activity could be proven.

[1385] SC_IDC_00102430 (Email from Danchenko to Former Danchenko Employer-1 Executive-1 dated 02/24/2016) (capitalization in original).

h. The FBI's handling of the prior counterespionage investigation of Danchenko

The failure of the FBI to assess properly the prior counterespionage investigation of Danchenko is incomprehensible. The investigation related to Danchenko's pitching a person he thought perhaps was going into the Obama administration for classified information. Although the conduct of certain FBI employees was, at best, negligent with respect to the prior investigation of Danchenko and his subsequent use as a CHS, we did not find any evidence that FBI personnel acted with specific intent – which the statute requires – to permit knowingly false information received from Danchenko to continue to be used in FISA applications. Prosecution, therefore, was not supported by the available evidence.

i. The recordings of Page, Papadopoulos and others

The Office carefully reviewed and analyzed the evidence related to, among other things, (i) the FBI's handling of the recordings made by CHSs and UCEs, (ii) the conduct of the CHSs and UCEs in making those recordings, and (iii) the FBI's failure to include key exculpatory material from those recordings in the Page FISA applications. As discussed more fully below, in determining whether the actions of individuals and entities warranted criminal prosecution, the Office adhered to the previously delineated Principles of Federal Prosecution.

i. *CHS-1's recordings of Page*

As discussed throughout this report, one of the key allegations contained in the Steele reporting, and which would later underpin the Page FISA applications, was the existence of "a well-developed conspiracy of co-operation" between the Trump campaign and Russian leadership. This alleged conspiracy purportedly was managed by campaign manager Paul Manafort using Page, and others, as intermediaries with the Russians.[1386] On its face, this was a shocking and serious allegation of collusion between the Trump campaign and the Russian government. However, as discussed in detail above, during the first recorded meeting between Page and CHS-1, Page never once indicated that he maintained a relationship with Manafort – despite several efforts by CHS-1 to establish such a relationship. In fact, Page explicitly denied ever having met or spoken with Manafort. While Page said he had sent a couple of emails to Manafort during his time on the campaign,[1387] he noted that Manafort did not respond to any of these emails. These assertions made by Page could have easily been corroborated through basic investigative steps and legal process, but were never undertaken.

Moreover, as discussed above, the Page FISA applications also relied on uncorroborated allegations from the Steele Reports that Page had met with Igor Sechin and Igor Divyekin in July 2016 to discuss the removal of certain sanctions against the Russian government. In his recorded meetings with CHS-1, however, Page denied meeting with Sechin or Divyekin and further denied even knowing who Divyekin was. Following the release of the *Yahoo! News* article on September 23, 2016 containing these same allegations, Page made similar denials in his letter to Director Comey and volunteered to be interviewed by the FBI regarding the accusations.

[1386] SCO-105084 (Documents Known to the FBI Comprising the "Steele Dossier") at 9, "Company Intelligence Report 2016/095" (capitalization in original).

[1387] As previously noted, on one of the emails Manafort was included on the TO: line and he was cc'd on two others.

Despite these recorded exculpatory statements made by Page and the denials contained in his letter to Comey, the FBI submitted its initial Page FISA application on October 21, 2016 containing the uncorroborated Steele Report allegations discussed above. The application inaccurately stated that "Page did not provide any specific details to refute, dispel, or clarify the media reporting [and] he made vague statements that minimized his activities." In fact, the only fair reading of Page's statements to CHS-1 regarding Manafort is that Page explicitly denied meeting or speaking with Manafort about any subject, to say nothing of the allegations regarding collusion with the Russian government. In the same vein, the only fair reading of Page's statements to CHS-1 regarding Sechin and Divyekin is that Page explicitly denied meeting with either individual, and, in fact, had never even heard of Divyekin. These multiple, explicit denials to CHS-1 were not included in the initial Page FISA application or subsequent renewals. Further, during the pendency of the Page FISA renewals, the FBI obtained additional information that should have cast further doubt on the allegations contained in the applications, including, but not limited to (i) Page's denials of the allegations during a series of interviews with the FBI in March 2017, and (ii) the FBI's interview of Steele's primary subsource (Igor Danchenko), which as discussed more fully below, cast further doubt on the nature of any alleged relationship between the Trump campaign and the Russian government.

The Crossfire Hurricane investigators did not correct the errors, omissions, and misrepresentations that were contained in the initial Page FISA application and subsequent renewals. When interviewed by the Office, one of the Crossfire Hurricane investigators stated, without further explanation, that he assessed Page's statements to CHS-1 to be "evasive." Similarly, when interviewed by the OIG, the investigator stated that Page "minimized, he kind of vacillated on some things. So, that's our, that was our, my assessment of what he said." Again, a fair reading of the transcripts of the recorded meetings between Page and CHS-1 reveal that Page was, if nothing else, explicit in his denials regarding Manafort, Sechin, and Divyekin. Based on a review of all the evidence, the Office concluded that the Crossfire Hurricane investigators, while aware of Page's explicit denials regarding the allegations, appear to have chosen to cloak those explicit denials in unsupported assessments to not endanger the viability of the Page FISA applications.

While the evidence assembled by the Office may have been sufficient to meet a negligence standard, in order to prove a criminal violation of Page's civil rights, the Government would be required to prove beyond a reasonable doubt that one or more persons acted *intentionally* to violate those rights. What in our judgement would be the admissible evidence in such a prosecution did not meet that standard.

In addition, in order to prove a false statement or perjury charge, such a prosecution would have to rest largely on not what was a provable, affirmative false statement, but rather on material omissions (*e.g.* Page's exculpatory statements to CHS-1). Given, among other things, (i) the reliance by the investigators on their professional assessments, (ii) the claimed inability to recall the details of important conversations, (iii) the lack of evidence as to who was responsible for information that was included or withheld in the FISA applications, and (iv) the inability to prove intent, the Office concluded that the standard of proof beyond a reasonable doubt could not be met. Accordingly, the Office did not seek criminal charges against any FBI or Department personnel in relation to the Page exculpatory material being withheld from the Page FISA applications.

ii.   Recordings of George Papadopoulos

The FBI also recorded meetings between Papadopoulos and FBI CHSs and UCEs. During the course of these meetings, Papadopoulos denied Russian assistance to the Trump campaign, notwithstanding repeated attempts by CHS-1 to link the WikiLeaks disclosures of DNC emails to the campaign – an assertion set forth in the Page FISA applications. In fact, when asked directly by CHS-1 if the campaign had advance knowledge about the WikiLeaks disclosures, Papadopoulos replied "no." Papadopoulos stated that the campaign "would [not] advocate for this type of activity because at the end of the day, it's, ah, illegal . . . and compromises the U.S. national security." Papadopoulos also stated that this type of activity is "espionage . . . treason." Papadopoulos also made repeated denials about the campaign's involvement with the WikiLeaks disclosures to a second CHS. These highly probative statements, some of which were made before the initial Page FISA application, were not included in that application or any subsequent renewals. Perhaps more importantly, these statements did not cause anyone in the FBI to question the initial predication for Crossfire Hurricane, namely Papadopoulos's alleged statements to the Australian diplomats regarding Russia's offer of assistance to the Trump campaign.

Similar to the Page exculpatory statements, the Crossfire Hurricane investigators chose not to credit Papadopoulos's statements and assessed them to be "weird," "rote," "canned," "rehearsed," and, without citing any evidence, the product of legal coaching.[1388] Indeed, when interviewed by the Office, one Crossfire Hurricane investigator repeated that assessment noting that Papadopoulos's statements were "curious," rehearsed, and therefore not authentic. Likewise, when interviewed by the Office, another investigator recalled briefing FBI executives about the Papadopoulos statements, including McCabe, and noted that the statements were deemed to be scripted to give a false impression.

For the same reasons stated with respect to Page, the evidence assembled by the Office in relation to the exclusion of the Papadopoulos statements in the Page FISA application may have been sufficient to meet a negligence standard but was insufficient to bring criminal charges against any FBI or Department personnel.

iii.   The conduct of CHS-1

As discussed above, on December 15, 2016, CHS-1 and Page had the third of what would eventually be four recorded meetings. In that meeting, CHS-1 and Page discussed, among other things, the potential formation of a London-based think tank focusing on Russia's relations with the West. Although the two discussed Secretary of State nominee Rex Tillerson's relationship with Igor Sechin and also briefly discussed a *Washington Post* column mentioning Page's purported relationship with Sechin, the subject of Page meeting Sechin and Igor Divyekin was not raised during this meeting. Nevertheless, a few days later, CHS-1 informed Case Agent-1 that Page, in fact, had told CHS-1 that he had met with Sechin on his most recent trip to Russia. According to Case Agent-1, CHS-1 purported to recall this information after reading about Sechin in the newspaper. A review of the transcript of this meeting and careful listening to the entire recording revealed no such statements made by Page,[1389] and reviewing the transcript or

---

[1388] *Redacted OIG Review* at 332-333.

[1389] Transcript of conversation between Carter Page and CHS-1 on 12/15/2016.

listening to the recorded conversation appears to have been a basic step that Case Agent-1 did not take. The Office examined whether CHS-1 made an intentional false statement to the FBI when he provided this information, but was unable to establish that CHS-1 intentionally lied to the FBI.

j. Certification of the FISA applications

The Office also assessed whether there were any criminal violations in the certifications made by senior government officials as part of the Page FISA applications.[1390] The certification addresses the foreign intelligence purpose of the application, such as a purpose of obtaining information "necessary . . . to protect against . . . clandestine intelligence activities by an intelligence service or network of a foreign power or by an agent of a foreign power" or "information with respect to a foreign power or foreign territory that . . . is necessary to . . . the national defense or security of the United States . . . or the conduct of the foreign affairs of the United States."[1391] The official must also certify that the foreign intelligence sought cannot be obtained by normal investigative techniques, and explain the basis for that certification.[1392] The certification of a FISA application does not cover the accuracy of the information in the application itself; that is addressed by a sworn statement from an FBI Agent.[1393]

The certifications met the requirements of FISA. Our investigation did not reveal that any certifier lacked a reasonable basis for believing that the assertions as to the purpose of the application were true. The examples and explanations provided in the certifications strongly supported the assertions that a significant purpose of the applications was to obtain foreign intelligence information.

The certifiers also certified that the foreign intelligence sought could not be obtained by normal investigative techniques. The certifications listed other techniques that might be used to investigate Page. Again, our investigation did not find that any certifier lacked a reasonable basis for believing that the assertions about the use of investigative techniques were true. The certifications explained the basis for the statements logically and in a manner that was relevant to the Page applications.

E. **The Alfa Bank and Yotaphone Allegations**

1. *Factual background – Alfa Bank*

a. Introduction

The Office's investigation identified evidence that certain individuals and entities sought to support the Clinton campaign by promoting allegations to law enforcement and the Intelligence Community related to Trump and his campaign. The Office considered

---

[1390] *In re Carter W. Page*, No. 16-1182, at 63; *In re Carter W. Page*, No. 17-52, at 76; *In re Carter W. Page*, No. 17-375, at 88; *In re Carter W. Page*, No. 17-679 at 98.

[1391] *See* 50 U.S.C. § 1801(e)(2). The certification requirements are discussed above in Section III.C.3.

[1392] 50 U.S.C. §§ 1804(a)(6)(C) and (a)(6)(E)(ii).

[1393] *See supra* §§ III.C.1; III.C.3.

whether the activities of these individuals or entities, as well as government officials, violated any federal criminal statutes. In particular, we examined the validity of the allegations and whether these individuals or entities conspired with the Clinton campaign to provide false or misleading information to law enforcement and the Intelligence Community.

First, the Office identified certain statements that Michael Sussmann made to the FBI and the CIA that the investigation revealed were false. Sussmann was a partner at Perkins Coie, the law firm that served as counsel to the Clinton campaign. A grand jury in the U.S. District Court for the District of Columbia found probable cause to believe that Sussmann lied to an FBI official and returned a one-count indictment charging him with making a materially false statement, in violation of 18 U.S.C. § 1001.[1394]

As set forth in the Indictment, on September 19, 2016 – less than two months before the 2016 election – Sussmann met with FBI General Counsel Baker. Sussmann provided Baker with data and white papers that allegedly demonstrated a covert communications channel between the Trump Organization and Alfa Bank, a Russia-based bank. The Indictment alleged that Sussmann lied in that meeting, falsely stating to Baker that he was not providing information to the FBI on behalf of any client. Instead, the Office's investigation revealed that Sussmann had assembled and conveyed the allegations to the FBI on behalf of two clients, Rodney Joffe, an executive at Tech Company-1[1395] and the Clinton campaign. After a two-week trial, a jury found that the case against Sussmann had not been proven beyond a reasonable doubt.

Second, as explained further below, the Office's investigation uncovered evidence of numerous actions by individuals and entities with ties to the Clinton campaign to promote the Alfa Bank allegations to the Intelligence Community and the government. The Office also uncovered evidence that individuals and entities with ties to the Clinton campaign promoted allegations that Trump or his associates were using, in the vicinity of the White House and other locations, one or more telephones from the Russian mobile telephone provider Yotaphone. The Office considered the validity of the allegations and evaluated whether the conduct of these individuals or entities constituted a federal offense and whether admissible evidence would be sufficient to obtain a conviction for such an offense. Ultimately, the Office concluded that our evidence was not sufficient to obtain and sustain a criminal conviction.

The Office also examined the FBI's actions in relation to the Alfa Bank and Yotaphone allegations. In doing so, the investigation assessed whether any FBI or other federal employee conspired with others to promote the allegations in order to benefit the Clinton campaign in a manner that would constitute a federal offense. The Office's investigation did not establish sufficient evidence that any FBI official or employee

---

[1394] *See Sussmann Indictment.*

[1395] *Sussmann* Tr. 05/17/2022 PM at 506:12-17. Tech Company-1 is a U.S. based company that provides internet-related services and products to both commercial and government clients. *Sussmann* Tr. 05/17/2022 PM at 502:2-506:8; OSC Report of Interview of University-1 Researcher-1 on 07/22/2021 at 4; OSC Report of Interview of Tech Company-1 Employee-1 on 02/02/2021 at 1-4.

knowingly and intentionally participated in a conspiracy with others to promote the allegations, to falsify government records, to obstruct justice, or to cause the FBI to open an investigation into them as part of such a conspiracy.

b. <u>Sussmann's attorney-client relationship with the Clinton campaign and Joffe</u>

As part of its investigation, the Office obtained billing records from Perkins Coie related to the firm's representation of various individuals and entities, including the Clinton campaign, Tech Company-1, and Rodney Joffe. The records reflect that Sussmann repeatedly billed the Clinton campaign for his work on the Alfa Bank allegations. In compiling and disseminating these allegations, Sussmann and Joffe also met and communicated with Marc Elias, another partner at Perkins Coie, who was then serving as General Counsel to the Clinton campaign.[1396]

By way of background, in April 2015, the Clinton campaign engaged Perkins Coie and Elias to provide "legal counseling and representation of [the Clinton campaign] in connection to its legal affairs, including the Federal Election Commission and other regulatory requirements and general organizational and compliance matters."[1397] A few months later, the DNC and the Democratic Congressional Campaign Committee engaged Perkins Coie to provide legal advice in connection with the "Federal Election Commission and other regulatory requirements and general organizational and compliance matters."[1398]

After these engagements, in the spring of 2016, Perkins Coie engaged Fusion GPS on behalf of the Clinton campaign. Fusion GPS was a Washington, D.C.-based consulting firm that provided research and strategic intelligence services to clients, including corporations and law firms. As set forth in the letter memorializing that engagement, the purpose was for Fusion to support Perkins Coie's legal advice to clients on "defamation, libel and similar laws in which accuracy is an essential legal element."[1399] Elias explained that Perkins Coie hired Fusion for research and investigative services to assist Elias and Perkins Coie in representing the Clinton campaign.[1400] As part of those services, Fusion provided research and other services that were used to, among other things, promote the Alfa Bank allegations to the media and the FBI.

c. The Alfa Bank allegations

i. *Actions by Sussmann, Perkins Coie, and Joffe to promote the allegations*

The Office's investigation revealed that beginning in late July or early August 2016, Sussmann, Joffe, and agents of the Clinton campaign together assembled and disseminated the Alfa Bank allegations and other derogatory information about Trump and his associates to the media and then to the FBI. Generally speaking, the Alfa Bank allegations pertained to

---

[1396] Joffe and Elias declined to be voluntarily interviewed by the Office.

[1397] *Sussmann* Government Exhibit 301 at 1.

[1398] SCO-021710 (Letter from Perkins Coie Attorney-1 to DNC Official-1 re: Legal Representation dated October 7, 2015) at 1.

[1399] *Sussmann* Government Exhibit 302 at 1.

[1400] *Sussmann* Tr. 05/18/2022 AM at 630:10-634:10.

assertions that a "secret" email server located in Pennsylvania was configured to allow email communications between Alfa Bank and the Trump Organization through a "TOR exit node" (*i.e.*, a node used for anonymized internet traffic) at Spectrum Health, a U.S.-based healthcare company located in Michigan.

Beginning in the summer of 2016, Joffe worked with Sussmann, Fusion GPS, a number of cyber researchers, and employees at multiple internet companies to assemble data and white papers. In connection with these efforts, Joffe used his access to non-public or proprietary internet data. Joffe also enlisted the assistance of researchers at a U.S.-based university ("University-1") who were receiving and analyzing large amounts of internet data in connection with a pending federal government cybersecurity research contract. Joffe tasked these researchers to mine internet data to establish a connection between Trump and Russia.

In particular, in late July and early August, Joffe commenced a project in coordination with Sussmann and Perkins Coie to support an "inference" and "narrative" tying Trump to Russia. For example, records show that on three days in August 2016, Joffe had meetings or conference calls with Sussmann and Elias.[1401] At about the same time, Joffe began tasking his own employees and associates to mine and assemble internet data that would support such an inference or narrative.[1402] Joffe expressly stated in emails that a purpose of this effort was to please certain "VIPs,"[1403] apparently referring to Sussmann, Elias, and the Clinton campaign.

Among others whom Joffe called was an executive of another technology company ("Tech Company-3 Executive-1"). Joffe had an ownership interest in Tech Company-3. Joffe instructed Tech Company-3 Executive-1 to search data maintained by his company and another affiliated company[1404] for information concerning the online activities of Trump and his associates.[1405] Joffe told Tech Company-3 Executive-1 that he was working with a person at a firm in Washington, D.C. with close ties to the Clinton campaign and the

---

[1401] *Sussmann* Government Exhibits 319, 327, 331-332, 553.4.

[1402] SC-00000473 (Email from Joffe to University-1 Researcher-1 & University-1 Researcher-2 dated 08/03/2016); SC-00000732 (Email from University-1 Researcher-1 to Tech Company-1 Employee-1 & Joffe dated 08/20/2016); SC-00000570 (Email from Tech Company-2 Executive-1 to Joffe, University-1 Researcher-1 & University-1 Researcher-2 dated 08/20/2016); SC-00000016 (Email from University-1 Researcher-1 to University-1 Researcher-2, Joffe & Tech Company-2 Executive-1 dated 08/21/2016); SC-00000665 (Email from Joffe to University-1 Researcher-1, University-1 Researcher-2 & Tech Company-2 Executive-1 dated 08/21/2016).

[1403] SC-00000573 (Email from Joffe to Tech Company-2 Executive-1, University-1 Researcher-1 & University-1 Researcher-2 dated 08/20/2016).

[1404] The affiliated company was Packet Forensics, a company that, among other things, places or gains access to sensors on the internet's infrastructure that allow it to collect large quantities of internet domain name system ("DNS") traffic from around the globe, which it then sells. *Sussmann* Tr. 05/24/2022 PM at 1981:7-14, 1985:19-1987:13.

[1405] OSC Report of Interview of Tech Company-3 Executive-1 on Aug. 12, 2021 at 2-4; *Sussmann* Tr. 05/24/2022 PM at 1990:3-1991:6, 1994:2-1997:1.

Democratic Party. Joffe also provided to Tech Company-3 Executive-1 a document containing the physical addresses, email addresses, Internet Protocol ("IP") addresses, email domains, and other personal information associated with various Trump associates, including information about some spouses and family members (the "Trump Associates List").[1406]

Tech Company-3 Executive-1 was highly uncomfortable with this task.[1407] Still, according to Tech Company-3 Executive-1, he and others complied with the instructions because Joffe was a powerful figure at these companies.[1408] The companies thereafter embarked on a data analysis and opposition research project concerning Trump and his associates, which they codenamed "Crimson Rhino."[1409] As part of the research project, Tech Company-3 Executive-1 and his associates drafted a report that they provided to Joffe. The report's "preliminary result" was that the researchers "observed no connection that clearly indicated direct communications between said individuals and Russia that would imply money transfers from Russia to the United States within the last 90 days."[1410]

Joffe also tasked others, including an employee of Tech Company-1 ("Tech Company-1 Employee-1"), to use resources at his companies to conduct opposition research about Trump.[1411] According to Tech Company-1 Employee-1, one of the services that Tech Company-1 provided was access to domain name system ("DNS") information.[1412] As part of these services, Tech Company-1 stored approximately 150 billion DNS transactions per day, which was approximately five terabytes of data.[1413] Although Tech Company-1 Employee-1 acknowledged that Tech Company-1 did not conduct political research as part of its business operations,[1414] during the 2016 campaign, Joffe asked Tech Company-1 Employee-1 to run searches of Tech Company-1's DNS data logs related to the Alfa Bank allegations.[1415] According to Tech Company-1 Employee-1, this included creating scripts to pull data related to various domains and IP addresses, including the domain trump-

---

[1406] *Sussman* Tr. 5/24/2022 PM at 1996:9-11; SC-00083453. The List included Carter Page, Sergei Millian, Paul Manafort, Richard Burt, Roger Stone, and Peter Petrina.

[1407] *Sussmann* Tr. 05/24/2022 PM at 1996:9-1997:12.

[1408] OSC Report of Interview of Tech Company-3 Executive-1 on Aug. 12, 2021 part 2 at 1.

[1409] *Sussmann* Tr. 05/24/2022 PM at 1997:3-1998:12.

[1410] SC-00083451 (Crimson Rhino paper) at 1.

[1411] OSC Report of Interview of Tech Company-1 Employee-1 on Feb. 2, 2021 at 4-5.

[1412] DNS is a naming system for devices connected to the internet that translates recognizable domain names, *E.g.,* http://www.google.com, to numerical IP addresses, *E.g.,* 123.456.7.89. *Sussmann* Tr. 05/17/2022 AM at 325:4-24. "A DNS look-up tells you that one computer looked up the IP address for a particular domain name." *Sussmann* Tr. 05/17/2022 AM at 339:17-18.

[1413] *Sussmann* Tr. 05/17/2022 PM at 504:11-20.

[1414] *Id.* at 506:9-11.

[1415] *Id.* at 508:4-19.

email.com and various domains that included the phrase "alfa" in them.[1416] Tech Company-1 Employee-1 could not recall conducting any other searches of Tech Company-1's DNS data for political projects or related in any way to specific political organizations, but Tech Company-1 Employee-1 never asked Joffe about the purpose of the project or whether these searches were on behalf a political campaign.[1417] Tech Company-1 Employee-1 has stated, in sum and substance, that he did not ask because he did not want to know.[1418]

Joffe similarly tasked Tech Company-2 Executive-1[1419] and other researchers with conducting opposition research regarding Trump. For instance, Joffe emailed these researchers the same Trump Associates List that he had provided to Tech Company-3 Executive-1.[1420] Among those whom Joffe and Tech Company-2 Executive-1 enlisted were researchers at University-1 who were assigned to a then-pending federal cybersecurity contract with the Defense Advanced Research Projects Agency ("DARPA"). At the time, Joffe was negotiating an agreement between Tech Company-1 and University-1 to sell large amounts of internet data to the university for use under the DARPA contract. The intended purpose of this agreement, and of University-1's sensitive work with DARPA, was to gather and analyze internet metadata to detect malicious cyberattacks.[1421] Both Joffe and Tech Company-2 Executive-1 worked with two of these University-1 researchers, University-1 Researcher-1 and University-1 Researcher-2, to mine internet data to conduct opposition research.

As part of these efforts, Sussmann and Elias began facilitating collaboration and information sharing by Joffe, Fusion GPS, and the Clinton campaign. For example, email records reflect that in August 2016, Sussmann began exchanging emails with personnel from Fusion and Elias containing the subject line, "connecting you all by email."[1422] (The contents of these emails have been withheld pursuant to asserted attorney-client privilege.)[1423]

[1416] *Id.* at 511:21-517:17; *Sussmann* Government Exhibits 111, 1600, 1602.

[1417] *Sussmann* Tr. 05/17/2022 PM at 514:14-17, 519:3-10.

[1418] *Id.* at 509:5-9, 519:3-10.

[1419] Tech Company-2 Executive-1 was the president and CEO of another company funded by Joffe. *Sussmann* Tr. 05/24/2022 PM at 1985:8-9; OSC Report of Interview of Tech Company-3 Executive-1 on Aug. 16, 2021 at 2. Tech Company-2 Executive-1 declined to be interviewed by the Office.

[1420] SC-00000578 (Email from Joffe to Tech Company-2 Executive-1, University-1 Researcher-1 & University-1 Researcher-2 dated 08/20/2016).

[1421] OSC Report of Interviews of University-1 Researcher-2 in July, August 2021 at 1.

[1422] SC-00108364 (Email from Sussmann to Simpson, Fritsch & Elias dated 08/11/2016).

[1423] Perkins Coie Privilege Log dated 09/07/2021, sheet 2 at lines 1-5. In the *Sussmann* case, Fusion GPS withheld over 1500 documents, claiming they were covered by attorney-client privilege as they were purportedly prepared to assist Perkins Coie in providing legal advice to law firm's clients, the Clinton campaign and Fusion GPS, in the event that then-candidate Trump sued them for defamation. Before trial, the government challenged their privilege claims and

Later that month, Joffe also began communicating with Fusion GPS personnel.[1424] Email records offered at the *Sussmann* trial and described in further detail below reflect that, in the ensuing months, Fusion GPS employees communicated with news reporters regarding the Alfa Bank allegations and urged them to publish articles about them.

Sussmann took additional steps to integrate the Alfa Bank-related allegations into the Clinton campaign's opposition research efforts. For example, in the summer of 2016, Sussmann met in Perkins Coie's offices with Fusion personnel and with Christopher Steele, whose Dossier-related activities are described above.[1425] Fusion had at the time retained Steele to conduct opposition research.[1426] Sussmann and Steele have each testified separately about the meeting and their accounts differ as to what occurred. Although Sussmann testified before Congress that the purpose of the meeting was to "vet" Steele for the Clinton campaign given Sussmann's knowledge of national security matters, Sussmann never acknowledged discussing the Alfa Bank allegations with Steele and has maintained that the contents of their meeting are privileged.[1427] In contrast, Steele testified under oath in a British legal proceeding that, during the meeting, Sussmann told him about the Alfa Bank allegations.[1428] Steele further testified that, after the meeting, Fusion personnel tasked Steele to research and produce intelligence reports about Alfa Bank, which he did.[1429]

---

successfully moved the Court to inspect a sampling of approximately 38 documents *in camera*. After reviewing the materials and receiving briefing not only from the government and Sussmann's counsel but also from Fusion GPS's counsel, counsel for the DNC and counsel for the Clinton campaign, the Court determined that 22 of 38 emails were improperly withheld as privileged. Specifically, the Court rejected their privilege claims because the emails at issue "solely related to disseminating the information they [Fusion GPS] and others had gathered." *United States v. Sussmann*, 21-CR-582, 5/12/2022 Order at 6-7.

[1424] *Sussmann* Government Exhibit 602 (Email from Joffe to Laura Seago & Sussmann dated 08/30/2016). Fusion GPS similarly withheld the contents of such communications as subject to attorney-client privilege. Fusion GPS Supplemental Privilege Log dated 03/22/2021.

[1425] U.S. House of Representatives Permanent Select Committee on Intelligence Interview of Michael Sussmann, (Dec. 18, 2017) at 74-75; *Steele Transcript* (Mar. 18, 2020) at 1:18-2:3. *See supra* § IV.D.1.b.

[1426] U.S. House of Representatives Permanent Select Cmte. on Intelligence Interview of Glenn Simpson, (Nov. 14, 2017) at 13, 19, 22-25.

[1427] U.S. House of Representatives Permanent Select Cmte. on Intelligence Interview of Michael Sussmann, (Dec. 18, 2017) at 75-76.

[1428] *Steele Transcript* (Mar. 18, 2020) at 1:23-2:3.

[1429] *Steele Transcript* (Mar. 18, 2020) at 1:18-2:6; SCO-105084 (Documents Known to the FBI Comprising the "Steele Dossier") at 23-24 (Company Intelligence Report 2016/112).

According to government records and public information, Steele also later provided the substance of the Alfa Bank allegations to State Department personnel, and Fusion GPS and Steele provided such information to Bruce Ohr, an official at the Department.[1430]

Emails, billing records, and testimonial evidence offered at trial show that during approximately the same time period – and *before* approaching the FBI about these matters – Sussmann provided the Alfa Bank allegations to Eric Lichtblau, a reporter for the *New York Times*.[1431]

Law firm records reflect that after providing the Alfa Bank allegations to the media, Sussmann apprised Elias of his efforts who, in turn, appears to have communicated with the Clinton campaign's senior leadership concerning these issues.[1432]

Emails and billing records further show that, during the same time period, Sussmann and Joffe worked together to draft a white paper, which summarized the Alfa Bank allegations and which Sussmann provided to the FBI during his September 19th meeting with James Baker. Sussmann billed significant time drafting this paper to the Clinton campaign.[1433] In addition, and as described in further detail below, Joffe also solicited input on this white paper from the University-1 researchers.

Sussmann incorporated at least one of the aforementioned researchers into his efforts to disseminate the Alfa Bank allegations to the media for the benefit of the Clinton campaign. For example, emails reflect that on September 17, 2016 – two days before his meeting with the FBI – Sussmann emailed University-1 Researcher-2, stating that "[w]e have a mutual acquaintance,"[1434] in context apparently referring to Joffe. Soon thereafter, Sussmann spoke with University-1 Researcher-2.[1435] During their conversation, Sussmann told University-1 Researcher-2 that the data underlying the Alfa Bank allegations had been lawfully collected, thus reflecting Sussmann's apparent knowledge concerning the data's origins.[1436] University-1 Researcher-2 also said that Joffe asked him to speak with the media about the Alfa Bank allegations, which he subsequently did.[1437]

[1430] *Steele Transcript* (Mar. 18, 2020) at 74:23-75:22; SCO-015117 (Notes from Meeting with Chris Steele dated 10/11/2016); SCO-015110 (Emails between Winer and Kavalec dated 10/12&13/2016); SCO-075792 (FBI Interview of Bruce Ohr on 12/12/2016).

[1431] *E.g., Sussmann* Government Exhibit 553.16 (M. Sussmann billing entry to HFA dated 09/06/16); SCO-092700 (Michael Sussmann Verizon record) at 10; SCO-092711 (Michael Sussmann Verizon record) at 3; *see also Sussmann* Tr. 05/18/2022 PM at 725:6-726:25, 747:12-749:14; 05/19/2022 AM at 844:24-845:10, 865:25-866:10, 903:8-14.

[1432] SC-00004312 (Email from Elias dated 10/09/16) at 1, 3.

[1433] *E.g., Sussmann* Government Exhibits 553.6, 553.12, 553.16, 553.22.

[1434] SC-00004278 (Emails between University-1 Researcher-2 & Sussmann dated 09/17/16).

[1435] SCO-092711 (Sussmann Verizon record) at 5.

[1436] OSC Report of Interviews of University-1 Researcher-2 in July, August 2021 at 3, 5.

[1437] *Id.* at 5.

ii. *Actions by Tech Company-2 Executive-1 and others and additional actions by Joffe*

The Office gathered emails and communications between Joffe, employees of various internet companies, and the other researchers regarding the use of internet data related to the Trump campaign. Among the internet data Joffe and his associates obtained was DNS internet traffic pertaining to (i) Spectrum Health, (ii) Trump Tower, (iii) Trump's Central Park West apartment building, and (iv) the Executive Office of the President ("EOP").

For example, Tech Company-2 Executive-1 referenced the Trump Associates that Joffe had provided:

Regarding this whole project, my opinion is that from DNS all we could gain even in the best case is an *inference*.

I have not the slightest doubt that illegal money and relationships exist between pro-Russian and pro-Trump, meaning actual people very close to Trump if not   himself. . . .

But even if we found what Rodney asks us to find in DNS we don't see the money flow, and we don't see the content of some message saying "send me the money here" etc.

I could fill out a sales form on two websites, faking the other company's email address in each form, and cause them to appear to communicate with each other in DNS. (And other ways I can think of and I feel sure [University-1 Researcher-2] can think of.)

IF Rodney can take the *inference* we gain through this team exercise . . . and cause someone to apply more useful tools of more useful observation or study or questioning ... then work to develop even an inference may be worthwhile.

That is how I understood the task. Because Rodney didn't tell me more context or specific things. What [Cyber Researcher-1] has been digging up is going to wind up being significant. It's just not the case that you can rest assured that Hil[l]ary's opposition research and whatever professional govts and investigative journalists are also digging . . . they just don't all come up with the same things or interpret them the same way. But if you find any benefit in what [he] has done or is doing, you need to say so, to encourage [him]. Because we are both killing ourselves here, every day for weeks.

. . . .

Trump/ advisor domains I've been using. These include ALL from Rodney's PDF [the Trump Associates List] plus more from [Cyber Researcher-1]'s work . . . .[1438]

[1438] SC-00000570 (Email from Tech Company-2 Executive-1 to Joffe, University-1 Researcher-1 & University-1 Researcher-2 dated 08/20/2016) (emphases added) (capitalizations in original).

The above email reflects the fact that Joffe's tasking likely triggered or affected the research efforts that ultimately culminated in Sussmann's meeting with Baker. Joffe's response states that the "task is indeed broad" and that the ability to "provide evidence of *anything* that shows an attempt to behave badly" would make "the VIPs . . . happy." According to Joffe, the "VIPs" were looking for a "true story that could be used as the basis for a closer examination," and any interactions between Trump and Alfa Bank "would be jackpot."[1439]

Joffe proceeded to disseminate the Alfa Bank allegations despite having previously expressed and received from others expressions of serious doubts and differing views about their strength, and purposefully crafted a written analysis to conceal the weaknesses of the allegations. For example, on August 21, 2016, Joffe urged the researchers to push forward with additional research concerning Trump, which he stated would "give the base of a very useful narrative." Later in the same email, Joffe expressed his own belief that the "trump-email.com" domain was "a red herring," noting that the host for that domain "is a legitimate valid [customer relationship management] company." Joffe therefore concluded that "we can ignore it, together with others that seem to be part of the marketing world."[1440]

On August 22, 2016, University-1 Researcher-1 expressed his view that Joffe's research project was flawed, stating that:

> Lets [sic] for a moment think of the best case scenario, where we are able to show (somehow) that DNS (MX[1441] or otherwise) communication exists between Trump and R[ussia]. *How do we plan to defend against the criticism that this is not spoofed UDP traffic we are observing?* There is no answer to that. Lets [sic] assume again that they are not smart enough to refute our "best case" scenario. Rodney, you do realize that we will have to expose every trick we have in our bag to even make a very weak association? Letsv [sic] all reflect upon that for a moment. [S]orry folks, but unless we get combine netflow and DNS traffic collected at critical points between suspect organizations, *we cannot technically make any claims that would fly public scrutiny.* This is not a typical attribution problem when the two parties (defenders vs. attackers) are clearly separated. In this case we will have not only the Trump folks trying to sho[o]t this down, but all the privacy freaks trying to come up with a crazy conspiracy theory on how we obtain the data. Sorry to say this, we are nowhere close coming [sic] with a plan to attack this problem that will fly in the public domain. *The only thing that drive [sic] us at this point is that we just do not like [Trump]. This will not fly in eyes of*

[1439] SC-00000573 (Email from Joffe to Tech Company-2 Executive-1, University-1 Researcher-1 & University-1 Researcher-2 dated 08/20/2016).

[1440] SC-00000665 (Email from Joffe to University-1 Researcher-1, University-1 Researcher-2 & Tech Company-2 Executive-1 dated 08/21/2016).

[1441] "Mail server." *Sussmann* Government Exhibit 247 at 2.

public scrutiny. Folks, I am afraid we have tunnel vision. Time to regroup?[1442]

On September 14, 2016, Joffe solicited the views of the researchers on the white paper, and asked these DNS experts to consider the paper not using their expertise, but conducting the reviews as if they were *not* experts:

> Please read as if you had no prior knowledge or involvement, and you were handed this document as a security expert (NOT a dns expert) and were asked: 'Is this plausible as an explanation?' NOT to be able to say that this is, without doubt, fact, but to merely be plausible. Do NOT spend more than a short while on this (If you spend more than an hour you have failed the assignment). Hopefully less. :)[1443]

University-1 Researcher-1 replied, endorsing Joffe's approach: "A DNS expert would poke several holes to this hypothesis (primarily around visibility, about which very smartly you do not talk about). That being said, I do not think even the top security (non-DNS) researchers can refute your statements. Nice!"[1444] University-1 Researcher-1 explained to our investigators that he endorsed Joffe's approach of downplaying the paper's weaknesses because Joffe was important to the success of the then-pending DARPA contract with University-1, and University-1 Researcher-1 therefore felt pressure to please Joffe.[1445] Apart from this email, however, University-1 Researcher-1 consistently maintained that the Alfa Bank data did not support any definitive conclusions.[1446]

The following morning, University-1 Researcher-2 responded to Joffe by disputing one of the paper's key findings, stating that, "Tor exit nodes, by definition route traffic for all users, since they do not know the origin of the traffic. To say that the Tor exit is exclusively used by Alfa Bank goes too far."[1447] Tech Company-2 Executive-1 responded to Joffe, stating, in part, that the paper's conclusion was "plausible" in the "narrow scope" defined by Joffe, and noting in part that: "if the whitepaper intends to say that there are communications between at least Alfa [Bank] and Trump, which are being intentionally hidden by Alfa [Bank] and Trump, I absolutely believe that is the case."[1448] University-1

[1442] SC-00000021 (Email from University-1 Researcher-1 to Tech Company-2 Executive-1, Joffe & University-1 Researcher-2 dated 08/22/2016) (emphasis added).

[1443] SC-00000023 (Email from Joffe to University-1 Researcher-1, University-1 Researcher-2 & Tech Company-2 Executive-1 dated 09/14/16) (capitalization in original).

[1444] SC-00000028 (Email from University-1 Researcher-1 to Joffe, University-1 Researcher-2 & Tech Company-2 Executive-1 dated 09/14/16).

[1445] OSC Report of Interview of University-1 Researcher-1 on July 22, 2021 at 1-2.

[1446] *Id.* at 1; 2-3; 4.

[1447] SC-00000758 (Email from University-1 Researcher-2 to Joffe, University-1 Researcher-1 & Tech Company-2 Executive-1 dated 09/16/2016).

[1448] SC-00000760 (Email from Tech Company-2 Executive-1 to Joffe, University-1 Researcher-1 & University-1 Researcher-2 dated 09/15/16).

Researcher-2 replied on the same date, stating that he believed that there was "a threshold of probable cause" for criminal and other federal violations.[1449]

On September 16, 2016, Tech Company-2 Executive-1 emailed these researchers, discussing, among other things, the draft white paper's allegation that there was a TOR exit node at Spectrum Health that Alfa Bank had used to communicate with the Trump organization. Tech Company-2 Executive-1 initially noted that University-1 Researcher-2 had given his "adversaries every courtesy" and that "[i]f everyone in America were as measured, fair and careful, what concerns could we ever have?"[1450] Tech Company-2 Executive-1 continued that she had no reason to think that Alfa Bank has a VPN somehow through mail1.trump-email.com. "That would suggest we are dealing with masterminds of the internet." Tech Company-2 Executive-1 added that she firmly believed that there were communications between the Trump organization and Alfa Bank and that she did not

> care in the least whether I'm right or wrong about VPN from Alfa Bank, [TOR] from Alfa Bank, or just SMTP artifact pointing to a 3-way connection. Rodney has carefully crafted a message that could work to accomplish the goals. Weakening that message in any way would in my opinion be a mistake.[1451]

Notably, TOR publishes a comprehensive list of exit nodes dating back to February 22, 2010. FBI experts we engaged examined this data for dates between February 22, 2010 and September 1, 2021. No instances of IP addresses in the range of 167.73.x.x (assigned to Spectrum Health) were ever indexed as TOR exit nodes. The FBI experts advised that historical TOR exit node data conclusively disproves this white paper allegation in its entirety and furthermore the construction of the TOR network makes the described arrangement impossible. Even if true or indeed possible, using the TOR network in the alleged manner would result in worse anonymization and security than simply using TOR in its default configuration. The experts explained that it would instead amount to a static proxy with a known endpoint that could be more easily correlated with traffic to the relatively small number of guard nodes allowing the identification or the true source IP much more easily than using a randomly selected exit node for each connection as the system is designed to do. It is entirely likely that one or more users, at some time, connected to both Spectrum Health and Alfa Bank using TOR and may have even come through the same exit node, but this in no way indicates any kind of correlation given the deliberately random nature of TOR routing.[1452]

[1449] SC-00000761 (Email from University-1 Researcher-2 to Tech Company-2 Executive-1, Joffe & University-1 Researcher-1 dated 09/15/16).

[1450] SC-00000031 (Email from Tech Company-2 Executive-1 to University-1 Researcher-2, Joffe & University-1 Researcher-1 dated 09/16/16).

[1451] *Id.*

[1452] *FBI Technical Analysis Report* 12-13.

iii. *Sussmann's meeting with the FBI*

The night before he met with Baker, Sussmann sent the following text message to Baker's personal cellphone: "Jim – it's Michael Sussmann. I have something time-sensitive (and sensitive) I need to discuss. Do you have availability for a short meeting tomorrow? *I'm coming on my own – not on behalf of a client or company – want to help the Bureau.* Thanks."[1453] Baker responded: "Ok. I will find a time. What might work for you?"[1454] To which Sussmann replied: "Any time but lunchtime – you name it."[1455]

The next day, Sussmann met with Baker at FBI Headquarters. According to Baker, the meeting occurred in Baker's office and lasted approximately 30 minutes.[1456] No one else was present. Baker explained that Sussmann said during the meeting that he had information regarding a "surreptitious communications channel" between Alfa Bank and the Trump organization and that he stated, "I'm not here on behalf of any particular client."[1457] Baker said that he was "100 percent confident" that Sussmann made this statement during the meeting.[1458] Because Baker considered Sussmann a friend and colleague, Baker believed that the statement was truthful. Baker also stated that Sussmann provided him with thumb drives containing data and "white papers" that explained the covert channel. Baker also noted that Sussmann said that major news organizations were aware of the Alfa Bank allegations and were intent on publishing about the issue relatively soon.[1459] As a result, Baker considered this to be an urgent matter because, if a news organization were to publish the allegations, any secret communications channel would likely disappear.[1460]

Thus, soon after he met with Sussmann, Baker spoke with Assistant Director for Counterintelligence Priestap and Deputy General Counsel Anderson, who handled counterintelligence and cyber matters. Baker believed that Priestap and Anderson needed to be aware of the allegations because they involved a Russian bank purportedly making an effort to communicate with the Trump organization. This "seemed to [Baker], on its face, to be a potential national security threat."[1461] Baker relayed to Priestap and Anderson the details of his meeting, including Sussmann's specific representation that he was not there on behalf of any client and a general explanation of the Alfa Bank allegations. Both Priestap

---

[1453] *Sussmann* Government Exhibit 1500 (James Baker iPhone screenshots) at 4 (emphasis added).

[1454] *Id.*

[1455] *Id.*

[1456] *Sussmann* Tr. 05/19/2022 AM at 840:23-841:19.

[1457] *Id.* at 842:9-14.

[1458] *Id.*

[1459] *Id.* at 845:4-10, 847:21-24.

[1460] *Id.* at 848:3-16.

[1461] *Id.* at 854:6-12.

and Anderson took contemporaneous notes. Priestap wrote in his FBI notebook[1462] that Sussmann "said not doing this for any client":

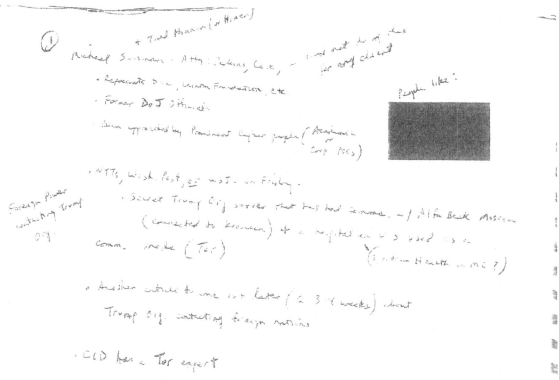

Similarly, Anderson took the following notes,[1463] which stated, in part, "No specific client but group of cyber academics talked w/ him about research":

Despite their notes, neither Priestap nor Anderson remembered receiving this information from Baker.[1464] Baker also recalled that he briefed both Director Comey and Deputy Director Andrew McCabe about the Alfa Bank allegations.[1465]

[1462] *Sussmann* Government Exhibits 2A, 2B, 2C, 243, 289.

[1463] *Sussmann* Government Exhibits 3A, 242.

[1464] *Sussmann* Tr. 05/23/2022 AM at 1445:22-1446:1; 05/24/2022 AM at 1786:15-25.

[1465] As noted previously, McCabe and Comey declined to be interviewed.

d. The FBI's Alfa Bank investigation

Following his meeting with Sussmann and briefings of FBI leadership, Baker recalled that he gave either Priestap or Strzok the white papers[1466] and thumb drives from Sussmann.[1467] The materials then made their way quickly to the Cyber Division. At trial, an FBI cyber agent ("Cyber Agent-1") testified that the agent and his supervisor ("Cyber Agent-2") were tasked to take custody of the Alfa Bank materials and to obtain signatures for the accompanying chain of custody form.[1468] A review of that form showed that Baker relinquished custody of the materials to Strzok, who then provided the materials to Eric Sporre, the Deputy Assistant Director of the Cyber Division.[1469] According to the form, Sporre thereafter transferred custody to Cyber Agent-2.[1470] Cyber Agent-1 testified that he was able to get signatures from Baker and Sporre for the form, but Strzok was unavailable and someone else obtained his signature.[1471]

i. The Cyber Division's review of the Alfa Bank allegations

Following the receipt of the materials, Cyber Agent-2 tasked Cyber Agent-1 to review the data provided on the thumb drives along with the white papers and identify whether there were any "cyber equities," such as an allegation of hacking.[1472] Cyber Agent-2 also tasked Cyber Agent-1 to review the data and compare it to the white paper and provide an assessment as to whether the data supported the white paper's findings.[1473] The white paper that Cyber Agent-1 reviewed, titled "White Paper #1 – Auditable V3,"[1474] contained an initial section titled "Findings" that stated:

> The Trump Organization is using a very unusually-configured 'secret' email
> server in Pennsylvania for current and ongoing email communications with
> Alfa Bank (Moscow), and with Alfa Bank (Moscow) through another

---

[1466] At his meeting with Baker, Sussmann provided three white papers to the FBI. Sussmann, Joffe, and possibly others drafted the first paper. *Sussmann* Government Exhibits 11, 319, 327, 331, 382, 553.6, 553.12, 553.16, 553.22; SC-00004255 (Email from Sussmann dated 09/06/2016); SC-00000023 (Email from Joffe to University-1 Researcher-1, University-1 Researcher-2, Tech Company-2 Executive-1 on 09/14/2016). The investigation determined that University-1 Researcher-2 drafted the second paper. Fusion GPS drafted the third paper. *Sussmann* Government Exhibits 687, 688, 689.

[1467] *Sussmann* Tr. 05/19/2022 AM at 878:8-15.

[1468] *Sussmann* Tr. 05/17/2022 AM at 365:20-366:7.

[1469] *Sussmann* Government Exhibit 282.

[1470] *Id.*

[1471] *Sussmann* Tr. 05/17/2022 AM at 370:6-10.

[1472] *Id.* at 371:20-372:4.

[1473] *Id.* at 372:8-24.

[1474] *Sussmann* Government Exhibit 217.

unusually-configured server (a 'TOR exit node') at Spectrum Health in Michigan.

These servers are configured for direct communications between the Trump organization and Alfa Bank to the exclusion of all other systems.

The only plausible explanation for this server configuration is that it shows the Trump Organization and Alfa Bank to be using multiple sophisticated layers of protection in order to obfuscate their considerable recent email traffic.

The white paper further stated that the "secret" email server domain was "mail1.trump-email.com [was] hosted by a Pennsylvania-based company, Listrak, which is a reasonably well known CRM [customer relationship management] company that provides large-scale distribution of marketing emails (usually sending emails to thousands of recipients hundreds of times a day)."[1475]

Within a day of receiving the Alfa Bank materials, Cyber Agent-1 and Cyber Agent-2 drafted a report of their analysis.[1476] The report's summary stated that they had "assess[ed] there is no CyD [Cyber Division] equity in this report and that the research conducted in the report reveals some questionable investigative steps taken and conclusions drawn."[1477] The report acknowledged that there was no allegation of hacking and so there was no reason for the Cyber Division to investigate further. The report also said that

> it appears abnormal that a presidential candidate, who wanted to conduct secret correspondence with the Russian government (or a Russian bank), would (1) name his secret server 'mail1.trump-email.com', (2) use a domain (trump-email.com) registered to his own organization, and then (3) communicate directly to the Russian bank's IP address (as opposed to using TOR or proxy servers).[1478]

Cyber Agent-1 testified that both he and Cyber Agent-2 did not agree with the conclusion in the white paper and assessed that (i) the authors of the white paper "jumped to some conclusions that were not supported by the technical data," (ii) the methodology was questionable, and (iii) the conclusions drawn did not "ring true at all."[1479] In interviews with the Office, both Cyber Agent-1 and Cyber Agent-2 said that they were proud of their work because they had both come to the same conclusion despite their own very different political views.

ii.   The opening of the FBI's investigation

After the Cyber Division's review, FBI leadership referred the matter to a squad in the Chicago Field Office responsible for investigating Eurasian counterintelligence and

---

[1475] *Id.* at 3.

[1476] *Sussmann* Tr. 05/17/2022 AM at 381:13-21.

[1477] *Sussmann* Government Exhibit 247.

[1478] *Id.* at 3.

[1479] *Sussmann* Tr. 05/17/2022 AM at 378:12-379:12.

cyber matters. The investigation was referred to a Chicago Field Office Agent ("Chicago Agent-1") who had worked on both the FBI's Mid-Year Examination investigation (the investigation related to Hillary Clinton's email server) and Crossfire Hurricane. Chicago Agent-1 was joined by a new FBI agent, Chicago Agent-2. Chicago Agent-2 was Chicago Agent-1's trainee and was the co-case Agent and primary lead for the Alfa Bank investigation. Chicago Agent-1 and Chicago Agent-2 opened a full investigation "into the network communications between a US-based server and the Russian Alfa Bank organization."[1480] A full investigation, as described above in section III.B.2, may be opened if there is "an articulable factual basis for the investigation that reasonably indicates that . . . [a]n activity constituting a federal crime or a threat to the national security . . . may be occurring."[1481]

According to the case agents and other records obtained during the investigation, it was FBI leadership who decided to open a full investigation. Indeed, two days after the meeting between Baker and Sussmann, Supervisory Special Agent-1, the Crossfire Hurricane supervisor, reached out to Chicago Agent-1. Supervisory Special Agent-1 told Chicago Agent-1 that "people on the 7th floor to include Director are fired up about this server."[1482] Supervisory Special Agent-1 further stated that, if the investigation had not been opened, he would have reached out to Chicago Agent-1's supervisor because "Priestap says it's not an option – we must do it."[1483] Chicago Agent-1 responded that the case team was "opening a CI case today."[1484] Still, the team was already skeptical of the allegations. Chicago Agent-1 noted that the team was "leaning towards this being a false server not attributed to the Trump organization" but that they would "run it down."[1485]

Chicago Agent-1 and Chicago Agent-2 memorialized the opening of the investigation in an EC.[1486] Chicago Agent-1 and Chicago Agent-2 later acknowledged that there were certain errors in this document. Of most importance to the Office was the representation made as to the source of the white papers. The EC stated that "the Department of Justice provided the FBI with a whitepaper that was produced by an anonymous third party."[1487] According to both Chicago Agent-1 and Chicago Agent-2, this

---

[1480] *Sussmann* Government Exhibit 200 (FBI EC from Chicago CG-CY-1, *Opening EC—ALFA BANK* dated 09/23/2016) at 1 (capitalization altered) (hereinafter "*Alfa Bank Opening EC*").

[1481] *AGG-Dom* §§ II.B.3.a; II.B.4.b.i.

[1482] SCO-006608 (Lync messages between Supervisory Special Agent-1 and Chicago Agent-1 dated 09/21/16).

[1483] *Id.*

[1484] *Id.*

[1485] *Sussmann* Government Exhibit 249.

[1486] *Alfa Bank Opening EC.*

[1487] *Id.* at 2 (capitalization altered).

representation was an error, and both recalled that they understood the allegations were presented to the FBI's General Counsel by an anonymous source.[1488]

iii.   The close hold on Sussmann's identity as a source

In evaluating the FBI's early actions related to the Alfa Bank investigation, one issue that the Office identified was the decision by the FBI to put a "close hold" on Sussmann's identity as the source of the allegations and to prevent its disclosure to the Alfa Bank case team. (A close hold is when the FBI's leadership protects specific information, such as the identity of a source, and prevents the "field" or investigative team from learning that information.) The investigation revealed that multiple members of the Alfa Bank case team were "frustrated" and "concerned" that they were prevented from interviewing the source of the allegations. Accordingly, the Office attempted to determine whether Baker or other senior FBI officials may have protected Sussmann's identity improperly to further the Alfa Bank allegations against Trump for political reasons or to mask Sussmann's ties to the DNC and the Clinton campaign.

During Baker's testimony at the Sussmann trial, and although not remembering having done so, Baker speculated that he may have attempted to protect Sussmann's identity and limited disclosure to only a few senior FBI executives.[1489] According to Baker, if he did so, it was because he considered Sussmann to be a source who "had in their possession very sensitive information that he was willing to give to [the FBI]."[1490] But, again, Baker testified he did not recall whether he had refused to provide this to any specific FBI personnel or who he would have instructed to put a close hold in place. Cyber Agent-1 testified that when he was obtaining Baker's signature on the chain of custody, he could not "distinctly recall what the conversation was" but that he was "frustrated" that Baker did not tell him who had provided the thumb drives.[1491] Cyber Agent-2 told the Office that he and Cyber Agent-1 considered filing a whistleblower claim about Baker's failure to provide the information but ultimately decided that they would not because the data provided was not formal evidence in a criminal proceeding.[1492] The FBI Headquarters Program Manager for the Alfa Bank case team ("Headquarters Supervisory Special Agent-3"), noted that FBI leadership, including Strzok, instructed him not to identify the source to the team.[1493] Headquarters Supervisory Special Agent-3 further explained that he believed that the investigative team did not need to interview the source as a first step and instead should

---

[1488] *Sussmann* Tr. 05/23/2022 PM at 1645:15-1646:19, 1687:15-1688:12; 05/24/2022 AM at at1820:19-1821:24, 1846:12-1847:7.

[1489] *Sussmann* Tr. 05/19/2022 AM at 879:6-880:13.

[1490] *Id.* at 879:16-880:20.

[1491] *Sussmann* Tr. 05/17/2022 AM at 370:14-19.

[1492] OSC Report of Interview of Cyber Agent-2 on Sept. 16, 2019 at 2.

[1493] OSC Report of Interview of Headquarters Supervisory Special Agent-3 on Dec. 15, 2020 at 2-3, 4, 6.

focus on the data and log files to make a determination as to the validity of the allegations.[1494]

The Office's investigation showed that the Alfa Bank investigative team made multiple requests to learn the identity of the source of the Alfa Bank allegations. Approximately a week after the FBI received the Alfa Bank allegations, Chicago Agent-1 sent Supervisory Special Agent-1 a message requesting that the investigative team interview the source of the white paper.[1495] Approximately a week later, Chicago Agent-1 and his supervisor again made requests to FBI leadership to interview the source of the allegations.[1496] As Chicago Agent-1 explained, this was important to the case team because the investigation had found that the allegations were unsubstantiated, and the team wanted to confirm their findings.[1497] Ultimately, the case team never learned that Sussmann was the source of the allegations nor that he was connected in any way to the DNC and the Clinton campaign.[1498]

The FBI's investigation ultimately concluded that it was unable to substantiate any of the allegations in the white paper that Sussmann provided to Baker:

> FBI Chicago assesses Alfa Bank and Trump Organization related servers almost certainly did not communicate intentionally or covertly, based on the results of an internal examination of Alfa Bank servers by [redacted] and subsequent preventative steps employed by the companies. FBI Chicago has high confidence in this assessment, which is based on a highly reliable sensitive source with excellent access and corroborates FBI investigative activity conducted to date.[1499]

In coming to that conclusion, the investigators took a number of steps. First, they conducted open-source research on the mail1.trump-email.com domain that was identified in the white paper. They learned that the domain was registered to a company called Central Dynamics ("Cendyn") and that the server was housed at a company named Listrak, located in Pennsylvania.[1500] As a result, the FBI reached out to both Cendyn and Listrak to request data and log files from each company and to conduct interviews as well. Both Cendyn and Listrak were compliant with these requests and provided log files and data that was analyzed by FBI analysts on the investigative team. Ultimately, the data and files provided nothing to substantiate the Alfa Bank allegations.[1501] In addition, the FBI reached out to Mandiant, a

---

[1494] *Id.* at 6-7.

[1495] *Sussmann* Government Exhibit 257.

[1496] *Sussmann* Government Exhibit 265.

[1497] *Sussmann* Tr. 05/24/2022 AM at 1841:7-21.

[1498] *Id.* at 1816:19-21.

[1499] SCO-006174 (Examination of Alfa-Bank Servers dated 10/03/2016); *Sussmann* Government Exhibit 233.

[1500] *Sussmann* Tr. 05/24/2022 AM at 1827:17-21.

[1501] *Id.* at 1831:7-13.

cybersecurity firm, that was hired by Alfa Bank to conduct an internal investigation and forensic analysis into the allegations.[1502] Mandiant provided the FBI with its findings, which too concluded that there was no evidence to support the allegations of a secret communications channel nor any evidence of direct communications between the Alfa Bank servers and Trump Organization servers.[1503]

In early October 2016, an Agent detailed to the National Computer Forensics and Training Alliance ("Cyber Agent-3"),[1504] contacted the Cyber Division at FBI Headquarters because he had received two IP addresses from an anonymous source who had requested that the information be provided to the FBI.[1505] According to Cyber Agent-3, the anonymous source told him that the information related to a *New York Times* story involving the upcoming election.[1506] Cyber Agent-3 was then put in contact with Chicago Agent-2. Cyber Agent-3 recalled that Chicago Agent-2 was dismissive of the information and Cyber Agent-3 interpreted Chicago Agent-2's response as if the investigative team was already aware of the information.[1507] Chicago Agent-2 explained that the case team performed open-source checks on these two IP addresses that resulted in identifying one IP address associated with Alfa Bank and one IP address associated with a home address in Moscow.[1508]

The Office's investigation revealed that the anonymous source who provided the two IP addresses to Cyber Agent-3 was, in fact, Joffe. The most likely reason Joffe decided to provide the two IP addresses to the FBI via Cyber Agent-3 anonymously was to create the appearance of corroboration. One plausible theory that the Office considered was that Joffe and others were attempting to promote the Alfa Bank allegations in such a way that the allegations appeared to be from multiple independent sources. Indeed, at this time, Joffe himself was an FBI CHS.[1509] But in this instance, Joffe decided to provide the Alfa Bank allegations and the two IP addresses to Cyber Agent-3, instead of his FBI handler, with instructions to keep his identity protected.[1510] Joffe's unwillingness to voluntarily meet with our investigators left unanswered his actual motive for providing some information to the

---

[1502] *Sussmann* Tr. 05/23/2022 PM at 1660:25-1661:12.

[1503] *Id.* at 1661:18-24; SCO-001891 (FBI Interview of Mandiant representative on 10/13/2016).

[1504] The National Computer Forensics and Training Alliance is a nonprofit partnership between the government and private industry to collaborate and cooperate in identifying and disrupting cybercrime. OSC Report of Interview of Cyber Agent-3 on Nov. 18, 2020 at 1.

[1505] OSC Report of Interview of Cyber Agent-3 on Feb. 13, 2020 at 1-2.

[1506] SCO-011023 (Email from Cyber Agent-3 to Chicago Supervisory Special Agent-1 dated 10/02/2016).

[1507] OSC Report of Interview of Cyber Agent-3 on Nov. 18, 2020 at 3-4.

[1508] *Sussmann* Tr. 05/23/2022 PM at 1662:6-23.

[1509] *Sussmann* Tr. 05/25/2022 AM at 2166:24-2167:3.

[1510] *Id.* 2167:19-2168:14.

FBI through Sussmann and the two IP addresses through Cyber Agent-3, and in both instances to remain anonymous.[1511]

Finally, the Alfa Bank investigators also received information in early October 2016 from a separate CHS regarding the Alfa Bank allegations. Chicago Agent-2 explained that, according to the handler, the CHS had access to the white paper and had made an initial assessment that the allegations were credible but that the data appeared incomplete.[1512] The CHS also explained that he/she had been contacted by University-1 Researcher-2, one of the white paper authors.[1513] In the correspondence from Chicago Agent-2, there is an indication that the FBI was interested in speaking with University-1 Researcher-2,[1514] however, that meeting never occurred.

In January 2017, the FBI closed the Alfa Bank investigation.[1515] Ultimately, the FBI was unable to substantiate any of the allegations in the white paper.[1516]

e. Actions by Fusion GPS to promote the Alfa Bank allegations

The Special Counsel's investigation also uncovered numerous communications in which Fusion GPS leadership and other personnel sought to discuss, advance, and disseminate the Alfa Bank allegations.

As noted, in April 2016, Perkins Coie engaged Fusion GPS in connection with the 2016 election.[1517] As part of Fusion GPS's work on behalf of Perkins Coie and the Clinton campaign, it collected, organized, and promoted opposition research on Trump's ties to Russia.[1518] Perhaps most notably, as described in Section IV.D.1.b, Fusion GPS retained Steele, who compiled the information and reports that became known as the Steele Dossier. Fusion GPS also drafted one of the white papers that Sussmann provided to Baker at their September 19, 2016 meeting. That white paper provided an overview of the parent

---

[1511] It is notable, however, that in November 2016, soon after the presidential election, Joffe emailed a colleague, stating, "I was tentatively offered the top [cybersecurity] job by the Democrats when it looked like they'd win." SC-00029962 (Email from Joffe to Tech Company-1 Employee-2 dated 11/17/2016).

[1512] *Sussmann* Tr. 05/23/2022 PM at 1665:8-16.

[1513] *Id.* at 1665:17-1666:4.

[1514] SCO-007853 (Emails between Chicago Agent-2, Headquarters Supervisory Special Agent-3, Chicago Agent-1, others in October 2016).

[1515] *Sussmann* Government Exhibit 233.

[1516] *Id.*

[1517] *Sussmann* Government Exhibit 302.

[1518] U.S. House of Representatives Permanent Select Cmte. on Intelligence Interview of Glenn Simpson, (Nov. 14, 2017) at 13, 19, 22-25, 59, 101-102; OSC Report of Interview of John Podesta on Jan. 19, 2022 at 2.

company of Alfa Bank and described ties to Russian government officials and certain U.S. persons and entities.[1519]

Following Sussmann's promotion of the Alfa Bank allegations to the FBI, Fusion GPS continued to promote these allegations to various media personnel. For instance, on October 18, 2016 – two weeks before news stories would first appear about the Alfa Bank allegations – Mark Hosenball of *Reuters* emailed Fusion GPS co-founder Peter Fritsch, stating in part, "anything new Russkie/Donald wise?," to which Fritsch responded, "do the [expletive] Alfa Bank secret comms story. It's hugely important. Forget the wikileaks side show."[1520] The reporter replied that the issue with the story was the inability of his "cyber expert colleagues" to confirm that some of the important data was authentic.[1521] Later on that day, Fritsch replied: "It's everyone's problem. Call [University-1 Researcher-2] at [University-1]."[1522]

On October 22, 2016, Franklin Foer, a reporter for *Slate* magazine, emailed University-1 Researcher-2 at his University-1 email address asking for assistance on the "Alfa Bank/Trump story".[1523] A few days later, Fritsch forwarded to Foer a tweet stating that the U.S. Senate Majority Leader had "talked w/ top NatSec officials who say that [the FBI Director] 'possesses explosive information' about Trump's ties to Russia."[1524] Fritsch's email stated: "time to hurry."[1525] Foer replied "Here's the first 250 words," and included in the email a partial draft of an article about Alfa Bank and Trump on which Foer was working for Fritsch's review.[1526] The reporter published an article shortly thereafter.[1527]

On October 31, 2016, media outlets published articles regarding the Alfa Bank allegations and the existence of an FBI investigation.[1528] As previously noted, within hours of these articles, the Clinton campaign issued tweets and public statements concerning the

---

[1519] *Sussmann* Government Exhibit 207. The Office has not seen evidence that Fusion was involved in originating the Alfa Bank data or were aware of its origination, but rather only promoted the allegations.

[1520] *Sussmann* Government Exhibit 652.

[1521] The email said: "[T]he problem with the [Alfa Bank] story at this point is that my cyber expert colleagues cannot satisfy themselves about the authenticity of some of the key data, which they say from what they can tell is NOT public data. We are in contact with your experts via different channels but my colleague [] in Silicon Valley still hasn't got the confidence he says he needs to understand where all the data originated. If you can help more with this pls do. . . ." *Id.*

[1522] *Id.*

[1523] SC-00018512 (Email from Foer to University-1 Researcher-2 dated 10/22/16).

[1524] *Sussmann* Government Exhibit 666.

[1525] *Id.*

[1526] *Id.*

[1527] *Sussmann* Government Exhibit 54.

[1528] *Sussmann* Government Exhibit 53; *Sussmann* Government Exhibit 54.

purported existence of a secret communications channel involving the Trump Organization and Alfa Bank.[1529]

f. Actions by the Clinton campaign to promote the Alfa Bank allegations

On October 31, 2016 – about one week before the election – multiple media outlets reported that the FBI had received and was investigating the allegations concerning a purported secret channel between the Trump Organization and Alfa Bank. For example, *Slate* published an article that discussed at length the allegations that Sussmann provided to the FBI.[1530]

Also on that day, the *New York Times* published an article titled *Investigating Donald Trump, F.B.I. Sees No Clear Link to Russia*.[1531] The article discussed information in the possession of the FBI about "what cyber experts said appeared to be a mysterious computer back channel between the Trump Organization and the Alfa Bank."[1532] The article further reported that the FBI had "spent weeks examining computer data showing an odd stream of activity to a Trump Organization server," and that the newspaper had been provided computer logs that evidenced this activity. The article also noted that at the time of the article, the FBI had not found "any conclusive or direct link" between Trump and the Russian government and that "Hillary Clinton's supporters . . . pushed for these investigations."[1533]

As noted above, in the months prior to the publication of these articles, Sussmann had communicated with the media and provided them with the Alfa Bank data and allegations.[1534] Sussmann also kept Elias apprised of his efforts.[1535] Elias, in turn, communicated with the Clinton campaign's leadership about potential media coverage of these issues.[1536]

For example, emails reflect that on September 1, 2016, Sussmann met with the reporter who published the *New York Times* article, Eric Lichtblau.[1537] Sussmann billed his

---

[1529] *Sussmann* Government Exhibit 52; @HillaryClinton 10/31/2016 8:36pm Tweet.

[1530] Franklin Foer, *Was a Trump Server Communicating with Russia?*, Slate (Oct. 31, 2016).

[1531] Eric Lichtblau & Steven Lee Myers, *Investigating Donald Trump, F.B.I. Sees No Clear Link to Russia*, N.Y. Times (Oct. 31, 2016).

[1532] *Id.*

[1533] *Id.*

[1534] *See, e.g., Sussmann* Government Exhibits 553.16, 553.23, 389.

[1535] *E.g., Sussmann* Government Exhibits 307, 327, 331, 367, 553.2, 553.16; *Sussmann* Tr. 05/18/2022 AM at 574:21-575:22.

[1536] *Sussmann* Government Exhibit 377 at 3.

[1537] *Sussmann* Government Exhibit 357; *Sussmann* Government Exhibit 358.

time for the meeting to the Clinton campaign under the broader billing description "confidential meetings regarding confidential project."[1538]

Emails further reflect that on September 12, 2016, just one week prior to Sussmann's meeting with Baker, Sussmann and Elias communicated about Sussmann's efforts to share the Alfa Bank allegations with the *New York Times*.[1539]

In addition, on September 15, 2016, Elias provided an update to the Clinton campaign regarding the Alfa Bank allegations and the not-yet-published *New York Times* article, sending an email to Jake Sullivan (HFA[1540] Chief Policy Advisor), Robby Mook (HFA Campaign Manager), John Podesta (HFA Campaign Chairman), and Jennifer Palmieri (HFA Head of Communications), which he billed to the Clinton campaign as "email correspondence with J. Sullivan, R. Mook, J. Podesta, J. Palmieri re: Alfa Bank Article."[1541]

On the same day that these articles were published, the Clinton campaign posted a tweet through Hillary Clinton's Twitter account which stated: "Computer scientists have apparently uncovered a covert server linking the Trump Organization to a Russian-based bank."[1542] The tweet included a statement from Clinton campaign advisor Jake Sullivan which made reference to the media coverage article and stated, in relevant part, that the allegations in the article "could be the most direct link yet between Donald Trump and Moscow[,] that "[t]his secret hotline may be the key to unlocking the mystery of Trump's ties to Russia[,]" and that "[w]e can only assume that federal authorities will now explore this direct connection between Trump and Russia as part of their existing probe into Russia's meddling in our elections."

During the Sussmann trial, both Elias and Mook said that the HFA campaign did not authorize Sussmann to take the Alfa Bank allegations to the FBI. According to Elias and Mook, the campaign did not trust the FBI due to Comey's announcement related to the FBI's Midyear Exam investigation, regarding Hillary Clinton's use of a private e-mail server during her time as Secretary of State.[1543] Mook also explained that top Clinton campaign officials were aware of the Alfa Bank allegations and favored providing the allegations to the media.[1544] Mook likewise noted that he had discussed the allegations with Clinton, who approved the dissemination of them to the media.[1545] Mook testified that the campaign did so before questions and potential doubts about the accuracy and reliability of the allegations had been resolved and without knowing the exact origins of the data.[1546]

[1538] SC-00004247 (Email from Sussmann dated 09/04/2016).

[1539] SC-00004312 (Email from Elias dated 10/09/2016).

[1540] "Hillary for America."

[1541] *Sussmann* Government Exhibit 386; *Sussmann* Government Exhibit 390.

[1542] *Sussmann* Government Exhibit 52; @HillaryClinton 10/31/2016 8:36pm Tweet.

[1543] *Sussmann* Tr. 05/18/2022 PM at 758:8-760:1, 05/20/2022 AM at 1256:2-1257:8.

[1544] *Sussmann* Tr. 05/20/2022 AM at 1264:25-1267:4.

[1545] *Id.* at 1267:5-1267:16.

[1546] *Id.* at 1205:22-1206:5, 1267:25-1269:1.

Although the campaign could not substantiate the allegations, they stated that they considered them "concerning" and wanted the media to vet the allegations because of concerns about Trump's association with Russia.[1547] Sullivan and Elias raised Trump's July 2016 "Russia, if you're listening" statement as one reason for the Clinton Campaign's concern about Trump's ties to Russia.[1548]

g. Sussmann's meeting with the CIA

The Office also gathered information related to a post-election meeting that Sussmann had with the CIA. On February 9, 2017, Sussmann provided an updated set of allegations – including the Alfa Bank data and additional allegations relating to Trump – to the CIA. The Office examined Sussmann's interactions with various CIA employees, including how he was able to secure a meeting with the CIA, what occurred during that meeting, and what materials he provided to the CIA.

The investigation revealed that in December 2016, Sussmann reached out to the CIA General Counsel and requested a meeting related to allegations against Trump.[1549] The General Counsel did not take the meeting and suggested to Sussmann that he provide the allegations to the FBI.[1550] Sussmann, however, ignored that suggestion and continued to pursue a meeting. On or about January 31, 2017, Sussmann met with a retired CIA employee ("Retired CIA Employee-1"). During the meeting, Sussmann told Retired CIA Employee-1 that he had a client who wanted to provide information to the CIA about Trump.[1551] Sussmann explained that his client "is an engineer with a number of patents" and was unsure whether his client would reveal his identity to the CIA.[1552] Sussmann further noted that his client did not want to provide this information to the FBI because the client did not trust the FBI and did not believe that the FBI had the requisite resources to deal with the allegations.[1553] Retired CIA Employee-1 also recalled Sussmann's statement that, should the CIA not investigate the allegations, he would provide them to the *New York Times*.[1554] Following the meeting, Retired CIA Employee-1 drafted a memorandum describing the meeting and sent it to active CIA officers, who then scheduled a meeting with Sussmann for early February 2017.[1555]

In the next meeting, Sussmann made a substantially similar statement to the one he had made to Baker regarding the source of the allegations. In particular, Sussmann asserted

---

[1547] *Id.* at 1268:4-1269:1; OSC Report of Interview of Jake Sullivan on Nov. 12, 2021 at 2-3.

[1548] *Sussmann* Tr. 05/18/2022 PM at 745:2-746:21; OSC Report of Interview of Jake Sullivan on Nov. 12, 2021 at 1-2.

[1549] SC-00004549 (Email from Sussmann dated 12/14/2016).

[1550] SC-00004559 (Email to Sussmann dated 12/20/2016).

[1551] *Sussmann* Tr. 05/20/2022 PM at 1333:3-1334:9; *Sussmann* Government Exhibit 809.

[1552] *Sussmann* Tr. 05/20/2022 PM at 1333:3-1334:9; *Sussmann* Government Exhibit 809.

[1553] *Sussmann* Tr. 05/20/2022 PM at 1334:15-1335:10; *Sussmann* Government Exhibit 809.

[1554] *Sussmann* Tr. 05/20/2022 PM at 1335:22-1336:10; *Sussmann* Government Exhibit 809.

[1555] *Sussmann* Government Exhibit 809; SC-00081639 (Email dated 02/08/2017).

that he was not representing a particular client in conveying the above allegations.[1556] Sussmann, however, was in fact continuing to represent at least Joffe – a matter Sussmann subsequently acknowledged under oath in December 2017 testimony before Congress (without identifying the client by name).[1557]

Sussmann provided a similar set of allegations to the CIA that he had previously provided to the FBI. Specifically, Sussmann provided the CIA with an updated version of the Alfa Bank allegations and a new set of allegations that supposedly demonstrated that Trump or his associates were using, in the vicinity of the White House and other locations, one or more telephones from the Russian mobile telephone provider Yotaphone. The Office's investigation revealed that these additional allegations relied, in part, on the DNS traffic data that Joffe and others had assembled pertaining to the Trump Tower, Trump's New York City apartment building, the EOP,[1558] and Spectrum Health. Sussmann provided data to the CIA that he said reflected suspicious DNS lookups by these entities of domains affiliated with Yotaphone.[1559] Sussmann further stated that these lookups demonstrated that Trump or his associates were using a Yotaphone in the vicinity of the White House and other locations.[1560]

The FBI DNS experts with whom we worked also identified certain data and information that cast doubt upon several assertions, inferences, and allegations contained in (i) the above-quoted white papers about the Yotaphone allegations, and (ii) the presentation and Yotaphone-related materials that Sussmann provided to the CIA in 2017. In particular:

- Data files obtained from Tech Company-2, a cyber-security research company, as part of the Office's investigation reflect DNS queries run by Tech Company-2 personnel in 2016, 2017, or later reflect that Yotaphone lookups were far from rare in the United States, and were not unique to, or disproportionately prevalent on, Trump-related networks. Particularly, within the data produced by Tech Company-2, queries from the United States IP addresses accounted for approximately 46% of all yota.ru queries. Queries from Russia accounted for 20%, and queries from Trump-associated IP addresses accounted for less than 0.01%.

- Data files obtained from Tech Company-1, Tech Company-2, and University-1 reflect that Yotaphone-related lookups involving IP addresses assigned to the EOP began long before November or December 2016 and therefore seriously undermine the inference set forth in the white paper that such lookups likely reflected the presence of a Trump transition-team member who was using a Yotaphone in the EOP. In particular, this data reflects that approximately 371 such lookups involving

---

[1556] *Sussmann* Tr. 05/20/2022 PM at 1366:13-16; *Sussmann* Government Exhibit 814.

[1557] U.S. House of Representatives Permanent Select Cmte. on Intelligence Interview of Michael Sussmann, (Dec. 18, 2017) at 29-30, 54-67.

[1558] "Executive Office of the President."

[1559] *Sussmann* Government Exhibit 817.

[1560] *Id.*

Yotaphone domains and EOP IP addresses occurred *prior* to the 2016 election and, in at least one instance, as early as October 24, 2014.

Two CIA employees ("CIA Employee-2" and "CIA Employee-3") prepared a memorandum summarizing the meeting they had with Sussmann in February 2017. The final version included Sussmann's representation that he was not representing any "particular client."[1561] In their interviews with the Office, both CIA employees specifically recalled Sussmann stating he was not representing a particular client.[1562] [1563]

During the meeting, Sussmann provided two thumb drives and four paper documents that, according to Sussmann, supported the allegations.[1564] The CIA analyzed the allegations and data that Sussmann provided and prepared a report to reflect its findings. The report explained that the analysis was done to examine whether the materials provided demonstrated "technical plausibility" of the following: "do linkages exist to any Russian foreign intelligence service; do linkages exist to Alpha [sic] Bank; are the provided documents/data based upon open source [] tools/activities; and is the provided

---

[1561] *Sussmann* Government Exhibit 814.

[1562] OSC Report of Interview of CIA Employee-2 on Aug. 13, 2020 at 1; OSC Report of Interview of CIA Employee-3 on June 29, 2021 at 3-4.

[1563] Complete resolution of these issues is difficult. The Office's investigation determined that Sussmann's billing practices were irregular. For example, prior to the 2016 election, Sussmann billed all Alfa Bank-related work to the Clinton campaign. Following the election, Sussmann appears to have retroactively billed some of his time for the Alfa Bank-related work to Joffe. The Office did not receive a satisfactory explanation from Perkins Coie for this practice.

Sussmann also engaged in questionable client record keeping. For example, and for reasons unknown, Sussmann's client retention letter to Tech Company-2 Executive-1 was addressed to a "Ms. Tina Wells" with the address of "1200 Pennsylvania Avenue, NW, Washington, D.C. 20004." Sussmann's letter memorializing his joint representation of Joffe and Tech Company-2 Executive-1 was addressed to "Ms. Tina Wells" and "Mr. Bob Hale." *See* Representation letters from Perkins Coie to Rodney Joffe and Tech Company-2 Executive-1 dated 4/12/2017 and 4/13/2017. These fake names are apparent references to the actors who played "Mary Ann" and the "Skipper" on the television series "Gilligan's Island." (Though "Mary Ann" was actually played by Dawn Wells and the "Skipper" was played by Alan Hale.) The address provided for "Ms. Wells" (Tech Company-2 Executive-1) is "1200 Pennsylvania Avenue, NW, Washington, D.C.," which is the William Jefferson Clinton EPA Headquarters and which has no apparent connection to Tech Company-2 Executive-1. The use of false names would appear to prevent a law firm from, among other things, conducting proper conflicts checks.

[1564] The titles of the four documents were: (i) "Network Analysis of Yota-Related Resolution Events"; (ii) "YotaPhone CSV File Collected on December 11th, 2016"; (iii) "Summary of Trump Network Communications"; and (iv) "ONINT on Trump Network Communications." The two thumb drives contained six Comma Separated Value (".CSV") files containing IP addresses, domain names and date/time stamps.

information/data technically conceivable."[1565] The CIA ultimately concluded that the materials that Sussmann provided were neither "technically plausible" nor did they "withstand technical scrutiny" and further, that none of the materials showed any linkages between the Trump campaign or Trump Organization and any Russian foreign intelligence service or Alfa Bank.[1566] The report also noted that one of the thumb drives contained hidden data, which included Tech Company-2 Executive-1's name and email address.[1567]

Accordingly, Sussmann's conduct supports the inference that his representations to both the FBI and the CIA that he was not there on behalf of a client reflect attempts to conceal the role of certain clients, namely the Clinton campaign and Joffe, in Sussmann's work. Such evidence also further supports the inference that Sussmann's false statements to two different agencies were not a mistake or misunderstanding but, rather, a deliberate effort to conceal the involvement of specific clients in his delivery of data and documents to the FBI and CIA.

h. Sussmann's Congressional testimony

On December 18, 2017, Sussmann testified under oath before the HPSCI and addressed his role in providing the Alfa Bank and Yotaphone allegations to the FBI and CIA. During the proceedings, the following exchange, in part, occurred:

Question:	Okay. Did you have any other meetings with any other administration officials regarding the information you conveyed to the FBI G(eneral) C(ounsel) and CIA GC? Was there anyone else you contacted that worked for the Federal Government?
Sussmann:	Not that I recall.
Question:	Okay. So those are the only two? Now, I want to ask you, what was the information about?
Sussmann:	The information was about communications, or potential communications between persons unknown in Russia, and persons unknown associated with the Trump Organization.
Question:	Information that was given to you by a client?
Sussmann:	Yes.
Question:	So that information was not given to you by any other source but the client you represented?
Sussmann:	Absolutely.

. . . .

[1565] SCO-074879 (Special Project – Trump Organization Yotaphone and Email Server Network Communications Analysis dated 02/15/2017 at 1).

[1566] *Id.*

[1567] *Id.* at 2.

Question:	No, that's fair. So let me ask you this question: When you decided to engage the two principles [sic] one, Mr. Baker in September, and the general counsel of CIA in December, you were doing that on your own volition, based on information another client provided you. Is that correct?
Sussmann:	No.
Question:	So what was -- so did your client direct you to have those conversations?
Sussmann:	Yes.
Question:	Okay. And your client also was witting of you going to -- in February to disclose the information that individual had provided you?
Sussmann:	Yes.
Question:	Back to the FBI. You obviously had a conversation or you had a meeting at the FBI with Mr. Baker. Was there anybody else in the room from the FBI in that room with you?
Sussmann:	No.
	. . . .
Question:	Okay. I want to ask you, so you mentioned that your client directed you to have these engagements with the FBI and - and to disseminate the information that client provided you. Is that correct?
Sussmann:	Well, I apologize for the double negative. It isn't not correct, but when you say my client directed me, we had a conversation, as lawyers do with their clients, about client needs and objectives and the best course to take for a client. And so it may have been a decision that we came to together. I mean, I don't want to imply that I was sort of directed to do something against my better judgment, or that we were in any sort of conflict, but this was -- I think it's most accurate to say it was done on behalf of my client.[1568]

Sussmann's congressional testimony concealed and obscured the origins and political nature of his work on the Alfa Bank allegations. Moreover, Sussmann's testimony was also misleading in that it conveyed the impression to Congress that Sussmann's only client for the Alfa Bank allegations was Joffe, when in fact he was billing the work to the Clinton campaign. Indeed, during points in the testimony not quoted above, Sussmann was specifically asked if Fusion GPS was his client in these matters.[1569] Sussmann's answer

---

[1568] U.S. House of Representatives Permanent Select Cmte. on Intelligence Interview of Michael Sussmann, (Dec. 18, 2017) at 59-67.

[1569] Id. at 74.

failed to disclose or volunteer that Fusion, in fact, had drafted one of the white papers that Sussmann gave to the FBI. Sussmann also failed to mention that the only client billed for Sussmann's pre-election work on those allegations was the Clinton campaign.

i. Perkins Coie's statements to the media

On October 4, 2018, Perkins Coie stated to multiple media outlets that "[w]hen Sussmann met with [the FBI General Counsel] on behalf of a client, it was not connected to the firm's representation of the Hillary Clinton Campaign, the DNC or any Political Law Group client."[1570] The following week, John Devaney, the Managing Partner of Perkins Coie, wrote to the editor of the *Wall Street Journal* and stated, "Mr. Sussmann's meeting with the FBI General [] was on behalf of a client with no connections to either the Clinton campaign, the DNC or any other Political Law Group client."[1571] The Office interviewed Perkins Coie leadership, including Mr. Devaney, regarding their knowledge of Sussmann's promotion of the Alfa Bank allegations and his billing entries related to the Clinton campaign. Each of the Perkins Coie employees denied knowing that Sussmann had in fact billed all of his time related to the Alfa Bank allegations to Clinton campaign.

Sussmann could have easily corrected Perkins Coie's mistaken belief that Sussmann's work on the Alfa Bank allegations "was not connected to the firm's representation of the Hillary Clinton Campaign, the DNC or any Political Law Group client." He chose not to.

j. Providing the Alfa Bank and Yotaphone allegations to Congress

The Office identified documents reflecting that in March and April 2017 – during the months after Sussmann provided the Alfa Bank and Yotaphone allegations to the CIA – the offices of at least two U.S. Senators received similar materials.

On March 22, 2017, Senators Jack Reed and Mark Warner wrote to Director Comey urging the FBI "to conduct an investigation" into reports that "a server belonging to the Trump Organization was purposefully communicating with servers belonging to a major Russian bank and the Spectrum Health organization in Michigan during the 2016 election.[1572] In support of its request, the letter attached an untitled white paper of unknown authorship. The paper included a summary of the Alfa Bank allegations, which was similar in substance to materials that Sussmann had provided to the FBI and CIA."[1573]

[1570] *See, e.g., Michael Sussmann, Hillary Clinton Lawyer, Gave FBI Russia Meddling Document,* Wash. Times (Oct. 4, 2018); *Lawyer for Clinton Campaign and DNC Gave FBI Documents for Russia Probe, Sources Say,* Fox News (Oct. 4, 2018).

[1571] John Devaney, *Our Michael Sussmann Is an Honorable Man,* Wall St. J. (Oct. 18, 2018).

[1572] SCO-012000 (Letter from Senators Jack Reed and Mark Warner to Director Comey dated Mar. 22, 2017 and attachment).

[1573] *Id.* at 2-8.

About a month later, Senator Reed sent a second letter to Comey about the Yotaphone allegations.[1574] Like the first letter, this one attached a white paper of unknown authorship.[1575] The paper stated that a small number of Yotaphones are sold globally and a very small number – in the dozens – presently operate in the United States.[1576] The paper noted that a group of internet technical experts had discovered a pattern of Yotaphone-like activity occurring within the Trump Organization and the Spectrum Health networks, which it correlated with Trump campaign and transition team visits to Michigan.[1577] The data also purportedly showed that Yotaphone-like activity continued at the Trump Organization until December 15th when the same activity began within the EOP, from which the experts inferred that the person or persons using this device in the Trump campaign were part of the transition team that began working within the EOP.[1578] The paper concluded that "[g]iven the broad concerns about the Trump campaign's connections to Russia, the existence and activity of the YotaPhone, as described here, stands out as an extraordinary oddity that warrants investigation."[1579]

Finally, on May 8th, a staffer to Senator Reed sent a follow-up memorandum to the FBI's Office of Congressional Affairs.[1580] The memorandum noted that the source of the analysis "insists on remaining anonymous, but is represented by an attorney." It went on to say that "[t]he source is willing, through counsel, to have extensive technical discussions with the Bureau's technical staff to explain the DNS records and the analysis that has been conducted." The memorandum also noted that Senator Reed continued to request that the FBI pursue the allegations and that the source's attorney was Michael Sussmann.[1581]

Because, however, either the FBI or the CIA, or both agencies, had already examined these allegations, the FBI did not take further investigative steps in response to these requests.[1582] The Office did not determine how, or from whom, Senators Reed and Warner received the above-described materials. An executive at Research Organization-1 ("Research Executive-1") appears to have learned about the allegations from Senator Reed's office and thereafter conducted work on these issues in coordination and consultation with Senator Reed's staff. Research Executive-1 was a former FBI analyst and Hill staffer and

---

[1574] SC-00081652 (Letter from Senator Jack Reed to Director Comey dated April 27, 2017 and attachment).

[1575] The paper was titled "An Unusual Russian Phone Operating on Trump Organization Networks and in the Executive Office of the President."

[1576] *Id.* at 1.

[1577] *Id.* at 3.

[1578] *Id.*

[1579] *Id.*

[1580] SC-00081658 (Memorandum from Senator Reed Staffer-1 to FBI Office of Congressional Affairs Employee-1 dated 05/08/2017).

[1581] *Id.*

[1582] SCO_007878 (Email from Moffa to Strzok, others dated 05/31/2017).

the founder of Research Organization-1. Research Executive-1's activities are further described below.

k. Tech Company-1's connections to the DNC and the Clinton campaign

The Office's investigation also identified evidence that the Clinton campaign and the DNC maintained or sought contemporaneous relationships with Tech Company-1 personnel, and used or considered using Tech Company-1 products and services, at around the same time as Joffe's efforts to promote the Alfa Bank and Yotaphone allegations. The campaign and the DNC considered Tech Company-1 a possible source of data, including telephone metadata, and there were a number of communications regarding Tech Company-1 data.[1583] The Office examined this information in considering whether the campaign or the DNC maintained broader relationships with Tech Company-1 that might have led or contributed to Joffe's Alfa Bank and Yotaphone activities. Although the Office identified multiple instances in which the campaign or the DNC maintained ties or communicated with Tech Company-1 and its employees, we did not identify evidence establishing that any such activities originated with Joffe or related to the Alfa Bank or Yotaphone allegations. Joffe was not copied or addressed on these communications, and the Office did not identify evidence of his awareness of these discussions. We also are not aware of any evidence that the campaign or the DNC used this data to conduct opposition research (*i.e.*, to gather information regarding an opposing candidate, as opposed to voter information) or otherwise target Trump or his associates.[1584]

The Office also considered whether any conduct related to the Tech Company-1 data constituted an illegal campaign contribution to the Clinton campaign by Tech Company-1 or other related criminal statutes. The Office did not identify any chargeable criminal conduct in this regard.

l. Other post-election efforts to continue researching and disseminating the Alfa Bank and Yotaphone allegations

In addition to the above efforts to disseminate the Alfa Bank and Yotaphone allegations to the FBI, the CIA, and Congress, the Office identified other efforts to generate

---

[1583] *See, e.g.*, SC-00013425 (Email from Clinton Campaign Official-1, to DNC Employee-1 and others, dated 05/13/2016) (referencing Tech Company-1 "who we use for digital stuff currently"); SC-00013423 (Email from DNC Employee-1 to Clinton Campaign Official-1 dated 05/13/2016) (stating "Yep, we're talking to [Tech Company-1] too"); SC-00013242 (Email from an employee of a data firm to a DNC employee and others dated 05/20/2016) (referencing Tech Company-1 "phone metadata"); SC-00014434 (Email from DNC Employee-2, to representatives of the Clinton campaign and others, dated 07/30/2016) (including Tech Company-1 data as among the data that the DNC would like to test).

[1584] In the course of our investigation, we also found evidence that Tech Company-1 or other private sector entities collected and sold certain other types of user data, such as telephone data, geolocation data, and other kinds of user information. *See, e.g.*, SC-00013383 (Email dated 05/27/2016). The scope and detail of the data raise privacy issues that may be of public interest but that are outside the scope of this report. We expect that today most major campaigns likely buy and use these kinds of data.

and disseminate research and other materials relevant to these allegations during the post-election period. These post-election activities included (i) continued efforts by employees of Tech Company-1 and Tech Company-2 (including Tech Company-2 Executive-1) to gather data and information concerning Trump, Russia, and other topics, and (ii) efforts by Research Executive-1 to conduct research and analysis through a non-profit organization that Research Executive-1 created in 2017 with the assistance of former HFA Chairman John Podesta, Fusion GPS founder Glenn Simpson,[1585] and others.

i. Continued efforts through Joffe-affiliated companies

Documents and other records that the Office gathered from private entities reflect that during or around the same time period as the aforementioned letters from Senator Reed and afterwards, Joffe was continuing to use Tech Company-1 resources and personnel to discuss research issues relating to Trump and Russia, including the Alfa Bank and Yotaphone allegations.

For example, emails and other evidence reflect that in early 2017 and afterwards, Joffe tasked Tech Company-1 Employee-1 to run searchers over Tech Company-1's DNS traffic to gather additional information concerning the Alfa Bank and Yotaphone allegations. In particular:

- According to Tech Company-1 Employee-1, at or around the time of Trump's inauguration, Tech Company-1 Employee-1 had been running queries for Joffe relating to Trump, including queries concerning Alfa Bank, Yotaphone, and the EOP.[1586] Joffe and Tech Company-1 Employee-1 intended to continue running certain of these queries after Trump's inauguration.[1587] Soon after the inauguration, however, Tech Company-1 Employee-1 and Joffe noticed that Tech Company-1's access to the EOP's DNS traffic had ceased.[1588] Tech Company-1 Employee-1 and Joffe never learned why Tech Company-1 no longer had access to the EOP's DNS data, but it was clear that Tech Company-5, the contractor that handled the EOP's DNS traffic and the company for which Tech Company-1 maintained the EOP's DNS servers, was no longer handling the EOP's data.[1589] The Office was unable to determine the reason such data access ceased.

- During the time period, Joffe also continued to direct Tech Company-1 Employee-1 to run Trump-related searches over Tech Company-1's data, and emails reflect the aforementioned end of Tech Company-1's access to EOP data.

- For example, on February 14, 2017—five days after Sussmann's meeting with the CIA—Joffe emailed Tech Company-1 Employee-1 with the subject line "for obvious reasons . . . ," and stated in the email: "Could you please run a search going back

---

[1585] Simpson declined to be interviewed by the Office.

[1586] OSC Report of Interview of Tech Company-1 Employee-1 on Feb. 25, 2021 at 2-5.

[1587] *Id.*

[1588] *Id.*

[1589] OSC Report of Interview of Tech Company-1 Employee-1 on July 9, 2021.

from Feb 1 to this moment (or later ;-)) searching for all activity (not just RCODE 0) for wildcard *.yota.* in recursive? Thanks!"[1590]

- That same day, Tech Company-1 Employee-1 uploaded data responsive to Joffe's request to a file transfer site and emailed Joffe: "feb 01-14 uploaded to sftp site. . . Note that these contain everything, including TLD queries."[1591]

- On the following day, Joffe replied: "[Tech Company-1 Employee-1], looks like no activity for EOP, right? Odd. Could you redo all of Jan so we can see when it disappeared."[1592]

- Later that day, Tech Company-1 Employee-1 responded to Joffe: "yeah – I only looked at a couple of hours on the first day but I noticed the same thing. Most of the recursive traffic was from Comodo address. I think I need to look at overall EOP volumes since Jan 20 to see if there have been significant volume changes."[1593]

- On February 16, 2017 Tech Company-1 Employee-1 emailed Joffe, analyzing location information for three IP addresses that Tech Company-1 Employee-1 had found communicated with Yotaphone IP addresses between January 6, 2017 and January 19, 2017. Tech Company-1 Employee-1 stated, in part:

    The resolver address in the queries is the address that is dedicated to [Tech Company-5] and was used for EOP traffic. Only the first client address maps to EOP. The others are:

    [IP address] – Haifa, Israel

    [IP address] – Madison, Wisconsin

    [IP address] – amazonaws

    The timestamps on the records are a bit confusing as well – two queries from two different addresses for the same qname as the exact same second in two different nodes (Chicago and Frankfurt). May be an error in processing but still odd.[1594]

- As of approximately five months later, Tech Company-1 Employee-1 was continuing to run Trump-related searches over Tech Company-1's DNS traffic. In particular, on July 18, 2018, Tech Company-1 Employee-1 emailed Joffe:

    I have 4 jobs that look specifically for Trump data

[1590] SC-00030423 (Email from Joffe to Tech Company-1 Employee-1 dated 02/14/2017).

[1591] SC-00030425 (Email from Joffe to Tech Company-1 Employee-1 dated 02/15/2017).

[1592] *Id.*

[1593] SC-00030424 (Email from Tech Company-1 Employee-1 to Joffe dated 02/15/2017)

[1594] SC-00030427 (Email from Tech Company-1 Employee-1 to Joffe dated 02/16/2017).

- clnt_ip='217.12.97.15' or clnt_ip='217.12.96.15' or clnt_ip='167.73.110.8'

- qname = 'trump1.contact-client.com'

- qname = 'mail1.trump-email.com'

- a query that looks for a bunch of alfa ban.ru domains[1595]

In sum, it appears that efforts to gather and mine data concerning Trump from Tech Company-1's DNS data continued for many months after the 2016 Presidential election.

ii.   Efforts by Research Executive-1 and others

The Office also gathered information reflecting that, soon after the 2016 election, a number of individuals with ties to the Clinton campaign or Democratic politics met, organized, and executed additional efforts through which they intended to ensure that research and dissemination of materials concerning election interference, including Trump's possible illicit ties to Russia, would continue. These efforts included continued work regarding the Alfa Bank and Yotaphone allegations. As described in further detail below, participants in these activities continued to provide materials to the FBI in an effort to trigger further investigations of Trump's ties to Russia.

In the days immediately after the election, former Clinton campaign Chair Podesta began speaking with associates about a specific potential research project, namely, to create a non-profit organization that would conduct research regarding election interference and would assist the U.S. government and the media in gathering information on this issue.[1596] Podesta spoke and met with Glenn Simpson, Research Executive-1, and others regarding his idea. (Podesta told investigators that he was unaware at that time, or at any time prior to October 2017, that Glenn Simpson and Fusion GPS had carried out opposition work on the Steele Dossier and related matters on behalf of Podesta's prior employer, the Clinton campaign. According to Podesta, he knew during the campaign that Perkins Coie was conducting opposition research for the campaign, but did not know who had been actually conducting that research until October 2017 when he learned specifically that Fusion GPS had been paid by both the campaign and the DNC.)[1597]

In approximately the late 2016 time period, former U.S. Senator Tom Daschle brokered an introduction between Podesta and Research Executive-1—who previously had worked as an FBI analyst, as a Senate Armed Services Committee staffer, and at a private firm founded by Daschle, the Daschle Group. By that time, Research Executive-1 had founded and was running Research Organization-1, which conducted research for private clients.[1598] Podesta assisted Research Executive-1 by helping him contact and vet numerous

---

[1595] SC-00030428 (Email from Tech Company-1 Employee-1 to Joffe dated 07/18/2017).

[1596] OSC Report of Interview of Research Executive-1 on Apr. 14, 2021 at 1.

[1597] OSC Report of Interview of John Podesta on Jan. 19, 2022 at 1-2.

[1598] OSC Report of Interview of Research Executive-1 on Apr. 14, 2021 at 1; OSC Report of Interview of John Podesta on Jan. 19, 2022 at 5.

potential donors on the West Coast who would ultimately fund Research Executive-1's research on election interference.[1599]

Also, at around this time, Glenn Simpson called Research Executive-1 and sought his/her assistance on Podesta's proposed election interference project. Research Executive-1 and Simpson initially met for coffee in Washington, D.C. In December 2016, Simpson briefed Research Executive-1 on the work he had been doing concerning Trump's purported ties to Russia and expressed concern for his own safety.[1600] According to Research Executive-1, Simpson did not mention – and Research Executive-1 did not know at this time – that Simpson had been doing work for Perkins Coie or the Clinton campaign.[1601]

In January 2017, Simpson and Research Executive-1 again met to discuss the potential research project.[1602] Also in January 2017, and as a result of these discussions, Research Executive-1 formed Research Organization-2, a non-profit organization that would continue researching election interference issues, including Trump's potential ties to Russia.[1603]

Following its formation, Research Organization-2 entered into a contract with Fusion GPS and hired a number of specialists to assist its research. Research Organization-2 also maintained a contract with Steele's firm, Orbis Business Intelligence, a/k/a "Walsingham Partners."[1604]

As noted above, among the research that Research Organization-2 conducted, and provided to the FBI, was an analysis of the Alfa Bank allegations. According to Research Executive-1, he first became aware of these allegations when Senator Reed's office contacted him in 2017 to inform him of them.[1605] Research Executive-1 learned from a staffer for Senator Reed, ("Reed Staffer-2") – whom Research Executive-1 knew from his time on the Senate staff – that there was a particular "client" who used the name "Max" and who was behind the allegations.[1606] Research Executive-1 also learned that Reed had requested further information from the FBI about its efforts to investigate this matter because multiple Senators were reportedly frustrated that, in their view, the FBI was not investigating the Alfa Bank allegations.[1607] Research Executive-1 agreed to research the issue through Research Organization-2. In conducting work on the Alfa Bank matter,

---

[1599] OSC Report of Interview of John Podesta on Jan. 19, 2022 at 5.

[1600] OSC Report of Interview of Research Executive-1 on Apr. 14, 2021 at 2.

[1601] Id. at 1-2.

[1602] Id. at 1.

[1603] Id. at 1-2.

[1604] Id. at 2.

[1605] Id. at 2.

[1606] Id. at 3.

[1607] Id.

Research Executive-1 isolated Fusion GPS from the project for reasons unknown to the Office.[1608]

As a result of receiving this information from the Senate Armed Services Committee, Research Executive-1 met in early 2017 with Sussmann at Perkins Coie's office.[1609] At the meeting, Sussmann discussed the allegations, including media reports concerning them.[1610] According to Research Executive-1, Sussmann did not identify his "client" by name, but stated that he (Sussmann) was dealing with the government on the issue; that he was persuaded by the data; and that he was frustrated by the FBI's dismissal of it.[1611] Sussmann also described to Research Executive-1 his interactions with the media and his frustration with their coverage of it.[1612]

Later that year, Research Executive-1 again met Sussmann at Perkins Coie regarding the Alfa Bank allegations. Sussmann's client, Joffe, was also present at this meeting. During their discussions, Sussmann and Joffe stated that they believed the FBI had sent the Alfa Bank allegations to the wrong investigative team.[1613] Research Executive-1 was told that Joffe was part of a multi-million-dollar program that collected DNS data, which was the source of the data underlying the Alfa Bank allegations.[1614]

During the same time period, Research Executive-1 had assembled an investigative team to examine the Alfa Bank allegations, including a number of DNS experts who had previously worked for multiple U.S. intelligence agencies. Research Executive-1's team tested Joffe's data and conducted their own analysis. The team was skeptical of the Alfa Bank data and found no evidence of a secret channel of communications, but Research Executive-1 said, "it was something."[1615]

Research Executive-1 also learned of the Yotaphone allegations from Sussmann. Research Executive-1's team did some, but not a lot of, work on these allegations. Research Executive-1 told our investigators that he was "totally" skeptical of the Yotaphone assertions.[1616] Research Executive-1 understood that the EOP's computer network was run by the Department of Homeland Security, which contracted out the services to an unknown vendor with access to the data that formed the basis of the Yotaphone allegations.[1617]

[1608] *Id.* at 2-3.

[1609] *Id.*

[1610] *Id.*

[1611] *Id.*

[1612] *Id.*

[1613] *Id.* at 3.

[1614] *Id.* at 4.

[1615] *Id.*

[1616] *Id.*

[1617] *Id.* at 3-4.

iii. Meetings between DARPA and University-1

In connection with its consideration of the Alfa Bank issue, the Office also gathered information about meetings between certain of the aforementioned University-1 employees and staff members of both the Senate Armed Services Committee and HPSCI. During at least one of these meetings, the participants discussed the Alfa Bank allegations, including the possibility that researchers under DARPA's Enhanced Attribution ("EA") program might assist HPSCI in investigating the allegations.[1618] The Office considered whether these activities might be relevant to a prosecution for contract fraud or abuse of government resources.

In early October 2018, a representative of the Senate Armed Services Committee requested via University-1's Government Affairs representative that researchers affiliated with the EA program provide a briefing to Committee staff members in Washington, D.C. Personnel at University-1 agreed to facilitate such a briefing.[1619]

In late October 2018, another University-1 researcher ("University-1 Researcher-3") and a DARPA Program Manager, ("DARPA Program Manager-1") traveled to Washington, D.C. to provide the briefing. Upon their arrival, University-1 Researcher-3 and DARPA Program Manager-1 met with Reed Staffer-2 and another Committee staffer in the Russell Senate Office Building. At the meeting, which lasted only a short time, University-1 Researcher-3 and DARPA Program Manager-1 provided a broad and brief overview of the EA program – which they understood to be the purpose of the meeting. At the conclusion of the meeting, which had been cut short due to scheduling conflicts, Reed Staffer-2 indicated to University-1 Researcher-3 that he would like to schedule a follow-up meeting with University-1 researchers in attendance so that the Committee staff could receive a more comprehensive briefing on the EA program.[1620]

The following month, in November 2018, University-1 Researcher-3 and University-1 Researcher-2 traveled to Washington, D.C. to provide a second briefing on EA for staffers for the Senate Armed Services Committee. University-1 Researcher-2 recalled that the night before the meeting, he spoke with Joffe, who told him that after the Senate briefing, there was going to be another meeting Joffe wanted him to attend. Joffe told University-1 Researcher-2 that there would be someone to meet him and take him to this other meeting.[1621]

The November 2018 meeting occurred in the Hart Senate Office Building with Reed Staffer-2 and two staffers present. At the meeting, University-1 Researcher-3 and

---

[1618] The Enhanced Attribution program is intended to bring transparency to the actions of malicious cyber actions undertaken by adversaries and other individual cyber operators. *See* https://www.darpa.mil/enhanced-attribution.

[1619] OSC Report of Interview of University-1 Researcher-3 on Aug. 10, 2021 at 2.

[1620] *Id.*

[1621] OSC Report of Interviews of University-1 Researcher-2 in July, Aug. 2021 at 4.

University-1 Researcher-2 gave an unclassified presentation regarding the EA program and the history of DNS.[1622]

Following the meeting in the Senate space, Reed Staffer-2 informed University-1 Researcher-3 and University-1 Researcher-2 that some other people were interested in speaking with them. University-1 Researcher-3 and University-1 Researcher-2 agreed to meet with these other people, who turned out to be HPSCI staffers, but the meeting needed to be quick due to University-1 Researcher-3's schedule. Reed Staffer-2 then brought them into the secure space of the HPSCI.[1623] Before the meeting, University-1 Researcher-3 told Reed Staffer-2 that University-1 Researcher-2 did not possess a security clearance, to which Reed Staffer-2 stated that the briefing would be unclassified.[1624]

After arriving in the HPSCI secure conference room, Reed Staffer-2 introduced University-1 Researcher-3 and University-1 Researcher-2 to several HPSCI staffers. During the meeting, University-1 Researcher-3 and University-1 Researcher-2 began to provide a similar presentation to that which they had given to the Senate staffers. Soon after the start of the presentation, however, the Committee staffers cut University-1 Researcher-3 off and showed him and University-1 Researcher-2 a news article about Trump, Russia, and Alfa Bank that University-1 Researcher-3 had not seen previously.[1625] The staffers asked University-1 Researcher-3 to read the article and said they wanted University-1's help with the matter, and Reed Staffer-2 said University-1 Researcher-3 ". . . could make it easier."[1626]

University-1 Researcher-3 said he responded by saying that it would be inappropriate for a public university to do that, and he suggested they contact DARPA. University-1 Researcher-3 told investigators that Reed Staffer-2 then said, "We are now in charge," and one of the HPSCI staffers said that their boss (Congressman Adam Schiff) would soon take over leadership of HPSCI.[1627] University-1 Researcher-3 took the comment as a mild threat. University-1 Researcher-3 said he then "dragged" University-1 Researcher-2 out of the meeting. University-1 Researcher-2 similarly recalled that University-1 Researcher-3 had quickly ended the meeting.[1628] University-1 Researcher-3 told investigators that he told University-1 Researcher-2, "Don't touch this with a ten foot pole, stay away from this."[1629] University-1 Researcher-3 said he had no recollection of

---

[1622] OSC Report of Interview of University-1 Researcher-3 on Aug. 10, 2021 at 2.

[1623] *Id.*

[1624] *Id.* at 2.

[1625] OSC Report of Interview of University-1 Researcher-3 on Aug. 10, 2021 at 2-3. University-1 Researcher-2 recalled that the staffers showed him articles about Trump's DNS ties to Alfa Bank, and they asked him and University-1 Researcher-3 if there was anything they could do to help with "this." OSC Report of Interviews of University-1 Researcher-2 in July, Aug. 2021 at 4.

[1626] OSC Report of Interview of University-1 Researcher-3 on Aug. 10, 2021 at 3.

[1627] *Id.*

[1628] OSC Report of Interviews of University-1 Researcher-2 in July, Aug. 2021 at 4.

[1629] OSC Report of Interview of University-1 Researcher-3 on Aug. 10, 2021 at 3.

University-1 Researcher-2 mentioning the work and research he (University-1 Researcher-2) already had done at University-1 regarding the Alfa Bank-related allegations.[1630]

University-1 Researcher-3 recalled that he informed DARPA Program Manager-1 of this request from the HPSCI staffers, including his objections to the nature of the request.[1631] University-1 Researcher-3 recalls that DARPA Program Manager-1 listened but did not react substantively to the information.[1632] When interviewed by the Office, DARPA Program Manager-1 denied learning of the Alfa Bank allegations other than through media reports.[1633] DARPA Program Manager-1 maintained that he was unaware of any role that University-1 personnel played in the Alfa Bank allegations.[1634]

iv.   *The relevant Trump Organization email domain and Yotaphone data*

This subsection first describes what our investigation found with respect to the allegation that there was a covert communications channel between the Trump Organization and Alfa Bank. It includes the information we obtained from interviews of Listrak and Cendyn employees. It then turns to the allegation that there was an unusual Russian phone operating on the Trump Organization networks and in the Executive Office of the President. We tasked subject matter experts from the FBI's Cyber Technical Analysis and Operations Section to evaluate both of these allegations.

With respect to the allegation that there was a covert channel of communication between the Trump Organization and Alfa Bank, FBI subject matter experts conducted technical analyses and made assessments of the passive DNS data and information that was provided to the FBI and CIA in the white paper[s].[1635] We also interviewed employees at the two contractors involved in managing the trump-email.com domain, Cendyn and Listrak. Cendyn, a customer relationship manager, or marketing services provider, registered the domain on behalf of the Trump Organization in 2009. The IP address associated with the domain, 66.216.133.29, is, and was, operated by Listrak, a subcontractor

---

[1630] *Id.*

[1631] *Id.*

[1632] *Id.*

[1633] OSC Report of Interview of DARPA Program Manager-1 on Feb. 11, 2021 at 3.

[1634] *Id.*

[1635] FBI Cyber Division Cyber Technical Analysis Unit, Technical Analysis Report (April 20, 2022) (hereinafter "*FBI Technical Analysis Report*") (SCO_094755). As explained by the FBI experts who assisted us in this area, DNS (Domain Name System) refers to a distributed system of computers on the internet that maintain the association between domain names and IP addresses. *Passive DNS* is an industry practice of cataloging and aggregating DNS queries at various observable points for research, analytical, marketing, and security purposes. *FBI Technical Analysis Report* at 5-6.

of Cendyn. Listrak provides marketing automation services, including sending bulk email.[1636]

Listrak personnel stated that the Trump Organization's IP address was one of numerous IP addresses assigned to a cluster of four to eight physical servers that handle all outbound email for thousands of Listrak clients. Significantly, Listrak informed us that the IP address and domain used for the Trump Organization were configured to only send *outbound* email.[1637] Moreover, Listrak explained that, as is customary for such services, no one in the Trump Organization had direct technical or system administrator access to Listrak servers.[1638] Indeed, the very notion of a "Trump Server" is a misnomer in that the servers involved did not belong to and were not controlled by the Trump Organization.[1639] To the contrary, the servers belonged to and were controlled by Listrak at all times.[1640] Listrak further stated that it never had, during this time period, a dedicated server (physical or virtual) to handle Trump Organization communications.[1641] Rather, the server that hosted the Trump Organization housed hundreds of other clients and that each server sent millions of emails out for clients.[1642]

Cendyn personnel told us that the Trump Organization's contract with Cendyn for digital and email marketing ended in 2015, but the domain name continued to be registered and pointed to the same IP address.[1643] Moreover, after Cendyn's contract with the Trump Organization expired in 2015, Cendyn continued to use the IP address to send emails out on behalf of other Cendyn clients.[1644] However, there was no data provided at the time, nor is such currently available, that shows which clients were sending email from the IP address during the May through September 2016 time period examined in the white paper.[1645] Cendyn, however, maintained technical control of the domain until March 2017.[1646] Similarly, Listrak maintained complete technical control of its servers during the same May through September 2016 time period.[1647]

[1636] OSC Report of Interview of Cendyn CEO and CTO on Nov. 17, 2021; OSC Report of Interview of Listrak Employee-1 and personnel on Oct. 27, 2021.

[1637] OSC Report of Interview of Listrak Employee-1 and personnel on Oct. 27, 2021 at 1-2.

[1638] *Id.*

[1639] *Id.*

[1640] OSC Report of Interview of Cendyn CEO and CTO on Nov. 17, 2021 at 1-2.

[1641] OSC Report of Interview of Listrak Employee-1 and personnel on Oct. 27, 2021 at 1-2.

[1642] *Id.*

[1643] OSC Report of Interview of Cendyn CEO and CTO on Nov. 7, 2021 at 2.

[1644] *Id.*

[1645] *Id.* at 1. Cendyn explained that it does not retain these outbound emails, as they are marketing emails, which are wiped from Cendyn's systems within 30 days of being sent.

[1646] *Id.* at 2.

[1647] OSC Report of Interview of Listrak Employee-1 and personnel on Oct. 27, 2021 at 2.

Because the Trump Organization had no access to the server or any of the systems involved, Listrak personnel told us that the only way any alleged covert communications channel could have existed would be if Listrak employees deliberately modified their mission critical servers with non-standard software or configurations. But they pointed out that making such changes would risk the integrity, reliability or availability of their systems. Moreover, Listrak told us that changing its servers to accommodate incoming messages would completely alter the core structure of its business operations, which is primarily to send outgoing mass marketing emails.[1648] Listrak employees responsible for the design and administration of these servers categorically stated this did not happen and that it would be impossible for it to have happened without their knowledge and without affecting other clients' account functions and operations.[1649]

In addition to investigating the actual ownership and control of the IP address, the Office tasked FBI cyber experts with analyzing the technical claims made in the white paper.[1650] This endeavor included their examination of the list of email addresses and send times for all emails sent from the Listrak email server from May through September 2016, which is the time period the white paper purportedly examined.[1651] The FBI experts also conducted a review of the historical TOR exit node data.[1652]

The technical analysis done by the FBI experts revealed that the data provided by Sussmann to the FBI and used to support Joffe and the cyber researchers' claim that a "very unusual distribution of source IP addresses" was making queries for mail1.trump-email.com was incomplete.[1653] Specifically, the FBI experts determined that there had been a substantial amount of email traffic from the IP address that resulted in a significantly larger volume of DNS queries for the mail1.trump-email.com domain than what Joffe, University-1 Researcher-2 and the cyber researchers reported in the white paper or included on the thumb drives accompanying it.[1654] The FBI experts reviewed all of the outbound email transmissions, including address and send time for all emails sent from the Listrak server

---

[1648] *Id.* at 2.

[1649] *Id.*

[1650] *FBI Technical Analysis Report* at 3-4.

[1651] *Id.* at 4, 10-11.

[1652] *Id.* at 5-6, 12-13. The Onion Router ("TOR") is an open source global anonymous communications platform, frequently used to access websites without exposing the IP address of the browser to the website or to intermediary observation. TOR publishes a list of TOR exit nodes, which are the last node in a TOR circuit and which provides an unencrypted connection to internet hosts. https://collector.torproject.org/archive/exit-lists/.

[1653] Our experts noted that the assertion of the white paper is not only that Alfa Bank and Spectrum Health servers had resolved, or looked up, the domain [mail1.trump-email.com] during a period from May through September of 2016, but that their resolutions accounted for the vast majority of lookups for this domain. *FBI Technical Analysis Report* at 6.

[1654] The USB drive that Sussman provided to the FBI on September 19, 2016, which was proffered as data supporting the claims in the white paper, contained 851 records of DNS resolutions for domains ending in trump-email.com. *FBI Technical Analysis Report* at 7.

from May through September 2016, and determined that there had been a total of 134,142 email messages sent between May and August 2016, with the majority sent on May 24 and June 23.[1655] The recipients included a wide range of commercial email services, including Google and Yahoo, as well as corporate email accounts for multiple corporations.[1656]

Similarly, the FBI experts told us that the collection of passive DNS data used to support the claims made in the white paper was also significantly incomplete.[1657] They explained that, given the documented email transmissions from IP address 66.216.133.29 during the covered period, the representative sampling of passive DNS would have necessarily included a much larger volume and distribution of queries from source IP addresses across the internet. In light of this fact, they stated that the passive DNS data that Joffe and his cyber researchers compiled and that Sussmann passed onto the FBI was significantly incomplete, as it included no A-record (hostname to IP address) resolutions corresponding to the outgoing messages from the IP address.[1658] Without further information from those who compiled the white paper data,[1659] the FBI experts stated that it is impossible to determine whether the absence of additional A record resolutions is due to the visibility afforded by the passive DNS operator, the result of the specific queries that the compiling analyst used to query the dataset, or intentional filtering applied by the analyst after retrieval.[1660]

The FBI experts also examined the white paper's claim that a particular "Spectrum Health IP address is a TOR exit node used exclusively by Alfa Bank, *i.e.*, Alfa Bank communications enter a TOR node somewhere in the world and those communications exit, presumably untraceable, at Spectrum Health."[1661] However, the FBI experts assisting us noted that TOR publishes a comprehensive list of exit nodes dating back to February 22, 2010.[1662] The FBI examined this data for dates between February 22, 2010 and September 1, 2021. No instances of IP addresses in the range of 167.73.x.x (assigned to Spectrum Health) were ever indexed as TOR exit nodes.[1663]

[1655] *Id.*

[1656] *Id.*

[1657] *Id.* at 11.

[1658] *Id.*

[1659] The data used for the white paper came from Joffe's companies Packet Forensics and Tech Company-1. As noted above, Joffe declined to be interviewed by the Office, as did Tech Company-2 Executive-1. The 851 records of resolutions on the USB drive were an exact match for a file of resolutions sent from University-1 Researcher-2 to University-1 Researcher-1 on July 29, 2016, which was referred to as "[first name of Tech Company-2 Executive-1]'s data." *Id.* at 7.

[1660] *Id.*

[1661] *FBI Technical Analysis Report* at 12-13.

[1662] https://collector.torproject.org/archive/exit-lists/.

[1663] *Id.*

The FBI experts who examined this issue for us stated that historical TOR exit node data conclusively disproves this white paper's allegation in its entirety.[1664] Moreover, the FBI experts further explained that the construction of the TOR network makes the arrangement described in the white paper impossible. Indeed, they added that even if true or possible, using the TOR network in the manner alleged in the white paper would result in worse anonymization and security than simply using TOR in its default configuration.[1665] Rather than allowing for clandestine communication, the setup described in the white paper would create a static proxy with a known endpoint that could be more easily traced with traffic to the relatively small number of guard nodes, and which would allow for the identification of the true source IP much more easily than using a randomly selected exit node for each connection as the TOR system is designed to do.[1666] In simpler terms, the FBI experts told us that using a TOR exit node in the manner described by the white paper would make a secret communication channel much easier to find, not harder. And, they further noted that although it is entirely likely that one or more users, at some time, connected to both Spectrum Health and Alfa Bank using TOR, and may have even come through the same exit node, this possibility in no way indicates any kind of correlation because of the deliberately random nature of TOR routing.[1667]

We also tasked the same FBI experts to review the white paper on Yotaphones that Sussmann provided to another government agency on behalf of Joffe.[1668] This white paper stated that there was "an unusual Russian phone" that was "operating on Trump Organization networks and in the Executive Office of the President."[1669] Its claims were based primarily on DNS resolution requests for the domains "client.yota.ru" and "wimax-client.yota.ru" from July 23, 2016 through January 15, 2017 from Trump-affiliated networks, coupled with the assertion that such YotaPhone resolution request activity was rare in the United States.[1670]

However, the FBI experts examined historical DNS query data for the yota.ru domains for the same time period as that analyzed in the white paper. Indeed, they examined data that the white paper researchers also had access to.[1671] In doing so, the FBI experts determined that, contrary to the claims set forth in the white paper, the DNS query data actually indicated that resolution requests for these domains were not at all rare from U.S.-based IP addresses, as compared with other countries.[1672] These experts further

---

[1664] *FBI Technical Analysis Report* at 12-13.

[1665] *Id.* at 13.

[1666] *Id.*

[1667] *Id.*

[1668] SC-00001940, Network Analysis of Yota-Related Resolution Events.

[1669] *Id.*

[1670] *Id.* at 2.

[1671] FBI Cyber Technical Operations Unit, *Trump/Alfa/Spectrum/Yota Observations and Assessment* (undated; unpaginated).

[1672] *Id.*

observed that the DNS query data used to support the white paper claims was deliberately filtered to select only those organizations in the United States with ties to Trump.[1673]

In sum, as a result of our investigation, the FBI experts advised us that actual data and information on YotaPhone resolution requests directly undermined or refuted several conclusions and inferences included in the Yotaphone white paper.[1674]

2. *Prosecution decisions*

We identified evidence that certain individuals and entities promoted the Alfa Bank and Yotaphone allegations to the Intelligence Community. We examined the validity of the allegations, conducted technical analyses, and assessed the data and information that was provided to the FBI and CIA. We examined this evidence in considering whether the activities by these individuals and entities, as well as government officials, violated any criminal statutes. In particular, the investigation examined whether these individuals and entities either on their own provided, or conspired with others to provide, false or misleading information to the Intelligence Community.

First, and as noted above, we identified certain statements that Sussmann made to the FBI and the CIA that the investigation revealed were false. Given the seriousness of the false statement and its effect on the FBI's investigation, a federal Grand Jury found probable cause to believe that Sussmann had lied to the FBI and charged him with making a false statement to the Bureau, in violation of 18 U.S.C. § 1001.[1675] Ultimately, after a two-week trial, a jury acquitted Sussmann of the false statement charge.

We also considered whether any criminal actions were taken by other persons or entities in furtherance of Sussmann's false statement to the FBI. The evidence gathered in the investigation did not establish that any such actions were taken.

Second, our investigation uncovered evidence of actions taken by individuals and entities with ties to the Clinton campaign to promote the Alfa Bank and Yotaphone allegations to the Intelligence Community and Congress. We evaluated whether any of these individuals made a false statement within the meaning of 18 U.S.C. § 1001 and whether admissible evidence would be sufficient to obtain a conviction for such an offense. We also considered whether actions taken by certain persons could have implicated federal election laws. We concluded that the evidence was not sufficient to obtain and sustain a criminal conviction.

We examined as well whether the actions and conduct of Sussmann and various other persons in advancing the Alfa Bank and Yotaphone allegations established a conspiracy to defraud the United States, in violation of 18 U.S.C. § 371. Ultimately, we concluded that our evidence was not sufficient to obtain and sustain a criminal conviction. We did not obtain admissible evidence likely to meet the government's burden to prove beyond a reasonable doubt that the individuals acted "willfully," *i.e.*, with general knowledge of the illegality of their conduct. We faced significant obstacles in obtaining

---

[1673] *Id.*

[1674] *Id.*

[1675] *Sussmann Indictment* at 27.

287

evidence because many of the individuals and entities involved invoked multiple privileges, including the attorney-client and Fifth Amendment privileges.

Third, we examined the FBI's actions in response to the Alfa Bank and Yotaphone allegations. We assessed whether any FBI or other federal official conspired with any other persons in promoting the Alfa Bank allegations to damage the Trump campaign or benefit the Clinton campaign. Our investigation did not find any evidence that any FBI official or employee knowingly and intentionally participated in some type of conspiracy with others to promote the Alfa Bank allegations or cause the FBI to open an investigation. Certain FBI officials, however, declined to be interviewed on the matter, and others professed a lack of recollection of it.

Finally, we considered the conduct of third parties and other government officials regarding actions taken following the election that involved the continued promotion of the Alfa Bank and Yotaphone allegations to law enforcement and other government bodies. We did not, however, develop sufficient evidence to charge false statements or conspiracy crimes in connection with any intentional misrepresentations in this regard because it was unclear, in numerous instances, when particular data searches involving the alleged activity at the EOP were run, and when specific data files came into possession of the relevant persons (*i.e.*, whether such data was searched or identified before or after materials were received by the CIA or Congress). In addition, because of the protections of attorney-client privilege and other impediments, we were unable to determine with precision or certainty who authored each of the relevant white papers. Accordingly, we did not charge any individuals[1676] with knowingly providing false information to the government in connection with the Alfa Bank and Yotaphone allegations.

V.   OBSERVATIONS

In making the observations that follow, we are mindful of the benefits hindsight provides and the hazards of possibly being unfair to individuals who were called upon to make decisions under real pressure and in unprecedented circumstances. That said, the objective facts show that the FBI's handling of important aspects of the Crossfire Hurricane matter were seriously deficient. Some FBI employees who were interviewed by our investigators advised that they had significant reservations about aspects of Crossfire Hurricane and tried to convey their misgivings to their superiors. Others had doubts about the investigation, but did not voice their concerns. In some cases, nothing was said because of a sense that there had to be more compelling information in the possession of those closest to the decision-making center of the case than had been made known to them. And there were still other current and former employees who maintained that they did the best they could to take reasonable investigative steps and acted within the FBI's various policies, procedures and guidelines.

As the more complete record now shows, there are specific areas of Crossfire Hurricane activity in which the FBI badly underperformed and failed, not only in its duties to the public, but also in preventing the severe reputational harm that has befallen the FBI as a consequence of Crossfire Hurricane. Importantly, had the Crossfire Hurricane actors faithfully followed their own principles regarding objectivity and integrity, there were clear opportunities to have avoided

---

[1676] As noted above, the Office charged Sussmann with lying to the FBI when he stated that he was not bringing the Alfa Bank allegations on behalf of any client.

the mistakes and to have prevented the damage resulting from their embrace of seriously flawed information that they failed to analyze and assess properly.

As described in section IV, both the OIG and the FBI's Inspection Division have reviewed aspects of the Crossfire Hurricane investigation into possible collusion between Russia and the Trump campaign and the FISA applications targeting Carter Page. The OIG also conducted a more limited audit of the accuracy of 29 FISA applications that were not connected to Crossfire Hurricane.

In 2020, the Department and the FBI provided the Privacy and Civil Liberties Oversight Board ("PCLOB") 19 of the 29 applications reviewed by the OIG. The PCLOB is an independent agency within the Executive Branch that was established by the 9/11 Commission Act of 2007. The Board's primary mission is to ensure that federal efforts to prevent terrorism are balanced with protecting privacy and civil liberties. The 19 applications were directed at counterterrorism targets and Adam Klein, the former Chairman of the PCLOB, reviewed the 19 applications.[1677]

Following the OIG's review and audit, both the Attorney General and the FISC directed that a number of changes be made. Outside commentators have also recommended numerous changes. In the FISA reform proposals put forth by various individuals and groups, there is division between those that would make all, or many, FISA surveillances more difficult or prohibit certain types of surveillances altogether and those that focus more specifically on the issues raised by the Page applications.

In making our observations, the Office considered but did not include proposals that would curtail the scope or reach of FISA or the FBI's investigative activities. We are concerned about the impact of such proposals in a time of aggressive and hostile terrorist groups and foreign powers. The FBI's priorities include protecting the United States against national security threats.[1678] Inevitably, that involves pursuing some targets and investigations that end up yielding few results. The OIG review of the September 11th attacks noted that "the FBI . . . failed to use the FISA statute fully" and that, in its investigation of Zacarias Moussaoui, a potential "19th hijacker," the deficiencies "included a narrow and conservative interpretation of FISA."[1679] More recently, for reasons that may include the COVID pandemic, the impact of the Page FISA applications, or changes in government priorities, the number of FISC orders using certain FISA authorities reportedly has declined sharply -- from 1184 to 430 -- over a recent four-year period.[1680]

[1677] *See* Adam Klein, PCLOB, Chairman's White Paper: *Oversight of the Foreign Intelligence Surveillance Act* (June 2021) (hereinafter "Klein, *White Paper*").

[1678] *See* https://www.fbi.gov/about/mission. *Cf. Sensitive Investigations Memorandum* at 1 ("[T]he Department must respond swiftly and decisively when faced with credible threats to our democratic processes").

[1679] OIG, U.S. Department of Justice, *A Review of the FBI's Handling of Intelligence Information Related to the September 11 Attacks* at 363, 378 (Nov. 2004).

[1680] George Croner, *New Statistics Confirm the Continuing Decline in the Use of National Surveillance Authorities*, Lawfare (May 24, 2022) (describing use of various FISA authorities

Former Assistant Attorney General David Kris has said that, in amending FISA, "you're doing surgery on a very complicated thing." He went on to say, "[t]hat may sound trivial, but it's actually very important for national security."[1681] Moreover, if amendments are not approached from a long-term perspective:

> I worry that in the not-too-distant-future we may find ourselves on the other end of the familiar national-security pendulum swing, reviewing a new inspector general or other report -- this time criticizing the Justice Department . . . for the proliferation of red tape or other restrictions, and the failure to stop an attack or other grave, hostile acts committed against our national security.[1682]

Senator Graham expressed the same thought succinctly: "I'd hate to lose the ability of the FISA court to operate at a time probably when we need it the most."[1683]

Thus, we first discuss below the prior review that the OIG conducted of the FBI's handling of the Robert Hanssen investigation, focusing on problems that appeared both in that investigation and Crossfire Hurricane. We then turn to measures to assist in the full and complete consideration of politically sensitive investigations and make FISA applications more understandable and complete for the officials and judges who review and approve them. We conclude with a discussion of bias and improper motivation and suggest one possible FBI reform for consideration by the Department. We do not try to review all the many changes that have already been made but rather seek to build on them.

A. The OIG's Prior Evaluation of Systemic Problems in the FBI's Counterintelligence Program (Robert Hanssen)

Robert Hanssen was "the most damaging spy in FBI history."[1684] For more than 20 years while he was assigned to the FBI's counterintelligence program, Hanssen betrayed the United States and gave the KGB enormous amounts of highly sensitive information, including the identities of dozens of human sources, some of whom were subsequently executed by the Soviet Union.[1685] The OIG conducted an extensive review of the FBI's failure to deter and detect Hanssen as a mole and concluded that Hanssen did not escape detection "because he was a 'master spy'" or "was extraordinarily clever and crafty" but rather because of "longstanding

---

from 2018 to 2021, and in earlier years), https://www.lawfareblog.com/new-statistics-confirm-continuing-decline-use-national-surveillance-authorities.

[1681] Bryan Tau and Dustin Volz, *Secretive Surveillance Court Rebukes FBI Over Handling of Wiretapping of Trump Aide*, Wall St. J., Dec. 17, 2019 (quoting Kris).

[1682] David Kris, *Further Thoughts on the Crossfire Hurricane Report*, Lawfare, Dec. 23, 2019, at 13-15 (hereinafter "Kris, *Further Thoughts*").

[1683] Charlie Savage, *We Just Got a Rare Look at National Security Surveillance. It Was Ugly.* N.Y. Times (Dec. 11, 2019), https://www.nytimes.com/2019/12/11/us/politics/fisa-surveillance-fbi.html?searchResultPosition=10.

[1684] OIG, U.S. Department of Justice, *A Review of the FBI's Performance in Deterring, Detecting, and Investigating the Espionage Activities of Robert Philip Hanssen* at 6 (Aug. 14, 2003) (hereinafter "*Hanssen 2003 Review*").

[1685] *Id.*

systemic problems in the FBI's counterintelligence program."[1686] For many years, the FBI focused on a specific CIA employee as the potential mole.[1687] Although its initial focus may have been reasonable, as time went on:

> The FBI should have seriously questioned its conclusion that the CIA suspect was a KGB spy and considered opening different lines of investigation. The squad responsible for the case, however, was so committed to the belief that the CIA suspect was a mole that it lost a measure of objectivity .... [W]hile FBI management pressed for the investigation to be completed, it did not question the factual premises underlying it."[1688]

One of the OIG's recommendations for the FBI's counterintelligence program in the Hanssen matter was that "supervisors must guard against excessively deferring to line personnel . . . and . . . must ensure that the Department . . . is properly briefed on the strengths and weaknesses of potential espionage prosecutions."[1689] A more cooperative relationship between the Counterintelligence Division and the Department, the OIG explained later, would make it "more likely case agents' analytical and investigative judgments in counterespionage cases will be adequately scrutinized."[1690] Other recommendations similarly concerned greater involvement for Department attorneys, including "a larger oversight role in ensuring the accuracy and fairness of factual assertions in FISA applications and . . . direct access to the case agent and the source information relied on in the application."[1691]

When considering Crossfire Hurricane, some of the OIG's recommendations continue to be relevant, particularly by analogy. Numerous reports clearly state that Russia was trying to influence the 2016 presidential election.[1692] This was also the prevailing view of the media and

---

[1686] *Id.* at 10.

[1687] *Id.* at 12.

[1688] *Id.* at 12-13.

[1689] *Id.* at 18.

[1690] OIG, U.S. Department of Justice, *A Review of the FBI's Progress in Responding to the Recommendations in the Office of Inspector General Report on Robert Hanssen* at 28 (Sept. 2007) (hereinafter "*Hanssen Progress Review*").

[1691] *Hanssen 2003 Review* at 16.

[1692] *See, e.g.*, 1 *Mueller Report* at 4 (Russia's Internet Research Agency carried out "a social media campaign designed to provoke and amplify political and social discord in the United States," and the campaign evolved "to a targeted operation that by early 2016 favored candidate Trump and disparaged candidate Clinton"); *Joint Statement from the Department of Homeland Security and Office of the Director of National Intelligence on Election Security* (Oct. 7, 2016) (The Intelligence Community "is confident that the Russian Government directed the recent compromises of e-mails from US persons and institutions, including from US political organizations").

it was widely accepted throughout open source reporting at the time that Russia was to blame for the unlawful intrusion into the DNC servers.[1693]

One of the chief errors from the start of Crossfire Hurricane was the poor analysis the FBI brought to bear on the critical pieces of information that it had gathered, as well as an over-reliance on flawed or incomplete human intelligence that only later was found to be plainly unreliable. In July 2016, the FBI received the most damaging of the Steele Reports but, mysteriously and unfortunately, these reports do not appear to have made their way to the Counterintelligence Division for analysis until after mid-September.[1694] Later in July, Australia provided the information from Papadopoulos to U.S. authorities.[1695] The FBI then appears to have formulated a hypothesis that the Trump campaign, or someone associated with it, was working with the Russians. Neither the *Crossfire Hurricane Opening EC* nor those responsible for the investigation in the Counterintelligence Division or upper management, however, appear to have recognized the crucial need to analyze and then assess the actual ambiguities in Papadopoulos's statements to the Australian diplomats. Instead, the FBI immediately opened a full investigation, an investigation that clearly had the ability to affect an approaching presidential election. Indeed, executive management of the FBI and its Counterintelligence Division appear to have taken the Paragraph Five information at face value in opening the matter as evidenced by the *Opening EC* citing the Paragraph Five information as essentially the sole basis for opening a full investigation on unnamed members of an ongoing presidential campaign. Then, when the Steele reporting finally was received by Crossfire Hurricane personnel in September 2016, it was immediately exploited, with no verification of its sensational allegations, and used in support of its initial request for FISA authority. The Steele reporting would eventually fall apart, but not before it had been continuously adopted by the FBI as supportive of its underlying theory regarding collusion.

The Intelligence Community's *Analytic Standards* say that analysts "must perform their functions with objectivity" and "employ reasoning techniques and practical mechanisms that reveal and mitigate bias."[1696] In the Hanssen investigation, the squad "responsible for the case . . . was so committed to the belief that the CIA suspect was a mole that it lost a measure of objectivity and failed to give adequate consideration to other

---

[1693] *See, e.g.,* David E. Sanger & Nick Corasaniti, *DNC Says Russian Hackers Penetrated Its Files, Including Dossier on Donald Trump,* N.Y. Times (June 14, 2016), https://www.nytimes.com/2016/06/15/us/politics/russian-hackers-dnc-trump.html; Ellen Nakashima, *Russian Government Hackers Penetrated DNC, Stole Opposition Research on Trump,* Wash. Post (June 14, 2016), https://www.washingtonpost.com/world/national-security/Russian-government-hackers-penetrated-dnc-stole-opposition-research-on-trump/2016/06/14; Daniel Strauss, *Russian Government Hackers Broke into DNC Servers, Stole Trump Oppo,* Politico (June 14, 2016), https://www.politico.com/story/2016/06/Russian-government-hackers-broke-into-dnc-servers-stole-trump-oppo-224315.

[1694] *See supra* § IV.D.1.b.iii.

[1695] *See supra* § IV.A.3.

[1696] Intelligence Community Directive 203, *Analytic Standards* at 2 (Jan. 2, 2015). *See supra* § III.B.3.

possibilities.[1697] The *SSCI Russia Report* observed that the FBI's analysts should endeavor "to check assumptions underpinning FBI operations, to apply the rigor of intelligence analysis to assessments and confidential human sources, and to create a culture where questioning previously held assumptions is acceptable and encouraged."[1698] The Office concurs with this recommendation.

Apart from analytic integrity, in seeking FISA authority in Crossfire Hurricane, investigators withheld key pieces of information from the OI attorneys. The OI attorneys are responsible for ensuring the accuracy and fairness of the information presented to the FISC, an impossible task without being provided with relevant information. Both the OIG's review and this review highlight the omissions, errors, and misstatements by FBI personnel, including the withholding of significant exculpatory statements, that should not have occurred had the Crossfire Hurricane investigators considered and treated the Department lawyers as full partners. Rather, Crossfire Hurricane reflects a struggle by OI to obtain straightforward answers about Steele's possible bias and leaks to the media and Page's relationship with another government agency. Nor was OI told about the significant differences between the Steele Reports and the statements Danchenko made to the FBI.

In the follow-on *Hanssen Progress Review*, the OIG quoted a Department official as saying that the Department "still has the occasional fight with the FBI to get full access to information, particularly information pertinent to the reliability of sources relied on in the FISA applications."[1699] The Crossfire Hurricane investigation shows that regrettably these struggles for accuracy and transparency were still occurring in 2016. Moreover, it is certainly to be hoped that, with the new post-Page requirements of the *Sensitive Investigations Memorandum*, the new guidelines governing the FBI's use of human sources, and other significant policy changes, there will not be a recurrence of the serious errors identified by the OIG, the Inspection Division, and our investigation. Absent continual reinforcement by FBI leadership of the need for integrity, accuracy, and objectivity in following these requirements, however, such is not a certainty.

B. FBI Investigations

1. The New York counterintelligence investigation

When the NYFO opened a counterintelligence investigation of Page in April 2016, at a time when he was a foreign policy adviser to the Trump campaign, the investigation likely should have been treated as a sensitive investigative matter because of Page's role in the campaign. The Attorney General has since addressed this issue in a desirable, though slightly different, way. The Attorney General must approve any investigation of a "senior presidential campaign staff member or advisor." A footnote explains that "this includes any person who has been publicly announced by a campaign as a staffer or member of an official campaign advisory committee or group."[1700]

[1697] *Hanssen 2003 Review* at 12.

[1698] *SSCI Russia Report*, pt. V, at 936.

[1699] *Hanssen Progress Review* at 9.

[1700] *Sensitive Investigations Memorandum* at 2 & n.3.

2. Predication of Crossfire Hurricane

The FBI opened the Crossfire Hurricane investigation as a full investigation "to determine whether individual(s) associated with the Trump campaign are witting of and/or coordinating activities with the Government of Russia."[1701] As described in section III, the standard for opening a full investigation is "an articulable factual basis for the investigation that reasonably indicates that . . . [a]n activity constituting a federal crime or a threat to the national security . . . *is or may be* occurring . . . and the investigation may obtain information relating to the activity."[1702]

The information that the FBI learned in July 2016 was that a Trump campaign advisor had suggested to the Australian diplomats that the campaign "had received some kind of suggestion from Russia that it could assist" the campaign. The *OIG Review* found that the FBI met the requirements of the *AGG-Dom* because the "articulable factual basis" standard for opening the investigation is a "low" one and the information from Australia, at least when considered along with what was known about Russia's efforts to interfere with the 2016 U.S. elections, met that standard.[1703] We are not confident, however, that this is the case. Our investigation gathered evidence that showed that a number of those closest to the investigation believed that the standard arguably had not been met. For example, both Supervisory Special Agent-1 and UK ALAT-1 described the predication for the investigation as "thin."[1704] Even Strzok, who both drafted and approved the *Opening EC*, said that "there's nothing to this, but we have to run it to ground."[1705] Strzok's view would seem to dictate the opening of the matter as an assessment or, at most, as a preliminary investigation. In any event, there are a number of other reasons to be concerned about the predication of Crossfire Hurricane.

Apart from the need to meet the standard in the *AGG-Dom* for opening a full investigation, Executive Order 12333 requires the use of "the least intrusive collection techniques feasible." FBI policy says that "when First Amendment rights are at stake" – which they clearly were in a major-party political campaign – "the choice and use of investigative methods should be focused in a manner that minimizes potential infringement of those rights."[1706] Moreover, the FBI will "[a]pply best judgment" necessary to achieve an objective.[1707] To assist FBI agents with their judgments, decision-making and the need to employ the least intrusive means, the *DIOG* includes precautions when opening and conducting investigations in order to, among other things, encourage careful evaluation of

---

[1701] *Crossfire Hurricane Opening EC* at 3-4.

[1702] *AGG-Dom* §§ II.B.3.a; II.B.4.b.i (emphasis added).

[1703] *Redacted OIG Review* at 351-52.

[1704] FBI-AAA-EC-00000365 (Lync exchange between Supervisory Special Agent-1 and UK ALAT-1 dated 08/11/2016).

[1705] OSC Report of Interview of UK ALAT-1 on June 4, 2019 at 2.

[1706] *DIOG* § 4.4.4.

[1707] *Id.* § 4.1.1.1(F) (bolding omitted)

facts and circumstances, as well as to assess risk, before proceeding with any investigative activity.

In implementing these standards, the FBI could have taken one or more of the following sensible steps:

- Under the least intrusive standard, rather than opening an investigation with a broad scope ("to determine whether individual(s) associated with the Trump campaign are witting of and/or coordinating activities with the Government of Russia"), the FBI should have focused, at least at the beginning, on Papadopoulos, the alleged source of the information from Australia. On the other hand, the Paragraph Five information was not only connected to Papadopoulos, but also to the campaign as an alleged recipient of "some kind of suggestion from Russia."

- Under the FBI's guidelines, the investigation could have been opened more appropriately as an assessment or preliminary investigation. FBI investigations opened as preliminary investigations, short of full investigations, include time limits and a narrower range of authorized techniques to mitigate risk and avoid unnecessary intrusion. If necessary and appropriate, a lower level of investigative activity may be escalated under the guidelines by converting to a full investigation with supervisory approval.

- In the subsequent investigation of Page under the Crossfire Hurricane umbrella, the FBI could have used additional, less intrusive techniques before seeking authority to conduct electronic surveillance under FISA. The paucity of information collected on key aspects of Page's activities would support such an approach.

Regardless of an investigator's preference for any of these steps, there are now additional requirements that apply to the opening of an investigation like Crossfire Hurricane. The *Sensitive Investigations Memorandum* requires the Attorney General to approve the opening of such an investigation. That an investigation like Crossfire Hurricane should require a concurring decision by the Department, rather than any one component or entity, seems appropriate. We also believe that the proposal described below in E for an identified Department official to challenge all stages of a politically sensitive investigation would be another valuable way of addressing concerns about the opening, continuation and intrusiveness of an investigation like Crossfire Hurricane.

3. *Opening of individual investigations*

The FBI opened full investigations of Papadopoulos, Page, Flynn, and Manafort in August 2016, as part of Crossfire Hurricane.[1708] Again, in addition to the requirements of the *AGG-Dom* and the *DIOG*, the approval requirements in the *Sensitive Investigations Memorandum* now would apply to these. The proposal in Section V.E would also potentially apply to them.

[1708] *See supra* § IV.A.1.e; *Redacted OIG Review* at 59-60.

4. *Compartmentation*

Unlike most FBI investigations, which are managed from FBI field offices, Crossfire Hurricane was managed from FBI Headquarters. The information it collected was not shared with or available to others in the FBI, including, as described above, the Directorate of Intelligence. The *OIG Review* says that:

> [B]ecause the information being investigated related to an ongoing presidential election campaign, the Crossfire Hurricane case file was designated as "prohibited" meaning that access to the file was restricted and viewable to only those individuals assigned to work on the investigation. Agents and analysts . . . used covert investigative techniques to ensure information about the investigation remained known only to the team and FBI and Department officials.[1709]

Moreover, at least at times, even those participating in the investigation had limited information available. Supervisory Special Agent-3, who was tasked to supervise the Crossfire Hurricane investigators as a successor to Supervisory Special Agent-1, stated:

> Contributing to the difficulties . . . was how compartmentalized the . . . investigation was, specifically the lack of information sharing between the intelligence analysts and the operational component . . . . Even as the team lead, I only had access to limited information, and from the start of my [temporary duty], I did not have a clear picture of everything going on in the investigation . . . . I was managing the day to day operations of the case without having complete information.[1710]

The investigation's compartmentation, and its unusual structure as a Headquarters investigation, may have limited the amount of oversight that it received. In the past, NSA's collection of the international communications of U.S. citizens and groups was also highly compartmented. A Senate committee chaired by Senator Frank Church investigated this activity. It reported:

> In 1969, NSA formalized the watch list program under the codename MINARET. The program applied not only to alleged foreign influence on domestic dissent, but also to American groups and individuals whose activities "may result in civil disturbances or otherwise subvert the national security of the U.S." At the same time, *NSA instructed its personnel to "restrict the knowledge" that NSA was collecting such information and to keep its name off the disseminated "product."*[1711]

[1709] *See Redacted OIG Review* at 58-59.

[1710] *FBI Inspection Division Report* at 290.

[1711] S. Rep. No. 94-755, bk. 3, at 739 (1976) (emphasis added and footnotes omitted).

The report found that "NSA placed more restrictive security controls on MINARET material than it placed on other highly classified foreign intercepts in order to conceal its involvement in activities which were beyond its regular mission."[1712]

In possible contrast to the FBI, the CIA may not have compartmented some of the information that it had. The Office learned at one point from Director Brennan that "[t]here was no effort at the CIA to restrict information because it was potentially embarrassing for Hillary Clinton. . . . Obama just wanted the right people involved."[1713]

In combination, an unusually compartmented investigation bearing on politics will always involve risk, especially when it is the subject of significant media attention. In any event, in opening and conducting a sensitive investigation, the FBI should consider ways to balance the need for secrecy against the need to have a full and informed evaluation of the case. Leaks can cause great harm, but so can a failure to understand the information collected or to take appropriate investigative steps.

5. Interaction with the Trump campaign

On August 11, 2016, the FBI met with CHS-1 who, as described earlier, was a longstanding FBI source. CHS-1 had decided not to join the Trump campaign but told the FBI that he/she was willing to refrain from notifying the campaign about this decision.[1714] The Crossfire Hurricane investigators were pleased or relieved that the source did not want to join the campaign.[1715] But as to whether the FBI encouraged or directed the source to avoid notifying the campaign, the *OIG Review* is less clear. Not notifying the campaign, of course, could in and of itself affect the campaign's staffing decisions or other activities.

On September 1, 2016, CHS-1 met with a high-level Trump campaign official who was not a subject of the Crossfire Hurricane investigation. This meeting was consensually monitored. The OIG notes that "FBI and Department policy did not require that the FBI obtain Department approval to consensually monitor this conversation."[1716]

Also in September 2016, CHS-1 met with Papadopoulos. The *OIG Review* says that, "[t]he OGC Unit Chief told the OIG that because the operation targeted Papadopoulos individually and wasn't directed at anything related to the campaign, she thought that it was appropriate."[1717] If the purpose of CHS-1's meeting with Papadopoulos was not to find out if the

---

[1712] *Id.* at 749.

[1713] OSC Report of Interview of John Brennan on Aug. 21, 2020 at 9 (capitalizations omitted).

[1714] *See Redacted OIG Review* at 315.

[1715] *Id.* at 315-16.

[1716] *Id.* at 327.

[1717] *Id.* at 330; *see also FBI Inspection Division Report* at 178

campaign or anyone on its behalf was conspiring or colluding with Russia, it is hard to know what the purpose was.

6. *Defensive briefings*

The *OIG Review* discusses the FBI's decision not to give candidate Trump or his campaign a defensive briefing concerning the allegations that the Crossfire Hurricane team was investigating. The *Review* does not discuss whether the decision was consistent with other decisions that the FBI has made about defensive briefings for political candidates. There are of course numerous investigations over the years that involve presidential and congressional candidates or campaigns, including allegations of foreign contributions, improper foreign influence, or other activities.[1718] Each one has unique facts. In 2020, the Department declassified some documents related to a 2015 investigation of possible illegal campaign contributions. In that instance, the FBI provided a defensive briefing to the Clinton campaign.[1719] Some have argued that the decisions to provide a defensive briefing in that investigation but not in the Crossfire Hurricane investigation were inconsistent.[1720] President Obama may also have thought that a defensive briefing for the Trump campaign was desirable, but his views may not have related to Crossfire Hurricane.[1721]

As described in section III, the FBI has now established a board, the FIDBB, to address defensive briefings; the Attorney General has directed the FBI to promulgate procedures on this subject; and the Attorney General has imposed additional, specific requirements in connection with politically sensitive FISA applications. These requirements, particularly the last one, require a serious consideration of the need for a defensive briefing, and we support them.

[1718] *See, e.g.*, Michael Finnegan, *Fundraiser for Trump and Obama Sentenced to 12 Years in Prison for Foreign Money Scams*, L.A. Times, Feb. 18, 2021 (describing "more than $950,000 in unlawful donations to political committees of Obama, Clinton, McCain and many others, nearly all of it from undisclosed foreign donors"); *Former Associate of Rudy Giuliani Convicted over Illegal Campaign Contributions*, The Guardian, Oct. 22, 2021 (describing conviction involving campaign contributions on behalf of Russian financier); Zach Montellaro & Myah Ward, *Campaign Finance Watchdog Issues Massive Fine for Foreign National's Trump Super PAC Donation*, Politico, April 8, 2022 (describing fine for contribution made by companies of a Canadian billionaire to a U.S. political committee).

[1719] *See supra* § IV.

[1720] *See, e.g.*, Sen. Lindsey Graham, *Newly Declassified FBI Materials Demonstrate Clear Double Standard for Clinton, Trump Campaigns* (Aug. 23, 2020), https://www.judiciary.senate.gov/press/rep/releases/newly-declassified-fbi-materials-demonstrate-clear-double-standard-for-clinton-trump-campaigns.

[1721] The *OIG Review* describes several White House briefings around the time in 2016 when the FBI opened Crossfire Hurricane. Notes of a meeting taken by Deputy FBI Director McCabe, who was not at the meeting itself, indicate that "President Obama stated that the FBI should think about doing defensive briefs," but McCabe did not believe that the Crossfire Hurricane information from Australia would have been discussed. *Redacted OIG Review* at 76-77 (internal quotations omitted).

C. **FISA Issues**

1. Clarity of applications

In 2020, the FBI and the Department provided 19 complete FISA applications to the PCLOB for review. Adam Klein, the Chairman of the PCLOB, commented that:

> The applications present the reader (most notably, the FISA court judge) with a great deal of factual information . . . . This information, however, is sometimes repetitive, and the organization does not necessarily facilitate critical analysis. The applications recite many facts related to the target's potential involvement with terrorism. But each fact's relative importance emerges only after very close reading.
>
> . . . .
>
> Overall, these applications provide a great deal of relevant information and generally aim to highlight potential question marks for the court. However, their clarity and organization could be improved . . . .[1722]

Former Chairman Klein has also written that "[s]teps to improve the clarity of applications . . . would help drafters think rigorously about which facts are essential to probable cause, which are merely supportive and why the surveillance is necessary in the first place."[1723] Similarly, the FBI's public strategy says that it will "improve data collection, accessibility, and analysis to better understand, anticipate, and mitigate threats."[1724] Although the PCLOB did not review the applications for surveillance of Page, as the applications did not involve terrorism, some of the *White Paper*'s observations are relevant.

a. Transparency of sourcing information

In the Page applications, much of the probable cause information was based on multiple layers of unverified sub-sourcing. Whenever that is the case, there is a greater possibility for bias or exaggerations to proliferate, even under ideal circumstances. We appreciate and support the effort the Department's OI Attorneys made, which may have prevented even larger problems, to describe the sourcing for the Page applications. In any application, the description of the sourcing information is of fundamental importance and should be as transparent as possible. It should include the FBI's insight, or lack thereof, into the

---

[1722] Klein, *White Paper* at 12.

[1723] Adam Klein, *What the Inspector General's Latest FISA Report Can (and Can't) Tell Us*, Lawfare, Oct. 19, 2021.

[1724] *FBI Strategy, Our Four Guiding Principles*, https://www.fbi.gov/about/mission/fbi-strategy (hereinafter "*FBI Strategy*").

reliability of each layer.[1725] This is even more the case where what is described is the central contention of the application.[1726]

In addition, the source and sub-source information might have been easier to understand, and been seen as having more importance, if it had been described in the text of the application rather than in a footnote. Although former Assistant Attorney General Kris correctly notes that the FISC "reads the footnotes" and that "[t]he government's disclosures enabled the court to take Steele's information with a grain of salt,"[1727] we see no reason not to lay out sourcing information as clearly as possible, particularly when it contains subjective assessments.

b. Information from Congress

That a member of Congress is concerned about the activities of a political opponent or someone in another political party or may have written to the Attorney General or the Director of the FBI about those activities, would rarely seem relevant to a discussion of probable cause, unless the member provides specific and credible information that is not available from other sources.[1728]

c. Masking of information

In a FISA application, it is clearly important to protect the identity of sources. This is typically done by giving them a number rather than providing a name. It also may be important to minimize or mask private or derogatory information about someone who is not the target of the application. The broader use of minimized identities, such as describing someone as "Candidate #1" or attributing a news report to "an identified news organization," may not conceal much and may instead make understanding the application more difficult.[1729] It may also (even unintentionally) encourage a reader to think that because one possible step to ensure legality has been taken others have been too. In fact, whether information is minimized or masked has no effect on whether the information itself is accurate and supports a probable cause finding.

d. Use of news reports

Former NSA General Counsel Stewart Baker has urged the FBI to avoid using media reports in FISA applications. The FBI has little knowledge of the reliability of the sources used by reporters, and reliance on press accounts risks shortcutting the process of establishing probable cause. If the FBI uses a media source, it should disclose the name of

---

[1725] *Cf. In re Carter W. Page*, No. 16-1182, at 20 (not addressing reliability of the sub-source information used on that page).

[1726] *See id.* at 10, 20 (providing information from a source that Page was part of "a well-developed conspiracy of co-operation" between the Trump campaign and "Russian leadership").

[1727] David Kris, *The Irony of the Nunes Memo*, Lawfare, Mar. 1, 2018.

[1728] *See In re Carter W. Page*, No. 16-1182, at 23-24 (discussing a news report and including the apparent views of members of Congress).

[1729] *See, e.g., id.* at 22 (minimizing identities).

the source "and any credible claims of bias that have been leveled against the news outlet."[1730] It might also disclose what, if any, efforts it has taken to verify the allegations.

e. Need to share important information

In January 2017, the FBI interviewed Igor Danchenko, Steele's primary sub-source. Danchenko said that Steele "misstated or exaggerated" the sub-source's statements "in multiple sections of the reporting."[1731] NSD, but not OI, was present at the interview.[1732] Because the interview involved an important sub-source used in a FISA application, OI should, at a minimum, have been informed of what the sub-source said.

2. *Completeness of applications*

The *OIG Review* concluded that FBI personnel "did not give appropriate attention to facts that cut against probable cause."[1733] The FBI has addressed this issue by requiring that both an agent and a supervisor must affirm that OI "has been apprised of all information that might reasonably call into question the accuracy of the information in the application *or otherwise raise doubts about the requested probable cause findings or the theory of the case.*"[1734] The FBI has also pledged that it "will adhere to the rule of law through attention to detail."[1735] Finally, the Attorney General has directed both the FBI and OI to conduct completeness reviews.[1736]

Implementation of the reviews may be difficult. An FBI CHS may have recorded dozens or hundreds of hours of conversations with the target or others engaged in related activities. For example, in the released transcripts of conversations among an FBI CHS, George Papadopoulos, and others, there is clearly a large amount of extraneous information, and it may not always be clear what is being discussed.[1737] Moreover, no one may have listened to all the recordings, or there may not be available transcripts. The FBI may also have a large volume of other raw

---

[1730] Baker, *Partisan Taint in the Trump-Russia Investigation,* Lawfare, Sept. 8, 2020 (hereinafter "Baker, *Partisan Taint*").

[1731] *See Redacted OIG Review* at 187.

[1732] *Id.* at 187 n.336.

[1733] *See Redacted OIG Review* at 413.

[1734] *Wray Declaration* at 3 (emphasis added).

[1735] *FBI Strategy.*

[1736] Attorney General Memorandum, *Augmenting the Internal Compliance Functions of the Federal Bureau of Investigation* at 1-2 (Aug. 31, 2020); *Supplemental Reforms Memorandum* at 3.

[1737] *See* FBI, U.S. Department of Justice, *Verbatim Transcription,* Task Nos. 628389 and 635144 (completed Dec. 22, 2016 and Jan. 9, 2016), *available at* https://www.judiciary.senate.gov/imo/media/doc/2020-05-05%20Submission %20SJC%20SSCI.pdf; FBI, U.S. Department of Justice, *Verbatim Transcription,* Task No. 620098 (completed Nov. 10, 2016), *available at* https://www.judiciary. senate.gov/imo/media/doc/2020-04-24%20Submission%20SJC%20SSCI.pdf. For links to these and other materials, *see* https://www.judiciary.senate.gov/fisa-investigation.

records related to an investigation. Any of these factors may make it hard to identify information that "raise[s] doubts about the requested probable cause findings or the theory of the case."

One possible way to implement the new requirement, at least in part, may be by asking on the FISA verification form or elsewhere if the FBI is aware of particular kinds of derogatory information about the target. An example might be whether the FBI has information about financial transactions between the target and others associated with a foreign power. If the FBI is not aware of such information, the government may tell the FISC that the FBI either has no such information or that, if it may have such information, it is choosing not to include it. The FISC could then consider the absence of such incriminating information in its assessment of whether the target is an agent of a foreign power.

Moreover, in the circumstance where the FBI has unreviewed data relating to an investigation, or data that is still being evaluated, OI may want to consider whether the FISA application should disclose that fact to the FISC.

3. *Reliance on prior FISA applications*

When the Page FISA applications were renewed, reviewing officials may have placed too much reliance on the prior authorization by the Attorney General and the FISC. Deputy Attorney General Rosenstein noted that at the time when the Page renewal application came to him many different Department officials had approved the prior applications and three different judges had found probable cause.[1738] At least some of the requirements found in the *Supplemental Reforms Memorandum* apply to both initiations and renewals of FISA surveillances.[1739] In addition, some kind of red-teaming, in cases with "partisan risk," might help here.

4. *Timely renewal requests*

Deputy Assistant Attorney General Evans has observed that the FBI should submit a request to renew FISA authority approximately 45 days before its expiration. In practice, "renewal requests often come over from the FBI to OI a week, week and a half, before the expiration." If the requests came earlier, there would be more time for the "robust back and forth" needed to develop the applications.[1740] Implementing this proposal would require a significant commitment by Department and FBI leadership.

Even if the FBI is not timely in submitting a renewal request, OI may be able to begin acquiring needed information by requesting it from the FBI (or possibly seeking it elsewhere) and asking to meet on a case 45 days before it expires. This may be worth the effort involved for a sensitive and important surveillance.

[1738] *See Redacted OIG Review* at 227.

[1739] *See Supplemental Reforms Memorandum* ¶ 1 (imposing requirements "[b]efore any application initiating or renewing the targeting" of a U.S. person is submitted to the FISC).

[1740] U.S. Senate Committee on the Judiciary, Interview of Stuart Evans – Redacted Version, at 214 (July 31, 2020).

D. **Bias or improper motivation**

The *OIG Review* of Crossfire Hurricane says that "[w]e did not find documentary or testimonial evidence that political bias or improper motivation influenced the FBI's decision to seek FISA authority on Carter Page."[1741] It also says that "[w]hile we did not find documentary or testimonial evidence of intentional misconduct on the part of the [FBI personnel], we also did not receive satisfactory explanations for the errors or problems we identified."[1742] David Kris has catalogued statements in the *OIG Review* like those above and discussed the tension between the statements about the lack of evident bias and the lack of explanation for the problems found.[1743]

In this report we have referred to the possible impact of "confirmation bias" on the Crossfire Hurricane investigation.[1744] Confirmation bias is widely understood as a phenomenon describing how information is processed by individuals and groups. It stands for the general proposition that there is a common human tendency – mostly unintentional – for people to accept information and evidence that is consistent with what they believe to be true, while ignoring or rejecting information that challenges those beliefs. In short, people tend to give more credence to information that supports what they already believe. The effects of confirmation bias can be amplified in groups operating in situations of high stress and under time pressures.[1745]

Throughout the duration of Crossfire Hurricane, facts and circumstances that were inconsistent with the premise that Trump and/or persons associated with the Trump campaign were involved in a collusive or conspiratorial relationship with the Russian government were ignored or simply assessed away. Indeed, as set forth in Sections IVA.2 and 3, from even before the opening of Crossfire Hurricane, some of those most directly involved in the subsequent investigation had (i) expressed their open disdain for Trump, (ii) asked about when they would open an investigation on Trump, and (iii) asserted that they would prevent Trump from becoming President. As discussed throughout this report, our investigation revealed that the stated basis for opening a full investigation "to determine whether individual(s) associated with the Trump campaign [were] witting of and/or coordinating activities with the Government of Russia"[1746] was seriously flawed. Again, the FBI's failure to critically analyze information that ran counter to the narrative of a Trump/Russia collusive relationship exhibited throughout Crossfire Hurricane is extremely troublesome. The evidence of the FBI's confirmation bias in

---

[1741] *See Redacted OIG Review* at vii; *see also id.* at iii-iv (similar statements about opening of Crossfire Hurricane and related investigations).

[1742] *Id.* at xiii; *see also id.* at 414.

[1743] Kris, *Further Thoughts* at 2-5.

[1744] *See, e.g.,* references at pages 18, 98, 305.

[1745] *See generally* ScienceDirect, *Confirmation Bias* (quoting Caleb W. Lack & Jacques Rousseau, *Comprehensive Clinical Psychology* § 11.04.4.1.1 (2d ed. 2022); Shahram Heshmat, *What Is Confirmation Bias?* in *Psychology Today* (Apr. 23, 2015), https://www.psychology today.com/us/blog/science-choice/201504/what-is-confirmation-bias; Bettina J. Cassad & J.E. Luebering, *Confirmation Bias*, in *Encyclopedia Brittanica* (Last updated Mar. 31, 2023).

[1746] *Crossfire Hurricane Opening EC* at 3-4.

the matter, includes, at a minimum, the following information that was simply ignored or in some fashion rationalized away:

- The Australian diplomats told Crossfire Hurricane investigators that Papadopoulos never stated that he had any direct contact with the Russians nor did he provide any explicit information about an offer of assistance.

- There was a complete lack of information from the Intelligence Community that corroborated the hypothesis upon which the Crossfire Hurricane investigation was predicated.

- The FBI generally ignored the significant exculpatory information provided by Carter Page, George Papadopoulos, and Trump Senior Foreign Policy Advisor-1 during recorded conversations with FBI CHSs.

- The FBI failed to pursue investigative leads that were inconsistent with their theory of the case (*e.g.*, Page's recorded denials of having any relationship with Paul Manafort, a fact about which there was available evidence).

- The FBI failed to take Page up on the written offer he made to Director Comey to be interviewed about the allegations contained in Michael Isikoff's *Yahoo! News* article and instead opted to seek FISA surveillance of Page.

- The FBI was willing to make use of the completely unvetted and uncorroborated Steele reporting in multiple FISA applications targeting a U.S. citizen, even after the Crossfire Hurricane investigators had determined that there were major conflicts between the reporting of Steele and his primary sub-source, Igor Danchenko – conflicts the FBI incredibly failed to resolve.

- The Crossfire Hurricane investigators did not even ask Steele about his role in providing information to Michael Isikoff as contained in the September 23, 2016 *Yahoo! News* article – information that essentially accused Carter Page of colluding with the Russians. And thereafter the same investigators demonstrated a willingness to contort the plain language of the article to suggest it was not Steele but Steele's employers who had given the information to Isikoff.

- The FBI ignored the fact that at no time before, during or after Crossfire Hurricane were investigators able to corroborate a single substantive allegation in the Steele dossier reporting.

- There was a complete failure on the part of the FBI to even examine – never mind resolve – the serious counterespionage issues surrounding Steele's primary sub-source, Igor Danchenko.

- The FBI leadership essentially disregarded the Clinton Plan intelligence, which it received at almost the exact same time as the Australian Paragraph Five information. This was despite the fact that at precisely the same time as the Clinton Plan intelligence was received (i) the Clinton campaign made public statements tying the

DNC computer hack to Russian attempts to help Trump get elected, (ii) the FBI was receiving the Clinton campaign-funded Steele Reports, and (iii) the Clinton campaign-funded Alfa Bank allegations were being prepared for delivery to the media and the FBI.

- The Crossfire Hurricane investigators essentially ignored information they had received as early as October 2016 regarding Charles Dolan, a longtime Democratic operative with ties to the Clintons who also possessed significant ties to Russian government figures who would appear in the Steele reporting, and never interviewed him.

- The Crossfire Hurricane investigators provided only partial, and in some instances misleading, information to Department attorneys working on the Page FISA applications while withholding other highly relevant information from those attorneys and the FISC that might cast real doubt on their probable cause assertions.

Finally, the results of the OIG's *Audit of 29 Applications* also establish significant problems in the Page FISA applications, problems that point to bias and other factors. Following the *Audit*, the Department and the FBI "notified the FISC that the 29 applications contained a total of 209 errors, 4 of which they deemed to be material."[1747] We note that because the *Audit* did not look for omitted information – a major issue in the Page applications – the results of the *Audit* and the review of the Page applications are not directly comparable. Nonetheless, at least on the surface, the difference is notable: in the four Page applications, there were a total of 17 material errors and omissions,[1748] far more than the four material errors found in the larger group of 29 non-Page applications.

Given the foregoing, and viewing the facts in a light most favorable to the Crossfire Hurricane investigators, it seems highly likely that, at a minimum, confirmation bias played a significant role in the FBI's acceptance of extraordinarily serious allegations derived from uncorroborated information that had not been subjected to the typical exacting analysis employed by the FBI and other members of the Intelligence Community. In short, it is the Office's assessment that the FBI discounted or willfully ignored material information that did not support the narrative of a collusive relationship between Trump and Russia. Similarly, the *FBI Inspection Division Report* says that the investigators "repeatedly ignore[d] or explain[ed] away evidence contrary to the theory the Trump campaign . . . had conspired with Russia. . . . It appeared that . . . there was a pattern of assuming nefarious intent."[1749] An objective and honest assessment of these strands of information should have caused the FBI to question not only the predication for Crossfire Hurricane, but also to reflect on whether the FBI was being manipulated for political or other purposes. Unfortunately, it did not.

[1747] *Audit of 29 Applications* at ii; *see also id.* at 10-11 (listing the material errors found).

[1748] *Redacted OIG Review* at viii – xiii (describing the errors in the Page FISA applications).

[1749] *FBI Inspection Division Report* at 33 n.15, 37.

E. **Possible FBI reform**

One possible way to provide additional scrutiny of politically sensitive investigations would be to identify, in advance, an official who is responsible for challenging the steps taken in the investigation. Stewart Baker proposes having a "career position for a nonpartisan FBI agent or lawyer to challenge the FISA application and every other stage of the investigation." This would be done in investigations that "pose partisan risk." In Baker's view, the Attorney General, through the *Supplemental Reforms Memorandum*, has already taken "a good step in this direction by requiring that politically sensitive surveillance and search applications be reviewed by a special agent from a field office not involved in the investigation."[1750] Similarly, Adam Klein said that "DOJ and FBI leaders should consider whether a regularized practice of internal redteaming in the most sensitive cases, whether within the FBI or in collaboration with attorneys at the National Security Division, could serve as an effective check on confirmation bias without unduly delaying time-sensitive applications."[1751]

As a way to ensure full consideration of the issues in applications that may present very difficult – and vitally important – issues, we recommend that the Department seriously consider Baker's proposal for an official to challenge both a politically sensitive FISA application and other stages of the investigation.[1752] "Nothing," former Attorney General Levi warned, "can more weaken the quality of life or more imperil the realization of the goals we all hold dear than our failure to make clear by words and deed that our law is not the instrument of partisan purpose."[1753]

[1750] Baker, *Partisan Taint*. Baker explains his proposal for the career official in more detail in Like It or Not, Trump Has a Point: FISA Reform and the Appearance of Partisanship in Intelligence Investigations at 12-13, Sept. 5, 2020.

[1751] *White Paper* at 24-25.

[1752] Baker also proposes that the career official should "take the lead in reporting on the investigation to majority and minority congressional leadership, not after the fact but as it proceeds." *Baker, Partisan Taint*. We do not endorse this aspect of the proposal, at least not without further consideration; we are concerned that it could lead to a politically motivated leak of a sensitive investigation.

[1753] Edward H. Levi, *Farewell Remarks* (Jan. 17, 1977), *quoted in* U.S. Department of Justice, *FYs 2022 – 2026 Strategic Plan* at 15.

Made in United States
North Haven, CT
04 June 2023